Scottish Surnames

Donald Whyte
F.H.G., F.S.G. Hon.

Birlinn

First published in Great Britain, 1996, by
Birlinn Limited
2nd edition, revised and enlarged, 2000
Birlinn Limited
Unit 8, Canongate Venture
5 New Street, Edinburgh EH8 8BH

© Donald Whyte, 2000

ISBN 1 84158 056 2

British Library Cataloguing in Publication Data
A catalogue record for this book is available from the
British Library

Typesetting by Textype, Cambridge
Printed and bound in Finland by
WS Bookwell

CONTENTS

◄◊►

ABBREVIATIONS

━◀◦▶━

adm.	Admitted
AD	Anno Domini
ADC	Aide de Camp
AFC	Air Force Cross
b.	born
Bt.	Baronet
ca.	circa, about
cr.	created
CA	Chartered Accountant
CBE	Commander, Order of the British Empire
CE	Civil Engineer
CIE	Companion, Order of the Indian Empire
COSLA	Convention of Scottish Local Authorities
d.	dead, died, death
DBE	Dame Commander, Order of the British Empire
DD	Doctor of Divinity
DFC	Distinguished Flying Cross
DSO	Companion, Distinguished Service Order
dy	died young
FRS	Fellow of the Royal Society
FRCS	Fellow, Royal College of Surgeons
HEIC	Honourable East India Company
HEICS	Honourable East India Company's Service
HMS	His or Her Majesty's Service
Junr.	Junior
KCB	Knight Commander, Order of the Bath
m.	married, marriage
MC	Military Cross
MD	Doctor of Medicine
MP	Member of Parliament
NATO	North Atlantic Treaty Organisation

NS	Nova Scotia [Order of Baronets]
NSW	New South Wales [Australia]
OBE	Officer, Order of the British Empire
ord.	ordained
PC	Privy Councillor
QC	Queen's Counsel
RA	Royal Artillery
RFA	Royal Field Artillery
RN	Royal Navy
RSA	Royal Scottish Academician
RSW	Member, Royal Scottish Society of Water-colourists
SCC	Solicitor to the Supreme Court (Scotland)
SRO	Scottish Record Office
UF	United Free [Church]
UK	United Kingdom
unm.	unmarried
USAAF	United States Army Air Force
WS	Writer to the Signet
Yr.	Younger

INTRODUCTION

◆

IT WAS WILLIAM CAMDEN, the first serious student of British surnames who wrote: 'Every person had in the beginning only one proper name,' and if we look at early record sources for Scotland we find that personal names predominate. In the charter of King Duncan to the monks of St Cuthbert, granted in 1094, no surnames appear. The monarch and the witnesses made their rude crosses, over which the learned scribe, Grento, added their names: Acaerd, Hermer, Hemming, Ulf, Aelfric, Malcol(m)b, Teobold, Duncan (the king), Eadger, Vinget and Earnulf.

'Sur' or additional names – not 'sire' names – are of comparatively late origin, and often appear in changed or corrupt form. They emerge slowly, and we can detect their evolution in early charters. That granted during the reign of David I (1124–53), by Waldeve, son of Cospatrick, to Helias, son of Huchtred, of the lands of Dundas, has among the witnesses, Waldeve, son of Baldwin, William of Copeland and Adam the Steward. Baldwin may have become a surname through the dropping of 'son of', but this is a written form, and such a conclusion would be dubious. However, Copeland – a place-name – emerged as a surname, and Steward did likewise, becoming Stewart. In small communities, personal names were sufficient and patronymics alone were all that custom required. The process grew with an increase in population and mobility in the 13th century. Surnames arrived late in the Highlands and Western Isles. In many parts of the world surnames are still a rarity. In Iceland the people are listed in directories under their given names, and the following is an example of how the system works. A man called Arnar might have a son named Gunnar

Arnarson, who might marry a woman called Sigurlin Asgeirsdotter. If they had a son he would be called Arnar Gunnarson.

Surnames may be divided into five groups, with some overlapping. There are those derived from the personal name of the father, more correctly termed surnames of relationship. Patronymics come into this class, although these produced surnames under varying circumstances. Then come names stemming from places, and these form a large group. Next are hundreds of trade and office names, usually referred to as occupational surnames. Into a fourth class come surnames flowing from a number of sources. Lastly, there are surnames derived from nicknames, personal traits and characteristics.

Easily recognised as emerging from personal names – themselves deriving from a variety of sources – are surnames such as Adam, Allan, Cecil, Henry and Thomas. Before the Christian era, personal names could claim numerical superiority; but since then, local, trade and divergent names have left these in the minority. Thousands might receive their names from a locality, but not even two could be called Jacob or Moses except through a second-hand use by adoption or popular application. Patronymics commonly indicate whose son a man is, and these were borne in ancient times as we can see from the *ben* and *bar* of the Semitic languages. In the Homeric lists of heroes they can be identified by the suffixes *ades* and *ides*. The Romans too, had their patronymic forms consisting of *praenomen* (e.g. Marcus), *nomen* (e.g. Tullius), and *cognomen* (e.g. Cicero), sometimes with two other designations of the father and the tribe. With the fall of the Roman Empire the system of nomenclature declined, and men came to be linked with the name of the father only – e.g. Hugonis Wilhelmus, meaning Hugh, son of William. The Teutonic nations added *sen* or *son* to the personal name, while the Saxon style was the addition of the suffix *ing*, as in Atheling (Athel's son). In Welsh, a form of the Celtic *mac* emerged, which the Cambrians made *mab* or *map*, shortened to *ap*. The Irish, being Celts, also used *mac*, 'son of', as a prefix, but often found greater charm in *ua*, originally for grandson, but by an extension of use came to mean any descendant and found more often as *O*, as in O'Brien.

In Scotland the Gaels used the prefix *mac* to denote 'son of', and often it was a remote ancestor of note, whose personal name was commemorated by the clan chiefs. For the ordinary clansman, patronymics such as Dhomnuil mac Challum, vic Alastair, vic Iain Bhain (Donald, son of Malcolm, son of Alexander, son of fair John) sufficed, and were meaningful in small communities. Surnames eventually triumphed and stabilised. Examples are MacAlpine (son of Alpin), Diarmaid (son of Dermid), MacLaren (son of Laurin) and MacPhail (son of Paul). Many derive from trades or offices: Maceachern (son of the horse lord), MacGowan (son of the smith), Maclellan (son of the devotee of St Fillan), MacIntosh (son of the leader), and MacIntyre (son of the carpenter). In ordinary English, *son* is often added to the Christian name, as in Thomson and Robertson. Some others require a little thought: names like Dawson, an abbreviation of Davidson, and Watson, a shortening of Walterson. Another class is still less obvious, the suffix being curtailed in names like Andrews, Edwards and Richards.

Numerous surnames have their origin in place-names: sheriffdoms or counties, provinces, lordships, baronies, towns, villages, hamlets, farms, estates, crofts and sheilings. Some are not easily recognised as they now appear in archaic or distorted form. Some territorial names have been romanticised through the custom of styling landowners by the names of their estates, or 'of that Ilk', which usually means their ancestors were the first private owners, and are always chiefs of the surname. The term is often used erroneously. In America, people will talk of 'Al Capone and his Ilk', meaning Al Capone and his kind, and even in Scotland there are those who think the term simply refers to the estate from which they derived the name. The meaning survives even when an owner sells or loses his estate, as they retain the name and arms, recorded in the Lyon Court. Names like Dundas of that Ilk, Moncreiffe of that Ilk, and Houston of that Ilk, run like a bright golden thread through the rich tapestry of Scottish history. Scottish chiefships abound in this book, as in olden times landowners were often patriarchal and held responsible in law for the behaviour of the people who resided on their estates.

When we consider national names we often find that a man had to move before these became applicable. A man from south of the border would be Englis, and modern forms are Inglis, English and England. There are more Scot(t)s in England than in Scotland. Wallace is thought to be very Scottish, but usually means origins in the old British kingdom of Strathclyde. Ireland is straightforward, and so is French. The lordly name of St Clair or Sinclair, may indicate a place in Normandy, but can come from a sinkler in the old cloth-making trade (the person who steeped the flax), or a tinker from Argyll. The non-resident principal can often be noted by record scholars. In Fife, for example, names such as Lothian and

Berwick appear frequently in old records. Dutch, found in the Firth
of Tay area, is said to derive from a survivor of a man-of-war from
Holland, shipwrecked near Tayport during the reign of Queen
Anne. People in the Orkneys called Mainland probably originated
in the largest island, called Pomona or Mainland.

Some of the great names in Scottish history have come from
provinces or districts such as Buchan, Galloway, Lennox, Mar and
Strathearn. Berwick, Lanark, Roxburgh and Stirling are usually
thought of as towns which had (or have) Norman style mottes or
castles, but these are also surnames of antiquity. A good number
have hardly changed at all, and point unmistakably to the places
which gave them life. Examples are Crawford, Cunningham,
Dunbar, Home, Morton, Romanes and Traquair. It should be
remembered that when a family has the name of a place, the latter
nearly always came first. There are a few exceptions, such as
Hamilton, Livingston, Riddell and Melville. Into the class of local
names are a number derived from features of the landscape: names
like Hill, Dale, Hope (in some cases), Moor or Muir, and Fields.

Medieval townships are clearly responsible for another group of
surnames originating in a central location and its four approximate
compass points, followed by the suffix *tun*, *ton* or *toun*, denoting a
dwelling-place, viz:

NORTON

WESTON—MIDDLETON—EASTON

SUTTON

Sometimes, although three or four geographical locations exist,
only one surname has evolved. In Mid Lothian, near Ingliston
Showground, there are places called Easter Norton, Norton Mains,
Middle Norton and Wester Norton, so a man named Norton may
have come from any of these. Names like Northgate and Southgate
generally come from gates of old walled towns, but are more
common in England than in Scotland, where the access and egress
points were known as 'ports'. The occupational name of Porter
usually comes from a source like this; sometimes from a doorkeeper
of a monastery, but others may have derived from a ferryman or
'phortair'.

Job-description is a much used (and occasionally abused) term today; but for many centuries the surnames of numerous officials and craftsmen proclaimed their calling. Frequently, as in the case of smiths, son succeeded father, because the tools of the trade were inherited. Curiously, the ancients were reluctant to change a name which recalled brave deed or hallowed relationship. Moreover, they may have been influenced by the fact that occupational names are sometimes indefinite. One man in a community might be called Jacob, while a number might be called Smith as the metal craft embraced a number of trades.

Many occupational names are easily understood, such as Gardener, Taylor, Baxter or Baker, Cook, Glover, Dyer, Skinner, Wright and Weaver. Likewise numerous official names are recognisable: Usher, Marshall, Steward, Page and Carver, all deriving from the multiplicity of functions in the great houses and establishments of the Middle Ages. Some others require thought. Barker is from the obsolete name for the man who prepared the bark of trees for the Tanner (another occupational name). Cordiner or Cordwainer comes from the men who made shoes of goatskin, which was supposed to come from Cordova, in Andalusia. With other shoemakers (Soutar is from this source) they formed fraternities in the old Scottish burghs. Potinger comes from potage and indicates a maker of soups. Stoddart comes from *stot-herd*, a 'stot' being a general term for a young bull or bullock.

Surnames derived from nicknames form a interesting group, but many have disappeared because of their courseness. Some can be taken literally, but others have contrary meanings, in the same way that Tiny is often used to denote a six-footer. Broadhead, Foot, Crookshank, Cudlipp, Longman and Hawkey, all describe physical attributes or peculiarities, while Careless, Loveless or Lovelace, Goodenough and Sharp, all particularise mental and moral character. Flett, Old Norse, meaning an eager fellow or a flayer or robber, is found in the Orkneys, as also is Scollay – from the same source – *skalli* meaning 'bald-head'. A few names which ended in 'head', have been curtailed to leave the suffix *ett*, as in Blackett, Brockett, Duckett and Stricket (*stirk-head*). Names of animals can be nicknames, but must be treated with caution. Lamb may denote weakness, and Bull great strength, but might come from a herd or keeper of these animals and may therefore be occupational surnames.

A large number of divergent surnames come from plants, flowers, animals and birds, examples being Mustard, Primrose (in some cases), Goodlamb and Swan. Many come from medieval pageantry and religious festivals, as in Prophet, Priest, King, Marquess, Duke, Bishop and Abbot. A few derive from costumes or adjuncts of these, examples being Staff, Clubb, Bracegirdle and Broadbelt. Then there are names like Brand (sword), and sometimes Randall (shield). The Rendalls of the Orkneys, however, take their name from a place in Westray. In England the name is said to be a form of Randolph. Another group are mythological or biblical. Whatever their origin they all add colour to the study of surnames.

A number of books deal only with clans or families with tartans, most of which are of dubious antiquity, and the history given is mixed with fact and folk-tale: shrubbery surrounded by a forest of myth and legend. All too often, Highland and Border families are treated as if Lowland families were totally different. In Gaelic, *clann* simply means children of family, offspring or descendants, and many Lowland families also have tartans. This book deals with some two hundred and twenty surnames, and includes many not treated in such books. The choice for inclusion must to some extent be arbitrary, but the surnames cover a wide cross-section of Highland, Lowland and Border families, with some others regarding which little has been written. This edition has been extensively revised and enlarged. Many long-standing myths have been scotched, including the statement in books by some respected writers that the last MacFarlane chief emigrated to America; that Robert Burns was of Campbell ancestry, and that there was no MacCrimmon college of piping in Skye. A number of surnames long classed as Norman, have been shown by Mrs Beryl Platts, in her books *Origins of Heraldry* (London: Proctor, 1980) and *Scottish Hazard* (2 vols, London: Proctor, 1985, 1990), to be Flemish, hence the families inherited a much different culture. It would be surprising if everybody agreed with her findings, but the writer is convinced that her highly original work is in the main correct. Books for further reading are suggested at the end of this volume, followed by some hints on commencing research, a list of local family history societies and the names of professional record searchers.

Donald Whyte

SURNAMES AND FAMILIES OF SCOTLAND

—◄◦►—

ABERCROMBY Sometimes rendered Abercrombie, the name is derived from the lands of Abercrombie, in Fife, meaning 'place at the mouth of the winding stream'. Anciently there was a family styled 'of that Ilk'. Francis Abercromby was a Lord of Session during the reign (1437–60) of James II. His descendants held the barony until it was sold to James Sandilands, who was created Lord Abercromby in 1647. The senior cadet of the family was Abercromby of Birkenbog, in Banffshire. Alexander Abercromby, descended from Humphrey Abercromby of Pitmeddan, had sasine of Pitmeddan and other lands in 1484. Another Alexander was falconer to King Charles I, and married Elizabeth Bethune. Their son Sir Alexander of Birkenbog was created a Baronet of NS in 1636. The honours descended to the 8th Baronet, Sir Robert Alexander Abercromby, an army officer, who was succeeded in 1972 by his kinsman, Ian George Abercromby, a great-grandson of the 5th Baronet A scion of the family, Alexander Abercromby of Fetternear, married Jean Seton and had three sons: Francis, John and Dr Patrick, author of *The Martial Achievements of the Scottish Nation*. The eldest son, Francis of Fetternear, having married Anne, Baroness Sempill, was given a life peerage as Lord Glasford in 1685. Their sons Francis, John and Hugh, were the 9th, 10th and 11th Lords Sempill. The dignity of Glasford, of course, became extinct. General Ralph Abercromby of Tullibody, 1734–1801, fought in France, Flanders, Holland, the West Indies and Egypt. His third son, James, was MP for Edinburgh and became Speaker of the House of Commons. He was created Lord Dunfermline in 1839.

ABERNETHY The surname derives from the Perthshire village of that name. Orme, son of Hugh, Abbot of Abernethy, had a grant in free forest of Dunlappie (an old parish joined with Stracathro in 1612), in Angus, during the reign of Malcolm IV (1153–65). He witnessed a charter by that monarch to Duncan, Earl of Fife, and his heir born of his wife Ada, the king's niece, of Falkland, Strathmiglo and Kingskettle, ca. 1162. During the reign of Robert the Bruce (1306–29), Alexander, Lord of Abernethy, left three daughters and co-heirs: Margaret, who married John Stewart, Earl of Angus, and brought with her the barony of Abernethy; Helen, who married Norman Lindsay of Crawford, who obtained the barony of Balinbreich; and Mary, who married Andrew Lesley of Rothes, who received the barony of Downie, in Angus. Those daughters were mothers of three great families: the Earls of Angus, Crawford and Rothes, all of whom marshalled the arms of Abernethy – a lion rampart Gules, debruised with a ribbon – with their own. Of the mail line of Abernethy was Laurence of Rothiemay, created a Lord of Parliament in 1455. His successors were usually styled Lords of Saltoun. Alexander, 9th Lord Saltoun, 1611–68, left no issue, and the title, after the death of a sister who never assumed it, was claimed by his cousin, Alexander Fraser of Philorth. His right was ratified. The present judicial title of Lord Abernethy, is borne by John Alastair Cameron, born 1938, who was admitted to the Faculty of Advocates in 1966. He was Vice-Dean of the Faculty, 1983–92, and became a Senator of the College of Justice in 1992.

AGNEW The name comes from followers of William the Conqueror called Agneaux, whose home was in the baronie d'Agneaux, in the Bocages of Normandy. Members eventually settled in Wigtownshire, and appear to have been oppressed for a time by the Earls of Douglas, who razed their old castle of Lochnaw. Andrew Agnew was restored to Lochnaw by Douglas of Leswalt in 1430/31, and became hereditary sheriff of Wigtownshire in 1451. He built a new castle, enlarged in 1663, and again in 1820. Quinten his son, married Marion Vaus, and they had a grant of the lands of Creachmore in 1469. Sir Patrick Agnew of Lochnaw was created a Baronet of NS in 1629. The shrievalty of Wigtownshire remained in the family until the abolition of the hereditary jurisdictions in 1747. The 11th Baronet is Sir Crispin Hamlyn Agnew, who is chief of the surname. He served in the Royal

Highland Fusiliers, attaining the rank of Major, and retiring in 1981. He studied to become an advocate at the Scottish Bar, and is Rothesay Herald at the Lyon Office; in 1995 he became a QC. Captain Alexander Agnew of Criech, an old cadet, matriculated arms in 1693, and was succeeded by his son, Lt. Col. Andrew Agnew of Lochryan, who served in the Royal Regiment of Dragoons. From another branch descends the baronets of Clendry, Kirkholm. An Irish family of O'Gnimhs, who were hereditary bards to the Clannaboy O'Neils, changed their surname to Agnew, causing much confusion among genealogists.

AITCHISON Names such as Aitchison, Acheson, Aitcheson and Atkinson, like Adamson, come from 'son of Adam'. Early forms are found south of the Highland line and in Cumberland. John Atkynson appears as a custumar in North Berwick in 1387, and another man of the same name appears at Aberdeen in 1402. W.R. MacDonald, in *Scottish Armorial Seals*, notes Thomas Atkinson of Bonkyll as bearing in 1430: On a chevron engrailed, three buckles. Also Thomas Atkinson of Sleichshouses as having in 1495, a seal blazoned: On a chevron, a buckle between two cinquefoils. Marc Aitchison is recorded at Prestonpans in 1609, and Mr John Echesone was schoolmaster at Kilbride in 1680. A family named Aitchesoun was associated with the Scottish Mint in the 15th and 16th centuries. James Aitchesoun, 'Maister Cunzear' was ordered to make bawbees in 1553. Sir Archibald Acheson, knight, was Secretary of State under Charles I, and at his death in 1634 was owed £1250 by the Treasury for his services, 1628–34. He had been granted lands in Ireland, and created a Baronet of N.S. in 1628. Sir Archibald was the progenitor of the Earls of Gosford, now represented by Sir Charles David Nicholas Alexander John Sparrow Acheson, 7th Earl, who resides in Fittleworth, Sussex.

AITKENHEAD The name comes from the old barony of Aitkenhead, in Lanarkshire, and has many variants, including Aikenhead, Aikynhead and Atkinhead. In 1372 the lands were confirmed to John de Maxwell. William de Akynhead was a bailie of Rutherglen in 1376. Three men called Akynhead held the castle of Dunbarton against the king in that year. David Aitkenhead, a staunch royalist, was Lord Provost of Edinburgh for three terms: 1620–22; 1625–29; and 1634–37. Mother Mary (Augustine) Aitkenhead, 1787–1858, was foundress of the Irish Sisters of Charity. She was born in Cork, the daughter of David Aitkenhead, a Protestant physician of Scottish descent, who married Mary Stackpoole, daughter of a Catholic merchant. She became a devout Catholic and in 1815 opened her first convent in Dublin. Other foundations followed in England, Scotland, Australia, Africa and America. Her unbounded zeal resulted in schools, hospitals, homes for orphans and the blind: indeed, for almost every need of the suffering poor. In 1958 the Eire government issued a commemorative stamp bearing her portrait. John M. Aitkenhead, 1910–88, was educated at Ardrossan and Glasgow, and in 1940 opened an unusual private school at Kilquhanity House, near Kirkpatrick-Durham, in Kirkcudbrightshire, which survived for over 50 years.

ALLAN It is generally agreed that the surname Alan, Allan or Allen, is of two-fold origin. In Old Gaelic it represents *Ailene* – the Ailenus of Adamnan, biographer of St Columbia – or *Ailin*, from *Ail*, 'rock', as seen in the old name of Dumbarton, 'Ail Cluade'. From this source comes *Alwyn*, the name of the first earls of Lennox, sometimes confused with the Old English *Aelwin*. A second origin is through the Norman French *Alan*, found at an early period as *Alamnvs* and *Alanus*. Alan, King of Brittany, is mentioned in 683. One of the leading Bretons who came to England with William the Conqueror in 1066 was Alan or Alain Fergant. The form *Alamnvs* points to *Alemannus*, the Germanic tribal name meaning 'all men', as the source of the personal name.

The name became popular in Scotland from its occurrence in the family of the Stewards (Stewarts) to the Kings of Scots, and eventually kings. Alan, son of Waldeve, witnessed charters by David I, in 1139. Alanus, brother of Galfridus Redberd, witnessed the sale of a tenement in Perth in 1219. Aleyn fitz Maucolum of Berwickshire, and John fitz Aleyn, burgess of Montrose, rendered homage to Edward I in 1296. Loughlan le fitz Aleyn, son-in-law of Alexander of Argyll, was received to the king of England's peace in 1301. Duncan Alowne was admitted burgess of Aberdeen in 1446, and Henry Alane was clerk of accounts in the royal household in 1498. The Allans of Bute appear on record as Callan, Callen, Macallan and Maccallen, and are properly MacAllans.

A few Allans became landowners, but more distinguished themselves as individuals. David Allan, 1744–96, son of a shoremaster at Alloa, became a historical painter. He studied at Glasgow and Rome, and his illustrations for collections of Scottish songs earned him the title of 'The Scottish Hogarth'. Another printer, William Allan, 1782–1850, was born in Edinburgh, and apprenticed to a coachmaker; but afterwards studied at the Trustees Academy and at the school of the Royal Scottish Academy in London. He went to Europe in 1805, and returned in 1812, resolved to become a serious historical painter. He became president of the Royal Scottish Academy in 1838, and in 1841 succeeded Sir David Wilkie as HM Limner for Scotland, being knighted at that time. Yet another Allan, Robert W., 1852–1942, a native of Alloa, studied at Glasgow and painted many watercolours and oils of harbours, landscapes and seascapes.

An interesting and talented family of Allans sprang from John Allan, who was born ca. 1590, and lived at Gogar. His grandson John farmed at Monshill, Dalmeny, and married Helen Cunningham, who bore him eight children. Thomas, the second son, was tenant of Little Barnbougle, and moved to Newmains, Kirkliston, before 1763. He married Agnes Reid, and their fourth son, Robert, 1745–1818, settled in Edinburgh, where he became a notable citizen. Robert founded a bank with David Steuart in 1775, but the partnership was dissolved in 1780 when Steuart became Lord Provost. The firm was afterwards known as Robert Allan & Co. He was a member and, in 1795, captain of the Honourable Company of Golfers. He won a number of prizes as a player. Robert married Ann Learmouth, and had nine children, the eldest of whom was Thomas, 1777–1833, of Laurieston Castle. He was proprietor of the *Caledonian Mercury*, and by his wife Christian Smith, left able descendants.

ANDERSON/MacANDREW The surname Anderson simply means 'son of Andrew', hence MacAndrew, but as borne by Lowland families means 'Servant of St Andrew', the patron saint of Scotland. The Lowland form influenced the Gaelic 'Gilleandrais', Gillanders, or St Andrew's *gille* or servant. Donald MacGillandrish, from Moidart, was ancestor of a group who settled at Connage of Petty, and were considered to be a sept of Clan Chattan. A family in Islay named Macillandrais adopted the Lowland form of Anderson. The name is prolific all over the Lowlands and the North-East. Curiously an Anderson was recognised as 'of that Ilk', in the 16th century, although there was no place-name. It seems that the Lord Lyon of the time wished to have someone who would be received in public ceremony as representer of the race or clan of Anderson. However, nobody can now identify the 'representer' with certainty.

Andersons appear in the 13th century in various parts of

Scotland. David le fitz Andreu, burgess of Peebles, and Duncan fitz Andreu, from Dumfriesshire, swore fealty to Edward I in 1296. John Anderson was prior of Fyvie in 1424. Early landowners were John of Balmaddy in 1479; John of Pitfour in 1490; John Struthers in 1576 and Herbert of Terraughty in 1577. Donald Makandro was one of the victims of the plundering of Petty in 1502. Mackallum MacAndro in Murthlac appears in 1550, and Dowgall McAndro Vuyear in Stuckvillage was fined for sheltering MacGregors in 1613. Iain *beag* MacAndrea, a servant of William Mackintosh in Kilravock, was an expert archer who demonstrated his skills against a raiding party of Macdonnels in 1670.

The Andersons of Dovehill can be traced back to 1540. John of Dovehill, 1636–1710, was eight times Lord Provost of Glasgow. In 1696 he purchased stock to the value of £1000 in the ill-fated Darien Scheme. Other estate owners were of Aucharnie, Bourtie, Candacraig, Bordland and Fingland, Montrave and Stobcross, and Tushielaw. Several Andersons appear in Stockholm, Sweden, about the close of the 16th century, and Col. Anderson, whose mother was a Sinclair of Murtle, was enobled there in 1668.

Many Andersons have distinguished themselves. Alexander Anderson, an Aberdonian, became a mathematician in Paris, and issued various treatises on geometrical science, 1612–19. Andrew Anderson, son of George Anderson, who introduced the art of printing to Glasgow, was invited to settle in Edinburgh, and became the King's Printer in Scotland in 1671. James Anderson, 1662–1728, achieved lasting fame as the compiler of *Selectus Diplomatum et Numismatum Scotiae* (1739), a work of learning never transcended in elegance. It was not, however, published in his lifetime. John Anderson, 1726–96, a native of Roseneath, became Professor of Oriental Languages at Glasgow in 1756, and of Natural Philosophy in 1760. He bequeathed money to found the Andersonian Institute. James Anderson, 1739–1808, an eminent agriculturist, was born at Hermiston. Dr Robert Anderson, 1750–1830, born at Carnwath, was editor and biographer of British poets, and William Anderson, 1805–66, was the industrious author of *The Scottish Nation*, first published in 1863. The MacAndrew baronets descend from Francis Glen MacAndrew, of Knock Castle, Largs, whose son Charles received the honour in 1959. An MP for several constituencies, he also served with distinction in the Ayrshire Yeomanry. His grandson, Sir Christopher, the 3rd Baronet, resides at Archdeacon Newton, near Darlington.

ANSTRUTHER The name comes from the old barony of Anstruther, in Fife, held before 1153 by William de Candela. His son, also William, was a benefactor of Balmerino Abbey. Their arms indicate Flemish origin, but they are said to have belonged to the Norman family of Malherbe, who held Candel, in Dorset, *in capite*, in the 11th and 12th centuries. It was probably Henry, son of the second William, who first assumed the territorial designation of Anstruther. A descendant of this ancient family, William de Anstruther, lived in the reign of Robert the Bruce (1306–29), and confirmed donations made by his ancestors to ecclesiastics. Andrew Anstruther, who obtained a charter of the barony in 1483, fought at Flodden in 1513. His grandson, Andrew, was killed at Pinkie in 1547. Sir Philip Anstruther, who died in 1702, had seven sons. The eldest, Sir William, a Lord of Session, was the father of Sir John of Anstruther, created a Baronet of NS in 1701. He married in 1717, Lady Helen Carmichael, eldest daughter of James, 2nd Earl of Hyndford, in right of whom the family inherited as heirs general, the estates and representation of the Earls of Hyndford. They thus came to be styled Carmichael-Anstruther of Carmichael and Anstruther. Sir John Anstruther, 4th Baronet, was also created a UK Baronet in 1798. The third son of Sir Philip, who died in 1702, Sir Robert of Balcaskie, was created a Baronet of NS in 1694. This family is presently represented by Sir Ralph Hugo Anstruther of Balcaskie, 7th Baronet, who, on the death of Sir William Eric Francis Carmichael-Anstruther, 11th Baronet of Anstruther, in 1980, inherited his NS baronetcy. He is also chief of the surname.

ARMSTRONG This Border surname comes from a personal attribute, 'strength of arm'. An ancient tradition says the progenitor was Fairbairn, an armour-bearer to the king, who saved his master when his horse was killed under him. He grasped the monarch by the thigh and set him on his own horse. The grateful king gave him lands in Liddesdale, and the name 'Armstrong'. The earliest reference to the surname occurs in 1235, when Adam Armstrong for causing a death, was pardoned at Carlisle. By the 14th century the name was prolific, having spread from Mangerton, in Liddesdale, into the 'debateable lands' along the English border. Gilbert Armstrong was a steward in the royal household, and an ambassador to England in 1363. Others were not so peaceable, and many marched into border legend. Armstrong of Gilnockie, a freebooter, was executed in 1529. James VI had a court jester named Archie Armstrong. 'Kinmont Willie'

Armstrong, aided by Scott of Buccleuch, escaped from Carlisle prison. The noted jazz musician, Louis 'Satchmo' Armstrong, and the astronaut, Neil Armstrong, who made the first moonwalk in 1959, gave the name prominence in America. Michael Armstrong is proprietor of the popular *Family Tree Magazine*.

BAIRD There can be little doubt that the Bairds (originally Baards) who first appear in Scotland as vassals of Baldwin of Biggar, who was made sheriff of Lanark by David I (1124–53), were of Flemish extraction. Early in the 13th century, Richard de Baard, gave lands on the River Avon to the monks of Lesmahagow, confirmed by his son of the same name. Robert Bard was witness to the confirmation charter of the churches of Innyrwic and Liggerwood, to the monks of Paisley, ca. 1275. Four individuals of the name rendered homage to King Edward I in 1296, and one of them, Fergus de Barde, of Lanarkshire, was probably ancestor of the Bairds of Kipp and Evandale. Robert Barde was made a prisoner of war in 1315, and is probably the man who had a charter of Cambusnethan and became sheriff of Lanark. John Barde is recorded in 1389, and Simone Bayard was town officer in Aberdeen in 1387. Bairds also appear at Aberchirder, in Banffshire, ca. 1500. The surname Bairdie, on record from the middle of the 16th century, may be a variant or simply a pet form.

Bairds were prominent in Lanarkshire. Alexander Baird, 1765–1833, of Lochwood, from whom descended the family of Elie and Muirkirk, was an ironmaster, and his son William founded the firm of William Baird & Co., of Gartsherrie. Robert Baird of Gartsherrie, who died in 1856, was Dean of Guild of Glasgow. Hugh Baird, 1770–1827, CE, constructed the Union Canal and was engineer for the Crinan Canal. Robert Baird of Bellfield was a partner of the Canal Foundry in Glasgow. The Bairds of Craigton intermarried with the Hamiltons of Airdrie, the Dunlops of Househill and the Dennistouns of Colgrain.

The Bairds of Saughton Hall descended from Andrew of Auchmedden, in Aberdeenshire, which family came to be represented as heirs of line by the Frasers of Findrack. William Baird of Newbych was created a Baronet of NS in 1680, but the baronetcy became extinct on the death of his son, Sir John, in 1745. Sir William's uncle, Robert Baird of Saughton Hall, was created a Baronet of NS in 1695. The 2nd Baronet, of Saughton Hall continued that line, and from his brother William descended the baronets of New Bythe (cr. UK, 1809), in East Lothian. The present and 5th Baronet is Sir David Baird, residing in Dumfries. Sir James Baird, 10th Baronet of Saughton Hall, resides at Guist, Norfolk.

The Rev. George Husband Baird, 1761–1840, born at Bo'ness, after being minister at Dunkeld and New Greyfriars, Edinburgh, became Principal of the University of Edinburgh. Several Bairds have had distinguished careers in the army. Sir David Baird, 1757–1829, descended from the Bairds of Pitmedden, entered the army in 1772, and rose to the rank of Lt. General, having served in India, South Africa, Denmark and Ireland. Edward Baird, 1864–1956, served in the 10th Hussars and with the Imperial Yoemanry. He soldiered in World War I (1914–18), and became a Brigadier-General in 1916. Sir Harry Baird, 1877–1963, entered the army in 1897, and served with the 12th Bengal Cavalry. In World War I, he served in the Argyll & Sutherland Highlanders, after which he fought in the Afghan War. He rose to the rank of General. Probably the best-known Baird was John Logie, 1888–1946, born in Helensburgh, who invented the television, the first practical televisor apparatus, in 1926. In 1928 he showed that colour TV was possible.

BEATON/BETHUNE Two families named McBeth and Beaton practised medicine in the Hebrides. The McBeths (*MacBheatha* – 'son of life'), were hereditary physicians of the Clan Donald, and were endowed with Ballinable and other lands in Islay as fee for their appointment. Fercos Macbetha appears in 1408, and Gilchrist McVeig, surgeon, is also on record. In 1609, another Fergus McBaithe appears as witness to a Gaelic charter, which he may have written. His son John succeeded him in 1628, but gave his lands to the Thane of Cawdor.

The Mull Beatons – possibly related – were hereditary physicians to the MacLeans of Dowart or Duart. Hector Maclean granted a charter to Andrew MacDonil Vikinollif ('son of the doctor') and his heirs, of Peincross and Brolas, in 1572. Another of the Mull family was Fergus McVeagh, whose medical manuscript is in the library of the University of Edinburgh. A cadet of this family settled in the Fraser country, and were at Glenconvinth before 1558, when James Beaton attended Lord Lovat. The family declined in the Aird before 1622.

Most authorities agree that the Skye Beatons were Bethunes from Fife, and that Dr David Bethune, a grandson of John, Vth Laird of Balfour, settled in 'the winged isle', ca. 1560. He left descendants, who intermarried with the best families in the islands. The last of this medical family was Neil Beaton, who died in 1763. Rev. John Bethune, 1751–1815, son of Angus in Brebost, Skye, emigrated to North Carolina in 1773, and became an army chaplain. In 1784 he went to Quebec, where he organised a Presbyterian congregation, then became minster at Williamston, in Glengarry County, ontario. Two of his sons, John and Alexander, were clergymen.

The Fife Bethunes were of Flemish extraction, deriving their name from a town in Flanders. Bethunes came to England with William the Conqueror in 1066, and appear in Scotland by 1165. Robert de Bethunia witnessed a charter registered at St Andrews, ca. 1180. In old records the name is frequently found as Beton or Betun, and by the 16th century became confused with the Gaelic Beatons. The Fife Bethunes owned land in that county and in Angus. Alexander de Bethune was slain at Dupplin in 1332. His son Robert married the heiress of Sir John Balfour of that ilk, and received the lands of Balfour, from which sprang several branches. The family failed in the male line in 1760, and the estate was inherited by William Congleton, who assumed the name Bethune. Eventually it descended to Admiral Charles Ramsay Drinkwater-Bethune, 1802–84, RN. The Bethunes of Blebo descended from David, XIth laird of Balfour.

James Beaton (?1475–1539), was of the Balfour line, and became provost of the Collegiate Church of Bothwell in 1503. After being Abbot of Dunfermline, Bishop of Galloway and Archbishop of Glasgow, he became Archbishop of St Andrews in 1523. The celebrated Cardinal David Beaton, 1494–1546, was his nephew, and one of the most influential men of his time. He was Lord Privy Seal in 1528, and Ambassador to France, 1533–37. He became a cardinal in 1538, and the following year, Archbishop of St Andrews. His inglorious death at St Andrews was a serious blow to the Roman Catholic church. Yet another Beaton, James, 1517–1603, a nephew of the Cardinal, became Archbishop of Glasgow in 1552. At the Reformation in 1560, he retired to France, where he became ambassador for Mary, Queen of Scots.

BELL In Scotland the surname Bell may have three derivations. A local origin accounts for most. Someone who lived adjacent to a church, or was the bell-ringer, might be called John at the Bell, or simply John Bell. Likewise, a tavern-keeper called William, whose sign was a bell, would easily become William Bell. A secondary origin seems likely, from someone who was handsome, just *bel* (Old French). Probably a third derivation is from the forename Isabel, or Bell.

The surname is prolific outwith the Highland line, and 'Tinker' Bells are almost as numerous as 'Nobby' Clarks. Dr Black says that in Islay and Kintyre, Bell is used as an Englishing of *Mac Illinamhaoil*. This is said to have arisen from the union of a MacMillan with a Miss Bell, taking her name in English, but retaining the old name in Gaelic.

A family named Bell seem to have been hereditarily associated with the church of Dunkeld. David Bell was a canon there in 1263, and William Bell was a dean there, ca. 1330. A little later Thomas Bell was a canon there. William Bell, vicar of Lamberton, witnessed a charter of the Priory of Coldingham in 1271. Adam and Richard Bell, from Berwickshire, swore fealty to Edward I in 1296. That same monarch deprived Gilbert Fitz Bell of his lands. He may have been the progenitor of the Annandale Bells, who spread themselves throughout the West March. A common phrase in Dumfriesshire for anything plentiful, drew a comparison with the Bells of Middlebie, scores of whom are buried in the old kirkyard there. Thomas Bell witnessed a charter to the Abbey of Jedburgh, ca. 1350. Numerous Bells appear in Angus, Fife and Perthshire in the 15th and 16th centuries. John Bell, 1691–1780, of Antermony, an Asiatic traveller, was born in Campsie parish, Stirlingshire, and went to Russia in 1714. He became physician to Russian embassies in Persia, Siberia and China, before returning to Scotland in 1746. His travel book was printed in 1763.

In the Borders the Bells were as unruly as any of the larger families under whom they lived. There does not seem to have been a unified clan, but David Bell, at the Water of Mylk, was called the 'Young King'. The leading family appears to have been the Bells of Blackethouse. William Bell of Blackethouse, called 'Reidcloke', had to find caution in the sum of 1000 merks, 1607, for his good behaviour. Blackethouse passed to a collateral branch of the family, and descended to Benjamin Bell, 1749–1806, an eminent surgeon, who sold the estate in 1775 to John Carruthers of Brae, whose wife was Grisel Bell of the Auldhill branch of the family. Benjamin Bell was the father of George and Joseph Bell, both surgeons, and he was the grandfather of Benjamin Bell, 1837–1911, another medical man, who was the original of novelist Arthur Conan Doyle's famous character, Sherlock Holmes.

Several Bells were of an inventive turn of mind. Henry Bell, 1767–1830, born near Torphichen, was the first man in Europe to apply steam to the purpose of navigation. He settled in Glasgow ca. 1790, and worked as a carpenter. In 1811 he induced John and

Charles Wood in Port Glasgow to lay down the keel of the celebrated steamboat, the *Comet*, launched in 1812. Reverend Patrick Bell, 1801–69, of Carmylie, in Angus, was the inventor of a reaping machine in 1827, improved in 1852. Alexander Graham Bell, 1847–1922, born in Edinburgh, emigrated to Canada with his father in 1870, and at Boston, Massachusetts, invented the articulating telephone, 1872–76.

BISSET The Bissets or Bissetts came to Scotland with William the Lion on his return from captivity in 1174, and were probably of French origin, *bis*, in Old French, meaning brownish grey, the colour of the rock-dove. The diminutive form was Bissie, leading to forms such as Bizet or Byset. They seem to have migrated from Nottingham to Selkirkshire before 1195. Henricus Biset there witnessed several confirmation charters by William the Lion between 1198 and 1210. His son John witnessed a charter relating to Melrose Abbey, in 1204. He may have been the man granted lands in the Aird, west of Inverness, and who founded a priory at Beauly in 1231. His uncle, Walter Bisset, was Lord of Aboyne. He gave to the Abbey of Coupar his saltworks near Aberdeen. Walter was succeeded by his nephew Thomas, ancestor of the Bissets of Lessendrum, near Huntly. Peter Bisset, ca. 1510–68, was Professor of Law in the University of Bologna. Rev Dr James Bisset, 1792–1872, was educated at Aberdeen for the church, but became master of the grammar school at Udny where, among his pupils, were the future historians, Joseph Robertson and John Hill Burton. James Bisset, 1742–1832, the artist and poet, born at Perth, removed to Birmingham and Leamington, where he established a museum and art gallery. Robert Bisset, 1759–1805, born in the Manse of Logierait, went to London, where he taught and wrote articles for the press. David W. Bisset, born at Motherwell in 1938, became a librarian, and is secretary of the Scottish Esperanto Federation.

BOGLE The name derives from Bowgyhill (Boglehold or Bogleshole), in the parish of Old Monkland, Lanarkshire. It became prolific in the west of Scotland, especially in and around Glasgow. An old saying was that Glasgow owed its prosperity to (Church) Bells, Bairds and Bogles. There were three large branches of the family, and a number of offshoots. George Bogle, died 1707, and Jean Park, were the progenitors of the Bogles of Dalmdowie and of Shettleston, probably also of those of Hamilton Farm. He was closely related to William Bogle, portioner of Bogleshole, who married Annabell Wardrop, and their son John went to Strabane, Ireland, ca. 1717. He married Mary Graham, whose brother William Graham claimed to be *de jure* Earl of Menteith, in 1761. They were the progenitors of the Bogle-French family of Cedar Valley, Antigua. John Bogle, WS, who died in 1743, was of the old Bogleshole stock. Other Bogles were property-owners at Annfield, Cowlairs, Gilmorehill, Greenfield House, Langside, Mains and Yorkhill House. William Bogle was schoolmaster at Cambuslang in 1707. Rev Andrew Nisbet Bogle, minister at North Leith UF Church in 1903, claimed descent from Capt. Archibald Bogle, second son of William Bogle, writer in Hamilton, descended from the Bogleshole family.

BORTHWICK In the 12th century what became the barony of Borthwick, lying along the water of that name, on the borders of Selkirkshire and Roxburghshire, appears to have been the home of the Borthwicks. Thomas de Borthwick, before 1367, had a charter of the lands of Ligertwood, near Lauder, in Berwickshire, and his son was in possession of Catcune, in Mid Lothian. This was the family who built, in 1430, the imposing Borthwick Castle on land formerly known as Loquhariot (? Low Heriot), Lochwarret or Lochorwort, in the parish called Borthwick. The third laird, Sir William Borthwick, was probably raised to the peerage in 1452, and sat in Parliament as Lord Borthwick, in 1454. In 1567, Mary, Queen of Scots and her husband Lord Bothwell, were at Borthwick Castle when the barons, with a thousand men, sought to capture them. Bothwell received warning and hastily escaped, and the Queen also fled, disguised as a man. The Lord Borthwick was then William, 7th holder of the title. On the death of John, 10th Lord, without male issue, the honours passed to Henry Borthwick, descended from the 3rd Lord, and Parliament upheld his right. The title had many vicissitudes. Henry, 14th Lord, died ca. 1811, and the succession opened to Patrick Borthwick, merchant in Leith, and *de jure* Lord Borthwick. His son Archibald, 1811–40, formally claimed the peerage, but he died without male issue and his only brother, John Henry Stuart Borthwick, 1905–96, of Crookston, succeeded in his claim to be the descendant of the second son of the 1st Lord Borthwick. The present and 24th Lord is his elder son, John Hugh Borthwick, chief of the surname.

From Thomas Borthwick, of Edinburgh, descended Sir Thomas Borthwick of Whitburgh House, Ford, Mid Lothian, who was created a Baronet of the UK in 1908. He died in 1912, when about to be created a Baron, and his son Thomas Banks Borthwick received the honour. When he died in 1967, the peerage became extinct, and his nephew, John Thomas Borthwick became 3rd Baronet. By his wife Irene he has issue.

BOSWELL The surname is probably best known in literary circles through James Boswell, 1740–95, the friend and biographer of Dr Samuel Johnson. He was the eldest son of Alexander Boswell of Auchinleck, Ayrshire, who had a good law practice before becoming a Lord of Session in 1754. James studied law at Edinburgh, Glasgow and Utrecht, and was admitted an advocate in 1766. He made the acquaintance of Johnson in 1763, and kept notes which were of prime importance later when he wrote the famous biography. The writings of James did much to influence the decision in the 'Douglas Cause', 1767. In 1773 he accompanied Johnson on the epic tour to the Hebrides, and wrote his interesting *Journal*, published in 1785. Two of his sons, Alexander and James, were also literary men.

It is acknowledged that the family is of French origin, having come from the Seine Valley. They came to England before 1136, and had estates in Yorkshire. The first of the family to appear in Scotland was Robert de Boseville, who was given lands in Berwickshire. He may have come north in the train of Ada de Warenne, whose marriage with Prince Henry was solemnised in 1139. The family arms, Argent, on a fess Sable, three cinquefoils of the field, indicate the Hainaut-Ghent origins of the Seine Valley people.

The Boswells of Balgregie, Fife, no doubt migrated from Oxmuir, in Berwickshire, and Roger, the first of that family, appears to have married a daughter of Sir Michael Wemyss of Wemyss. James Boswell, 4th of Balgregie, acquired Balmuto, and David Boswell, 2nd of Balmuto, by his first marriage with Grizel Wemyss, had two sons: David, who died before him, and Sir Alexander, who was killed at Flodden in 1513. The latter left issue who continued his line of the family. By his second marriage in 1480, with Lady Elizabeth Sinclair, he had four other sons: William of Lochgelly; Thomas; George of Craigside, and Robert, a clergyman. Thomas had a charter of the Barony of Auchinleck, in 1504, but he too was slain at Flodden. He left a son David, whose son, John of Auchinleck, was ancestor of the Boswells of Duncansmuir, from whom descended the Craigston family and the Knockroon family, which ended in an heiress, who married her cousin, John Boswell. James Boswell, 4th of Auchinleck, was indicted for 'abiding from the raid at Dumfries' in 1600. With three sons who soldiered under Gustav Adolph of Sweden, he also had a son David, who carried on the family of Auchinleck. His grandson, David, 6th Laird, had two sons: James, who succeeded him, and John, who purchased Balmuto from his kinsman, Andrew Boswell, WS, in 1722. Alexander, 7th of Auchinleck, was the father of Alexander, 8th of Auchinleck, father of James, the friend of Samuel Johnson.

Alexander, eldest son of James Boswell, was created a Baronet of the UK in 1821. His son, Sir James, 2nd Baronet and 11th Laird, sold the estate to his kinsman, John Douglas-Boswell of Garrallan, and died without male issue in 1857, when the baronetcy became extinct. James Boswell's eldest son, by a second marriage, was Dr John Boswell, an eminent physician in Edinburgh, whose eldest son, Robert Boswell of St Boswells, WS, was Lyon Depute and Keeper of the Records of the Court of the Lord Lyon, 1770–95. He was interim Lord Lyon King of Arms, 1795–96. From him descended the 16th heir male of the Auchinleck family, David Rutherford Boswell, born 1927, educated at Epsom College and Guy's Hospital, who served in the dental branch of the RAF.

BOYD It is thought that the surname Boyd is derived from the Gaelic for the island of Bute, rendered *Bod* or *Boid*. The earliest known Boyds were vassals of the de Morevilles in the regality of Largs, and may have come with them from England. They were landowners in Renfrewshire during the reign of Alexander III (1249–86). Sir Robert Boyd witnessed a contract between Bryce de Egluntune and the burgh of Irvine in 1205. Alan de Bodha appears at Dumfries, ca. 1214. Robert Boyd fought at Largs in 1263. Another Robert Boyd was a supporter of Robert the Bruce, and one of his commanders at Bannockburn in 1314. He was granted lands at Kilmarnock and elsewhere in Ayrshire, and was ancestor of the Earls of Kilmarnock. His descendant, Robert Boyd, sat in Parliament as Lord Boyd in 1454. Thomas, his eldest son, married Princess Mary, sister of King James III (then a minor), in 1467, and was created Earl of Arran. He was later attainted and the estates reverted to the crown. His son James died unmarried, and his uncle, Robert, *de jure* 4th Lord Boyd, was restored to the honours and estates in 1549. It was the 10th Lord Boyd who was created Earl of Kilmarnock in 1661, and he had a new charter of the Barony of Kilmarnock in 1672. The 4th Earl, William, 1705–46, was a supporter of the Young Pretender, and was taken prisoner at Culloden, and executed, with forfeiture of all his honours. In June 1831, the then Earl of Errol was created a Peer of the UK as Baron Kilmarnock, and since then the honour has been used by eldest sons as a courtesy title.

Mark Alexander Boyd, 1562–1601, a native of Galloway, was educated at Glasgow and Paris, where he appeared as scholar, poet and lecturer. He entered the French army and served against the King of Navarre in 1587. Reverend Zachary Boyd, ca. 1585–1653, became minister of Barony Church, Glasgow, in 1623, and was twice Rector of the University. He preached against Cromwell in his presence, and wrote *Zion's Flowers*, and other devotional works. Another minister, Rev. Andrew Kennedy Hutchison Boyd, 1825–99, studied at Glasgow and Paris, and was ordained to the ministry in 1851. He was successively pastor of Kilpatrick-Irongray; St Bernard's, Edinburgh; and at St Andrews. He was awarded the degree of DD by the University of Edinburgh in 1874. Reverend Boyd was the author of *Recreations of a Country Parson*.

BRODIE The surname Brodie is said to be derived from the barony of that name, in Morayshire, but their armorial bearings indicate Flemish origins. They were probably descended from the Counts of Boulogne, and came to Scotland via England, in the train of Freskin and Berowald. Brothie comes from the Flemish word for brother, cognate with the Dutch *broeder*. Information about the early lairds is scanty: the family muniments having been burnt by Lord Lewis Gordon in 1645. Malcolm, Thane of Brodie, appears ca. 1285, and he had two sons: David, who succeeded him, and Alexander of East Grange, ancestor of the Brodies of Lethen. There is some hiatus here, as Michael de Brothie had a charter of the lands in 1311, as heir to his father. It is possible he was an elder brother of David, who had several sons. Thomas de Brothie was a juror at Inverness in 1376–7. His son John appears in 1380. John Brodie of Brodie appears as a witness in 1492, and Thomas Brodie of that ilk was a juror at Inverness in 1546, and that year he and his wife, Agnes Shaw, had a new charter of the Lordship of Brodie.

A descendant, Alexander Brodie, was a Lord of Session, 1657–61, and several other Brodies were in the legal profession in Edinburgh. Lord Brodie had a son John, who married Lady Mary Kerr. They had a large family, of whom their daughter Amelia married her cousin, James Brodie of Asleisk, and were the parents of Alexander Brodie of Brodie, Lord Lyon, 1727–54. His direct descendant, Montague N.A. Brodie, married Helena P.M. Budgeon in 1939. Their son Alastair married in 1968, Mary L.F.D. Johnson, with issue: Alexander, Phaedra and Edward. The imposing castle of Brodie was sold to the National Trust for Scotland in 1978, and since then the family have been at loggerheads.

Among cadets of the Brodies of Brodie are those of Lethen and Glashaugh. The Lethen branch descend from a younger son of David of that ilk, who purchased the estates of Pitgavenie, Eastgrange and Lethen in 1634. Of this line was Thomas Brodie, WS, who was Lyon Depute, 1769–70. The family is now represented by Ewen John Brodie of Lethen, who succeeded in 1966. Sir Benjamin Collins Brodie, of the Glasshaugh line, was surgeon to William IV and Queen Victoria, and was created a Baronet in 1834. The present Baronet is sir Benjamin David Ross Brodie.

Brodies were prominent in Edinburgh from the close of the 16th century. One 'Mr' James Brodie married Anna Forrett at Edinburgh in 1599. Alexander Brodie of Brodie was admitted a burgess and guildbrother of Edinburgh in 1648. Alexander and James Brodie graduated at Edinburgh University in 1687. Ludovick, son of Francis Brodie of Milnton, in Moray, was admitted WS in 1706. A daring Edinburgh burglar, Deacon William Brodie, was undetected until he raided the Excise Office. He fled to Holland, but was apprehended and brought back for trial. Brodie was hanged in 1788. Brodies also appear in Aberdeen. Elizabeth Brodie was the wife of Thomas Denman, a physician there in 1783, father of Lord Chief Justice Denman, and of two daughters who married Dr Mathew Baillie and Sir Richard Croft, another physician. Brodies were also quite numerous in the west. Sarah Brodie, wife of Rev. Archibald Sydserff of Dunbarton, died in 1730, and Robert Brodie of Hazelhead died in 1753.

BROWN/BROUN It is believed that the surname Brown is derived from an adjective meaning in Old English, brown or dark red. In Scotland the main variant is Broun, and in England Browne. In Old High German the name was rendered *Brun*, and was borrowed into French to give *Le Brun*. Brun occurs in English charters from ca. 970, but is not recorded in Scotland until early in the 12th century. Walterus le Brun was on an assize at Glasgow in 1116, and Sir David le Brun witnessed the foundation charter of the Abbey of Holyrood in 1128. He may have been the ancestor of the ancient family, Broun of Colstoun, East Lothian. Robert Brune witnessed a grant to the hospital of Soltre (Soutra), about 1260, and Richard Broun witnessed a charter of Donald, Earl of Mar, ca. 1285. Richard de Broun and others of the surname swore fealty to Edward I in 1296.

It is remarkable that the Brouns of Colstoun can trace their ancestry for over 850 years. Possibly they came from France, but it is uncertain if they descended from a knight shown as 'Braine' on the *Roll of Battle Abbey*. They were well established at 'Cummyrcollyston' (Colstoun) by 1385, when David Broun had a charter of the lands of Westersegarystoun. He and his wife Agnes resigned the lands of Colstoun in 1361, in favour of their son David. In the reign of James I (1406–37), William Broun of Colstoun married Margaret de Annand, co-heiress of Sauchie, in Stirlingshire. Later in the 15th century Sir William Broun of Colstoun was Warden of the Middle Marches, and took part in a battle at Dornock, in Annandale, against the English, led by Sir Marmaduke Langdale. Both commanders were slain. Patrick Broun of Colstoun was created a Baronet of NS in 1686. Through subsequent unions his successors were related to the Hays of Yester, the Murrays of Stanhope, and other influential families. The 13th and present Baronet is Sir William Windsor Broun, born 1927, who lives in NSW, Australia.

The family of Agnes, 1732–1820, mother of the poet Burns, also favoured the spelling Broun. She was the eldest daughter of Gilbert Broun, tenant of Craigentoun, Kirkoswald, by his first wife, Agnes Rainie, and married William Burnes, a native of Kincardineshire, in 1756. Their son Robert, who was to become Scotland's greatest lyric poet, was born in 1759.

A number of Brown families have been small landowners. The Browns of Lochton, Perthshire, were descended from John Brown of Muirside, Forfar, who married Janet Walker. A later member of the family, James Brown of Lochton, was Provost of Dundee, 1844–47. The family came to be represented by the Wemyss-Browns of Cononsyth. The Browns of Fordell, in Perthshire, were descendants of Sir John Brune, High Sheriff of Aberdeenshire in 1368. Of this family came James Brown, 1786–1864, a Director of the Bank of Scotland, who married Anne, daughter and eventual heiress of Lt. Col. William McKerral, VIIth of Hillhouse, and the McKerral-Browns of Peasenhall, Suffolk, came to represent them. The Browns of Newhall and Carlops, Peeblesshire, descended from Hugh Brown, a Glasgow merchant, whose son Robert, an advocate, purchased those estates in 1783. He published an edition of Alan Ramsay's *The Gentle Shepherd* in 1808. His grandson, Hugh Horatio Brown, was an accomplished man of letters. The Orkney author, the late George Mackay Brown, whose novels include *Greenvoe, Magnus, Time in a Red Coat*, and *The Golden Bird*, won the James Tait Black Prize in 1988.

BRUCE The story of the Bruces runs like a bright gold thread through the rich tapestry of Scottish history. They appear to have been of Flemish extraction, and settled at Brus (now Brix) – hence the surname – near Cherbourg, in Normandy, about the time that Matilda of Flanders married William the Conqueror, an event which explains why so many Flemish noblemen took part in the invasion of 1066. Their progenitor in Normandy was Adam, and it may have been his son Robert who fought at Hastings. His descendant, Robert de Brus, was probably a companion at the English court of Prince David, who, soon after succeeding to the throne of Scotland, granted him extensive lands in Annandale. The family already held estates in England, and there may have been a distant relationship with Maud or Matilda, who became the Scottish queen in 1124. His great-grandson, Robert de Brus, brought the family closer to the royal line through his marriage to Isabel, daughter of David, Earl of Huntingdon, younger brother of King Malcolm IV and King William. Indeed this was how their son, Robert, became a competitor for the crown in 1286. It was his grandson, Robert, Earl of Carrick, who was crowned King of Scots in 1306. He is usually referred to as 'Robert the Bruce'. His brilliant victory over Edward II of England at Bannockburn in 1314, led to the famous *Declaration of Arbroath* in 1320, and to the independence of Scotland. His daughter Marjory married Walter Stewart, and they were the ancestors of the Stewart kings.

The direct royal line died out, but branches of the family settled in Fife and Clackmannanshire. Edward Bruce of Easter Kennet, was granted the Lordship of Kinloss in 1600/01, and from him descended the Earls of Elgin and Kincardine. Of the Carnock line of the family was the Hon. Alexander Bruce, who was exiled in Holland with Charles I. In 1662 he conducted experiments with Christian Hugyens at The Hague, and at sea, on short pendulum clocks, with a degree of success. The same year he succeeded as 3rd Earl of Kincardine. Charles, 9th Earl of Kincardine, succeeded to the Earldom of Elgin in 1747, after the death of his kinsman, Charles, 4th Earl of Elgin and 2nd of Ailesbury. The present 11th Earl of Elgin and 15th of Kincardine, Lord Andrew Bruce, the clan chief, lives at Broomhall, near Dunfermline. He served in World War II with the Scots Guards, and was Grand Master Mason of Scotland, 1961–65.

The Bruce family has many offshoots. One of the most important was that of Airth, in Stirlingshire, descended from the Bruces of Clackmannan. Sir Edward Bruce having married Agnes, heiress of Airth, before 1417, gained that estate. They also owned Stenhouse, in the same county. In 1628, Sir William Bruce of Stenhouse was created a Baronet of NS. His descendant, the present and 12th Baronet, is Sir Michael Bruce, who served in the US Marine Corps, 1943–46, and lives at Newport Beach, California. Another branch of the Airth family descended from Rev. Edward Bruce, who went to Ireland ca. 1609, and whose family obtained the estates of Kilroot, Co. Antrim, and Scoutbush, Carrickfergus. James Bruce, ca. 1730–94, of Kinnaird, the explorer of the Nile, was also descended from the Airth line.

Sir William Bruce, ca. 1627–1710, of Balcaskie, created a Baronet of NS in 1688, purchased the Barony of Kinross in 1671, and became the King's Surveyor and Master of Works. He designed the fine mansion of Kinloss, completed in 1690. Sir William restored part of Holyroodhouse, and was the architect of Moncreiffe House and the central part of Hopetoun House. To him belongs the credit for the change from baronial to classical architecture in Scotland.

BUCHANAN Clarinch, an island in Loch Lomond, opposite Balmaha, was granted in 1225 by the Early of Lennox, to Absolon or Anselan, son of MacBeth. He took his name from lands on the shore supposed to mean in Gaelic, 'house of the canon'. He may have belonged to one of the old families of the Celtic Church. 'Clarinch' became the war cry of the Buchanans. Tradition tells us that the chief's surname was originally McAuselan, a name retained by a collateral line. Those of the 'stem' family adopted a territorial designation: *Mac-a Chanonaich*, in Gaelic.

In 1282, the Earl of Lennox granted a charter to Maurice de Bouchannane, confirming him in his lands and giving him the right to hold courts. The Buchanan chiefs held the lands for another 400 years. Maurice, son of Maurice, had a charter of the carucate of land called Bouchannane, with the land of Sallachy, by Donald, 6th Earl of Lennox, confirmed under the Great Seal in 1371. His descendant, Sir Alexander, went to France with the Earl of Buchan to assist against the English, and was killed at Verneuil in 1421. He was succeeded by his brother, Walter of Buchanan. A younger brother, John, was ancestor of Henry Buchanan of Leny, from whose daughter descended the Buchanans of Lany and Bardowie. Walter married Isobel, daughter of Murdoch, Duke of Albany, and had two sons: Walter, his heir, and Thomas, progenitor of the Buchanans of Drumakill, from whom descended George Buchanan, 1506–82, the great Latinist. Walter's eldest son, Patrick was killed at Flodden in 1513, and his eldest son George succeeded to Buchanan. From his younger son Walter, descended the Buchanans of Spittal. George was sheriff of Dunbartonshire, and fought at Pinkie in 1547. His son John died before him, and was succeeded by his son Sir George Buchanan, from whose half-brother, William came the Auchmar family. Sir George's grandson, also Sir George, was involved in the Civil War, and died a prisoner of Cromwell in 1651. John Buchanan, the last laird, sold his ancestral estate in 1682 to the Marquess of Montrose.

From the Spittal and Lany lines of the family descended Dr Francis Hamilton Buchanan, who established his claim to the chiefship in 1826, but his grandson John died in 1919, without issue. A branch of the Buchanans of Lany held the estates of Ardinconnal and Auchintorlie, in Dunbartonshire, and four brothers – George, merchant in Glasgow; Andrew of Drumpelier; Neil of Hillington, and Archibald of Auchintorlie – were the promoters of the Buchanan Society in 1725: the oldest organisation of its kind. From Archibald descended Sir Andrew Buchanan, created a Baronet of the UK, in 1878. The 5th Baronet of Dunburgh is Sir Andrew George Buchanan, Lord Lt. of Nottinghamshire since 1991. The Leith (-Buchanan) baronets (created UK, 1763), descend from Alexander Leith, of Aberdeen. The additional surname of Buchanan was added by Sir Alexander Leith, 3rd Baronet, who married in 1832, Jemima, daughter of Hector MacDonald Buchanan of Ross.

Dugald Buchanan, 1716–68, son of a Strathyre miller and farmer, became a teacher at Kinloch Rannoch, and wrote Gaelic poetry of high quality. James Buchanan, 1791–1868, 15th President of the USA, was son of James Buchanan, who emigrated from Donegal, Ireland, to Pennsylvania, and is said to have been a descendant of Thomas Buchanan, an Ulster-Scot.

BUDGE The surname Budge is found mainly in Caithness, Orkney and Skye. According to Hugh MacDonald, the Skye seannachie who wrote during the reign of Charles II (1660–85), they were associated with Clan Donald. When Angus Og of of Islay, a friend of Robert the Bruce, married Margaret, daughter of Guy O'Cathlan, an Ulster baron, he received as her dowry seven score of men, doubtless welcome as he had lost many followers harrying English fleets. A later historian calls them *Tochradh Nighean a Chathanaich*, 'The dowry of the daughter of O'Cathlan'. They received grants of land. Those who became known as *Butikes* or Budges, formed a small clan. One member, who fled to Caithness when pursued for slaughter, founded a family there in the latter part of the 14th century. Walter, Earl of Caithness, granted the three-penny land of Toftingall to Nicholas Budge in 1403. His son Magnus was infeft in the three-penny of Toftingall and in tenements in Wick, in 1415. Another son, Henry, supplicated for the treasureship of Ross in 1430, although he held a canonry and prebend of Caithness. This church office does not appear to have been very secure, and in 1432 there was a dispute about the office with Henry de Rynd. Budge died in 1444. The family had disputes with the Baynes and other local families, who probably looked upon them as interlopers.

The Budges established themselves firmly at Toftingall, in Watten parish, and it has been claimed there were twelve generations from Nicholas in 1403, to Donald, who registered arms in 1703, blazoned: Argent, a lion passant, Azure, armed and langued Gules. Crest, a hand holding a dagger, proper. Motto: *Stricita Parata Neci*. A Budge/Murray Threipland of Fingask marriage resulted in a quartering of 1826, showing the arms of Murray of Penyland, and of Thriepland of Fingask. In the Orkneys the Budges were prominent in South Ronaldsay. Marion Budge, spouse of the deceased Robert Edmonson in Wydwall, died ca. 1611, leaving children Patrick, Adame, Andro, Christian and Marioun. The testament of Magnus Budge in South Ronaldsay was confirmed in 1663. A number of Budges from South Ronaldsay served in Canada with the Hudson's Bay Co., between 1793 and 1850. One of those, William, a labourer in 1811, rose to be a clerk and trader. He cared for his books in a satisfactory manner, but a propensity to liquor kept him in a subordinate position. John Budge in Oxsetter, Northmavine, Shetland, died in 1613. Isabel Budge in Edinburgh, married Steven Hutcheson, a weaver, in 1662. In 1690, John, son of Daniel Budge in Tastingell, Caithness, was indentured apprentice to John Lowson, tailor-burgess of Edinburgh.

A branch of the family settled in Skye. According to tradition, William Budge, serving in a volunteer regiment, mended a damaged canon, and was invited by Col. MacDonald of Lyndale to become his estate blacksmith. Later, Lord MacDonald gave him lands at Balgown previously held by the MacRuries. He married Christian MacDonald, and had two sons. James, the elder, was a blacksmith and farmer. By his second wife, Margaret MacDonald, he had a large family. His second son, Donald, followed the family trade, and his eldest son, also Donald, became a hotelier at Dunvegan. The business was in the family from 1910–46. Donald's eldest son, another Donald, graduated in arts at Glasgow and became minister at Cumnock. During World War II he served as an army chaplain. In 1949 he was called to Jura. Rev Donald married and American lady, Eleanor B. Melchior, and died in 1978, without issue.

BURNS Whenever this surname is considered, the name of Robert Burns, 1759–96, is remembered. He was undoubtably Scotland's greatest lyric poet. It is fashionable today among intellectuals to compare him with Hugh McDiarmid (Christopher M. Grieve), 1892–1978, but the work of the latter, with all its literary merit, will never be as popular as that of Burns. The Ayrshire bard wrote for the common man: McDiarmid did not.

The surname Burns or Burnes appears in English records as early as the 11th century, but not in Scotland until early in the 17th. Burn, however, is a surname of great antiquity, and it seems probable that in many cases it became Burns. It certainly did with the Burn family who occupied the lands of Carntoun, near Tillicoultry, for around 200 years. John Burn sold the lands, ca. 1738, and became a schoolmaster in Glasgow, adopting the name Burns. He was the father of Rev. John Burns, 1744–1839, minister of Barony parish, and father of a remarkable family.

It is likely that the surname Burns is formed from a compound word, Burnhouse, a dwelling near a burn of stream. There are numerous Burnhouses in Scotland, and unrelated families of the name. Because most of the early ones were on the land as tenants and cottars, their appearance in records is late. James Burns, son of John Burns in Easter Gellat (?Dunfermline), was apprenticed in 1631 to John Quhippo, baker in Edinburgh. When he was admitted a burgess of the city in 1641, his name was recorded as Burne. John Burns, hammerman in Glasgow, was admitted burgess in 1641, for performing four days work for the commonweal every year, *gratis*. His son John was admitted burgess and guildbrother in his right in 1661. The testament of James Burns, maltman in Dundee, and Elizabeth Bouman his wife, was registered in 1665.

In Kincardineshire, families who appear as Burnes, Burnas, Burnace and Burness, are possibly descended from a common ancestor. In 1637, John Burnes, servitor to Sir Alexander Strachan of Thorntoun, witnessed a bond in favour of his master by the Earl of Traquair. Patrick Burness, clerk to the Presbytery of Brechin, attested a bond granted to the parish reader at Lochlea in 1659. Robert Burnace in Arbuthnott had a son Robert, born in 1633, who was placed by his father in a farm on the estate of Glenbervie. He married Elspeth Wise in 1655. In leasing the farm he was to neighbour persons of his name and kin, who had farmed there for generations. John Stuart, 1813–77, advocate in Aberdeen, a historian and genealogist, whose ancestor, David Stuart of Inchbreck, fought at Pinkie in 1547, stated there were Burnes or Burness tenants on the estate at that time. When the parochial registers begin, they are quite numerous. Walter Burness in Glenbervie parish, had a son of the same name who leased the farm of Bogjordan, on the estate of Inchbreck, and about them a false tradition has gained credence Walter, senior, is supposed to have been an Argyll Campbell who had given offence to his landlord, and moved with his son to Stonehouse of Mergie, and adopted the surname Burness, from the name of his previous home. The story is at variance with recorded facts. Walter, junior, had by his first wife sons William and James, who farmed Bogjordan. James, 1656–1743, married Margaret Falconer. Their son Robert married Isabel Keith, and he farmed at Clochnahill, Dunottar. The had with other issue a son William, 1721–84, who migrated to Ayrshire and married Agnes Broun, from Kirkoswald. Their famous son, the bard Robert, was born in the *auld clay biggin'* at Alloway.

BUTLER Like some other occupational names, butler is an old name which comes from servants in the great homes of the Middle Ages. The name is found in England as well as Scotland from the latter part of the 12th century. It derives from the Old French *buteiller* or *buteiler*, and refers to the person who had charge of the butts or casks of wine. Forms such as Boteler may have come from the makers of leather bottles and/or from the 'Botlers' who filled them. The Latin form of the name is usually *pincerna*, which can also mean cup-bearer. Hugo, pincerna, was a witness to charters from 1173 to 1207. Warinus, pincerna of the Bishop of Glasgow, appears between 1208 and 1213. Several Botillers swore fealty to Edward I of England in 1296. In Scotland the name seems largely to have been ousted by Spence, 'custodian of the larder'. Elizabeth

Butler, only daughter of 'Thomas, 8th Earl of Ormonde and Ossory, and widow of Theobold, Viscount Butler of Tulleophelim, married the royal favourite, Richard Preston, who rose from 'domesticus servitor regis' to be a landowner and knight. He accompanied King James to London in 1603, and was created Lord Dingwall. His father-in-law settled his estates on his heir male, Richard Butler, and he refused to give these up to Lord Dingwall, who was created Baron Dunsmore, Co. Kilkenny, and Earl of Desmond, in 1610. There were some other titled Butler families in England and Ireland, which seem now to be extinct. The name is not prolific in Scotland, and some who bear it may be of English or Irish stock.

CAMERON The Camerons, according to the late Sir Iain Moncreiffe, derive their name from *Cam-brun*, 'crooked hill', an elevation in Cameron parish, Fife. A knightly family in the Tay Valley in the Middle Ages, he suggested they were a branch of the Macduffs, the premier clan among the Gaels. Dr G.F. Black, however, in his monumental work, *The Surnames of Scotland*, says the name is of two-fold origin, Highland and Lowland, pointing out that besides the Fife place-name, there is Cameron (Toll), near Edinburgh, and Cameron, in the Lennox. He took the name to mean *cam-shron*, for 'wry' or 'hook nose'. Mrs Platts points out that Cambron, one of the earliest forms of the name, is a small place in Hainaut, less than five miles from Lens, where Count Lambert had his home, and that the arms of Cameron of Lochiel differ only in the tinctures to those of the great family of Oudenarde, nobles of Flanders.

The surname is certainly of great antiquity. Adam de Kamerun witnessed a charter by William de Haya to the monks of Cupar, before 1249. Hugh Cambrun was sheriff of Forfar in 1229. The Camerons of Lochaber became the most distinct group, and appear there by the beginning of the 15th century. The eponymous ancestor is given as Gillespick, son of Angus, who lived in the 11th century, but the patronymic of their Lochiel chief, *MacDhomnall Dubh*, derives from Donald *Dubh* (dark or swarthy), who lived in the first half of the 15th century. His son Allan was styled 'Captain of the Clancamroun'. Other small tribes attached themselves to the Camerons, particularly the MacMartins, MacGillonies and MacSorlies, while other small groups became auxiliaries to Lochiel, including Macphees, MacLachlans and MacIntyres. The stem line also settled cadets in Lochaber.

Allan Cameron, 12th chief and Constable of Strone Castle,

adopted the title of Lochiel in 1528, when his lands were erected into a barony. The succeeding chiefs came from his first marriage with a daughter of Celestine MacDonald of Lochalsh, while the Erracht line descended from his second marriage with Marjory, daughter of Lachlan MacIntosh. The Camerons were a warlike race and had fought at Harlaw in 1411. Sir Ewan Cameron, 1629–1719, was the last highland chief to hold out for Charles II against Cromwell. In old age he fought at Killiecrankie in 1689, but took the oath of allegiance to William and Mary. Donald Cameron, 'The gentle Lochiel', is held to have been the noblest of all highland chiefs. He brought 700 clansmen to Glenfinnan to aid Prince Charles, and it was his support that took the Young Pretender so far, only to lose at Culloden in 1746. His brother, Dr Archibald Cameron, was also involved, and the family estates were forfeited. They were restored in 1784. The military tradition emerged also in the Erracht line, and in 1793 Allan Cameron raised the 79th Regiment, which became in 1881 the Queen's Own Cameron Highlanders (the Queen's Own Highlanders, 1960). Donald Walter, the 25th chief, served in the South African War and in World War I, when he led his own battalion at Loos. The present chief, Donald Cameron, served with the Lovat Scouts in 1945, and as Colonel-in-Chief of the 4/5th Battalion, Queen's Own, 1958–69. The heir is his eldest son, Donald Angus Cameron.

The Hon. Lord (Sir John) Cameron, son of an Edinburgh solicitor, was a Lord of Session, 1955–85, and his son, Kenneth John, was created Baron Cameron of Lochbroom (Life Peer) in 1984. He was Lord Advocate, 1984–89, and in 1989 became a Lord of Session.

CAMPBELL OF ARGYLL Norman, Flemish, Celtic, British or Norse? The origin of the name has been variously stated: even traced back to the legendary Arthur of round table fame! Flemish origin is not far fetched when we now know that for ages historians have described all of William the Conqueror's followers as Normans, but his wife was Matilda of Flanders, and many armigerous Flemish nobles fought at Hastings in 1066. Not all were entered on the *Battle Abbey Roll*. The ancestors of those who were later named Campbell bore the Flemish name of Erkinbald, written in Scotland as Archibald (in Gaelic as *Gilleasbuig*), and descendants bore arms blazoned gyronny of eight, Or and Sable: the bearings of the Baldwins, Counts of Flanders. Mrs Platt, in *Scottish Hazard*, says pointedly that with a strong Flemish presence at the Scottish court, 'there could be no possibility of any arms of Flanders . . . being borne by a man not of that blood'. Erkinbald, like other Flemish men did, settled in Strathclyde and in the Lennox. He married Eva, daughter of Paul O'Duine, the native Lord of Lochawe, descendant of Diarmid. Their son Duncan is mentioned in 1369 in a charter to a descendant, and his son Colin appears to have been the father of Archibald, who held the lands of Menstrie in 1263. His son, Colin *Mor*, or Big Colin, was knighted in 1263, and it is from him that the patronymic of the Campbell chiefs, *Macailen Mor*, is derived. The name Campbell evolved from a nickname, *Cam-beul*, meaning 'Crooked Mouth'. There is no equivalent in Gaelic for 'Clan Campbell', the term always being *Clann O'Duibhne*.

While the Campbells may have gained a footing in Lochawe before 1330, it was under Robert the Bruce that they became a power in Argyll. Sir Neil, son of Colin *Mor*, led his clan at Bannockburn in 1314, and probably died two years later. He had married the king's sister, Mary, and had issue. His eldest son, by a previous wife, was Colin, who had a charter of the barony of Lochawe in 1315, and Archibald, son of Colin, received from the Countess of Menteith, a charter of her lands in Cowal, including Kilmun, which became the burial place of the chiefs. He had a further grant in 1369, of lands at Melfort, Strachur and elsewhere, 'with all rights enjoyed by his ancestor Duncan MacDuine'. The star of the Campbells rose after the forfeiture of the MacDougals, enemies of Bruce. The family lived on an island in Loch Awe, but in the 15th century founded Inveraray, giving them easy access to the islands. Sir Duncan Campbell of Lochawe became Lord Campbell in 1445, and his grandson, Colin, was created Earl of Argyll in 1457.

The Campbells played a great part in national affairs. Archibald, 2nd Earl, led his clan at Flodden in 1513, and perished there. Colin, 3rd Earl, fought at Pinkie in 1547. Above all, successive earls supported the Government and acted as its agents in the West Highlands. They also looked after their numerous cadets. Archibald, 8th Earl, created Marquess in 1641, and his son Archibald, 9th Earl, departed from the royalist traditions, becoming involved in the Civil War and the covenants, and both died on the scaffold. The Revolution of 1688 altered matters, and Archibald, 10th Earl, was created Duke of Argyll in 1701. Successive dukes have distinguished themselves. John, 2nd Duke, became a Field-Marshall, as was John, 5th Duke. George, 8th

Duke, was a Liberal politician, and George, 9th Duke, who married Princess Louise, Queen Victoria's daughter, was Governor-General of Canada, 1878–83. Ian, 12th and present Duke, is Hereditary Master of the Royal Household in Scotland, and Admiral of the Western Coast and Isles.

CAMPBELL OF BREADALBANE The leading branch of the Campbells is that of Breadalbane, a district in Perthshire extending from Lochaber and Atholl on the north, to Strathearn and Menteith on the south. It is scored by deep glens and contains Loch Tay and numerous torrents. The progenitor of this family was Sir Colin Campbell of Glenorchy, eldest son by his second wife, Margaret Stewart, of Sir Duncan Campbell of Lochawe. The patronymic of the House of Breadalbane is *Mac-Cailean-Mhic-Dhonnachaid*, 'son of Colin, son of Duncan'. Glenorchy, from which the MacGregors were ousted, was given to Sir Colin by his father in 1432. Other lands, including Lawers, in Perthshire, were bestowed on him and his fourth wife, Margaret, daughter of Luke Stirling of Keir, by James III, in recompense for his services in capturing Thomas Chalmers, one of the assassins of James I. He built Kilchurn Castle, at the north-east end of Loch Awe.

Sir Duncan Campbell, the eldest son, obtained a charter of the lands of the Port of Tay, 1492 and 1498, and of Finlarig in 1506. His lands of Finlarig, Shian, Balloch, Crannich and others, were incorporated into the barony of Finlarig by charter, 1513. He was slain at Flodden the same year, and was succeeded by his eldest son, Sir Colin, who built the chapel of Finlarig. He died in 1523. Sir John Campbell, 6th of Glenorchy, left no male issue, and was succeeded by his brother Colin, who purchased lands in Glendochart. When he died in 1583, he was succeeded by Duncan, elder son by his second wife, Catherine, daughter of Lord Ruthven. He was known as 'Black Duncan with the cowl', and added to his estate lands in Menteith and in Strathgartney. He had the power of 'pit and gallows', and amended statutes drawn up by his father for various courts held within the Lordship of Glenorchy, Discher and Toyer. There were severe penalties for shooting deer and wild fowl: a fine of £20 Scots for the first offence; the loss of an arm for the second, and hanging for the third. Persons found guilty of the third offence were hung with a 'widdie', a rope made of willow or birch twigs. Duncan was created a Baronet of NS in 1625. He engaged the Scottish artist, John Jameson, 1586–1644, to paint some family portraits and an illustrated genealogical chart, now in the National Portrait Gallery.

The 5th Baronet, Sir John Campbell, was MP for Argyll, 1669–74, and in 1681 was created Earl of Breadalbane and Holland. By his first wife, Mary, daughter of Henry Rich, 1st Earl of Holland, he had two sons. Duncan, the elder, was weak-minded and was passed over in the succession in favour of his younger brother, Sir John, 2nd Earl. The line failed with John, 3rd Earl, whose two sons predeceased him. The nearest heir was his third cousin, John, eldest son of Colin Campbell of Carwhin, descended from the 3rd Baronet. He was a distinguished soldier and agricultural improver, and in 1806 was created Baron Breadalbane. He was advanced to the dignity of Earl of Ormelie and Marquess of Breadalbane in 1831. His son John, 2nd Marquess, died without issue, when his UK titles became extinct. The Earldom of Breadalbane devolved on his cousin, John Alexander, son of William Campbell of Glenfalloch. His son Gavin was created Baron Breadalbane of Kenmore in 1873, and in 1885, Earl of Ormelie and Marquess of Breadalbane (UK). He, too, died without issue, and the Scottish earldom devolved on his nephew, Ian Edward, 8th Earl, who died in 1923, by which time Taymouth and part of the estates had been sold. Ian Edward was succeeded by his kinsman, Charles, descended from the 6th Earl. John Romer, his son, succeeded in 1959 as 10th Earl and 14th Baronet.

CAMPBELL OF CAWDOR

Clan Campbell has numerous branches, some titled, and most of them armigerous. The Countess of Loudon (Barbara Huddleston Abney-Hastings), represents a very old branch, descended from Duncan, a grandson of Colin *Mor* Campbell, knighted in 1280. Her heir is Lord Mauchline. Several branches possess baronetcies, including Auchinleck, Aberuchil, Succoth and Balcardine. Non-titled families still in existence include Glenduarel, Achallader, Airds Bay, Kilmartin, Strachur, Arduaine, Auchendarroch, Dunstaffnage, Jura, Kilberry and Skerrington. The Inverneil branch – 'Clan Tarlich' – produced the eminent folklorist, the late John Lorne Campbell, and the deceased Colin Campbell, family historian and armorist.

No branch has shed more lustre on the clan than the Campbells of Calder or Cawdor, in Nairnshire. Their story began with a flame-haired little girl, Muriel, daughter of John Calder of Calder and Isabella Rose. She became heiress in 1498, when an infant. The 2nd Earl of Argyll, having obtained a grant of the wardship and marriage of the heiress, sent sixty men under Campbell of Inverliver, to bring her to Argyll. They were pursued by the girl's uncles, Alexander and Hugh, and their men, who killed seven of Inverliver's sons in Strathnairn. When asked if this was too high a price to pay, as the infant, too, might die, Inverliver grimly replied that the heiress would never die, 'sae lang as there is a red-haired lassie on the shores of Loch Awe'. In 1510, when she was barely thirteen years old, she was married to Sir John Campbell, 3rd son of the Earl of Argyll, who thus gained possession of Cawdor and its old stronghold.

Muriel's grandson, John, 3rd Thane of Cawdor, early in the 17th century sold Croy, and disponed Ferintosh to Lord Lovat, in order to purchase or conquer the island of Islay, which remained in the family, 1612–1726, when it was bought by Daniel Campbell of Shawfield. Sir Hugh Campbell, 5th Thane of Cawdor, built a carved fireplace to commemorate the Campbell/Calder marriage of 1510. Sir John Campbell, son of Sir Alexander, 7th of Cawdor, married Mary, co-heiress of Lewis Pryse of Gogirthen, and died in 1777. In 1796 his grandson, John was elevated to the peerage (UK) as Baron Cawdor of Castlemartin, Pembrokeshire.

The first and second barons were Fellows of the Royal Society. In little more than a century, descendants have been awarded twelve mentions in despatches, three brevets, three *Croix de Guerre* (one with palm and star), the Legion of Honour four times, one AFC, one DFC, the MC twice, the DSO fifteen times, and three Victoria Crosses: an amazing record which does not include ordinary scholastic honours. John Frederick Campbell, 2nd Baron, was created Earl of Cawdor in 1827 and died in 1860. His grandson, Frederick Archibald, was First Lord of the Admiralty, 1905, and a member of the Council of the Prince of Wales, 1908–11. The 5th Earl, his grandson John, served in the Royal Navy in World War I, and in World War II as Lt. Col. of the 4th Battalion of the Queen's Own Cameron Highlanders. He was Chairman of the Historic Building Council for Scotland, and a Trustee of the National Museum of Antiquities. Hugh John, 1952–93, the 6th Earl, was an underwriting member of Lloyd's. His son Colin, 7th Earl and 26th Thane, takes a lively and benevolent interest in the affairs of Cawdor village. The family is proud of their feudal castle, which is the only privately inhabited stronghold in Scotland with its old drawbridge. The castle was popularised in Shakespeare's *MacBeth*, and is said to be haunted by the ghost of Lady Caroline, a daughter of the 1st Lord Cawdor.

CARLISLE The most prolific spellings of this name are Carlisle, Carlyle, and Carlile, and derive from Carlisle, in Cumberland. Walter, Prior to Carlisle, is on record ca. 1160, and about the same time, Odard de Carlyle – presumably from Carlisle – witnessed a charter by Uchtred, son of Fergus, Lord of Galloway. He seems to have possessed the lands of Hoddam. Evdone de Karleolo witnessed a charter by Eustace de Vesey, of twenty shillings out of the Mill of Sprouston, to the Abbey of Kelso, ca. 1207. Gilberd de Karlel and Beatrice Karlele swore fealty to Edward I of England in 1296. In 1451, William of Carlile was one of the conservators of the truce between Scotland and England. Probably the best-known of the name was Thomas Carlyle, 1795–1881, the industrious essayist and historian, who married Jane Baillie Welsh, 1801–66, whose letters have been published. Among Carlyle's finest works are *The French Revolution* (1837), and *Frederick the Great* (1858–65). Carlyles in Pennersaughs, in Middlebie parish, Dumfriesshire, formed an interesting group. John Carlyle, 1705–88, married Jane, heiress of John Bell of Satur, and left issue. William Carlile, 1746–1829, was Provost of his native Paisley, 1817–21, and a kirk elder for over 60 years.

CARMICHAEL From the lands of Carmichael, in Lanarkshire, comes this surname and a family who bore it were long in possession of the barony thereof. Robert Camitely (a mis-spelling) resigned his claim to the patronage of the kirk of Cleghorn, ca. 1220. By 1250 he had undoubted right of lordship of the lands of Cleghorn. John Carmichael of this family, escaped the carnage of Verneuill in 1424, and was appointed Bishop of Orleans. Another John Carmichael, who was knighted, was one of the warriors who fought for Charles VI of France at Baughé in 1442. John Carmichael of Meadowflats was ancestor of Sir John Carmichael of that ilk, Warden of the West Marches, who was killed by the Armstrongs in 1600. When his grandson, also Sir John, died ca. 1649, his estates passed to his cousin, John Carmichael of Park, whose family obtained the lands of Hyndford. Sir James Carmichael was created a Baronet of NS in 1627, and Lord Carmichael in 1647. His grandson, Sir John, was created Earl of Hyndford in 1701. The title has been dormant since the death, unmarried, of Andrew, 6th Earl, in 1817. He was succeeded in his paternal estate of Mauldslie by his nephew, Archibald Nisbet of Carfin, while the estates of Carmichael devolved on Sir John Anstruther, Baronet of Anstruther, the heir general. Since 1981 the recognised chief of the surname is Richard

John Carmichael, Baron of Carmichael, who is a member of the Supreme Council of Scottish Chiefs. Carmichael has been used as a translation of the Gaelic *Macgillemichael*, a name once prolific in Lismore. A family of Carmichaels from Greenock were pioneer settlers around Escuminac, in Bonaventure County, Quebec Province, Canada.

CARNEGIE Undoubtedly the most famous bearer of this surname was Andrew Carnegie, 1835–1919, a native of Dunfermline, who emigrated to America in 1848, settling at Allegheny, later at Pittsburgh. He acquired interests in oil and steel and became a multi-millionaire and philanthropist. His benefactions include libraries in North American and Britain, 'hero' funds, and the Palace of Peace at the Hague. The surname derives from the lands of Carnegie, in Angus, which came into the possession of a family styled of Balinhard, who adopted the surname Carnegie. Sir David Carnegie, 1575–1658, was created Lord Carnegie in 1616, and 1st Earl of Southesk in 1633. The 12th Earl is David Charles Carnegie, chief of the surname, whose home is Kinnaird Castle, Brechin.

CHISHOLM The earliest reference to the surname Chisholm in Scotland is in 1248/49, when Alexander de Chesholm witnessed a charter. The name comes from the barony of Chisholm, in Roxburghshire, said to mean 'waterside meadow good for producing cheese', or simply 'Cheeseholm', hence the surname. The lands are on the south bank of the Borthwick Water. It is interesting to note that the Chisholm arms: Gules, a boar's head couped Or, langued Azure, indicate that the family were connected at the dawn of heraldry with others who also carried boars' heads: Gordons, Elphinstones, Nisbets, Rollos, Trotters, Hoggs and Swintons (perhaps the leading family). They appear to have had some ancient association with the Anglo-Saxon rulers of Bernicia.

In the reign of David II, probably ca. 1330, Sir Robert Chisholm went north to become Governor of Urquhart Castle. By his wife Margaret, he left sons: John, who left an only daughter; Alexander; and another son who continued the Border line. Alexander married in 1368, Margaret, heiress of Godfrey del Ard de Ercles, and Isabella Fentoun. Their agreement regarding lands caused a long dispute with William Fentoun of Baky. A son Thomas, married Margaret, daughter of Lachlan Mackintosh of Mackintosh, and had two sons: Alexander, who died without issue, and Wyland (from which name Valentine evolved) of Comar, in Strathglass. Wyland, son of Wyland, flourished at the beginning of the 16th century and was called *An t'-Siosal*, 'The Chisholm'. The title Chisholm of that ilk was frequently assumed by the Border family, one branch of which owned the estate of Cromlix, in Perthshire, and provided three pre-Reformation bishops of Dunblane: James, son of Edmund; half-brother William; and their nephew William, who was loyal to Mary, Queen of Scots. By the marriage of Jane, daughter of Sir James Chisholm of Cromlix, to James, 2nd son of David, 2nd Lord Drummond, before 1600, their lands passed to that family. Another branch held Stirches, near Hawick, and had alliances with the Rutherfords, Andersons and Scotts. Robert Scott of Montpelier Park, Edinburgh, who married Isabella Chalmers at Edinburgh in 1818, had a family registered in Roberton parish, and he assumed before 1834 the style of Chisholm of Chisholm.

The barony of Comarmore, Strathglass, erected by King James V, was held almost continuously by the Chisholm family from 1538 to 1937. The lands held by this clan embraced the glens of the rivers Glass, Affric and Cannich: fairly productive land. The main cadets were Kinneries, Leitry, Knockfin and Mackerach. The fighting strength of the clan was around 200. Roderick, 'The Chisholm', brought the clan to Sheriffmuir under his cousin John of Knockfin in 1715. He was forfeited, but pardoned in 1727. The clan were 'out' again in 1745. Factors affecting the economy after the '45 caused families to leave Strathglass, but Alexander Chisholm, urged by his daughter Mary (from whom the present chief is descended), resisted evictions. However, his half-brother, William, did evict tenants in 1801, and they sailed with others to Nova Scotia on the ships *Sarah* and *Dove*, from Fort William. Jemima, daughter of this chief, married in 1845, Edmund Chisholm Batten of Thornfalcon, and it was to that family the estates went in 1935, when the female Chisholm line failed. Erchless Castle and other properties were sold. The chiefship, however, passed to James Chisholm Gooden-Chisholm, who died in 1793. In 1943, Alastair Hamish Wyland Andre Fraser Chisholm, succeeded his grandfather as chief.

CLAN CHATTAN The Clan Chattan is a conforederation of clans in Lochaber, Strathnairn and Badenoch, under the leadership of the Mackintosh chief, whose ancestor, Angus, 6th chief of that clan, married in 1291, Eva, daughter of Dugal Doul. The latter was the 6th chief of the old Clan Chattan, whose ancestry stretched back to the kings of Dalriada. Their first chief,

Kellehathon, or Gillichattan *Mor*, was the son of Bethoc, daughter of Malcolm, Earl of Atholl, by Hextilda, heiress of King Donald *Ban*, who reigned 1093 and 1094–97. Gillichattan means *St Cathan's servant*, and he would be baptised under the special protection of the saint. St Cathan was venerated by the chiefs of the Cinel Lorne, and they built a shrine for him at Ardchattan. The name means 'little cat', and the wildcat figures prominently in the heraldry of the clan.

Gillichattan *Mor* had a son Dugal or Diarmid, who left two sons: Gillichattan, the 3rd chief, and David *Down* of Inverhaven, ancestor of *Clann Da'idh*, or the Davidsons. The 3rd chief had two sons, Kenneth, who appears not to have succeeded him, and Muriach, Prior of Kingussie, who left the church when the succession opened to him, and he became 4th chief. He married a daughter of the Thane of Cawdor, and had four sons: Gillichattan-Patrick, 5th chief; Ewan *Ban*, ancestor of the Macphersons (from 'son of the parson'); Neil from whom some Smiths are descended; and Ferquhard, the eponymous ancestor of the MacGillivrays. Gillichattan-Patrick left a son, Dugal *Doul*, father of Eva. On her marriage to Angus Mackintosh he became 7th chief of Clan Chattan.

Eventually families claiming to be the blood of the old Clan Chattan, formed a confederacy under Mackintosh hegemony. Conspicuous among these were the Macphersons of Cluny, who at one period disputed the chiefship of Clan Chattan. They were powerful enough to be noticed separately from the Mackintoshes in 1587, and they had many cadets. The Davidsons, or *Clann Da'idh*, were recognised, and other claimants were the MacBeans, *Clann Vean*; the Cattanachs of Lochaber, and the Macphails or *Clann Phail* of Invernairnie. Other clans who joined were the MacLeans of the north, including those of Dochfour; the Smiths or Gows in the clan territory; the Rosses, or *Clann Andrish*; the Andrews or MacAndrews, possibly an offshoot of the Rosses; the Clarks or *Clann Clerich*; the Shaws of Rothiemurchus; the Farquharsons of the north-east, and the McCombies or *Clann Thomas*. There are numerous sept names of the principal groups.

Much has been written by Sir Walter Scott and others about a conflict staged on the North Inch at Perth in 1396, at the instance of the Earl of Moray and the Lindsay chief, ostensibly to prevent an all out clan war. This was the battle between the 'Clan Qwhevil' and the 'Clan Yha', with thirty men on either side (including Hal o' the Wynd, the Perth blacksmith, for 'Clan Qwhevil'). The clans might be identified as the Shaws of Rothiemurchus and the Davidsons or *Clann Da'idh*, but nobody has done so with certainty. The late Sir Iain Moncreiffe suggested the combatants were the Cummins and Mackintoshes, and pointed to their dispute about the lands of Meikle Geddes and Castle Rait, in Strathnairn. A clan MacMillan historian and Gaelic scholar, the late Rev. Somerled MacMillan, claimed that the 'Clan Qwhevil' were Lochaber MacMillans known as *Clann 'ic illemhaoil*.

CLARK(E)/CLERK The style *clericus* was given in Latin texts to scholars and minor clergymen who wrote charters and other documents. Roger Clericus held land between 1172–78, and Thomas Clericus was one of those appointed in 1246 to determine the marches of Wester Fedale. A charter by Richard de Bancori, of land in Dumfriesshire in 1249, was witnessed by James the clerk. Johanne le Clerke de Rokesburghe, burgess of Berwick, is mentioned in a safe conduct to John le Brun de Hollesleigh, in 1291. Nine persons described as clerics swore fealty to Edward I in 1296, including Petrus le Clerke de Norton, Edinburghshire, whose lands were restored.

Clerk appears to have stabilised as a surname around 1400, and it was nationwide. It also became a prolific surname in England, often as Clarke. John Clerc possessed a tenement in Edinburgh in 1400, and Adam Clark was a burgess of Dundee in 1406. Hugh and Alan Clerk were burgesses of Irvine in 1418. In 1446, John Clerk of Leith, shipmaster, had a safe conduct into England. John Clerk was prior of Scone in 1524. Alan Clerk, a smith, was admitted burgess and freeman of Glasgow in 1588, and John Clerk, a cordiner, was admitted likewise in 1594. The name was prolific in the north-east, and in the west country. Alexander Clark, from Garioch, graduated at King's College, Aberdeen, in 1675, and became schoolmaster of Raine. Clarks were numerous at Kilwinning early in the 18th century.

Three Clerks or Clarks have been Lord Provosts of Edinburgh. Alexander Clerk of Balbirnie held the office, 1579–84, and his second son, later Sir Alexander Clerk of Stenton, was Lord Provost in 1619. The Clarks, styled 'of Edinburgh', descend from Sir Thomas Clark, Lord Provost, 1885–88, who became a partner in the printing and publishing firm of T&T Clark. He was created a Baronet (UK) in 1886. His son John, 1859–1924, 2nd Baronet, was Colonel of the Royal Scots, and the 3rd Baronet, Sir Thomas, also served in that regiment. The 4th and present Baronet, Sir John Douglas Clark, resides in Edinburgh.

The Clerks of Pennicuik, descend from John Clerk of Kilhuntly, in Badenoch, whose grandson, John, 1611–74, purchased the barony of Pennicuik, in Mid Lothian, from Dr Alexander Pennicuik. His son John was created a Baronet of NS in 1679. The 3rd Baronet, Sir John, 1676–1755, was one of the Barons of Exchequer and a noted antiquary. His seventh son, John Clerk of Eldin, was a geologist and student of naval tactics. The 10th and present Baronet, Sir John Dutton Clerk, is a Member of the Royal Company of Archers.

Clarks in Paisley, descended from the family of Dunlambert, Belfast, have been associated with threadmaking in Paisley. John Clerk of Gateside, Paisley, died in 1864, and his son Stewart purchased the estate of Dundas, in West Lothian. His son, John Stewart Clark, was created a Baronet (UK) in 1918. He had a pedigree dairy herd at Dundas Home Farm. The 4th and present Baronet, Sir John Stewart-Clark, is a member of the European Parliament.

The surname Clerk passed into Gaelic, and gave the name *Mac a chleirich*. Malcolm McCleriche is recorded in 1461. The most common form today is MacCleary. Clarkson is derived from son of the clerk or scholar, and occurs in Aberdeen as early as 1402. Professor Joseph Andrew Clarke, of the Department of Environmental Engineering at the University of Strathclyde, was the recipient of a Royal Society Esso Energy Award in 1989.

COCHRANE Cochran or Cochrane is a territorial surname derived from the lands of Coveran or Cochrane, near Paisley. The first to appear on record is Waldeve de Coueran, possibly of Bernician extraction, who witnessed a charter granted in 1262 by Dugal, son of Syfyn (MacSwein), to Walter Stewart, Earl of Menteith, of lands in Kintyre. William de Coughrane, Lanarkshire (Renfrew not then a sheriffdom), appears on the *Ragman Roll* in 1296, and Cosmus de Cochrane is recorded between 1367 and 1371. His son William had a grant of the 10 merk land of Langnewton, in Roxburghshire, in 1360. By his wife Mary he had a son Robert, and possibly another, John de Cochrane, who served abroad for Edward I.

The first of the family to be styled 'of that Ilk', was James, son of Allan, so described in a sasine of 1486. His son James obtained license under the Privy Seal to sell or mortgage his lands of Nether Cochrane, in Renfrewshire, and Pitfour, in Perthshire, in 1509. The male succession failed on the death of his grandson, William, who made additions to Cochrane Castle. He had three daughters, two of whom must have died young. The third daughter, Elizabeth, married Alexander, a younger son of Alexander Blair of that Ilk, who assumed the name and arms of Cochrane. Their eldest son, Sir John, soldiered in Ireland, where he married Grace Butler, apparently without issue, as his brother William, 1605–85, succeeded. A royalist, he was created Lord Dundonald in 1647. During Cromwell's protectorate he kept a low profile, and at the Restoration was appointed a Privy Councillor. In 1669 he was advanced to be Earl of Dundonald, Lord Cochrane of Paisley and Ochiltree.

It was Thomas Cochrane, a descendant of the 1st Earl, who became the 8th Earl when the senior line failed in 1758. His grandson, Thomas, had a remarkable career. He served in the Navy, and in 1807 was returned to Parliament as MP for Westminster. Making charges of abuse against the Admiralty, he was falsely accused of swindling and struck off the Navy List. In 1817 he accepted an invitation from Chile to organise and command their navy, which played an important part in both Chile and Brazil, securing independence from Portugal. In 1832, a more liberal government at home restored his naval rank, and in 1854 he was Rear Admiral. Lord Dundonald promoted the use of steam and screw propellors, and urged the Admiralty to study the problems of naval architecture.

From the 11th Earl descended the baronets of Cults, Cupar, currently represented by Ralph Henry Vere Cochrane, 4th Baronet Douglas Mackinnon Baillie-Hamilton Cochrane, 12th Earl of Dundonald, had a notable military career. He went to Sudan in command of a detachment of the Camel Corps in the expedition for the relief of Khartoum. He was decorated and breveted Lt. Colonel. In 1889 he was a full Colonel, and in 1896 commanded the 2nd Life Guards. During the South African War of 1899 he had command of a mounted brigade. In 1902 he commanded the Canadian Militia, and brought out a scheme for re-organisation. The 15th and present Earl is Iain Alexander Douglas Blair Cochrane, residing at Lochnell Castle, Ledaig, Argyll.

Some MacEacherns who migrated from Moidart and Ardnamurchan to the lowlands, adopted the surname of Cochrane, apparently to conceal their origin. This has misled some people into thinking there is a link between the names, or that Cochrane is derived from an old spelling MacKauchern.

COCKBURN Not many families can rival the Cockburns for producing famous men. The family take the name from a place in the eastern Borders, known in the reign of William the Lion (1165–1214), as Cukoueburn (*Gowk's Burn*), which lay in the lands of Clifton, Roxburghshire, belonging to the Abbey of Melrose. Their origin is obscure, but they may have been of Bernician extraction. There are no earlier references to the surname further south. Peter de Cockburne witnessed a grant to the hospital of Soltre (Soutra) before 1220. The marriage of a daughter of Sir Robert de Cockburne is mentioned in 1266. Peter de Kokeburne, who witnessed a resignation of lands in 1285, is probably Peeres de Cokeburne, who swore fealty to Edward I in 1295. Another who signed the *Ragman Roll* was Thomas de Cokeburn, Roxburghshire. One of those men was probably the father of Alexander Cockburn, who lived in the reign of Robert the Bruce (1306–29). He was twice married and his sons were: Sir Robert Alexander, styled 'of that Ilk', who was Usher of the White Rod in 1373, and Keeper of the Great Seal, 1390–91; John, progenitor of the Cockburns of Ormiston; and Edward, ancestor of the extinct line of Skirling.

Sir William Cockburn of that Ilk, descended from Sir Alexander, was slain at Flodden in 1513. By his wife, Anna Home, he had several sons: William of that Ilk, Alexander, killed at Flodden; Andrew, Robert and probably Christopher, ancestor of the extinct Choicelee branch. From William of that Ilk descended John, who married Elspeth Oliphant, and had at least two sons: William, who died without issue in 1663, having sold the family estates to his brother James, who was created a Baronet of NS in 1671. Sir James married Grizel Hay, and had two sons: Sir William, 2nd Baronet, and John, of Kilkenny. Sir James, the 3rd Baronet, fought at Quebec, and was served heir to his father in Langton and the office of Usher, in 1754, but sold these in 1757. Lieutenant Col. Sir William Cockburn, 11th Baronet, served in the South African War and in World War I. His son, Sir John, 12th Baronet, 1925, married Gloria Mullings, and has issue, the heir being his eldest son, Charles.

John Cockburn, a Lord of Session, who was knighted in 1591, had a son John, MP for Haddington, and father of Adam, another Lord of Session, who married Susan Hamilton. Their son John, 1679–1758, was MP for Haddington, but is better known as an agricultural improver. His *Letters to his Gardener*, printed by the Scottish History Society, show that he was more interested in turnips, onions and trees than in politics. Although deeply in debt, he built a new mansion at Ormiston, but was forced to sell his estates to the Earl of Hopetoun and reside with his son, George, Comptroller of the Navy, in London.

Alicia Rutherford, 1712–94, wife of Patrick Cockburn, advocate, and a son of Adam Cockburn of Ormiston, wrote a version of *Flowers of the Forest*. Lord Henry Cockburn, 1779–1854, of the Cockpen branch of the family, and a Senator of the College of Justice, was author of the fascinating *Memorials* of his time (Edinburgh, 1856).

COLQUHOUN Umfridus de Kilpatrick had a grant of the lands of Colquhoun (probably derived from *Cuil cumhann* = 'narrow corner'), in Dunbartonshire, before 1241. The first to bear the name was Robert de Culchon, recorded in 1259. The lands of Luss, on the western shores of Loch Lomond, are said to have come to the family through marriage with the 'Fair Maid of Luss', heiress of Luss of that Ilk. Her husband was Sir Robert Colquhoun, who held the lands of Colquhoun towards the middle of the 14th century. Sir John Colquhoun of Luss was Governor of Dunbarton Castle in the reign of James II (1437–60), and in 1583, Sir Humphrey Colquhoun of Luss was made hereditary coroner of Dunbartonshire. In 1625, a descendant, Sir John Colquhoun, was created a Baronet of NS. The 5th Baronet, Sir Humphrey Colquhoun, left a daughter Anne, who married in 1702, Sir James Grant of Pluscardine. Their eldest son inherited the Grant estates, and the Luss lands went to the second son, James, who carried on the Colquhoun line and was created 1st Baronet of Luss in 1786. He built the modern mansion of Rossdhu. Sir James Colquhoun, 4th Baronet, was MP for Dumbartonshire, 1837–41. The 8th Baronet, and octogenarian chief of the Clan Colquhoun, is Sir Ivar Colquhoun. His heir is second surviving son, Malcolm Rory Colquhoun. A number of Colquhouns achieved fame in Sweden, and Walter Colquhoun, a 16th century cannon-founder, has left descendants under such names as Cahun and Ghan. Henry Cahun was appointed physician to the Swedish Navy in 1781. In Gaelic the Colquhouns are known as *Mac a Chounich*.

CRAUFORD/CRAWFORD Reginald, youngest son of Alan, 4th Earl of Richmond – descended from Galfride, Duke of Brittany, who had Flemish connections – had grants of land including Ardoch, in the Barony of Crauford, Lanarkshire, from which his family took their surname. He died a young man, and his widow (name unknown) married Baldwin of Biggar, Sheriff of Lanark. John, son of Reginald, was probably brother of Sir Gregan Crauford, and father of Sir Reginald, sheriff of Ayr; and of Galfride. Sir Reginald married Margaret, heiress of Loudon, and had five sons: William; Adam; John, from whom came the Craufurds of Craufurdland, near Kilmarnock; Hugh of Crosbie; and Reginald, parson of Strathaven. Hugh had a son Hugh, of Loudon, whose 'carnal brother', Reginald of Crosbie, was progenitor of the Craufurds of Kerse. By his wife Alicia, Hugh, younger, had a son Reginald, Sheriff of Ayr, murdered in 1297, and a daughter Margaret, mother of the patriot, Sir William Wallace. Reginald of Loudon had three sons: Reginald, whose heiress married Sir Duncan Campbell, ancestor of the Campbells of Loudon; Hugh, of Crosby, from whom came the Craufurds of Auchinames; and another son, ancestor of the Craufords of Baidland, afterwards of Ardmillan.

John Crauford of Craufurdland's son James, was an adherant of his kinsman, Sir William Wallace, and assisted in the appointment of the latter as Guardian of Scotland, in 1297. His grandson, John, had a charter of confirmation of the lands of Ardock, in 1391. He had two sons: William of Craufurdland, knighted by King James I, and John of Giffordland, progenitor of the Birkhead line. From Archibald Craufurd, who lived in the reign of James III (1360–88), descended the families of Auchenairn, Beanscroft, and Powmill. His son John was killed at Flodden, but left a son John, from whom came some other branches of the family. A later John Crauford was twice married, first to Robina, heiress of John Walkinshaw of that Ilk, and next, to Eleanora Nicolson. John assumed the additional surname of Walkinshaw, and was succeeded by his son, Lt. Col. John Walkinshaw-Craufurd, who left his estate to Thomas Coutts, the banker. This was contested by his aunt, Elizabeth, and the deed was reduced. By her second husband, John Houison of Braehead, she had a daughter Elizabeth, who married Rev. James Moodie, who assumed the additional names of Houison and Craufurd, and was succeeded by his son, William Houison-Craufurd. This old family still hold Craufurdland Castle.

The Craufurds of Auchinames had many branches. Thomas, alive in 1401, married Margaret, heiress of Malcolm Galbraith, and had two sons: Archibald of Auchinames, and Malcolm of Easter Greenock, from whom came the Craufurds of Jordanhill. Archibald, who died in 1467, had also two sons: Robert of Auchinames, slain at Flodden in 1513; and Archibald of Previck and Thirdpart, ancestor of the baronets of Kilbirney, Stirling (created 1781), now represented by Sir Robert James Craufurd, 9th Baronet, who lives in London. Robert Craufurd, killed at Flodden, was succeeded by his eldest son, James, who lost his life at Pinkie in 1547. He was succeeded by his brother William, who died in 1582. William's granddaughter married her second cousin, Patrick Craufurd of Drumsoy. Intermarriage of descendants with other cadets kept the Auchinames representation going into the present century, when Hugh Ronald George Crauford, born 1873, sold his estates and emigrated to Canada, where he died without male issue.

CUMMING Of Flemish stock, and descended from a Count of Pol, the Comyns or Cummings as they became, appear in Scotland during the reign of David I (1124–53). It has been suggested that the surname derives from a humble herb called *cummin*. William Comyn was Bishop of Durham and Chancellor to King David. His nephew, Richard, married Hextilda, daughter of Uchtred, son of Waltheof, and was confirmed in lands in Tynedale and Roxburghshire. Later, the family received lands in Buchan and Speyside, and became the most powerful barons in Scotland. This provided Nigel Tranter with material for some of the incidents portrayed in the first of his Bruce novels, *The Steps to the Empty Throne*. Richard Comyn's wife was granddaughter and heiress of King Donald Ban, deposed in 1079, and after Richard's death she married the Earl of Atholl, by whom she was maternal ancestor of Gillichattan, progenitor of Clan Chattan.

William, son of Richard, married Marjory, heiress of Fergus, the last Celtic Earl of Buchan, and obtained that title. Their son Alexander was Constable of Scotland. Another Comyn became Earl of Menteith, and yet another was Earl of Angus. John Comyn, Earl of Buchan, became one of the guardians of the realm in 1286, and his son John, the 'Black' Comyn, was a competitor for the throne in 1291, claiming as a descendant of Donald *Ban*. This enhanced the claims of his son, the 'Red' Comyn, who was slain by Robert the Bruce in a Dumfries church in 1306. Bruce afterwards carried out a raid on the Buchan lands, greatly weakening the position of the Comyns. He gave Slains Castle and the hereditary office of Constable to Lord Hay of Errol. The office remains with a descendant today.

On the borders of Badenoch, a branch of the family became a clan. Their chiefs, the Cummings of Altyre, claim descent from Sir Robert, an uncle of the 'Red' Comyn. They received grants of land and became powerful in Moray. They had a long dispute with Clan

Mackintosh, mainly over disputed ownership of Rait Castle, in Strathnairn. A descendant, Alexander Cumming, became heir to Sir William Gordon of Gordonstoun, and assumed the name. He was created a Baronet in 1804. The present representative is Sir William Gordon Cumming, born 1928, who resides at Altyre House, Forres.

About the middle of the 15th century, some Cummings, for a reason unknown denied their family burial-place, changed their names to Farquharson, and the families of Balthog and Haughton were among their descendants. In the time of Gilbert Cummin of Glenchearnach, it is said that oppressed people from a neighbouring glen were baptised as his clansmen at a hen-trough and afterwards known as 'Cummins of the hen-trough', to distinguish them from those of the true blood. Other branches of the old family were the Cummings of Inverallochy, Logie, Auchry, Culter, Dumphail and Relugas. Sir William Cumming of Altyre was Lord Lyon, 1512–19. One James Cumming was a herald painter, 1770, and became Lyon Clerk Depute. The Rev. Patrick Cumming, 1695–1776, of the Relugas family, distinguished himself as Professor of Divinity at Edinburgh.

Lieutenant Col. Alastair Michael Cumming, born at Singapore in 1941, has had a notable military career. He was commissioned in the Gordon Highlanders in 1962, and has served in Northern Ireland, Hong Kong and Germany. Now of The Highlanders, he is Regimental Secretary at Cameron Barracks, Inverness.

CUNNINGHAM As a surname, Cunningham is derived

from the Ayshire district of that name. It is now widespread. The eponymous is believed to have been Wernebald, a vassal of Hugh de Morville, who came to Scotland in the 12th century, and he obtained Cunningham from his superior. His son Robert gave the church of Kilmaurs to the monks of Kelso. In 1462, Sir Alexander Cunningham, Lord Kilmaurs, was created Earl of Glencairn. The 5th Earl was a promoter of the Reformation in 1560. John, 15th Earl, died without issue in 1796, since when the title has been dormant. He had served as an officer in the 14th Regiment of Dragoons, and afterwards took orders in the Church of England. Like his father, he was a friend of the poet Burns. The chiefship may lie with descendants of Andrew Cuningham of Corsehill, descended from Andrew, second son of the 4th Earl of Glencairn. Sir Alexander Cuningham of Corsehill, was created a Baronet of NS in 1672. The present and 12th Baronet is Sir John Christopher

Cuninghame. Another baronetcy (NS, 1701/2) is possessed by the Cunynghames of Milncraig, who claim descent from the 5th Earl of Glencairn. The Fairlie-Cuninghames of Robertland, also have a baronetcy of NS, conferred on David Cuningham in 1630, and they claim descent from the 1st Earl of Glencairn.

DALLING This surname appears in various parts of the Lowlands, and is conjectured to come from Dalling, in Norfolk; but in some cases it may have derived from Dowling, near Fiddown, in Kilkenny, Ireland. Robert Dawling in Leith appears on record in 1567. Other forms of the name are Dawline, Dalin, Dallin, Daillin and Dowlin, all recorded in the 17th century. Jeanna and Helena, daughters of James Dawling, burgess of South Queensferry, were retoured as his heirs in 1668. Matthew Douling appears as a maltman in Bo'ness in 1691, and Thomas Dauling was served heir to Thomas Dauling in Edinburgh, in lands in the Barony of Cumnock, Ayrshire, 1695. Further south, at Balmaghie, in Kirkcudbrightshire, there was an interesting family of Dawlings at Threave Grange. John Dawling there had a *guid gangin' plea* against James Kennan and his heirs about 1670, and it lasted over a century, doubtless impoverishing the family. Dr Robert Dalling, FRCSE, of Glasgow, has been consulting surgeon at Stobhill Hospital since 1978.

DALZELL/DALYELL This is another territorial name, from the old barony of Dalzell, in Lanarkshire, and is found in a variety of spellings. Hugh de Dalzell was sheriff of Lanark in 1288, and Sir William Dalzell was ancestor of the family styled 'of that Ilk', from 1446. A later laird was loyal to Mary, Queen of Scots, and his son, Sir Robert, was elevated to the peerage in 1628 by the title of Lord of Dalzell. In 1639 he was created Earl of Carnwath. He was succeeded by his eldest son, Robert, and his second son, John of Glenae, was created a Baronet of NS in 1666. The 16th Earl, Ronald Arthur Dalzell, 1883–1931, was succeeded by his uncle, Sir Arthur Edward Dalzell, 1851–1941, a distinguished soldier. Since his death the title has been dormant. The Binns family descend from the Lanarkshire Dalzells, but favour the spelling Dalyell. General Tam Dalyell, 1615–85, was an officer in the Russian Army, and on his return fought against the Covenanters. He has marched ferociously into legend. After Rullion Green in 1666, Covenanters swore they had seen pistol balls rebound off his chest and fall into his jackboots. He built the Mansion of The Binns, which is now the property of the

National Trust for Scotland. The General is said to have played cards with the devil, and on one occasion when the latter lost he hurled the table at the General. It missed and landed in the Sergeant's Pond. Folks who scorned this story must have had second thought when, in the dry summer in 1878 a solid carven marble-topped table was retrieved from the mud! The General's son, Thomas, was created a Baronet of NS in 1685. The present representative, who does not use the title, is Tam Dalyell, the well-known MP for Lithlithgow, whose book, *Devolution: The End of Britain* (London, 1977), posed the famous 'West Lothian Question', regarding voting at Westminster; relevant today, when Scotland has achieved devolution. Andrew Dalzell, 1742–1806, son of a Kirkliston carpenter, became Professor of Greek in the University of Edinburgh.

DAVIDSON

DAVIDSON Occasionally, a non-Gaelic form of patronymic was adopted in the Highlands. Davidson, 'son of David', is a good example. They came to form *Clann Da' idh*, associated with Clan Chattan, but their early history is obscure. According to tradition, the Davidsons of Invernahaven, in Badenoch, were originally a branch of the Comyns, but in a troublous period (perhaps in 1308, when Robert the Bruce defeated the Comyns at Inverness), they attached themselves to Clan Chattan. Donald Dhu, the eponymous ancestor, is said to have married a daughter of Angus Mackintosh, the 6th chief, and to have become a leading member of the confederation. The Davidsons were once powerful, but became involved in clan feuds, which did nothing for their prosperity. Some historians believe they were involved in the famous clan battle at Perth in 1396, but this is uncertain. At any rate, their influence diminished, and afterwards they are found in small groups.

The Davidsons who owned Tulloch, in Ross-shire, from 1762 to early in the present century, were considered to be of the ancient stock. Their recorded ancestor was Donald Davidson, in Cromarty, whose son was Alexander, father of William, who married in 1719, Jean, daughter of Kenneth Bayne, nephew and heir of Duncan Bayne of Tulloch. Their son Henry purchased Tulloch in 1762. His brother and successor was Duncan Davidson, MP for Cromarty, 1760–96. Duncan's son Henry was succeeded in 1827 by his son Duncan. As 'Younger of Tulloch', he had been MP for Cromarty, 1826–30, and 1831–32. He was married five times, and left eighteen children. Duncan was succeeded by his eldest son, Duncan Henry, 1836–89, whose son Duncan, 1865–1917, matriculated arms in 1906.

The Davidsons of Cantray, Inverness, descended from Sir David Davidson, born ca. 1788, only son of David Davidson and Marie Cuthbert. This family seems to have ended with an heiress, Edith Mary Davidson, born 1892. Another northern group, the Davidsons of Inchmarlo, Deeside, descended from John Davidson of Tillychetly, who died in 1802. His son Duncan, an advocate in Aberdeen, succeeded to Tillychetly, and purchased Inchmarlo. He was succeeded by his son Patrick, also an advocate, father of Duncan whose second son, Leslie, served in the Royal Artillery in World War I. The association of Davidsons with Aberdeen, was of long standing. Robert *filius* David, or Davidson, Provost of Aberdeen, was killed at the Battle of Harlaw in 1411. There were Davidsons at Auchinhamper, in the 15th century, and at Newton, Tillymorgan and Carnbogie. Alexander Davidson of Newton assumed the name and arms of Gordon of Gight, and this line ended with an heiress, the mother of Lord Byron.

Clearly there are other Davidsons in no way connected with those of the north. John Andrew Davidson, born 1928, 2nd Viscount Davidson, is descended from John Davidson, 1808–93, a native of Scone, who emigrated to Argentina. In Ayrshire there were Davidsons at Drumley, Greenan and Pennyglen. Davidsons in Roxburghshire seem to have formed a small independent clan in the 16th and 17th centuries. The chief family was seated at Samieston, and the male line ended with James Davidson, whose four nieces were co-heiresses in 1670. There was an influential Davidson family at Currie, Mid Lothian. From another family, many of whom were clergymen, descended the Most Rev. Randal Thomas Davidson, 1848–1930, Archbishop of Canterbury.

DEWAR In medieval times the person who had custody of the relic of a saint was called *deoradh*, a word originally meaning pilgrim or stranger, from the fact that such relics were taken to distant places to obtain divine intervention. In time the word became a surname and is found in various forms: Dear, Dior, Deoir, and finally Dewar. The Macindeors derive their name from a man who escorted the daughter of Walter Buchanan to Argyll to marry a Campbell of Ardkinglas. There being no others of his own surname there, he was called Deoir, meaning 'stranger', and his offspring became Macindeors.

The families of Dewars of Glendochart and Strathfillan are of great interest as they held the seven relics of St Fillan. These were the Crozier or *Coigerach*; *Na Bhernane* or bell; *Na Mais* or Chalice;

Na Miosach or Gospels; *Na Man* or Arm Bone; *Na Faerechd* or Mallet; and *Na Clach* or Healing stones. The Dewar custodian of the crozier, was the senior Dewar; he was also co-arb of St Fillan, and in the reign of William the Lion is referred to as the Abbot of Glendochart, where he ranks with the Earls of Athole and Menteith. At the Inquest of 1428 ordered by King James I, it was found that the Dewar Cogerach was the co-arb (or heir) of St Fillan in that office. During the troubled period of the Reformation all the relics were buried at various locations in Glendochart and Strathfillan, and only three survived: the bell, and two parts of the coigerach. Those relics will normally be seen in the Royal Museum of Scotland, following their purchase by the former Museum of Antiquities from a Dewar family in Canada. Those Dewars are not of the family of the Hereditary Dewar Coigerach, Co-arb of St Fillan, who are still in existence and are recognised in the offices by the Court of the Lord Lyon.

Patrick Dewar in Cambuskenneth, whose descendant Peter, tacksman of the King's Park, Stirling, purchased the farm of Craigniven in 1834, and was probably of Perthshire extraction. Peter married in 1827, Jean Chrystal, and had a large family, now represented by David Dewar of Broomhill, Kiambu, in Africa. Of this family is also Peter de Vere Beauclerk-Dewar, genealogist. Another Perthshire family is that associated with John Dewar & Sons, whisky distillers in Perth. John Dewar, born 1860, who married Jane Gow, had sons James, John Alexander, Charles Arthur and Thomas Robert. The later was created a Baronet in 1927, but died unmarried in 1930, when the title became extinct. His brother, John Alexander, was created Baron Forteviot in 1917. John James Evelyn Dewar is the 4th and present baron.

The Lowland Dewars derive their name from a farm in Heriot parish, Mid Lothian. In 1296, Peres de Dewar and Thomas de Dewere, signed the *Ragman Roll*. Taking their name from the place, the family styled themselves 'of that Ilk'. The testament of James Dewar of that Ilk, was confirmed in 1600, and in 1618 William Deware 'de eodem' occupied part of Harper-rig. The Dewars of Vogrie descended from James Dewar, ca. 1672–1740, possibly son of James Dewar, farmer in Kippielaw. The direct line failed in 1975, and in 1989, Lt. Col. Malcolm Dewar, residing in Sussex, was recognised not only as Dewar of Vogrie, but as chief of the surname, or 'of that Ilk'. It is thought that the Dewars, formerly of Doles, Andover, Hampshire, come from the same stock. The Rt. Hon. Donald Dewar, born Glasgow, 1937, is First Minister of the new Scottish parliament.

THE BLACK DOUGLASES

The surname Douglas is writ large upon the pages of Scottish history. The first of whom any certain record has been found was William Douglas, who witnessed charters between 1174 and 1200. He held lands at Douglas ('black water'), in Lanarkshire, from which he took his surname. William was probably related to Freskin the Fleming, who came to Scotland before the end of the reign of David I (1124–53), and was given lands at Strathbrock (Linlithgowshire) and at Duffus (Morayshire). He may have been his brother-in-law, and the family may also have come from Flanders: perhaps connected with the House of Boulogne. His eldest son, Archibald, was given lands at Hermiston, in Lothian. He had two sons: William, his successor, who also had lands in England, and Sir Andrew, progenitor of the Earls of Morton. William was succeeded by William *le Hardy*, Lord of Douglas, an adherant of Sir William Wallace. The next Lord was called 'the good Sir James', and next to Robert the Bruce was the greatest patriot of his time. He attended Bruce at his death, and promised to take his heart to the Holy Land, but was killed at Tebus de Ardales, in Spain, in 1330, fighting for King Alfonso against the Saracens. The heart, enclosed in a casket, was brought back to Scotland and buried at Melrose Abbey. William, son of Sir James, was killed in 1333, and left a natural son, Archibald. Hugh Douglas, his uncle, succeeded and, although a clergyman, held estates in Douglasdale and in the Borders. His successor was a nephew, William, and he became Earl of Douglas, ca. 1356. His son William was slain at Otterburn in 1388, and the lands of the 'Black Douglases' passed to Sir Archibald, 'The Grim', natural son of 'the good' Sir James. He was captured by the English at Poitiers in 1356, but escaped and survived until ca. 1400.

It was not only in Scotland and England that the Earls were renowned as warriors. Archibald's son, also Archibald, 4th Earl of Douglas, fought against the English in France for Charles VII, and was rewarded with the Duchy of Touraine. He died in battle and his grandsons were seized in Edinburgh and executed. The House of Douglas was becoming too powerful! After the deaths of the 5th and 6th Earls, James, second son of Archibald 'The Grim' succeeded as 7th Earl. Misfortune struck in the time of his sons. William, 8th Earl, displeased King James II, who had a hand in his death at Stirling in 1542. The same monarch obtained the submission of James, 9th Earl, and spitefully raised a charge of treason against his family. He was taken prisoner, and died in virtual retirement at Lindores. The Douglas estates were forfeited ca. 1455, and the earldom extinguished.

The Earls of Morton descend from Andrew Douglas, son of Sir Archibald, Lord of Douglas. He was ancestor of Sir William Douglas, the 'Knight of Liddesdale', killed by a kinsman in 1353. His brother Andrew, who succeeded, was ancestor of the Douglases of Dalkeith, from whom descended James, Earldom (cr. 1458), and Henry, from whom came the Douglas family of Lochleven, ancestors of the later earls. Of the Lochleven line was the heroine known as 'Kate Bar-lass' (actually she was Elizabeth), who, in an attempt to prevent the murder of King James in 1436/37, barred a door with her arm. Sir William, of the same family, was the custodian of Mary, Queen of Scots, at Lochleven, and in 1588 became the 5th Earl of Morton. The 14th Earl obtained from George III the money to finance Capt. Cook's voyage of discovery, but died just before the *Endeavour* set sail in 1768. This historic family is still very much in existence, and is represented by John, 21st Earl, a director of Dalmahoy Farms.

THE RED DOUGLASES When the star of the Black Douglases was waning, that of the Red Douglases was waxing. George, a natural son of William, 1st Earl of Douglas, by his sister-in-law, Margaret, Countess of Mar and Angus, having succeeded to the estates of his mother, became Earl of Angus. He was taken prisoner by the English at Homildon Hill in 1402, and later died of the plague. The 5th Earl, Archibald, occupies an interesting place in history as 'Bell the Cat'. Both nobles and commons had grievances against King James III, and an impasse having been reached, Archibald 'Belled the Cat' by seizing some of the king's favourites and putting them to death. Not surprisingly, his relationship with the monarch deteriorated. His castle of Tantallon was besieged in 1491, and he was forced to give up Liddesdale and Hermitage. He retained Ewesdale and Eskdale, and later obtained the lordship of Crawford. Even at Flodden in 1513, he had a dispute with James IV, and left the field, where two of his sons were killed. Another son, Gavin, who became Bishop of Dunkeld in 1516, was a renowned Latin scholar and translated Virgil's *Aeneid*.

Archibald, 6th Earl, had care of the young King James V, and fought at Melrose and Linlithgow Bridge to retain custody. He died ca. 1590, and was succeeded by his nephew, David, son of Sir George Douglas, who had married Elizabeth Douglas, heiress of Pittendreich. David was succeeded by his son Archibald, 1555–88, a peaceloving noble, who left no male issue. The title passed to William Douglas, a great-grandson of the 1st Earl, by decision of the Court of Session. His eldest son, William, became 11th Earl, and his second son, James, became Lord Mordington (title dormant since 1791). William was created Marquess of Douglas in 1633. Archibald, his eldest son was created Earl of Angus and Ormond in 1651, and his son James became 2nd Marquess of Douglas.

The 3rd Marquess, Archibald, son of James, was a child when he succeeded his father, and at the age of nine Queen Anne conferred on him the titles of Duke of Douglas, Marquess of Angus, Earl of Angus and Abernethy, Viscount Jedburgh Forest, Lord Douglas of Boncle, Preston and Roberton. In 1707 he received a charter which erected the Douglas and Angus estates into a dukedom and regality. After his death in 1761, Archibald James, elder son of Lady Jane Douglas, his sister, and Col. John Stewart of Grandtully, succeeded, but his right was strongly contested. He and his twin brother, Sholto Thomas, had been born in France when the mother was fifty years old. There were three separate actions, conjoined by the Court of Session, and the House of Lords finally found in favour of Archibald James. This was the celebrated *Douglas Cause*. Three of his sons became successively 2nd, 3rd and 4th Lords Douglas, but all died without issue, and the representation passed through a daughter to Cospatrick, 11th Earl of Home. The 14th Earl, Alexander Douglas Home, 1903–95, disclaimed his peerage to become Prime Minister of Great Britain, 1963–64. He became Baron of Coldstream in 1974 (Life Peer), and in 1998, a statue of him, on a stone plinth, was erected inside the gates of The Hirsel, the family home near Coldstream.

DOUGLAS OF DRUMLANRIG

The Douglases of Drumlanrig, Dumfriesshire, later Earls, Marquesses and Dukes, descend from William, 2nd Earl of Douglas, killed at Otterburn in 1388. He left a natural son, William, upon whom he conferred the barony of Drumlanrig and other lands. In 1412, he was deputed ambassador to England to negotiate the release of King James I. The same year he had a charter confirming him in the baronies of Drumlanrig, Hawick and Selkirk. He died fighting in France in 1427.

William Douglas of Drumlanrig was present at the siege of Roxburgh Castle in 1640, when King James II was killed by the bursting of a cannon. He was slain in a conflict at Lochmaben in 1484, and succeeded by his grandson, Sir James, who added to his estates. In 1602 he was acquitted of killing two men found guilty of sheep-stealing. They were actually hanged later! Sir William

Douglas, the eldest son, was created Viscount of Drumlarig in 1628, and in 1633 elevated to Earl of Queensberry. His eldest son, who succeeded, had four sons, of whom William succeeded, and James, who was an army officer, and adhered to the Covenants. William was raised to Marquess of Queensberry in 1682, and to Duke of Queensberry, with subsidiary titles, in 1684. The eldest son, James, succeeded, and is known as the 'Union Duke', having played a conspicuous part in bringing about the Union of the Parliaments in 1707. He was rewarded by a pension of £3000 per year (in effect a bribe), and in 1707 he was created Duke of Dover. Doubtless he was in the mind of Robert Burns when he wrote *Such a parcel of rogues in a nation*. His third son, Charles, 3rd Duke, was also created Earl of Solway in 1796. He outlived his sons, and was succeeded by his great-grandson, William, Earl of March, and in right of his mother, Earl of Ruglen, by which titles he was known until he became 4th Duke. When he died unmarried in 1810, the title Earl of Ruglen became dormant. The other honours passed by charter to the heir male of Jean, Duchess of Buccleuch; the title of Earl of March passed to the Earl of Wemyss, while the marquessate and earldom of Queensberry devolved on William Douglas of Kelhead, second son of the 1st Earl of Queensberry.

Sir James Douglas, Younger of Kelhead, 1639–1708, was created a Baronet of NS in 1628, and it was his grandson, Sir Charles, 5th Baronet, who continued the senior line of the family when he became 4th Duke of Queensberry in 1810. In 1833 he was created a peer of the UK by the title of Baron Solway of Kinmount. The 9th Marquess and 8th Baronet, John Sholto Douglas, is remembered as the originator of the 'Queensberry Rules', which govern pugilistic contests. The present representative is Sir David Harrington Angus Douglas, who is 12th Marquess of Queensberry, Earl of Queensberry, Viscount Drumlanrig, Lord Douglas of Hawick and Tibbers, and 11th Baronet of Kelhead. His heir is Sholto, elder son by his second marriage to Alexandria Sich.

DRUMMOND According to tradition, Maurice, progenitor of the Drummonds who became earls of Perth, came to Scotland with the Anglo-Saxon exiles, who included Prince Margaret, who married Malcolm *Canmore*, King of Scots. Traditions must be treated with some reserve, but the essential part of the story can scarcely be doubted, and all of them received lands. However, since Hungary is landlocked, they probably sailed from northern Europe. Possibly they resided for a time in Flanders, and married into

Flemish families. The Drummond arms: Or, three bars wavy Gules, indicate some link with the great Flemish family of Oudenarde, cadets of Petegem, and peers in their own right. The descendants of Maurice took their name from the lands of Dromyn (Drymen), in Stirlingshire. Maurice had a son, Malcolm *Beg*, who had two sons: Malcolm, who succeeded to his estates, and John, who left no male issue. Malcolm had two sons: Gilbert, probably killed at Dupplin in 1332, and Malcolm, who succeeded his father. He appears on record as 'Malcomo de Drummond', and had two sons: John, of Dummond, and Maurice, coroner of Lennox. He also had a daughter, who, as widow of John Logie, became the mistress, then consort of David II, King of Scots. After this alliance, the Drummonds had further grants of land. John, the heir, was styled 'of Concraig', and he had two sons: Malcolm, who had a licence to build a fortalice at Kindrocht, or Braemar; and Sir John, who succeeded his brother. John also had a daughter, Annabella, who married John Stewart of Kyle, who became King of Scots, assuming the forename of Robert.

John Dummond's great-grandson, Sir John, of Cargill and Stobhall, was created a Lord of Parliament about 1488. He was forfeited and imprisoned for striking the Lord Lyon of the time, but later pardoned and restored to his lands. James, 4th Lord Drummond, is said to have been created Earl of Perth ca. 1605. The 4th Earl, also James, was one of the twenty-four proprietors of East New Jersey, and encouraged emigration to that colony. He followed the fortunes of James VII, who created him Duke of Perth, but he was forfeited and his son, James, was titular Duke. His elder son, James, 3rd titular Duke, commanded the right wing of the Jacobite army at Culloden in 1746, and was wounded. On the death of Edward, 6th titular Duke, the direct line ended, and the heirs male to the Dukedom expired. He was succeeded by his kinsman, James Lundin or Drummond, grandson of the 1st Earl of Melfort, who, but for the attainder, would have been 10th Earl of Perth. His son James was created Lord Perth and Baron Drummond of Stobhill in 1797. This line ended in 1902, when the succession opened to William, 11th Viscount Strathallan, descended from James Drummond, created Lord Madderty in 1610. The 4th Lord Madderty was created Viscount Strathallan in 1686, and the representation is still vested in his descendants.

Among the principal branches are Drummond of Hawthornden, Mid Lothian (baronets), and Drummond of Blair Drummond, represented by the Home-Drummonds. The Hawthornden line is descended from the Dummonds of Carnock, and produced the eminent historian, poet and inventor, William Drummond, 1585–1649. He lamented the death of Prince Henry in *Tears on the death of Meliades*, in 1613, and wrote a *History of Scotland (1423–1524)*.

DUNBAR The first to use the name Dunbar were descendants of Gospatrick, Earl of Northumberland, 1067–72, and took their name from lands meaning 'fort on the point'. His third son, also Gospatrick on record in 1119, was known as Earl or Lord Dunbar. The last Earl was George, forfeited in 1434. William Dunbar, 1460–1520, was a distinguished poet, and Gavin Dunbar was Bishop of Aberdeen in the reign of James IV (1488–1513). An eminent Greek scholar, George Dunbar, was born at Coldingham in 1774, and succeeded Professor Dalzell at Edinburgh. There are a number of titled families, including Dunbar of Hempriggs (baronets of NS, 1706) and Dunbar of Mochram (baronets of NS, 1675). A former jockey, who once worked in the rag trade and served as a sergeant in the US Army, was recognised as 13th Baronet in 1984. He was Sir Jean Ivor Dunbar, 1918–93, who was succeeded by his elder son, Col. Sir James Michael Dunbar, USAF, 14th Baronet and also clan chief.

DUNCAN The surname derives from a Gaelic personal name: the early Irish form meaning 'brown warrior'. Dunchad, Abbot of Iona, is recorded by Adamnam as having died in AD 717. Dunnchad Ua Robbacain was coarb of Iona, 986–89. Two Scottish kings bore the name. Duncan, son of Crinan the Thane, was King of Scots, 1034–40, and Duncan, son of Malcolm III and Ingiborge, was king in 1094. The name became popular both as a forename and surname, and spread to the Lowlands. It appears as a surname as far south as Berwick by the middle of the 14th century. A number of Duncans have distinguished themselves, perhaps the best known having been Adam Duncan, 1731–1804, son of Alexander of Lundie and Helena Haldane, heiress of Gleneagles. He entered the Navy and rose to the rank of Rear Admiral of the Blue. Following his victory over the Dutch fleet in 1797, he was awarded a government pension, and created Viscount Camperdown. He became Admiral of the White in 1799. His grandson, Rt Hon. Adam Duncan, Earl of Camperdown, advocated repeal of the window tax, abolished in 1851. Andrew Duncan, 1744–1828, a native of St Andrews, was a renowned author and physician, and his son Andrew, Junr., 1733–1832, became a physician at the Royal Dispensary, in Richmond Street, Edinburgh. Rev Henry Duncan, 1774–1846, minister at Ruthwell, was the founder of savings banks in Scotland, and John Duncan, ca. 1802–49, a native of Wigtownshire, was a notable African traveller. The artist, Thomas Duncan, 1807–45, whose works include 'Old Mortality' and 'Auld Robin Gray', was a pupil of Sir William Allan. Archibald Alexander McBeth Duncan, born 1926, is a leading Scottish historian, and was Professor of Scottish History and Literature at the University of Glasgow, 1962–93.

DUNDAS The antiquity of the Dundas family is unquestionable. The lands, near South Queensferry, meant 'South Fort', Gaelic *dun deas*. These were owned by the family of Gospatrick, ancestor of the Earls of March, and his lands of Inverkeithing lie north of Dundas. The lands were granted by Waldeve, son of Gospatrick, to Helias, son of Huchtred, before 1145, for the service of 'half a knight'. It was justly remarked that any Prime Minister could raise a man to the peerage, but it took seven centuries to make a Dundas of Dundas. The estate was sold in 1874 to James Russell, a rich commoner, who re-sold, in 1899, to Stewart Clark, of the famous Paisley threadmaking firm. The Dundas of Arniston family, generations of whom followed the legal profession, is the main branch, descended from George Dundas of that Ilk (served heir, 1554/55), and his second wife, Katherine, daughter of Lord Oliphant. There are important offshoots. Henry Dundas, 1742–1811, fourth son of Robert Dundas of Arniston, Lord President of the Court of Session, was the most powerful Scottish statesman of his time, and was created Baron Duneira and Viscount Melville in 1802. Another offshoot of the Arniston branch is that of Beechwood, Mid Lothian. James Dundas, a younger son of Robert Dundas by his second wife, Janet Hepburne was a merchant in Edinburgh, from whom descended Robert Dundas, one of the principal clerks of the Court of Session, who was created a Baronet in 1821. The family ended with Sir Robert Whyte-Melville Dundas, 6th Baronet, who died in 1981. The Dundas family of Ochtertyre descend from James Dundas, 1752–1831, WS, son of Ralph Dundas, merchant in Edinburgh. A Victoria Cross, awarded to Capt. James Dundas, 1842–79, who 'covered himself with blood and glory' while dealing with an uprising by Himalayan tribesmen in 1865, was sold in March, 1997, for £43,700. Capt. Dundas was son of George Dundas, of the Manour family, a Senator of the College of Justice.

DUNLOP The well-known Ayrshire surname of Dunlop comes from lands in the district of Cunningham. Anciently the property of Dunlop Place was owned by the de Morvilles, but it is not known when it passed to the ancestors of the Dunlop family. In 1260, Willelmus de Dunlop witnessed an indenture between Godfrey de Ross – possibly the previous heritor – and the burgesses of Irvine. Neel fiz Robert de Dullop, Ayrshire, appears on the *Ragman Roll* in 1296, and he appears in an inquest held at Berwick on the lands of Lady Elena la Zouch in Conyngham. The property of Dunlop seems to have been alienated from them ca. 1300, probably on account of their support for John Baliol, but by the middle of the 14th century the lands had evidently been restored to James de Dunlop. Alexander, his grandson, was the first to be recorded using the style 'of that Ilk'. Constantyn Dunlop of that Ilk, is mentioned in 1483 and 1496. He died in 1505, leaving a daughter Janet, who married James Stewart, Sheriff of Bute, grandson of Robert II. Constantyn was succeeded by his brother Alexander, whose nephew, John Dunlop, had sasine of the lands in 1507. He married Marion Douglas, and died in 1509.

Alexander Dunlop, XIIth of that Ilk, was accused in 1558 of killing his son Alexander. In happier times, James Dunlop of that Ilk was a supporter of the Presbyterian cause, and to secure his estate from forfeiture he executed a deed of resignation in favour of his next brother, John Dunlop of Garnkirk. John took possession of the lands, but resigned these in favour of his nephew, James, son of his brother. James, who married Elizabeth Cunningham, also supported the Presbyterian cause, and ca. 1667, made over part of his estate to the Earl of Dundonald. He was imprisoned from 1645 to 1667, when he signed a bond to keep the peace. His son Alexander failed to recover the lands. He married Antonia, daughter of John Brown of Fordell, and emigrated to South Carolina in 1684, having made over his estate to his son John, who died unmarried. His brother, Lt. Col. Francis Dunlop succeeded and, when he died in 1748, was succeeded by his son John, whose wife, Frances Ann Wallace, was a friend of the poet Burns. The estate was eventually sold to Thomas Dunlop, a Glasgow shipowner and grain merchant, whose son Thomas was created a Baronet in 1916. The 3rd Baronet is Sir Thomas Dunlop, residing at The Corrie, Kilmacolm, Renfrewshire. Robert Wallace Dunlop, grandson of John, XXIVth of Dunlop, married Elizabeth Sandwich, and their eldest surviving son, Keith Wallace Dunlop, born 1862,

emigrated to the USA, and became a naturalised citizen.
The family papers of the Dunlops of Garnkirk are in the Mitchell Library, Glasgow. The Dunlops, formerly of Lockerbie House, claim descent from Constantine, third son of John Dunlop, IXth of that Ilk. Those of Househill descended from Thomas, a younger son of James, XIIth of Dunlop. The Doonside family descended from Magdalen, daughter of Francis, XVIIIth Laird, who married Robert Dunlop, RN. Their son David married the MacGregor heiress of Clober, in Stirlingshire.

DUNSMORE Variants of this surname include Dunsmure and Dunsmuir, and originate with the lands of Dundemore, near Lindores, in Fife. The meaning is obscure, but may mean 'strong fort'. Patrick de Dundemer of Fife swore fealty to Edward I of England in 1296, but the old family supported Wallace and Bruce during the War of Independence. The main line ended with an heir female, ca. 1330. There are several other places called Dunmore, and the earldom of Dunmore, in the Forest of Atholl, was bestowed in 1686 on Lord Charles Murray, a son of the Earl of Atholl, who was created 1st Earl of Dunmore. The 12th Earl is Malcolm Kenneth Murray, who lives in Tasmania. The name became prolific in the west. One James Dunmore took the hated 'Test' in Covenanting times, and Robert Dunmore was a merchant-burgess of Glasgow in 1793. A Dunsmuir family worked in coal mines around Glasgow in the 18th century. Some members migrated into Ayrshire. Robert Dunsmuir, 1825–88, from Hurlford, went to British Columbia in 1851 as a coal consultant. He became a coalmaster and industrialist, and in 1882 was elected a Member of the Legislative Assembly. His son James, 1851–1920, was Premier of the Province, 1900–1902. Others went to Ulster and the USA.

DURIE There was an old family, Durie of Durie, in Scoonie parish, Fife, and most people who bear the surname probably have some link with the family or estate. The lands passed by marriage to a Kemp family, from whose posterity these were purchased in 1614 by the eminent lawyer, Sir Alexander Gibson. On being appointed a Lord of Session in 1621, he assumed the judicial title of Lord Durie. Although the Duries lost the estate there is still a Durie styled 'of Durie', in the person of Andrew, son of the late Lt. Col. Raymond V. Dewar Durie, who had a distinguished military career with the Argyll & Sutherland Highlanders. He claims descent from George

Durie, the last Abbot of Dunfermline. The name comes from the Gaelic *dobharach*, 'little stream', and the earliest references to it appear between 1258 and 1271, when Duncan de Durry witnessed charters. John Durie, a monk of Dunfermline, was imprisoned for heresy, and became minister of Colinton in 1569. John Durie, from Edinburgh, published a pioneer work on Librarianship at London in 1650.

DURWARD The office of door-ward to the king (in Latin documents *Ostiarii regis*) was prestigious, and in the 13th century was hereditary in the family of de Lundin, probably from Lundin, in Fife. The first to hold the office appears to have been Thomas de Lundin, who lived in the early part of that century. The family once laid claim to the earldom of Mar, through the female line, and obtained lands on north Deeside. Alan, son of Thomas, married a natural daughter of King Alexander II (reigned 1214–49) and, during the minority of Alexander III, was regent of the kingdom. He died before 1275, and his estates were divided among three daughters. Many lordly ecclesiastics had door-wards, including the abbots of Arbroath. Thomas le Durward was a burgess of Arbroath in 1452, and the name spread throughout the north-east. Sir Walter Scott's novel, *Quentin Durward* (1823), is based on the story of one of King Louis' Scottish Guard, forced by circumstances to serve in France. He was selected to escort the Countess of Croye and her aunt from Plessis-de-Tours to Liege, and his courage and truth won her love. However, he gave up all his gay hopes to further serve his royal master. Joseph Durward was an expert clockmaker-burgess of Canongate, Edinburgh, 1775–1819.

ELIOTT Some seventy spellings of this name have been recorded, the most prolific being Eliot, Eliott and Elliott. The name was originally Elwald or Elwold, in Old English *Aefwald*, and anciently was used frequently as a forename. The Border clan of the Middle March had a chief in the late 15th century called Robert Elwald, who was Captain of Hermitage Castle. His son was slain at Flodden, 1513, and his son Robert was also Captain of Hermitage Castle. His brother Archibald was ancestor of the Elliots of Arkleton. The main forms of the name appear in an old rhyme:

> The double L and single T
> Descend from Minto and Wolflee,
> The double T and single L
> Mark the old race in Stobs that dwell,

The single L and single T
The Eliots of St Germains be,
But double T and double LL
Who they are nobody can tell.

The Stobo branch are held to be the senior line of the Border clan, descended from Gavin Eliott, who lived in the late 16th century. The next heir, Gilbert of Stobo, celebrated as *Gibbie wi' the gowden gartens*, married a daughter of Scott of Harden, and his fourth son, Gavin Eliott of Grange, was father of Sir Gilbert Eliott, 1st Baronet (cr. NS, 1700) of Headshaw and Minto. The 4th Baronet, Sir Gilbert, an eminent ambassador, was created Earl of Minto in 1751. This line is now represented by Gilbert Edward George Lariston Elliot-Murray-Kynynmound, 6th Earl, who resides at Minto House, Hawick. The 11th Baronet of Stobo, Sir Arthur Francis Augustus Boswell Eliott, the family historian, died in 1989, and was succeeded by his cousin, Charles Joseph Alexander Eliott, born 1937. Some of the surname may have derived from the village of Eliot, in Angus.

The Rt Hon. Walter Elliot, 1888–1958, son of William Elliot, Muirglen, Lanark, was a distinguished politician, who was Secretary of State for Scotland, 1926–29, and the recipient of many honours. His second wife, Katharine, 1903–94, daughter of Sir Charles Tennant, Baronet, was active in public life, and was created CBE in 1946 and DBE in 1958. She was also created Baroness Elliot of Harwood of Rulewater, Roxburghshire in 1958.

ERSKINE, EARLS OF MAR AND BARONS GARIOCH

The ancient mormaers of Mar were probably of Pictish origin, and they became the premier earls of Scotland. By 1014 the dignity passed to a scion of the Norse race of Ivar, and it descended to Thomas, 9th Earl of Mar and Lord of Garioch. His eventual heiress, Isabella, Countess of Mar, married as her second husband, Alexander Stewart, a natural son of the 'Wolf of Badenoch'. In 1404 she gave him the earldom in liferent and, after her death in 1408, he resigned it to the Crown. He fought against the Lord of the Isles at Harlaw in 1411, and although possessing only a lifererent, received in 1426, a re-grant of the earldom. The Earl died in 1435, and was succeeded by the heir of his late Countess, Robert, 1st Lord Erskine. His surname was territorial: derived from the barony of Erskine, in Renfrewshire. The family may have originated in Flanders, descended from a younger son of Gilbert of Ghent. Mrs Beryl Platts has commented on the similarity of their arms.

Robert's right to the honours was recognised in 1395, and he was retoured as heir to half of the earldom. He was later divested on the grounds that the earldom had passed to the Crown as *ultimus haeres* of the Countess Isabella, and the title was borne by various members of the Royal Family between 1459 and 1562. Parts of the lands were alienated. The Court of Session, in 1626, described the grant of 1426 as a pretended provision of tailzie, and ruled that the Crown had no right to the earldom. By his first wife, Janet Keith, Robert left two sons: Thomas, his heir, and Nicol (some say Malcolm) of Kinnoul.

John Erskine, *de jure* 18th Earl of Mar and 11th Lord Garioch, was high in favour with Mary, Queen of Scots, who entrusted him with the care of her son, Prince James. In 1565 he received a charter restoring him *per modum justitae* as Earl of Mar, with destination to heirs general. His captaincy of Stirling Castle was destined to heirs male. The charter was ratified in 1567. John, 23rd Earl and 16th Lord Garioch, was forfeited in 1716 for his part in the Jacobite rising, but his grandson, John Francis Erskine was restored by Parliament in 1824 as 24th Earl of Mar and 17th Baron Garioch. John Francis Miller Erskine, 1795–1866, 26th Earl of Mar and 19th Baron of Garioch, proved his claim to the earldom of Kellie in 1835, on failure of the male line of the 1st Earl, Alexander, second son of John, 4th Lord Erskine, descended from Sir Robert Erskine, 13th Earl of Mar. When he died without issue in 1866, the earldom of Kellie passed to his cousin and heir male, Walter Coningsby Erskine, and the earldom of Mar devolved on his nephew and heir-general, John Francis Goodeve Erskine. Walter Coningsby, an army officer, claimed the Earldom of Mar, as created in 1565, but died before the Lords decided on the case. His son, Walter Henry, was allowed the honours in 1875, becoming 11th Earl of Mar and 13th of Kellie. The ancient earldom was carried on by his nephew, John Francis Goodeve Erskine, and his son, John Francis Hamilton Erskine, has been numbered as 28th Earl of Mar and 23rd Baron Garioch. The 30th Earl and 23rd Baron Garioch was James Clifton, of Mar, whose son David died unmarried in 1967. His sister Margaret became Countess of Mar and Lady Garioch in her own right. She married in 1959 Edwin Noel of Mar (recognised in the surname by warrant of the Lord Lyon), son of Edwin Artiss, but they were divorced in 1976. There is one daughter of the marriage, Lady Susan Helen, Mistress of Mar. The Countess maintains a private officer of arms, called Garioch Pursuivant.

ERSKINE, EARLS OF MAR AND KELLIE

The Erskine succession to the Earldom of Mar and Lordship of Garioch, can best be understood by grasping details relating to Gratney, 7th Earl. He married Christian, daughter of Robert the Bruce, and besides Donald, his heir, had a daughter Ellen, who married Sir John Monteith. Their daughter, Christian, married first, Sir Edward Keith; and secondly, Sir Robert Erskine, who had married Beatrix Lindsay. By her first marriage Christian had a daughter Janet, who married her stepbrother, Sir Thomas Erskine. They had two sons: Robert, who succeeded Alexander Stewart as the 13th Earl; and John, ancestor of the Erskines of Dun and Pittodrie. The barony of Dun descended through the male line to John Erskine, who married in 1770, Mary Baird of New Byth. Their co-heiress, Margaret, married Archibald Kennedy, 12th Earl of Cassilis, and from them came the Kennedy-Erskines.

Robert Erskine became a Lord of Parliament, and the family stoutly asserted their claim to the Earldom of Mar, but the succeeding 14th, 15th, 16th and 17th Earls can only be described as *de jure*. John, 5th Lord Erskine, *de jure* 17th Earl, married Margaret, daughter of Archibald, 2nd Earl of Argyll, and had with other issue, John, the heir, and Alexander, father of the 1st Earl of Kellie. In 1565 he was granted the earldom of Mar, with its seat at Alloa, where generations of the family are buried. His heir, John, 2nd Earl (numbering from 1565) and 7th Lord Erskine, had by his first wife a son John, 3rd Earl, and by his second wife had issue, of whom James was ancestor of the Earls of Buchan; Henry was progenitor of the Lords of Cardross, and Charles was ancestor of the Erskines of Alva, now St Clair-Erskines, Earls of Rosslyn. Alexander Erskine, son of John, 4th Lord Erskine, was the father of Thomas, created Earl of Kellie in 1619. Alexander, 5th Earl, was involved in the Jacobite Rising of 1745. On the death of Methven, 10th Earl, he was succeeded by his distant kinsman, John Francis Miller Erskine, 9th Earl of Mar, who thus became 11th Earl of Kellie. He was succeeded in the earldom of Kellie by his cousin, Walter Coningsby Erskine, who claimed the earldom of Mar (created 1665), allowed to his son, Walter Henry, in 1875. John Francis Erskine, 13th Earl of Mar and 15th of Kellie, died in 1993, and the dowager countess, Pansie Constance Thorne, died in 1996. The present holder of the titles is their eldest son, James Thorne Erskine.

James Erskine, son of the 7th Earl of Mar, by his second wife, married Mary, only child of James Douglas, 6th Earl of Buchan, and had a son James, who succeeded as 8th Earl of Buchan. His son William, 9th Earl, never married, and Henry, another son of the 7th Earl of Mar, had a son who succeeded as Lord Cardross, a title conferred on his grandfather in 1610. His son Henry, 3rd Lord Cardross, was half-brother of John Erskine of Carnock, father of the eminent jurist, Professor John Erskine, author of standard textbooks. Henry was succeeded in turn by his son David, 4th Lord Cardross, who succeeded to the earldom of Buchan on the death of William, his father's second cousin. David Stewart Erskine, 11th Earl of Buchan, founded the Society of Antiquaries of Scotland in 1780. His brother, Henry of Almondell, was the famous legal wit who coined the phrase for the snuffmaker's carriage: 'Wha wad hae thocht it, that noses had bocht it'. He was the father of the 12th Earl. From him also descend the Barons Erskine of Restormel Castle, Cornwall. The 17th Earl of Buchan is Malcolm Henry Erskine, who is also Lord Auchterhouse, Lord Cardross and 7th Baron Erskine.

FALCONER The surname derives from the office of falconer, one who breeds and/or trains falcons and hawks for sport. Falconers appear in Kincardineshire during the reign of William the Lion (1165–1214). Mattheus the Falconer witnessed a charter ca. 1202, and around the same time, William the Falconer granted land to the Abbey of Arbroath. In the vernacular he may have been called 'the hawker'. While his descendants took the surname Falconer, the family home was Halkerton. In 1211, Ranulph the Falconer, son of Walter of Loutrop, had a grant of lands in the Mearns (Kincardineshire), including Balemacoy (?Balmakellie) and Lacherachgeich Kennie (which may have become Halkerton). Gervase the Falconer was taken prisoner at Dunbar in 1296, and was still in an English prison in 1307. A contemporary, Robert le Fauconer de Kyncardyn, signed the *Ragman Roll* in 1296. His seal shows a falcon striking a small bird. The arms of the Falconers and their cadets have undergone many changes, but the falcon has always been the dominant charge.

Subsequent Falconers were styled of Lethens, then of Halkerton. David of Halkerton was one of a jury in an inquisition in 1448, and his grandson, Sir Alexander, was ancestor of the Falconers of Innerlochtie, Kincorth, Dinduff and Phesdo. In 1646, Sir Alexander Falconer, 1594–1671, was created Lord Falconer of Halkerton. His brother, Sir David of Glenfarquhar, had a son Alexander, created Baronet and his son, Sir Alexander, 2nd Baronet succeeded as 4th

Lord Falconer in 1724. He died without issue in 1727, when the baronetcy became extinct, but his cousin David, a Lord of Session, became 5th Lord Falconer. Another brother of the 1st Lord was Sir John of Balmakellie, Master of the Minthouse. By his first wife, Sybil Ogilvy, he had a son David, an Edinburgh merchant and Quaker, whose son Gilbert, emigrated to Maryland. By a second wife he had further issue, including Sir John, 1636–86, Warden of the Mint. Sir David of Halkerton married in 1703, Catherine, daughter of William Keith, 2nd Earl of Kintore. Their grandson, Anthony Adrian Falconer, 8th Lord Falconer, inherited the Kintore peerage in 1778.

The two peerages continued in the family until the death in 1966, without issue, of Arthur George, 10th Earl of Kintore and 13th Lord Falconer of Halkerton. The Scottish title of Lord Falconer then became dormant, and the earldom passed to his sister, Ethel Sydney. She married Lawrence Baird, created Viscount Stonehaven, in 1925. He was a son of Sir Alexander Baird, created 1st Baronet of Urie in 1897. Their son, James Ian, succeeded as 12th Earl in 1974. He married in 1935, Delia Loyd, and died in 1989. She is the present Countess of Kintore, and her son, Sir Michael, is the 13th Earl and 4th Baronet. He assumed the surname Keith in lieu of Baird, and succeeded to the Viscountcy of Stonehaven, and – through his grandfather – the baronetcy of Urie.

There are Falconers in many parts of the world who are of Scottish descent, and a few may have a claim to the title, Falconer of Halkerton. The matter would not be easily resolved. An octogenarian English architect, Peter Serrel Falconer, has long styled himself 'heir presumptive', claiming descent from Patrick of Newton, a younger son of Alexander Falconer of Halkerton, who died in 1595.

FARMER The earliest known reference to the surname Farmer appears in Latin form in 1262 when Richard Fermarius was a juror at Peebles. The name is now widespread, but for long was most strongly represented in East Fife. It originally meant a farmer of the revenue, rather than an agriculturist, but many came to be tillers of the soil. Alan Fermour witnessed a document at St Andrews in 1391, and James Fermour attended the university there in 1424. A notable farming family descended from Thomas Farmer in Over Carnbee, who married Elizabeth Imrie in 1813. Their eldest son farmed at Drumrack, Crail, and three younger sons emigrated to New Zealand. One of these, James, made his fortune there and returned to Scotland in the 1880s and purchased the desirable farm of Brownhills, near St Andrews. Another branch settled in Edinburgh.

FARQUHARSON

Clan Farquharson claim descent from Farquhar, fourth son of Alexander *Ciar* Shaw of Rothiemurchus, a sept of Clan Chattan. The family took up residence in Aberdeenshire, and eventually assumed the surname of Farquharson. A descendant, Donald, married Isobel Stewart, heiress of Invercauld. Their son was the famous Findla *Mor*, 1st of Invercauld, who was killed at Pinkie in 1547, bearing the royal standard. After him the Farquharsons are known as *Clann Fhionnlaidh*. He was succeeded by Robert, son of his first marriage with Beatrix Garden. From them also descend the Farquharsons of Whitehouse, represented by Capt. Colin Andrew Farquharson, Lord Lieutenant of Aberdeenshire. Robert's grandson, Alexander, married Isabella, daughter of William Mackintoch of that Ilk, and died in 1681. His second son, John of Ivercauld, joined the Clan Chattan Regiment in 1715, and was taken prisoner at Preston, where he remained for ten months. John was married three times and, by his third wife, Margaret Murray, of the Atholl family, had with other issue, James of Invercauld, and Anne, who married William Mackintosh, XXIst of that Ilk, who held a commission under King George. Lady Anne, then only twenty years old, raised the Clan Chattan Regiment in 1745 for the Young Pretender.

James Farquharson died in 1750, and was succeeded by his son Capt. James, who had served in the Hanovarian army at Culloden. The Farquharsons were led by Francis Farquharson of Monaltrie, who mustered 300 men. Capt. James died in 1806, and was succeeded by his surviving daughter, Catherine, who married in 1798, Capt. James Ross, RN (second son of John Lockhart Ross of Balnagown), who assumed the surname of Farquharson, and died in 1810. Their grandson, James Ross Farquharson, XIIIth of Invercauld, died in 1888, and his son, Alexander Haldane Farquharson, became chief of the clan. On his death, the undifferenced arms were confirmed to his daughter Myrtle, by decree of Lyon Court. Her nephew, Capt. Alwyn Farquharson, was recognised as chief in 1949.

The stem family produced many branches, among them Monaltrie, Whitehouse, Haughton, Allargue, Breda and Finzean. The Farquharsons of Inverey were a celebrated Jacobite branch, of whom the 'Black Colonel', John, lives on in Deeside legends and ballads. His eldest son by his first wife, Margaret Gordon, was Peter or Patrick, who was appointed in 1715 by Lord Mar to raise Farquharson vassals, and he was made Colonel of Mar's Regiment. He narrowly escaped forfeiture, and died in 1737. Charles Farquharson, his full brother, also took part in the '15 Rising, as did James, their half-brother and Charles, of Balmoral, their uncle. The Whitehouse branch and others were also Jacobites, and rose for Prince Charles in 1745. They included Donald of Auchriachan; Francis of Monaltrie (who became a model landlord); Gregor of Tombae and his son Cosmo; James of Balmoral; John of Allargue; Lewis, farmer in Tarland; Robert in Tullich, Glenmuick; and William, of the Auchindryne family.

Joseph Farquharson, 1845–1939, a celebrated artist, was of the Finzean branch, currently represented by Angus Durie Miller Farquharson, OBE. Charles Anderson Farquharson, of Logie Coldstone, Aberdeenshire, who died in 1929, was father of the Rt Hon. Sir Donald H. Farquharson, OBE, a distinguished barrister in London.

FENTON While the earliest known person of this surname was John de Fenton, Sheriff of Forfar in 1261, the name derives from an old barony near North Berwick, in East Lothian. The Fentons, however, had lands in Forfar. Janet, heiress of Walter de Fenton, Lord of Baikie, in Angus, is on record in 1448. Sir William de Fentone married before 1270, Cecilia, daughter of Sir John Bisset of Lovat, and received the estate of Beaufort and some lands in Ireland. This man, or a son, gave lands at Lynros to the chapel of Baikie, in 1362. Probably the family of Fentons who appear in the Aird, west of Inverness, before 1422, were related. The Angus Fentons ended with co-heiresses around 1450. One married a Lyndsay and the other a Halket. These Angus Fentons have their name preserved in Fenton Hill, near Lindertis. Anciently there was a family so named in possession of the rich East Lothian lands of Fenton. Sir Alexander de Fentoun gave a donation to Dryburgh Abbey, ca. 1330. William de Fenton, Lord of that Ilk, acquired lands in Clydesdale in 1413. William Fenton of Fenton appears in 1450, and John Fenton of that Ilk, is recorded in 1473. Alexander (Sandy) Fenton, CBE, D.Litt., a native of Shotts and a graduate of the University of Aberdeen, is well known to Scottish historians and antiquaries. He was a director of the Museums of Scotland, 1978–85, and has been Honorary Professor of Antiquities in the Royal Museum of Scotland since 1996. Dr Fenton is the author of many books, pamphlets and articles.

FERGUSSON/FERGUSON
It is very unlikely that all Fergussons and Fergusons descend from a common ancestor. The name appears in various parts of Scotland from the 12th century onwards. The Gaelic form was *MacFhearghuis*, which became Englished as Ferguson-son, but corrupt forms such as Mackerras and MacHerries appear. Fergushill was an old variant. In many cases the suffix 'son' has been dropped, to give Fergus, Fergie, Ferrie and Ferries. According to tradition, the West Highland Fergussons descend from Fergus MacErc, King of Dalriada in AD 503. Possibly, some in the south-west took their name from Fergus, Lord of Galloway, who died in 1161.

The Fergusons of Craigdarroch, Dumfriesshire, appear on record during the reign of David II (1329–71). Several members of this family were parliamentarians before and after the Union of 1707. Two 18th century Fergusons have achieved fame in verse. Anna, died 1764, daughter of Sir Robert Laurie of Maxwellton, and wife of Alexander Ferguson of Craigdarroch, is the heroine of Lady John Scott's famous song, *Annie Laurie*. Her grandson, another Alexander Ferguson, a Dumfries lawyer, was the winner of the contest which gave rise to Robert Burns' racy ballad, *The Whistle*. The Craigdarroch line ended with an heiress, Ella Ferguson, who married in 1918, Col. Wallace Smith Cunninghame of Caprington. Cadets of the Craigdarroch family probably include the Fergussons of Spittalhaugh, Peeblesshire. Sir William Fergusson, 1st Baronet of Spittalhaugh, created UK, 1866, was an eminent surgeon in London, attending Queen Victoria and her Consort. This family is now represented by Sir James Colyer-Ferguson, 4th Baronet, who resides in London.

From the banks of the Tummel to Strathardle and Glenshee, the Fergussons of Dunfallandy, with their numerous cadets, were influential. They first appear in the 15th century, styled 'of Derculich', but must have obtained Dunfallandy, Logierait, by 1620. Several lairds were called barons, but unofficially. The Baledmund branch descended from Finlay Fergusson and Grizel Bruce, on record ca. 1602. A later Finlay of this line was tried for treason after the '15 Jacobite Rising, and acquitted. He seems also to have been involved in the '45.

In Strathyre and Balquhidder, the Fergusons were prolific, but not landed proprietors. Like their neighbours, the MacGregors, they were often in trouble with the authorities. Duncan Ferguson and several others in Strathyre were accused of killing deer in the forest of Glenfinglas, and put to the horn. On Lochearnside there was a dynasty of Ferguson masons. In Cowal and Kintyre, Argyll, the name Fergusson is ancient, and often appears as MacKerras. At Glenshellish, near the head of Lock Eck, a family of Fergussons held the lands for over 200 years. The last to own the lands was Daniel, who sold his farm in 1803. From a family long resident in Inverkeithing, descend the Munro-Fergusons of Raith, who have produced soldiers and statesmen. The Fergussons of Kilkerran in Ayrshire appear as a landed family in 1464, and may be descended from the Lords of Galloway. John Fergusson of Kilkerran was created a Baronet of NS in 1703, and his successors came to be regarded as chiefs of the surname. Sir Adam, 3rd Baronet, is referred to by the poet Burns in *The Authors Earnest Cry and Prayer*. The 7th Baronet, Sir Charles, was a high-ranked soldier for nearly 40 years, and was Governor of New Zealand, 1924–30. Sir James, 1904–73, 8th Baronet, was Keeper of the Records of Scotland, 1949–69. His son Charles is the 9th Baronet.

FLEMING Countless lives have been saved by 'a triumph of accident and shrewd observation', by a Scottish physician and bacteriologist, Alexander Fleming, 1881–1955. The son of an Ayrshire farmer, he studied at the medical school of St Mary's Hospital, London, and at London University. After a brilliant student career, he worked under Sir Anwoth Wright, pioneer in vaccine therapy. During World War I (1914–18) he served as a captain in the RAMC, and was mentioned in despatches. As professor in the Royal College of Surgeons he continued research on antibacterial substances, and his first reward was the discovery of the antibiotic, lysozyme. The 'accident' was with some mould having been allowed to develop on a plate on which bacteria was being cultured. The 'observation' was that the mould was so destructive of the bacteria that even when diluted hundreds of times, it still destroyed them. Fleming's epoch-making discovery of the mould from which penicillin is made, brought him numerous honours. He was knighted in 1944, and awarded the Nobel Prize for Medicine in 1945, along with Sir Howard (later Lord) Florey, and (Sir) E.B. Chain.

The surname Fleming sufficiently denotes the nationality of the people who bore it in Scotland in the 12th century. The earliest Fleming of note was Baldwin of Biggar, Sheriff of Lanark, who had a grant of land and was a powerful baron around 1160–1170. He seems to have come from Bratton, in Devonshire, and his forbear was Stephen Flandrensis, a Latinised form of the name. Several others who came to Scotland may have been related. A family of Flemings lived in Boghall Castle, Biggar. Theobald the Fleming held land on Douglas Water, and Jordan Fleming was taken prisoner at Alnwick in 1174, along with King William the Lion.

Robert Fleming, ancestor of the earls of Wigtown, rendered fealty to the English monarch in 1296. His son, Malcolm of Fulwood and Cumbernauld, was granted lands in Wigtownshire, with the title of Earl of Wigtown, in 1341. His grandson Thomas, 2nd Earl, sold his whole rights to Archibald Douglas, Earl of Galloway, in 1372, and certain of his lands were granted to Sir James Lyndsay. The title was also lost. His lands at Lenzie devolved on his cousin, Sir Malcolm Fleming, Sheriff of Dumbarton. A descendant, Sir Robert of Cumbernauld and Biggar, was created a Lord of Parliament, ca. 1452. Malcolm, 3rd Lord Fleming, who fell at Pinkie in 1547, was the father of Mary one of 'the four Maries' who tended Mary, Queen of Scots. John, the 6th Lord, was advanced to the dignity of Earl of Wigtown, Lord Fleming and Cumbernauld, in 1606. His eldest son was granted lands in Peeblesshire. John, 6th Earl, died without male issue. The estates of Cumbernauld and Biggar were inherited by his daughter Clementina, and the title devolved on his brother Charles, who died in 1747, since when the honour has been dormant. Clementina married Charles, Lord Elphinstone. Her grandson, Charles, heir to the lands, became an Admiral and assumed the surname of Fleming. He was the father of John, 14th Lord Elphinstone.

Another link with the Elphinstone family is found in the marriage of Marjory, only daughter of Sir Gilbert Fleming of Ferme, near Rutherglen, who married James, Master of Elphinstone, and died without issue in 1784. Archibald Fleming of Ferme was created a Baronet of NS in 1661. Another old Fleming family was seated at Auchintoul, in Banffshire. Patrick, of this family, is credited with having been the finest swordsman in the Jacobite army of 1745.

FLETCHER The name derives from Old French *flechier*, a person who attached the *fleches* or feathers to arrow shafts, but generally became arrowmakers. In Gaelic the name is *fleisdear*, and gave the surname *Mac an Fhleistear*, which was Englished as Fletcher. Fletcher is an ancient surname in Islay, and generations of them were arrowmakers to the Lords of the Isles. Arrows were a vital part of Clan Donald's equipment, not only in battle but in killing deer and and other game. The name is well represented in West Perthshire, and those of Glenlyon were arrowmakers to the MacGregors of Glenorchy, later in Glenstrae and Balquhidder. Possibly they also made arrows for the Campbells of Breadalbane. Archibald Fletcher, 1746–1828, a native of Glenlyon, after attending school at Kenmore, pursued his studies at Edinburgh. In 1778, being a Gaelic speaker, he was deputed to negotiate with some MacRaes – subjects of the House of Seaforth – who called themselves 'MacKenzie's shirt of mail'. They were no cowards, but objected to embarking at Leith for service in America. Fletcher himself favoured the cause of American Independence. This remarkable man became 'the father of Burgh reform', and was sent to London in 1787 as a delegate of the Scottish Burghs, where he gained the friendship of Charles Fox. In 1790, then in his mid-forties, he qualified as an advocate, and was greatly admired in the legal profession. Andrew Fletcher, 1653–1716, son of Sir Robert Fletcher of Saltoun, East Lothian, became a celebrated writer and patriot, notably for his resolute opposition to the Treaty of Union in 1707. A nephew of his, Andrew Fletcher, was admitted advocate in 1717, and in time became a Lord of Session under the title of Lord Milton. The Fletchers of Saltoun descend from Sir Andrew Fletcher of Innerpeffer, who purchased the lands ca. 1650. The XIth Laird, John Theodore Talbot Fletcher, died without issue in 1995.

FLETT An Orcadian of the 12th century appears in the *Orkneyinga Saga* as Thorkel *Flettir*. The nickname may be connected with the Old Norse *flett*, to 'fla' or 'to rob', and with Nyorsk *fletta*, 'an active, eager fellow'. There was a Dane of the same period called Harold Flettir, in 'Heimskringla', and one or two Norwegians had the same name. Throkel Flettir was a farmer on the island of Westray, and the saga tells us he was 'quarrelsome and overbearing'.

The Fletts were among the chief landed families in Orkney in the later Norse period, and the surname had clearly became stabilised by the 15th century. Kolbein Flett was one of those who laid charges against David Meynor of Weem in 1427. The name of Ioni Blatto, one of the prominent men of that time, is thought to be a mis-spelling of Flett. Mawnus Flett is recorded at Kirkwall in 1480, and Jhone Fleytt of Hare was a member of an assize there in 1509. William Flett of Howbister is mentioned in 1516, and George Flett, husbandman in the parish of Orphir, was retoured as heir to Robert

Flett, merchant in Kirkwall, in 1665. A number of Fletts appear in the *Orkney Register of Testaments*. John Sklaitter in Arquyle, parish of Rendall, died in 1592, and Mareoun Flett, his widow, is mentioned along with his son Johnne, executor. Margaret Flett, widow of Nicoll Lesk, who died in 1605, in Grindwater, Orphir parish, acted for their children, Andro, Alexander, Katherin and Barbara. William Flet in Clouk in Costa, parish of Evie, died in 1609, survived by his widow, Elizabeth Houston, and daughters Mareoun and Christian. Jasper Flett in Howbister is mentioned in 1607, and Hutcheon Flett is recorded in 1613, also Alexander Flett. Another Alexander, in Sabay, St Andrews parish, was a debtor in 1614.

There is a place-name Flett in Shetland, from *flotr*, a strip of land, and the surname itself appears in Shetland records. It is one of the most prolific in the Orkney Islands, and has been especially associated with Netherbrough, in Harray parish. It appears in New Zealand and in the USA, where the spelling Flatt is recorded. Numerous Orcadians were employed in Canada with the Hudson's Bay Company. Among them was William Flett, who went out in 1782 and became a canoe builder and buffalo hunter. George Flett, 1775–1850, from Firth parish, arrived at York Factory in 1796, and was a labourer-boatman. He retired to the Red River Settlement in 1823, and married Peggy, daughter of James Peter Whitford. Another Flett – Thomas from Harray – was an interpreter and postmaster at Ft Colville, 1838–53. James Flett, 1824–99, from Rousay, was a fisherman and canoeman in the Athabasca district, and after a spell as a clerk there, he retired to Edmonton on a pension.

Sir John Smith Flett, 1869–1947, Director of the Geological Survey of Great Britain, and of the Museum of Practical Geology, was a distinguished Orcadian who received much recognition. Ian Stark Flett, an Aberdonian, now retired and living in Kirkcaldy, after serving in the Signals and Intelligence Branch of the RAF, became a leading figure in the field of education in various parts of Britain. Ian Flett, of Dundee District Archives, is one of Scotland's best-known record keepers, lecturing and writing on associated matters. The Rev. William Nugent Flett, a clergyman in New Zealand, is undoubtedly of Scottish ancestry. His talented wife, Ethel Snelson Flett, is the author of a number of books, including *New Zealand Inheritance* (1957), and *The Essie Summers Story* (1974). She has contributed to newspapers and periodicals, including *The Scots Magazine*.

FLUCKER/FLOCKHART   This surname is a late development of Flucker: common in Fife, and not unknown among the fisherfolk of Newhaven, Edinburgh. Curiously, a flucker or fluker was a fisherman, specifically catching flatfish related to the turbot. In medieval times, the Nethergate of Dundee was known as the Fluckergate, and significantly the name appears most often in coastal towns. The name appears in 1316, when Dominus Patricius dictus Floker, was appointed master and guardian of the Hospital of Polmade (Balmadie), juxta Ruglen. Michael Flucker was custumar of Inverkeithing in 1359, and another man of the same name was vicar of Kirkcaldy in 1448. David Flucare held land in Edinburgh in 1486. The testament of Isobel Fleukar, widow of William Nicoll in Edinburgh, was confirmed in 1790. By this time many Fluckers were being recorded as Flockharts, possibly because it sounded like the surname Lockhart. James Fluckart, weaver in Edinburgh, married Janet Aitkine in 1679. Henrietta, daughter of the deceased Archibald Flockhart, married in 1796, Charles Bowman, clerk of hornings and inhibitions. John Flockhart, watchmaker in Edinburgh, married in 1797, Margaret Orrock, from Leith. Robert ('Daddy') Flockhart, ca. 1777–ca. 1857, was a street preacher in Edinburgh. The Edinburgh chemists, Duncan Flockhart & Co., made up cloroform for Dr James Y. Simpson, 1811–70, following a suggestion made by Dr David Waldie, 1813–89, surgeon and chemist, and a native of Linlithgow, in 1846.

FORBES   The surname Forbes is derived from the lands of Forbes, Donside, Aberdeenshire, and comes from the Gaelic *forba*, a field or tract of ground, with the place-name suffix, *ais*, possibly Pictish. Duncan de Forboys, who rendered homage to Edward I in 1296, was probably a Forbes. John Forbes appears in an English roll of 1306. Sir John de Forbes, justiciary of Aberdeenshire, 1394, was the father of Sir Alexander, 1st Lord Forbes (1445), and of Sir William Forbes, ancestor of the Pitsligo branch of the family. Over the next three centuries the Forbes family had disputes with the Gordons. James, 2nd Lord Forbes, was permitted to fortify the tower of Drymynour, commonly called Forbes, and in 1467 the 3rd Lord, 'Grey Willie', entered into a mutual bond with the heads of the cadet houses of Pitsligo, Tolquhoun and Brux, and Duncan Mackintosh, Captain of Clan Chattan, for defence and protection against all but the king and their respective superiors.

William, 7th Lord Forbes, was faithful to Mary, Queen of Scots, and in 1573 received a charter of the lands of Corsindae. He married Elizabeth, the daughter and co-heiress of Sir William Keith of Inverugie. One of their daughters married George Johnston of Caskieben, and was mother of the celebrated physician and Latin poet, Arthur Johnston, 1587–1641. William Forbes, 1570–1606, would have been 9th Lord, but entered the Capuchin monastery at Ghent in 1589, as 'Brother Archangel'. His brother John was also partial to the monastic life and, when he died in 1606, was succeeded by his half-brother, Arthur, 9th Lord. Lt. Gen. Alexander Forbes, 10th Lord, soldiered under Gustav Adolph of Sweden. William, 12th Lord, was a supporter of the Union of 1707 (for a bribe of £50!). James Ochoncar Forbes, 17th Lord, had a distinguished military career, and for some years commanded the army in Ireland. One of his daughters, Charlotte, married Sir John Forbes of Craigievar. Walter, his eldest surviving son, fought at Waterloo, and commanded a company of the Coldstream Guards in the defence of Hougoumont. Atholl Laurence Cunyngham Forbes, 21st Baron, served as a major in the Grenadier Guards in World War I. His son, Sir Nigel Ivan Forbes, born 1918, is the 22nd Baron, and was a major in the same regiment during World War II. He was Minister of State at the Scottish Office, 1958–59, and is chief of the clan. The heir is his son, journalist Malcolm Nigel Forbes.

During the Jacobite Risings several clansmen distinguished themselves. Rev Robert Forbes, 1708–75, Rector of the Episcopal Chapel at Leith, recorded the main events of the '45, and his collection of material was printed by the Scottish History Society, in 3 volumes, 1895–96, under the title of *The Lyon in Mourning*. Alexander, 4th Lord Pitsligo, a Jacobite, raised a troop of horse for Prince Charles in 1745. His estates were forfeited, and the title has remained under attainder. The male heirs are probably the Forbes family of Newe, baronets. Sir John Stewart Forbes, the 6th Baronet, died without male issue in 1984, and was succeeded by his cousin, Major Hamish Stewart Forbes, 7th Baronet, whose heir is his son James Thomas Stewart Forbes. The most distinguished Forbes of the Jacobite period was Duncan of Culloden, President of the Court of Session. The 1st Baronet of Craigievar (created NS, 1630), built the outstanding castle there, now in the care of the National Trust for Scotland. The baronetcy of Monymusk (created NS, 1626), was conferred on Sir Stewart Forbes. This family is now represented by Sir William Daniel Stuart-Forbes, 13th Baronet.

FORDYCE The name stems from the parish of Fordyce in Banffshire, and derives from the Gaelic *fothair deas*, 'south slope', and is associated mainly with the north-east. John Fordise was vicar of Athy in 1460, and may be the Johannes Fordys who became vicar of Garvok. The Fordyces were regarded as a sept of the Clan Forbes. Helene Fordyce of Tarcastell and Edinquheill, Elgin, died in 1541, and her lands reverted to the Crown. John and James Ffordyce appear on a valuation roll of Rothiemay parish in 1690. George Fordyce of Broadford, 1663–1733, was Provost of Aberdeen, 1718–19. He had twenty-one children by two marriages. His son George was Provost, 1722–23. Son William, an army surgeon, was knighted in 1782. Another son, Alexander, became a banker in London, with sufficient standing to marry in 1770, Lady Margaret, a daughter of the Earl of Balcarres. He went bankrupt, causing widespread ruin. William Dingwall Fordyce of Culsh, 1745–1834, advocate in Aberdeen, was progenitor of a notable legal family in that city. Alexander Dingwall Fordyce, 1786–1852, son of Arthur Dingwall Fordyce and Janet Morison, emigrated to Nicol Township Wellington County, Ontario, in 1836, and was a farmer and merchant.

FRASER Volumes have been written about the Frasers, and more could be added, along with notes on their interesting heraldry and the numerous titles held. They probably came from France into England after the Norman Conquest, and from the Seigneury of Freseliere, in Anjou. The seigneurs were called Fresel, and variants of the name found their way to Scotland. Cinquefoils, which have prominence in the Fraser arms, descend from those found in 12th century noble families of St Omer, in Flanders. The first on record in Scotland was Simon, who gave the church of Keith to the Abbey of Kelso. He is probably the man styled 'son of Malbet' and sheriff of Traquair in 1184. His son, Sir Gilbert, also sheriff, appears to have been a brother of Udard, who married a daughter of Oliver, son of Kylbert, and obtained Oliver Castle. Udard was succeeded by a nephew, Adam, from whom descended Sir Simon Fraser, an adherant of Sir William Wallace. He left a son, John, father of Alexander of Cornhill, Stirling, and of Richard of Touch-Fraser, progenitor of the Frasers of Philorth, in Buchan.

Richard's grandson, Sir Alexander, married Lady Mary, sister of Robert the Bruce, and their grandson, Alexander of Durris, by his marriage to Joanna, daughter of William, Earl of Ross, obtained Philorth, with a home at Cairnbulg. Sir Alexander Fraser of Philorth founded the town of Fraserburgh, and the IXth Laird married Margaret Abernethy, daughter of the 7th Lord Saltoun. On the expiry of the Abernethy line in 1668, their son Alexander was confirmed as heir. The title has descended to Flora Margaret, daughter of the 19th Lord Saltoun. She sits in the House of Lords and is chief of Clan Fraser. Alexander of Cornhill was ancestor of the Frasers of Muchal, in Mar, of whom Andrew built the imposing Castle Fraser in 1617. He was created Lord Fraser in 1633, which caused a dispute about the chiefship, but the title was confirmed, and in 1672 Lord Fraser was awarded the arms of chief of the family. Charles, 5th Lord, took part in the 1715 Jacobite Rising, and died in 1716, when the peerage expired and the chiefship fell to the Philorth or Saltoun line.

The Lovat chiefs descend from Hugh Fraser, about whose ancestry genealogists disagree, some deducing his line from the Frasers of Oliver Castle, and others from the Touch-Frasers, making them collaterals of the Philorth family. William Fraser, IVth Laird, appears as Lord of Lovat prior to 1464. The line continued to Hugh, 9th Lord, on whose death his daughter Amelia was adjudged Baroness Lovat, to the chagrin of the heir male, Simon Fraser of Beaufort, who obtained the dignity in 1730. This Simon, 11th Lord, notorious in Jacobite intrigue, was created a Duke by the Chevalier in 1740, but was imprisoned and executed after Culloden. The representation passed to Thomas Fraser of Strichen, who was created a Baron (UK) in 1857, when the Scottish title was also restored. The titles descended to World War II hero, Simon Christopher Fraser, 1911–95, who served in the Lovat Scouts, and was in command of the 1st Special Service (Commando Brigade) on D-Day, 1944, leading from the front. Tragedy struck in 1994, when he eldest son, Simon, Master of Lovat, who had sold parts of the estate, was killed when drag-hunting. The youngest son, Andrew, was killed the same year, when hunting in Kenya. When the veteran Lovat chief died in 1995, the family debts were high and most of the lands were sold. Beaufort Castle, and its contents were purchased by Ann Gloag, millionaire partner of Stagecoach Holdings, plc. The 16th Baron Lovat is the great soldier's grandson, Simon Christopher, born 1977, who still owns about 6500 acres.

GALBRAITH This surname is made up of two Gaelic words, *Gall Bhreatnaich*, or 'strange Briton'. The ancestors were probably of the British race, who settled among the Gaels, who called them *Clann-a-Breatanuich*. The family were once influential in the Lennox. Gillescop Galbrait witnessed a charter by Malduin, Earl of Lennox, of the church of Kamsi (Campsie) to God and St

Kentigern, ca. 1211. Early in the reign of Alexander II (1214–49), the same earl gave a charter to Maurice, son of Gillescop or Gillespic, of the lands of Bathernock (Baldernock). The lands were conveyed to his son, Arthur Galbraith, ca. 1238, with the power of pit and gallows. From the Galbraiths of Baldernock, chiefs of the surname, descended the Galbraiths of Culcreoch, Greenock, Killearn and Balgair. In the *Ragman Roll*, 1296, appears Arthur de Galbrait, Wigtownshire. The principal family were later styled 'of Gartconnel'. Joanna, eldest daughter of William of Galbraith, and heiress of Dalserf, married a son of Sir John de Keith, and died in 1301. William Galbraith of Gartconnel, probably son of William, is noted, ca. 1350, as 'a person of good account'. This William left three heiresses who all made good alliances. A Galbraith was Governor of Upper Dunbarton Castle in the reign of James II (1437–60). A family of Galbraiths settled on Gigha under the Lords of the Isles, after 1590, and were ancestors of the Galbraiths of Machrihanish and Drumore, Argyll. People move about and mingle like clouds, and Galbraiths are found in various parts of the country. Hugh de Galbraith was Provost of Aberdeen in 1342. Robert Galbraith was rector of Spot, 1534–36, and his seal bears: on a chevron between three bear heads erased and muzzled, a crescent. A Scottish judge and advocate to Queen Margaret Tudor, Robert Galbraith was murdered by John Carkettle in 1543. James Galbraith was Deacon of the Tailors in Canongate, Edinburgh, in 1554. Patrick Galbraith was parochial chaplain of Garvald in 1569, and appears as reader there in 1574. Numbers of Galbraiths from Islay, Colonsay and mainland Argyll emigrated to Ontario, Canada, 1830–52. The Harvard economist, John K. Galbraith, was born in Ontario, a descendant of Scottish emigrants. James Galbraith was a wholesale clock and watch maker in Trongate, Glasgow, 1880–86. The Hon. Sir Thomas Galbraith, 1917–82, was Unionist MP for Hillhead, Glasgow from 1948, and Dr Sam Galbraith has been Labour MP for Strathkelvin and Bearsden since 1987.

GARDEN The surname Garden is thought to be a variant of Gardyne, derived from the old barony of that name, in Kirkden parish, Angus. Some authorities, however, make it cognate with the occupational surname of Gardener, with its several variants. The Gardyne barony was long held by a family styled 'of that Ilk'. The name is prolific in the north-east, where some Garden families owned land. William Gardeyn of Angus, and William du Gardyn of

Edinburghshire, swore fealty to Edward I in 1296. Patrick Garden *de eodem* was a witness in 1450. 'Mr' Gilbert Garden was minister at Monifieth in 1565, later at Fordyce and Cullen. In the local Angus dialect the name is often clipped to Gairn. A celebrated centenarian was Peter Garden, who died in January, 1775, aged 131 years. He died near Chapel of Seggat, Auchterless, having retained his memory to the last. Peter lived under ten rulers (if we count the Cromwells), and could remember cutting boughs for spears during the Civil Wars. An old engraving of him appears in Granger's *Wonderful Museum*, vol. IV. Francis Garden, 1721–92, Lord Gardenstone, an advocate engaged in the famous *Douglas Cause*, was an agricultural improver, and founded the village of Laurencekirk. Alexander Garden, 1730–91, botanist and zoologist, studied at Edinburgh, and went to South Carolina to practise as a physician. He investigated the botany of that country, and published many learned papers. A family of Gardens were prominent professors in Aberdeen, and a long line of them were advocates there. Mary Garden, 1874–1967, from Aberdeen, went to America when only four years old, and studied in Chicago and Paris to become a celebrated opera singer. She shocked the supposedly liberated America of the 1920s with her revealing costumes when on stage, and by taking a succession of lovers.

GARMORY A scarce surname, said by Dr George F. Black to belong to the Stewartry of Kirkcudbright, and to be a short form of Montgomery. His earliest notice of the name is 1684, but there are examples of Garmory, with variants such as Garmorie and Germerie, in the 16th century. Fergus Garmorie in Spottis, was probably a bailie or notary, to whom a precept of sasine relating to the lands of Blakat, in Urr parish, was directed in 1588. A place-name, Garmoran (perhaps 'rough stream'), has been noted near Loch Morar. However, some Garmories around Urr, obviously believed they were originally Montgomerys. The idea may have come from a printed source.

GIBSON The name simply means 'son of Gib', a diminutive form of Gilbert, and is cognate with Gibbieson. Thomas Gibbieson was charged with breaking parole in 1358, and in 1390 Sir James Douglas of Dalkeith bequeathed £10 to John Gibson. Thomas Gibson held land in Dumfries, 1425, and in 1473 a merchant, John Gibson, had a safe conduct into England. The surname was prolific in Edinburgh, and those of Caithness and Orkney mainly originated there. The most distinguished family were the knightly Gibsons of Pentland, in Mid Lothian, and Durie, in Fife.

Alexander Gibson of Pentland became a clerk of Session in 1594. In the early part of the 17th century he had charters of various lands, including the barony of Durie, in Fife. He was made a Lord of Session in 1621, and is wrongly stated to have been made a Baronet of NS in 1628. In 1633 he was knighted and had his arms confirmed as Gules, three keys barways Argent. He died in 1644, and was succeeded by his eldest son, Alexander, who was knighted in 1641, and made a Senator of the College of Justice in 1646. He was deprived in 1649, and died in 1656. Another Alexander Gibson, PC, was knighted, but died without issue in 1661, when he was succeeded by his brother John, of Durie, who registered arms, 1672–78. His son Alexander died without issue in 1699. The first Lord Durie had a second son, Sir John, an ardent Royalist, who had three sons: Sir Alexander of Pentland; Sir John, Governor of Portsmouth; and Thomas of Keirhill, created a Baronet in 1702. This baronetcy was twinned with another, created in 1831.

Sir Alexander Gibson of Pentland, Clerk of Session, died in 1706, having married Helen, daughter of Sir James Fleming of Rathobyres, with issue: Sir John of Pentland; Sir Alexander, of Durie; Thomas, who married Anna Wright, heiress of Cliftonhall; and Lt. Gen. James Gibson, in Hungarian service, Sir John Gibson married Helen Carmichael, and died in 1767, leaving issue: Alexander of Durie; William, merchant in Edinburgh, and father of Sir James Gibson, 1765–1850, created a Baronet in 1831, who assumed the additional surname of Craig on succeeding to Riccarton as heir of entail; Thomas; and Margaret, who married Alexander Gibson Wright of Cliftonhall, from whom descended the Ramsay-Gibson-Maitlands. John, son of Alexander, sold Durie in 1786, and he succeeded to the estate of Skirling on the death of his grand-uncle, John, 4th Lord Hyndford, in 1787. Sir James Gibson-Craig of Riccarton was succeeded by his elder son, Sir William, Lord Clerk Register in 1862. The baronetcies devolved on his descendants, now represented by Sir David Peter William Gibson-Craig-Carmichael, 15th Baronet (cr. NS, 1702) and 8th Baronet (Cr. UK, 1831).

Patrick Gibson, 1782–1829, a native of Edinburgh, was an accomplished painter, etcher and art critic, who trained under Alexander Naysmith. In Glasgow, a Gibson family of Hillhead descended from Thomas Gibson in Meikle Govan, who died ca. 1544. By the end of the 16th century, the family was styled 'of Over

Newton'. Capt. James Gibson, of this family, commanded the ship *Caroline*, which transported Covenanters to America, and was also master of the *Rising Sun*, involved in the Darien Disaster. Andrew Gibson, 1st of Hillhead, died in 1733. His descendant, James, 1800–62, left a daughter Mary, who married John Dougan, a surgeon. Rev. Dr James Gibson, 1799–1871, a native of Crieff, distinguished himself in the study of Hebrew and church history at Glasgow and, after a spell as a tutor, became assistant minister at Glasgow College parish. Kingston Church was built for him in 1839, but he seceded at the Disruption, 1843, and became Professor of Church History and Systematic Theology. He was the author of many religious tracts.

GILCHRIST *Gillie Criosd* (*Gillachrist*) means 'servant of Christ'. Gilliecrist mac Finguni and Gillecrist mac Cormaic witnessed Gaelic grants in *The Book of Deer* before 1132. The exquisitely carved St Martin's Cross at Iona was the work of a mason named Gillacrist. Gillecrist mac Gillewinin witnessed a charter by Uchtred, son of Fergus, of the church of Colmanuele to the Abbey of Holyrood, ca. 1165. Gilchrist, Earl of Mar, 1179–1204, disputed the legitimacy of his predecessor, Morgund, and established himself in possession of property to the exclusion of Morgund's line. Gillecryst, a serf of the Earl of Angus, was one of the perambulators of the lands of Kynblathmund in 1219. Maldouen, 3rd Earl of Lennox, gave to his brother Gilchrist, the lands of Arrochar during the reign of Alexander I (1224–49). Patrick Gilchristes and Kilschyn Gilchrist swore fealty to Edward I of England in 1296, and appear to have been the earliest to use Gilchrist as a surname. As a forename it has occasionally been Englished as Christopher. See also MacGILCHRIST.

GORDON The people who came to call themselves Gordons arrived in Scotland after the Norman Conquest, and following a period in England. They are recorded as having been in Berwickshire about the middle of the 12th century, and they took their name from Gordon, a place-name, probably *Gor-dun*, meaning 'hill fort'. Nearby is Huntlywood and Huntlyburn, and when Gordons went to Aberdeenshire, they transplanted the name Huntly to the centre of the lordship of Strathbogie, granted to them by Robert the Bruce.

The Gordons also held lands in Galloway, and Sir Adam de Gordon gave these to a younger son, who founded the family of

Lochinvar, of whom Sir John was created a Viscount in 1633. The 6th Viscount, William, a Jacobite, was attainted in 1716, and beheaded. The attainder was reversed in 1824, but the peerage became dormant in 1847 on the death without issue of Adam, 11th Viscount. The Gordon baronets of Earlston are descended from Alexander, second son of William Gordon, VIth of Lochinvar. The Gordons of the south-west have always remained separate from their distant kinsmen in the north-east.

Through marriage the Gordons of Strathbogie gained Aboyne. Sir Adam's great-grandson, another Sir Adam, was killed at Homildon Hill in 1402. The legitimate line of the family was carried on by the Gordons of Lochinvar, but the chiefship passed to his daughter Elizabeth, who married Alexander Seton. Their son Alexander was created Earl of Huntly ca. 1445, and assumed the surname of Gordon. He settled the earldom on George, his second son, who became chief of the clan. Sir Adam had an elder brother, John Gordon, styled 'of that Ilk', but he left only natural sons, Jock and Tam, from whom descended several chieftains of the Buchan Gordons.

The 6th Earl of Huntly, George, was created Marquess of Huntly in 1599, and the 4th Marquess was created Duke of Gordon in 1684. The 13th Earl and 5th Duke, Col. George, was made Baron Gordon of Huntly in 1807, and when he died the dukedom and other titles became extinct. The Marquessate went to the Earl of Aboyne (cr. 1660), descended from a younger son of George, 2nd Marquess. The present Marquess, Granville Charles Gordon, is 'cock of the north', and chief of the Gordons. The Huntly estate passed in 1876 to the Duke of Richmond and Lennox, created Duke of Gordon that year. Aboyne Castle remains the seat of the Marquess and Earl of Aboyne.

From Jock Gordon, mentioned above, descended the Earls of Aberdeen (cr. 1682), through Patrick Gordon of Methlic, killed at Arbroath in 1445. John, 1st Marquess and 7th Earl, was Governor-General of Canada, 1893–98. Another branch of the family are the Gordons of Abergeldie, Upper Deeside, descended from Sir Alexander Gordon, second son of the 1st Earl of Huntly, and now represented by John Howard Seton Gordon. In the neighbourhood of Abergeldie, Gordons were once numerous, particularly around Khantore; in Glenmuick; and in Glengirnock, where the farms are now derelict.

Two regiments were formed from the Clan Gordon: the old 81st, disbanded in 1783, and the 100th Regiment of Foot, raised in 1794, renumbered the 92nd. In 1881 the 75th (Stirlingshire)

Regiment became the 1st Battalion of the 92nd or Gordon
Highlanders, formed as the 2nd Battalion. The uniform of the 75th
was altered to the full Highland garb as worn by the 92nd. The
Gordons had a proud military record, having served in the Egyptian
Wars, the South African War and in the present century in both
World Wars. Sadly, in 1994, as a result of government policy, they
were amalgamated with the Queen's Own Highlanders to form The
Highlanders.

GOURLAY Ingelram de Gourlay came to Scotland from
England with Prince William in 1174, and received lands in
Clydesdale and Lothian. The name may have come from a lost
place-name in Picardy. Hugh, son of Ingelram, possessed lands in
Fife, and ca. 1190 witnessed a charter to Arbroath Abbey. Hugh
and William Gurle attended a conference at Roxbugh in 1254, and
the following year lost their place on the King's Council. In 1296
Adam de Gurle of Roxburghshire signed the *Ragman Roll*, and Sir
Patrick Gourlay, a clergyman, witnessed charters before 1320. The
old family of Gourlay of Kincraig, in Fife, held the lands for 600
years. The estate descended to heirs female: Gertrude Gourlay, who
died in 1908, and her sister Susan, who lived in Bath. Robert
Fleming Gourlay, 1778–1863, emigrated from Ceres, Fife, to Upper
Canada, ca. 1815. He was a pioneer, but also a controversial
journalist and published at London in 1817 a *Statistical Account of
Canada*.

GRAHAM The surname Graham appears in England at an
early period, and those who came to bear it – from Grantham, in
Lincolnshire – are usually stated to have been of Anglo-Saxon
origin. It is more likely they came from Flanders and were
descendants of the Counts of Hesdin. William de Graham
accompanied David I (1124–53) to Scotland on his return from
England, and received from him the lands of Dalkeith and
Abercorn. His son John was at the court of William the Lion in
1200 when William Comyn resigned his claim to certain lands in
favour of the church of Glasgow. Sir Patrick, a descendant, was sent
to negotiate the marriage of Prince Alexander of Scotland with
Margaret, daughter of Guy, Earl of Flanders, in 1291. The family
were prominent during the War of Independence.

Sir David Graham of Kincardine and Old Montrose was one of
the Scottish barons engaged in arrangements for the release of
David II, made prisoner at the Battle of Durham in 1346. His great-

grandson, Patrick Graham, was made a Lord of Parliament before 1445, and his grandson, William, was created Earl of Montrose, 1504/5. The 5th Earl, William, was created Marquess of Montrose in 1644, and distinguished himself as a soldier during the Wars of the Covenant. His kinsman, John Graham of Claverhouse, was the military leader who defeated the Covenanters at Bothwell Brig in 1679. The 4th Marquess was raised to the Dukedom, in 1707, as a reward for supporting the Union (plus a bribe of £200). His grandson, James, 3rd Duke, campaigned for the repeal of the legislation which banned the Highland dress.

Malise Graham, the first of the name to bear the title of Menteith, was a grandson of Sir Patrick Graham, ancestor of the earls and dukes of Montrose. He was styled Earl of Strathearn, but was deprived of that title and created Earl of Menteith in 1424. However, William, the 7th Earl, was served heir to David, Earl of Strathearn, and was styled Earl of Strathearn and Menteith. He was deprived of those titles and in 1633, created Earl of Airth, to which he appended 'and Menteith'. John, his eldest son, bore the junior title of Lord Kinpont, and suffered a fate which prompted Sir Walter Scott to write his *Legend of Montrose*. In 1646, when Montrose took the field against the Covenanters, he was joined by Lord Kinpont. When encamped at Collace, some angry words passed between him and a friend, James Stewart of Ardvoirlich, and Stewart plunged his dagger into Lord Kinpont's heart. He fled to the Covenanting Army, where Argyll gave him a command as major. Lord Kinpont was interred at the priory of Inchmahone, in the Lake of Menteith, and Stewart was pardoned the following year. Kinpont's son succeeded as earl, but left no issue and was succeeded by his sister Mary, who married Sir John Allandyce of that ilk.

Although not a Highland clan, the Grahams owned lands along the fringes of Gaeldom. The Montrose line were feudal superiors of the MacFarlanes of Arrochar. Captain John Graham of Larbert, 1847–1926, descended from the Grahams, formerly of Auchencloich, served in the 1st Lanarkshire Volunteer Rifles, and was created a Baronet. The present representative is John Alexander Noble Graham, 4th Baronet. Several families along the English border, including the Grahams of Esk, baronets, are said to descend from John of Kilbride, a younger son of Malise, Earl of Menteith. The representatives of this family now live at Long Island, New York.

GRANT The ancestors of the Grant chiefs were in Flanders in the 11th century. The name simply means *le Grand*, or 'Big'. They came to England after the Norman Conquest, and possessed estates in Nottinghamshire bordering those of the Bissets, who introduced them to the north. Sir Laurence le Grant was Sheriff of Inverness in 1285, and is probably the same man who appeared with Robert Grant that same year as witness to an instrument by which John Byset, younger, was enabled to give the church of Conveth to the Priory of Beauly. It seems likely there had been intermarriage between the Bissets and the Grants.

Lands which the Grants held in the west of Stratherrick came later to the Lovat Frasers, perhaps by marriage as the Frasers quartered the three antique crowns of the Grants with their own armorial bearings. The Grants also held lands in Urquhart and Glenmoriston, but gained a firm footing in Speyside through the marriage of Sir Ian Grant, their chief by 1434, and Maud, the heiress of Gilbert of Glencarnie. Thus Freuchie became their home.

The IVth Laird, John Grant, succeeded his father in the lands of Glencarnie in 1553, and as bailie of the Abbey of Kinloss. From his second son, Patrick, descended the Grants of Rothiemurchus, to which family belonged Elizabeth Grant, 1797–1885, author of the fascinating *Memoirs of a Highland Lady*. The Rothiemurchus family is now represented by John Peter Grant. From his line sprang the Grants of Ballindalloch. Other cadets included Arneidle, Easter and Wester Elchies, Lurg and Moyness, Duthil, Corriemony, Ballintomb, Kinchurdie and Gartenbeg. The Grants had occasional feuds with neighbours, and fought alongside the Campbells of Argyll against the Gordons of Huntly at Glenlivet in 1594. During the persecution of the MacGregors, the Grants sheltered many of them and incurred the wrath of the Privy Council.

The Grants of Freuchie came to be known as the Lairds of Grant. Ludovick, second son of Sir James Grant of Grant, married Anne Colquhoun, heiress of Luss, and succeeded to the lands and baronetcy, but on the death of his elder brother, Humphrey, unmarried, took up the succession, the Luss chiefship passing to his second son. Lewis Grant, his grandson, was created Earl of Seafield in 1811, and assumed the additional surname of Ogilvie. The 7th Earl was created Baron Strathspey in 1858, and his descendant, the 11th Earl, died leaving an heiress, Nina Caroline, who succeeded as Countess of Seafield, and married Derek Studley Herbert, who assumed the additional surnames of Ogilvy-Grant. Their son, Ian Derek Francis-Ogilvy-Grant, is the 13th and present Earl. The barony of Strathspey went to her uncle, Trevor, who thus became the 4th Baron, holder of the baronetcy (NS), and chief of the clan. The 5th and present baron is the Hon. Michael Francis Ogilvy-Grant.

The Grants of Monymusk, baronets (NS, 1705), descend from Archibald Grant of Balentomb, a younger son of James Grant, IIIrd of Freuchie, and the Grants of Dalvey, baronets (NS, 1688), are descended from Duncant Grant of Gartenbeg, Duthil, whose family were known as *Clann Donochy*. Sir James Francis Grant, 1863–1953, author or editor of a long list of books, was Lord Lyon, 1929–45, and Dr Isabel Frances Grant, 1887–1983, founded the Highland Folk Museum at Kingussiue. She was author of a number of books and articles, including a brief history of *The Clan Grant* (1955). A biography and bibliography of her works appears in *Review of Scottish Culture*, No. 2, 1986.

GREGORY Derived from a Greek word, Latinised as *Gregorius*, meaning 'watch-man', the name was appropriately used by early churchmen. Gregory, Bishop of Dunkeld, appears as *Gregorius de duncallden* ca. 1147. Gregory, Bishop of Ross, appears 1171–84 and Gregory, Bishop of Moray, witnessed the foundation charter of the Abbey of Scone, 1114. Gregory, Bishop of Brechin, died ca. 1242. Gregory, son of Gregory the Sheriff, is possibly the same as Gregory de Melville, whose son Richard exchanged his lands of Granton for lands at Ednam, Roxburghshire, ca. 1186. William, son of Gregory, was Provost of Crail in 1330, and one Thomas Gregory was accused of deforcing in 1569. Rev John Gregory was minister at Drumoak, 1621–52, and progenitor of a remarkable academic family, who claimed descent from the MacGregors of Roro and Glenlyon. Alexander, the minister's eldest son, was assaulted by Viscount Frendraught, along with James Crichton of Kinnairdy and his son Francis, and died soon afterwards. It seems his wounds were not the cause of his death, and Francis Crichton was pardoned. Alexander's brother, David, was retoured as his heir, 1644, and had a new charter of Kinnairdy in 1673. His younger brother James, Professor of Mathematics at St Andrews and Edinburgh, invented the reflecting telescope. David, a physician, eventually settled in Aberdeen, and died in 1720, aged 95, having made over Kinnairdy to David, 1661–1708, who was Professor of Mathematics at Edinburgh in 1683, and in 1692 became Savilian Professor of Astronomy at Oxford. As an absentee laird, his old castle at Kinnairdy fell into disrepair, and the estate was conveyed to Thomas Davidson. John Gregory, 1724–73, grandson of the inventor, was elected to the Chair of Philosophy at Aberdeen in 1747, and to that of medicine in 1756. He became Professor of Physic at Edinburgh in 1765. His son, Dr James Gregory, 1753–1821, was appointed Professor of the Theory of Physic at Edinburgh in 1776, and in 1790 became Professor of the Practice of Physic. Donald Gregory, sometime secretary of the Society of Antiquaries of Scotland, and of the Iona Club, wrote a *History of the Western Highlands and Islands*, published in 1836, the year of his death.

GREIG/GRIEG The surname Gregg, Greig, with several variants, appears in Fife and along the east central coast in the 17th century, and is probably a shortening of Gregory. Some of them, however, like the family of the Gregory minister of Drumoak, had a tradition of descent from MacGregors, in various cases from proscribed MacGregors who had settled in Glengairn. The earliest record is of Walter Greg, long before the Macgregors came to Aberdeenshire: in fact ca. 1218, when he witnessed a charter by Malcolm, Earl of Fife. Patrick Grige was admitted a burgess of Aberdeen in 1488, and Johannes Greg was a councillor there in 1502. William Gregg, of Scottish origin, was a clerk in the office of Robert Harley, Secretary of State, in 1706, and was hanged at Tyburn in 1708, for passing copies of important documents to the French minister, Chamelart. A family with roots in Inverkeithing, distinguished themselves in Russia. Sir Samuel Greig, 1735–88, was one of five British naval officers sent to Russia in 1763 to improve their fleet. He was made a Rear-Admiral after defeating the Turks, and he reorganised the whole navy. His son, Alexis, was also in the Russian Navy, and commanded the fleet at the sieges of Varna and Anapa in 1828. Woronzow Greig, son of Alexis, was aide-de-camp to Prince Menschikoff during the Crimean War. He was killed at Inkerman in 1854. Alexander, son of John Grieg in Cairnbulg, Aberdeenshire, emigrated to Norway before 1770, and was ancestor of Edvard Grieg, 1843–1907, the famous composer. Andrew Greig, a native of Bannockburn, was Writer-in-Residence at the University of Edinburgh, 1993–94, and writes in prose and verse.

GUNN The Gunns were a warlike clan in Caithness and Sutherland, deriving their name from the Norse *gunnr*, meaning 'war'. The first of the name associated with Caithness was Olaf, a

12th century chief. For generations the Gunns had a feud with the Keiths. To reconcile the feud it was agreed that the two sides meet at the chapel of St Tayr in Caithness, with twelve horses. The Gunns arrived at the appointed time, but their foes, under George Keith of Ackergill, came with two men on each horse: twenty four against twelve, with devastating results. George Gun(n), the Coroner, called *Fear N'm Braisteach-more*, from the great brooch he wore as his badge of office, was killed in this encounter. His son James succeeded as chief, and moved with his family and many followers into Sutherland. Later, William McKames, a kinsman of the Gunns, killed Keith of Ackergill, his son, and several others at Drummoy. In modern times, James A. Gunn, 1882–1958, distinguished himself as Professor of Pharmacology at Oxford. Neil Gunn, 1891–1973, enriched Scottish literature with *The Silver Darlings* and other novels.

HALDANE The surname Haldane is held to derive from *Healf-dene*, meaning 'Half-Dane'. The name was associated with the Hocingas and Secgans, who took part in the campaign against Finn in the lay of *Beowulf*, and it later became an Old English personal name. Halden *filius* Eadulf was a witness at Earl David's inquest into the church of Glasgow ca. 1124. A younger son of the Halden family in the Borders came to own the estate of Gleneagles by his marriage to an heiress. Aylmer de Haldane of Gleneagles swore fealty to Edward I in 1296. The family held the estate until Robert Haldane, who purchased the estate from his brother Patrick in 1760, made an entail by which the 3rd Earl of Camberdown came into possession in 1766. The Haldane-Duncan line failed in 1933, having in 1918 made over the estates in favour of the senior heir male, James Brodrick Chinnery-Haldane, 1868–1941. He was succeeded by his son, Capt. Alexander Napier Chinnery-Haldane, who served with the Royal Scots in World War II. His son, Alexander Chinnery-Haldane, 1907–84, was quite a character, running around his lands on a Triumph motorcycle. He waged war on anyone who associated Gleneagles Hotel with Gleneagles estate. Alexander also named as his heir, his cousin, James Martin Haldane, the present and 26th Laird, in preference to his brother, Brodick Vernon Chinnery-Haldane, 1912–96, the homosexual society photographer, who numbered among his subjects, G.B. Shaw, Charles Chaplin and Marlene Dietrich. John Scott Haldane, 1858–1936, a distinguished scientist, was a kinsman. His daughter Naomi, 1897–1999, married Richard Mitchison (life peer, 1964), and was a prolific writer.

HALIBURTON This surname springs from the lands of Haliburton, in Berwickshire. Towards the close of the 12th century, David, son of Tructi, gave the church of Haliburton to the monks of Kelso, confirmed ca. 1230 by his son David. The Haliburtons of Dirleton claimed descent from David. John Haliburton, sheriff of Berwick, son of Sir Walter Haliburton of Dirleton, was created Lord Haliburton ca. 1440, and certainly appears as Lord Haliburton in a charter of 1450. Patrick, the 5th Lord Dirleton, was succeeded by his daughter Janet, who married ca. 1515, William, 2nd Lord Ruthven. On her death 1550, the title descended to her son Patrick, 3rd Lord Ruthven, whose son, William, Lord Ruthven and Dirleton, was created Earl of Gowrie in 1581. He was attainted and executed. The honours were restored to his son James in 1586, but he died young. His brother John succeeded, but lost his life in the mysterious Gowrie Conspiracy of 1660. Posthumously, he was found guilty of high treason, and his honours again forfeited. The Haliburtons of Pitcur were an old family in Angus and Perthshire, from whom descended James Hallyburton, 1518–88, Provost of Dundee, and a Reformation leader. Another group were the Halyburtons of Foderance, in Angus. Sir Walter Scott's ancestor, Robert Scott of Sandyknowe, married in 1728, Barbara, daughter of Thomas Haliburton of Newmains.

HAMILTON The noble family of Hamilton appear to have come to Lanarkshire from Northumberland in the 13th century. There, the Umfravilles held sway, and Gilbert was a popular name among them. Gilbert, progenitor of the earls and dukes of Hamilton, may have been a scion of the Umfravilles, and (surnames were then beginning to emerge) took his designation from Hameldone or Hamilton, a Northumbrian place-name. The earlier origins may go back to Flanders or France: perhaps to Amfreville, in the Seine Valley.

Walter Fitz Gilbert is recorded in 1294, and in 1296 he signed the *Ragman Roll* in token of fealty to Edward I. However, like other Scottish barons of the time, his sympathies were with Scotland, and he joined Robert the Bruce before Bannockburn, and in 1315 was granted the lands of Machan (Dalserf). Later he received the lands of Cadzow, in Lanarkshire, along with Kinneil and other lands in West Lothian. He died ca. 1346, leaving by his wife Mary Gordon, two sons: David, his heir; and John, ancestor of the Earls of Haddington. The territorial designation of Hamilton was in use before 1445, and the name was given to the town and parish previously called Cadzow. In that year, James Hamilton was made a Lord of Parliament. By his second marriage to Princess Mary, sister of King James III, the Hamiltons became the family in Scotland nearest to the Royal Stewarts, and honours came thick and fast. James, 2nd Lord Hamilton, was created Earl of Arran, and on the death of King James V in 1542, became Governor of Scotland. In 1549 he was granted the valuable Duchy of Chatelherault, in France. His son John was created Marquess of Hamilton, Earl of Arran and Lord Evan in 1599. James, the 2nd Marquess, was created Earl of Cambridge and Lord Innerdale in 1619, and two years later was made a Knight of the Garter. The 3rd Marquess, James, 1606–49, became Duke of Hamilton, Marquess of Clydesdale, Earl of Arran and Cambridge, Lord Avon and Innerdale in 1643. William, 2nd Duke, was created Earl of Lanark in 1639. In 1651, he joined Gen. Leslie in his march into England, and was fatally wounded at Worcester.

Anne, Duchess of Hamilton in her own right, eldest daughter of the 1st Duke, married William Douglas, Earl of Selkirk, in 1656. Life in her household is well told in Rosalind Marshall's book, *The Days of Duchess Anne* (Collins, 1973). King Charles created her husband Earl of Selkirk in 1646, and in 1660 he was created Duke of Hamilton, Marquess of Clydesdale, for life. The Duchess resigned her titles in 1698, in favour of her eldest son, James, Earl of Arran, who became 4th Duke. He was opposed to the Union of 1707, but was chosen a representative peer and created Duke of Brandon. Unfortunately, he engaged in a duel with Lord Charles Mohun in 1712, and both parties were killed.

The 5th Duke, James, maintained great state in his new home of Chatelherault, near the old tower of Cadzow, and the 6th married Elizabeth, one of the beautiful Gunning sisters. James George, 7th Duke, through his guardian, asserted his right to the Douglas and Angus estates, leading to the celebrated *Douglas Cause*, but in 1769 the Lords decided in favour of Archibald, alleged twin son of Lady Jean Douglas, born in France when she was fifty years old. After the Napoleanic War, the 10th Duke built a new palace at Hamilton, but it was demolished a century later. The 11th Duke, married a cousin of Napolean III, and the 14th piloted the first aircraft over Everest in 1933. Angus Alan Douglas-Hamilton, the 15th Duke of Hamilton, resides at Lennoxlove, near Haddington, and is interested in motor speed records. His brother, Lord James, was MP for West Edinburgh, 1974–97, and after the death in 1994 of George, Earl of Selkirk, and litigation in Lyon Court against his cousin, Alasdair, styled Master of Selkirk, was awarded the title of Earl of Selkirk, which he disclaimed in order to remain in the Commons. The arrangement was that his son, John Andrew, would on his death become 12th Earl of Selkirk.

HAMILTON, EARLS OF HADDINGTON The

Hamilton Earls of Haddington descend from John, a younger son of Walter Fitz Gilbert, progenitor of the Earls and Dukes of Hamilton. John Fitz Gilbert, witnessed charters between 1365 and 1381, and he married Elizabeth, daughter of Sir Alan Stewart of Darnley and Crookston. Sir Alan's son John granted them lands at Ballencrieff, Bathgate. Alexander, their son, came into possession of Innerwick, East Lothian, though his marriage, ca. 1381, with Elizabeth, co-heiress of the Earl of Angus. Their grandson, Alexander of Innerwick, married Isobel Schaw, and had issue. Their eldest son, Hugh, carried on the Innerwick line, and Thomas, the youngest son, was ancestor of the Earls of Haddington.

Thomas Hamilton acquired the lands of Orchardfield, Edinburgh, and married Margaret, daughter of Adam Cant, from whom he purchased the estate of Priestfield. Their elder son, Thomas, merchant-burgess of Edinburgh, exchanged with his cousin James of Innerwick, the lands of Ballancrieff for those of Balbyne and Drumcarne, in Perthshire. He was killed at Pinkie Cleuch in 1547. His eldest son, then a minor, was the father of Thomas, who became Earl of Haddington. This remarkable man was admitted advocate in 1587, and in his time held the offices of a Lord of Session and Lord Advocate. In 1617, as Lord Binning he entertained the king in that house from which he earned the *soubriquet*, Tam o' the Cowgate. In 1619 he was created Earl of Melrose, Lord Byres and Binning, and in 1627 was made Earl of Haddington. He was married three times and had at least ten lawful children, the eldest being Thomas, 2nd Earl of Haddington.

The 5th Earl, Charles, 1650–85, married in 1674, Margaret, elder daughter of John Leslie, Earl (later Duke) of Rothesay. She became Countess of Rothes in her own right, and her eldest son, John, by the Earl of Haddington, became 9th Earl of Rothes, while their second son, Thomas, became 6th Earl of Haddington. He sold Byres to the Earl of Hopetoun, and became an agricultural improver, planting some 800 acres of his Tyninghame estate with trees. His eldest son, Charles, author of several poems, was the father of Thomas, 7th Earl. The 9th Earl, Thomas, served as MP for various English seats, and in 1827 was created Baron Melrose of Tyninghame. The UK honour became extinct at his death in 1858, when he was succeeded as 10th Earl by George Baillie of Jerviswood and Mellerstain, who obtained license to add the additional surname of Hamilton. He was a representative peer of Scotland. His son George, when still Lord Binning, obtained license to assume the surname of Arden. He had married in 1854, Helen, daughter of Sir John Warrender of Lochend, Baronet, by his wife, Frances Arden, daughter of the Lord Chief Justice, Baron Alvanley. Her brothers all died without issue, and she became heiress to the Alvanley estates. Their children did not assume the surname Arden, except the youngest, Henry, who inherited the Alvanley estates. Lord Binning succeeded his father as 11th Earl in 1870, and was a representative peer, 1874–1917. He became a Knight of the Thistle in 1902. The Earl was succeeded in 1917 by his grandson, George Baillie-Hamilton, 1894–1986, who soldiered in two World Wars. He was a Trustee of the National Library and of the National Museum of Antiquities. The 13th Earl is his son, John George Baillie-Hamilton, who lives at Mellerstain, Gordon, Berwickshire.

HAMILTONS OF ABERCORN
Claud Hamilton, Lord Paisley, youngest son of James, 2nd Earl of Arran, by his wife, Lady Margaret Douglas, was ancestor of the Earls of Abercorn. He married Margaret, daughter of George, Lord Seton. Their eldest son was James Hamilton, Sheriff of Linlithgowshire, who had a charter of the lands of Abercorn and others, in 1601. He was created a peer by the title of Baron of Abercorn in 1603, and in 1606 was advanced to the dignity of Earl of Abercorn. He was one of the 'undertakers' who received land in Ulster, and his eldest son James became Lord Hamilton, Baron of Strabane, in 1616. As the Irish estates were willed to his younger brothers, he resigned his Irish title in favour of his brother Claud in 1633. George, 4th Lord Strabane, was the father of Claud, 5th Lord Strabane and 4th Earl of Abercorn. Claud commanded a regiment of Horse for King James, at the Boyne, and after the defeat was killed on his way to France. His estate and title of Strabane was forfeited, and the earldom of Abercorn devolved on his brother Charles.

Charles, 5th Earl of Abercorn, obtained a reversal of his brother's attainder in 1692. He died without issue and the honours devolved on James Hamilton, descended from Sir George Hamilton of Donalong, Tyrone, fourth son of the 1st Earl of Abercorn. His

son, Col. James Hamilton, was MP for Strabane, and father of
James of Donalong, created Baron of Mountcastle and Viscount of
Strabane in 1701. He succeeded the 6th Earl of Abercorn, and his
son James, 8th Earl, was created a peer of Great Britain as Viscount
Hamilton of Hamilton, in the county of Leicester. This is
interesting, bearing in mind that most authorities state that
Leicester was the home of the first Hamilton to come to Scotland.
James was a noted agricultural improver. He inherited the Lordship
of Paisley, but resided mainly at Duddingston, in Edinburgh. The
Viscount built an imposing mansion at Baron's Court, Strabane,
but died unmarried, when his nephew John became 9th Earl of
Abercorn. In 1790 he was created Marquess of Abercorn, and
made a Knight of the Garter. By his first wife, Catherine Copley, he
had several children, the eldest of whom, James, 2nd Viscount, was
the father of James, 10th Earl and 2nd Marquess of Abercorn. This
nobleman was a fine scholar and received several honorary degrees.
He was served heir to the 1st Duke of Chatelherault, and as heir-
male asserted his right to the original title. James became Governor-
General of Ireland from 1866 to 1868, when he was created Duke of
Abercorn and Marquess of Hamilton. His son James, 2nd Duke of
Abercorn, served as High Constable of Ireland and at the coronation
of King Edward VII. James Albert Edward Hamilton, his eldest son,
became 3rd Duke, and was Governor-General of Ireland, 1922–45.
His son, the 4th Duke, died in 1979, having married Lady Mary
Kathleen Crichton, Mistress of the Robes to Queen Elizabeth the
Queen Mother, from 1964, until her death in 1990. Their son Sir
James is the 5th Duke, holding a number of subsidiary titles.

From the three noble houses treated there are numerous
offshoots, including the Barons Dalzell, Hamilton baronets of
Silvertonhill, Lanarkshire, and the Stirling-Hamiltons of Preston,
East Lothian. Readers seeking the origins of cadets are referred to *A
History of the House of Hamilton*, a well-researched work by Lt.
Col. George Hamilton (Edinburgh, 1933).

HAY The first of the Hay family to appear in Scotland was
William de la Hay, who probably came with his uncle, Ranulph de
Soulis, who appears as butler at the royal court ca. 1153. The office
at that time was probably a life appointment, and William held it
during most of the reign of William the Lion (1165–1214). He
became 1st Baron of Erroll, and married Eva, heiress of Pitmilly,
and died ca. 1201, in her lifetime. The family derived their name
from La Haye, in the Cotentin peninsula of Normandy. In Latin

documents the name is written *de Haya*. It was rendered into English as Hay and into Gaelic as *Garadh*.

William was progenitor of the Hays of Erroll, and his second son may have been ancestor of the Hays of Yester. The Erroll Hays descend through his grandson, Gilbert, and from his son William came the Hays of Leys and those of Megginch, ancestors of the Earls of Kinnoull. Sir Gilbert, 5th Baron of Erroll was given the important post of Hereditary Lord High Constable of Scotland by Robert the Bruce in 1324. Sir William Hay of Lochloy, who died ca. 1420, was ancestor of the Hays of Mayne. William Hay, the 9th chief, was belted Earl of Erroll in 1452. His wife, Lady Beatrix, daughter of James, 7th Earl of Douglas, was ultimately co-heiress of her brother, the last 'Black Douglas'. George, 7th Earl of Erroll, was prominent during the reign of Queen Mary. His grandson, Francis, 9th Earl, was a leader of the Counter-Revolution, and with his allies, the Earls of Huntly and Angus, he entered into a treaty with King Philip II of Spain, to depose Queen Elizabeth I, and place King James VI, who was to be converted, on the throne of a united Catholic Britain. Later, the king went against them and destroyed their strongholds. The Erroll stronghold of Slains has been a ruin ever since.

In 1745, Mary, 1685–1758, Countess of Erroll in her own right, raised her followers for Prince Charles Stewart. She married in 1720 (as his second wife), Alexander Falconer of Hillhead, who took the name of Hay of Delgaty. The Countess died without issue and her great-nephew, James, succeeded to the honours in 1758. His descendant, Diana Hay, 1926–78, Countess of Erroll, married as his first wife, the late Sir Iain Moncreiffe of that Ilk, a brilliant historian and genealogist, but the marriage was dissolved by divorce in 1964. Their son, Sir Merlin Serald Victor Gilbert Hay, is 24th Earl, and chief of the Hays.

Peter Hay of Megginch, who died in 1596, was the father of George, created Earl of Kinnoull in 1633. His grandson, George, 3rd Earl, followed Montrose and fought at Tippermuir in 1644. The 6th Earl, William Hay, resigned his titles in the hands of Queen Anne, and obtained a charter in 1704, limiting the honours to himself during life, and at his death to his kinsman, Thomas, Viscount Dupplin, descended from a younger brother of the 1st Earl. His son George was the 8th Earl, and the 15th and present earl is Arthur William Hay, who lives in London.

John Hay of Yester appears as a Lord of Parliament in 1488. A descendant became Earl of Tweeddale in 1646, and his son John was advanced to the dignity of Marquess in 1694. The 13th Marquess is Edward Douglas John Hay, born 1947, who is Hereditary Chamberlain of Dunfermline. Captain Jock Hay, 1906–97, of Delgaty, was a nationalist and socialist, who claimed to be chief of the Hays. Many Hays have been in the legal profession – Writers to the Signet and Advocates.

HENDERSON The surname Henderson is cognate with Henryson, 'son of Henry': a prolific name all over Europe in the Middle Ages, and borne by many families. Henderson – with intrusive 'd' – became the most common form, but some families have retained the Christian name as a surname; hence Henry and again with the intrusive 'd', Hendry, leading to Henderson. The surnames now appear all over Scotland, but at one time there were three quite distinct groups.

Henryson appears in Aberdeen as early as 1317, when John, *filius* Henry was a burgess. In 1370, James Henrisson, an Aberdeen merchant, complained that his shop had been wrecked by the English. William Henrison was chamberlain of Lochmaben Castle, in Dumfriesshire, in 1374, and Walter Henrison was 'sergeand' in Edinburgh, in 1467. Robert Henryson, 1430–1505, was a well-known poet, along with William Dunbar and Gavin Douglas, one of the 'makars'. He taught law at Glasgow in 1462, and prior to his death was a schoolmaster at Dunfermline. Many words of humanistic appearance were introduced by him, and he made good use of humour and alliteration. His finest poem was *The Testament of Cresseid*, which is a kind of supplement to Chaucer's work on the same subject.

The Hendersons of Fordell, in Dalgety parish, Fife, were the chief Lowland family of the name. Robert Henderson appears to have wadset the lands to Alexander Drummond of Ardmore, before 1478, but the subjects were redeemed by his son James, King's Advocate, in 1510. His descendant, John, was created a Baronet of NS in 1664. John's line ended with an heiress, Isabella, who succeeded to Fordell in 1817, and married Admiral Sir Philip Durham. Her kinsman, George Mercer, on succeeding to Fordell, assumed the surname of Henderson. Georgina Duncan, granddaughter of his brother Douglas, assumed the name and arms of Mercer-Henderson, and married in 1888, Sidney, Earl of Buckinghamshire, whose family inherited Fordell. Rev. Alexander Henderson, 1583–1646, minister at Leuchars, and a prominent Presbyterian leader, is supposed to have been a cadet of the Hendersons of Fordell. The old castle there was restored by the late Sir Nicholas Fairburn, QC, who died in 1995.

The following year the castle and 80 acre grounds were sold to William Inglis and his wife Lorraine, for over £500,000.

A branch of Clan Gunn bears the name Henderson. According to tradition they descend from Henry, a younger son of George Gunn, a 15th-century chief who lived with 'barbaric pomp' at Clyne. After a devastating feud with the Keiths, a family dispute, probably about the succession, led to Henry separating himself from his brothers and settling in the lowlands of Caithness. In 1594 there is mention of a champion of the clan, Donald MacWilliam MacHendrie, 'who may have had something to say in the matter of the Henderson patronymic'. A third distinctive group, a sept of the MacDonalds of Glencoe, Englished their name from *MacEanruig*. They claimed a fabulous descent from one Eanruig Mor Mac Righ Neachan, 'Big Henry, son of King Nechtan', who succeeded to the Pictish monarchy ca. 706. A more acceptable claim would be descent from Dugal MacEanruig, who flourished ca. 1340.

In modern times, Dr Hamish Henderson, of the School of Scottish Studies, now retired, has done much to recover the folksongs and stories of the travelling folk. During World War II he served as an infantryman in North Africa, Sicily and Italy, and was mentioned in despatches.

HOG/HOGG As the surname, Hog or Hogg (variants Hogges, Hoge, and Hoog), is found in early times in Scotland and England, later in Ireland, it cannot be supposed that all who bear it descend from a common ancestor. In the eastern border counties of Scotland, where the name is most prevalent, the name almost certainly derives from the animal which, in its wild state, typified courage and ferocity. It is worth noting that other families in the same area – Gordons, Nisbets, Redpaths and Swintons – all displayed boar's heads on their seals and shields.

Early examples of the surname include Adam, son of Henry del Hoga (i.e. 'of the hog'), who was given as a bondsman to the Abbey of Kelso by Andrew Fraser, ca. 1280. The croft of Henry del Hoga is recorded as early as 1250, and ca. 1270, John de Grantham, son of Emma, heiress of Saloman del Hoga, made a grant from her lands at Berwick to the monks of Kelso. Adam del Hoga held a croft in the time of Lady Alicia de Gordun (ca. 1280). At one time it was thought that the Hogs of Harcarse and Bogend, in Berwickshire, descended from Hogs in Morayshire, and there was certainly a place there called Hogstoun. However, the name which evolved around what is now Gordonstoun was Ogstoun. There was an aristocratic family of Hogs in Denmark, and at Frue Kirk, Aalborg, there is a fine monument, dated 1647, in memory of Sir Erik Hog and his wife, Dame Sophia Lange. There the surname is said to mean 'falcon', and to 'go the whole hog', as the saying goes, the name must be written with a spole or spoke through the vowel.

It seems likely that the Hogs of Harcarse and Bogend descended from John Hog, an Edinburgh burgess who swore fealty to Edward I in 1296. His descendants rose to prominence in the burgh and in 1359 Roger Hog loaned money to the King of Scots. Walter, son of Simon Hog, held the lands of Hogiston, adjacent to the burgh muir, in 1402. A portrait of the law lord, Sir Roger Hog, 1635–1700, by David Scougall, is in the hall of the old Parliament House in Edinburgh, and there is another in the quaint little church of Fogo. He was the progenitor of the Hogs of Ladykirk and Cammo, and of Newliston and Kellie. Roger Hog, 1715–89, a rich banker, purchased Newliston in 1753, and later the lands (but not the castle) of Kellie. Because of his wealth and standing he was recognised as chief of the surname in 1783, when he matriculated arms: Argent, three boar's heads erazed and armed Or. His descendant, Major Roger T.A. Hog, last of Newliston, died in 1979, without issue, and the present chief appears to be Eric J.G. Hog, residing at Renoir, Paris, France.

One of the best-known Hoggs was James, 1770–1835, 'The Ettrick Shepherd', a son of Robert Hogg, tenant of the small farms of Ettrick Hall and Ettrick House, in Selkirkshire. The parochial registers show that the spelling Hog was common up to ca. 1800, after which, as with the surnames Ker, Tod and others, the final letter was duplicated. James Hogg rose to become a famous poet and novelist, and has aptly been named 'The Poet Laureate of Fairyland'. His best known poem is *The Queen's Wake*, containing the beautiful episodal tale of 'Kilmany'. His finest prose work is *Confessions of a Justified Sinner*. Two of his brothers, David, 1773–1854, and Robert, 1776–1833, emigrated to America in 1833. Robert died at sea, and the families settled at Binghampton, in New York State. There are numerous descendants in various states. In a renovated byre at Aikwood Tower, the Border castle restored by Lord Steel of Aikwood, there is a permanent exhibition of the life and work of 'The Ettrick Shepherd'.

HOUSTON Many writers of books on clans and tartans make the Houstons a sept of Clan Donald. This erroneous assumption arises from the fact that the patronymic of the Macdonalds of Sleat is *Clann Huisdein*, i.e. 'children of Hugh', who was a son of Alexander, Earl of Ross and Lord of the Isles. The Houstons belong to Renfrewshire, and if they must be allotted a tartan it should be Stewart Ancient or Lennox District, as the Houstons were vassals of the Earls of Lennox.

Hugo de Pad'inan, progenitor of the Houstons of Houston was granted a charter of the barony of Kilpeter, in Strathgryfe, by Baldwin of Biggar, probably ca. 1160. He witnessed charters between 1165 and 1180. Hugo was of Flemish extraction, and before settling in Kilpeter had occupied some lands at Romanno, in Peeblesshire. It was from his grandson Hugh, son of Reginald, that the lands became known as Houston (Hugh's town), and the family so called. In 1225 he had a dispute with the monks of Paisley, over his lands of Auchinhoss, and compromised by paying the lordly ecclesiastics half a merk annually towards keeping the tomb of St Mirren illuminated with wax candles.

Portraits of Sir John Houston, IXth Laird, and his lady, Dame Maria Colquhoun, who died respectively in 1400 and 1405, once graced the church of Houston, and have been cited as proving that painting was so prevalent in Scotland as to be employed in funeral monuments not only of great peers, but even of knights of no great eminence nor fame. John, the XIIth Laird, had a charter of half of the lands of Lenny, in Mid Lothian, in 1468. His son Peter was slain at Flodden in 1513, fighting along with the men of Lennox on the right wing of the Scottish army. Patrick, son of Peter, was killed in battle at Linlithgow Bridge, in 1525. The Houstons were a turbulent family. Patrick Houston, XVIth of that Ilk, was implicated in the slaughter of Robert, son of Robert Mure of Caldwell, in 1550, and in 1564 appeared before the High Court at Edinburgh, charged with assaulting Andrew Hamilton of Cochno. Nevertheless, he was knighted in 1556 by Mary, Queen of Scots. Here it is worth noting that one Margaret Houston, Widow Beveridge, nursed Queen Mary through childbirth in 1566, and with a slap on the rump of Prince James, heralded the Union of the Crowns.

The XIXth Laird, Patrick, was created a Baronet of NS in 1668. Sir John, the 3rd Baronet, suffered losses through having Jacobite sympathies, and after his death at London in 1722, the estate of Houston was sold. The 4th Baronet, Sir John, died without issue, leaving his remaining lands to his kinsman, George Houston of Johnstone. The title, however, passed to the heir male, Patrick Houston, who had emigrated to America, ca. 1735. There are descendants in Georgia, but they have not assumed the baronetcy since 1795. Some early Houstons migrated to Wigtownshire, and from there to Ulster. Sam Houston, 1793–1863, of Texas fame, was a descendant. The ancestors of Sir William Houston, created a Baronet in 1836, were at Cotreoch, in Wigtownshire. His heir, Col. Sir George, of the Grenadier Guards, married a daughter of Thomas Boswall of Blackadder, and assumed the additional surname of Boswall. The 8th and present Baronet is Sir Thomas A. Houston-Boswall, who lives in New York.

HUME/HOME The name is of territorial origin: from the old barony of Home, in Berwickshire. In early times it was spelled indifferently Home or Hume. The family of Polwarth adopted the Hume spelling, while the principal family retained the Home spelling. David Hume, 1711–76, always favoured the 'u' spelling, but his brother, John of Ninewells, preferred the 'o' spelling. The ancestor of the Earls of Home is supposed to have been William, son of Patrick of Greenlaw, who married (as her third husband) after 1225, his cousin Ada, daughter of Patrick, 5th Earl of Dunbar, whose dowry was the lands of Home. The evidence for this union is very slim.

We are on surer ground when Gilbert, son of Alden of Home, first appears on record between 1172 and 1178. About 1198, he is styled as seneschal to Earl Patrick. William of Home, probably his grandson, had a dispute with the Abbey of Kelso about a piece of land which the monks claimed had been given to them by Ada, daughter of Patrick, Earl of Dunbar, and Home claimed the land. This may have given rise to the story of a marriage (her third) between Ada and William of Greenlaw. Galfridus or Geoffrey de Home, the next on record, signed the *Ragman Roll* in 1296. The family increased their possessions by subsequent unions. Sir Thomas Home's marriage with Nicola, heiress of Dunglas, in East Lothian, brought prosperity, and their grandson, Sir Alexander Home, was engaged in diplomatic missions to England, which increased the standing of the family.

Sir Alexander's eldest son, another Sir Alexander, was created a Lord of Parliament under the title of Lord Home, in 1473. He too, made an advantageous first marriage to Mariota, heiress of Landells in Berwickshire. Alexander, 3rd Lord Home, invaded England with 3000 men in 1513, and was completely routed at Millfield, with heavy losses. Lord Home escaped, with the loss of his banner, and this defeat influenced King James IV to make an incursion into England the same year, with a large army, only to be defeated at Flodden. Lord Home, along with the Earl of Huntly, led the advance, but was repulsed. He has been accused of cowardice, but he was the only Scots commander to hold his position when the English cavalry rendered it impossible to rescue his impetuos sovereign. This brave Lord had a dispute with the Duke of Albany, which resulted in his execution and forfeiture in 1516. His brother George was restored to his title and most of his estates.

Alexander, 6th Lord Home, was created Earl of Home, with subsidiary titles, in 1604/5. His son, James, 2nd Earl, died without issue, but by this time Homes had numerous branches, including Wedderburn, from whom came the Earls of Marchmont, now dormant, and the family of Blackadder, created Baronets of NS, 1671, and still existing. The nearest heir male in 1633 was James Home of Cowdenknowe, descended from the Homes of Whiteriggs, and he was recognised as 3rd Earl in 1636. Succeeding earls played prominent parts in Scottish affairs. Alexander, 7th Earl, was chosen one of the representative peers of Scotland in 1710, but was suspected of Jacobite sympathies and imprisoned in Edinburgh Castle, but released in 1716. The 10th Earl, Alexander, married in 1798, Elizabeth, daughter of Henry, Duke of Buccleuch, and their eldest son, Cospatrick Alexander, 11th Earl, was created a peer of the UK in 1873, under the title of Baron Douglas of Douglas, in Lanarkshire. The 14th Earl, Sir Alexander Douglas Home, 1903–95, disclaimed his titles in order to enter the Commons as an MP, and was Prime Minister, 1963–64. See also article THE RED DOUGLASES. His son, David Alexander Cospatrick Home, is the 15th Earl, residing at The Hirsel, Coldstream.

Outwith the titled families, many Homes or Humes have distinguished themselves. Henry Home, 1696–1782, passed advocate in 1724, and was raised to the bench as Lord Kames in 1752. John Home, 1722–1808, the dramatic poet, was the author of *Douglas*, performed at Edinburgh in 1756. David Hume of Godscroft, ca. 1560– ca.1630, was a noted historian, poet and controversial writer. Better known perhaps, was David Hume, 1711–76, philosopher and historian, brother of the Laird of Ninewells. Joseph Hume, 1777–1855, was a politician, statesman and national economist.

HUNTER The surname is derived from the chase and, as the name is widespread, there is no reason to think there was a common ancestor. Instances of the name appear as early as 1124.

The Hunters of Hunterston, Ayrshire, thought to be of Norman origin, appear to be the oldest family. Precedence was disputed by the Hunters of Polmood, in Tweedsmuir, but significantly the Ayrshire family were styled 'of that Ilk', which means not only 'of Hunterston', but chiefship. Robert Hunter of Hunterston subscribed the bond in defence of the reformed religion in 1562. Michael Hunter of Polmood was outlawed for a raid on Belstone Tower. An heiress of the family married her cousin, Robert Caldwell, who assumed the surname of Hunter. The present chief is Neil A. Hunter, residing in Andorra, in the Pyrenees. The brothers William, 1718–83, and John Hunter, 1728–93, distinguished themselves in the medical profession, and the 'collections' of William are in Glasgow's Hunterian Museum. Samuel Hunter, 1769–1839, born at Stoneykirk, Wigtownshire, was an army surgeon who took up journalism, and was editor and part proprietor of the *Glasgow Herald*, 1803–37. William Hunter, 1755–1815, a native of Montrose, joined the medical service of the East India Co., and was secretary of the Asiatic Society, 1784–94.

IMRIE The surname Imrie and variants such as Imray are abbreviated forms of the Germanic personal name *Amalric*, a compound of 'work' and 'rule'. It came early to Scotland. Emeric, a Lombard from Flanders, is recorded at Berwick in 1329. The escheat of Ade Emry, burgess of Dunblane, took place in 1424. Walter and Thomas Ymery were tenants in Condland, in Stirlingshire, in 1513. James Immerie resided in Dunfermline ca. 1568. John Imrie, freeman cordiner, was admitted burgess of Glasgow in 1611. The name is more prolific in the eastern Lowlands. Dr John Imrie, 1923–96, a native of Oldhamstocks, near Dunbar, was an erudite historian who was Keeper of the Records of Scotland, 1961–96. He did much towards the preservation and publication of records, and his death was a sad loss to the world of archives.

INNES The distinguished Innes family descend from Berowald the Fleming, who received a charter of lands in the district of Elgin called Innes (from which their surname is derived), and Etherurecard (? Nether or Easter Urquhart), from Malcolm IV in 1160, in fee and heritage, with one toft in the burgh of Elgin, for the service of one knight at Elgin Castle. One of the witnesses was Willelmo filio Frisgin (Freskin the Fleming), to whom Berowald may have been related. A grandson, Walter of Innes, had a charter by Alexander II in 1226. Sir Robert Innes, 1364–81, 8th of Innes, was the father of Sir Alexander, who married Janet, daughter of the Thane of Aberchirder. Sir Robert, 11th Laird, was Sheriff-Depute of Moray, and father of four sons: Sir James, who entertained King James IV at his castle in 1490; Walter of Innermarkie, ancestor of the baronets of Balvenie; Patrick, ancestor of the Innes baronets (1686) of Coxton, now represented by Sir David Innes, 12th Baronet and Thomas, of Elrick.

William, 15th of Innes, styled 'of that Ilk', sat in the Reformation Parliament of 1560. His son Alexander was executed by the Regent Morton in 1578, but left a son, John, who resigned the chiefship to Alexander Innes of Cromney, grand-nephew of Alexander, 13th Laird. This chief was murdered by a kinsman of the Innermarkie line. Robert, son of Alexander, founded the burgh of Garmouth in 1587, and is said to have dabbled in witchcraft. His son, Sir Robert, 20th chief, was a prominent Covenanter, and was created a Baronet of NS in 1625. He entertained Charles II at his home at Garmouth in 1650. Sir Robert built Innes House, 1640–53, and raised a regiment for Charles II. Sir James, 3rd Baronet, married in 1666 Margaret, daughter and co-heir of Harry Ker, styled Lord Ker, only surviving son of Robert, 1st Earl of Roxburgh, who died in his father's lifetime. In 1694, Sir James resigned his estates to his son, Sir Harry Innes, whose grandson, Sir James, 6th Baronet and 24th chief, became, after protracted litigation, 5th Duke of Roxburgh, in 1812. His son James Robert, 1816–95, was created a peer of the UK in 1837, as Earl Innes. Sir Guy David Innes-Ker is 10th Duke, 11th Baronet and 26th chief, residing at Floors Castle, Kelso.

From Robert Innes, 2nd of Innermarkie, sprang the Innes family of Balvenie and Edingight. Sir Robert Innes, 5th of Innermarkie and 1st of Balvenie, was created a Baronet of NS in 1628. From Robert Innes, 2nd of Innermarkie, descended Sir Thomas Innes, 1893–1971, of Learney, who was Lord Lyon King of Arms from 1945 to 1969. He was probably the most colourful holder of the office since Sir David Lindsay of the Mount, Lord Lyon, 1542–55, and author of *A Satyre of the Three Estates*. Sir Thomas was the author of *Scots Heraldry, The Tartans and Clans of the Families of Scotland* and other authoritative works. The present holder of the office of Lord Lyon is his third son, Sir Malcolm R. Innes of Edingight, who is also Secretary to the Order of the Thistle, and President of the Scottish Genealogy Society.

Sir George Innes, 4th Baronet of the Innermarkie line, was a grandson of Robert Innes, and was a RC priest, who died in 1698, when the baronetcy devolved on his cousin, Sir James Innes of Balvenie, father of the 6th, 7th and 8th Baronets. The present 17th Baronet is Sir Peter Alexander Berowald Innes, a consultant civil engineer, who lives at The Wheel House, Nations Hill, Kings Worthy, Winchester.

The Innes clan (recognised as such in 1579) produced two excellent antiquaries. Father Thomas Innes, 1662–1744, a priest of the Scots College at Paris, produced his *Critical Essay* in 1729, which laid the foundations for genuine Scottish historical research. He was descended from the family of Innes of Drainie. Cosmo Innes, 1798–1874, Professor of Constitutional Law at the University of Edinburgh, was the author of *Scottish Legal Antiquities* (1872), and other learned works. He was a cadet of the family of Innes of Leuchars and Dunkinty, Keepers of Spynie Castle.

IRVINE/IRVING The Irvines, Irvings, Irwins and many other variants, are said to be of Celtic origin, and descended from Duncan, hereditary lay abbot of Dunkeld (of the kin of St. Columba), who was killed at Duncrub in 965. His son Duncan, Abbot of Dunkeld, is thought to have fought at Luncarty in 990. He had sons: (1) Crinan the Thane, who married Princess Bethoc, heiress of Malcolm II, King of Scots, and had a son, King Duncan, killed in 1040; (2) Grim of Strathearn; and (3) Duncan of Cumbria. From the latter descended William Irvine, armour-bearer to Robert the Bruce; and Robert, witness to a charter to James Douglas, of lands in Roxburghshire, ca. 1320. From Robert descended the Irvines of Bonshaw. The brothers took their surname from an old parish in Annandale. William received a charter of part of the Forest of Drum, then in Kincardineshire. He was Clerk of the Rolls, 1328–31. His son William, was one of the barons who sat in the Parliament held at Perth in 1369. He was probably dead by 1398, when his son Alexander had a charter of the Park of Drum, which remained with the family until 1737. He went to France in 1408 with the Earl of Mar, to join the Duke of Burgundy, and returned a knight. Alexander was killed at Harlaw in 1411.

The Vth laird, Alexander Irvine, was deprived of his office of Sheriff of Aberdeenshire in 1471, for attacking with a force of men the house of Sir Walter Lindsay of Bewfort. His son and heir, Alexander, married Janet Keith, and by her had a son Alexander, and two daughters, Mary and Elspeth. By Nan Menzies he had four natural children: David, Alexander, John and Agnes, for all of whom he made provision in 1493. The Irvines of Drum were the undoubted chiefs of the surname, recognised as such by Parliament in 1664, when a birthbrief was issued for Capt. John Irvine, soldiering in France, son of Robert Irvine of Fedderet. Alexander, XIIth chief, inherited debts and a reduced estate, and when he died in 1696, his kinsman and executor, Alexander Irvine of Murthill, intruded himself as laird of Drum. However, on the death of his grandson, John, without issue, the rightful heir of entail, Alexander Irvine of Artamford, succeeded. The XXVth laird, Lt. Col. Charles Francis Irvine, served in the Gordon Highlanders in World War II (1939–45).

The Dumfriesshire chieftains did not come into prominence until the 16th century. Christopher Irving of Bonshaw and a son were killed at Flodden in 1513. From the time of his successor, Edward, the family is well documented. Various members were involved in the municipal affairs of Dumfries. Edward married Blanche Graham, and was succeeded in 1605 by his son William, who died ca. 1647. Descendants in Canada come from Aemilius Irving, of Quebec, and from his father's younger brother, John Beaufin Irving, 1844–1925, whose son Sir Robert Beaufin Irving, 1877–1954, was Commodore of the Cunard-White Star Line, and captain of the *Queen Mary*. William's second son, Francis, married Agnes, daughter of Raining, Provost of Dumfries. His son, John of Friars Carse, was Provost of Dumfries, 1634 and 1646, and a Covenanter. A descendant, Richard Francis Irving, emigrated to Australia in 1874. By his second marraige to Annie M. Tindale, he had, with a daughter Heather, a son Malcolm James Irving of Barwhinnock and Lango Downs, Charleville, Queensland.

Dr J. Bruce Irving, of Bonshaw Tower, Kirtlebridge, is chairman of the Dumfries & Galloway Family History Society. The Bell-Irving family of White Hill, Lockerbie, descend from Richard Irving, who had a charter of lands in Hoddam, in 1549.

ISBISTER The Orkney surname of Isbister comes from the lost place-name of Isbister, in the parish of Harray, and also from Isbister, in Birsay parish. There are places so named in South Ronaldsay, and at Northmavine and Whalsay, in Shetland, and the name probably means 'river mouth farm'. Robert Ysbuster appears at Harray in 1557, and again in 1565, as Robert Ysbister 'of that Ilk', so his was considered to be the principal family. Malcolm Ysebuster was a baillie of Harray in 1607, and he may have been the same as Malcolm Isbuster, of Harray parish, who died in

February, 1613. At least seventeen men of this surname were employed in Canada by the Hudson's Bay Co. between 1709 and 1860. One of those, Thomas Isbister, began as a labourer, and rose to having charge of a trading post at Nelson River. He was killed by a bull in 1836. His eldest son, Alexander K. Isbister, graduated at the University of Edinburgh in 1858, and became a schoolmaster with the Company.

JAMIESON The surname Jameson or Jamieson simply means 'son of James'. It is worth noting that a family named Jamieson or Nelson held the office of Crowner of Bute from early in the 14th century to the 17th, and this may explain why some authorities list Jamieson as a sect of the Stewarts of Bute. Some others, with less conviction, make them a sect of Clan Gunn. As James was a prolific name in mediaeval times, and the name of seven Stewart kings, there must be many unrelated families of the surname in various parts of Scotland.

Early references to the surname include Alexander Jamison, who had a safe conduct to trade with England in 1445. William Jamyson was a tenant in Pollock in 1472, and in the same year, John Jameson was a freeman of Irvine, Robert Jacobi was in Brechin in 1493, but the surname James is rare in Scotland. James Jameson was reader in Kettins Church in 1563, and Sir Mark Jamieson was vicar pensioner of Currie in 1567.

George Jameson, 1586–1644, was a native of Aberdeen, and was apprenticed to John Anderson, an Edinburgh painter in May, 1612. Later, he applied himself to portrait painting, occasionally practising in history and landscape. He was patronised by the Campbells of Breadalbane, and among other work for them, executed a large pedigree chart, with miniature portraits, which is now in the Museum of Scotland. Other portraits by him are possessed by the University of Aberdeen, and he has been called 'The Scottish Vandyke'.

A distinguished naturalist, Robert Jameson, 1774–1854, was born at Leith. In boyhood he showed a market interest in natural objects, and he entered the Humanities Class at Edinburgh in 1788. Later he studied medicine and visited London, where he met members of the Linnaean Society. He studied geology on the Orkney and Shetland Isles, and on the island of Arrran, and in 1804 was appointed Professor of Natural History at Edinburgh. Robert was the author of a number of scientific books.

John Jamieson, 1759–1836, a native of Glasgow, studied Latin and Greek there, and became pastor of a Secession congregation at Forfar. He was translated to Nicolson Street Church, Edinburgh in 1792. At an early stage in his career he received the degree of Doctor of Divinity from the College of New Jersey. Dr Jamieson was a prolific writer, but is best remembered for his *Etymological Dictionary of the Scottish Language* (1808).

There are several armigerous Jamieson families in Scotland. John Jamieson of Croy, merchant-burgess of Glasgow, had a grant of arms in 1865, and about the same time his nephew, Michael James Jamieson, matriculated arms. Michael's brother, Robert Jarvie Jamieson, followed in 1869. Douglas Jamieson, 1880–1952, a grandson of John of Croy, was Solicitor-General for Scotland, 1933–35, and Lord Advocate, 1935. His daughter Barbara married Kenneth C. Cook, who recorded his bearings at the College of Arms, in London. Others who bear arms include Dr Arthur Jamieson of Barnach, residing at Hillcrest, Beith, Ayrshire, who was chairman of the Glasgow & West of Scotland Family History Society, 1977–88. James Jamieson, who died in 1736 in Essex County, Virginia, bore arms which indicate a Scottish origin, and others are found throughout the United States of America.

JOHNSTONE OF ANNANDALE Johnson, Johnston

or Johnstone is a surname with at least three derivations. Johnstone parish in Dumfriesshire, means *John's Toun*, or the dwelling place of John, who, before the surname stabilised, received a grant of lands from Robert de Brus, ca. 1170. This was the foundation of the great Border clan. The lands 'in valle de Anand' (Annandale), were confirmed to John Johnstone by William the Lion in 1172. It has been claimed the ancestors were old Celts of the Border, who intermarried with Norman settlers. Some others had their names from places. Perth, often called St Johnston, gave its name to a number of inhabitants, as did Jonystoun, now Johnstonburn, at Humbie, in East Lothian. The surname Johnson, 'John's son', is often confused with Johnston or Johnstone.

John, father of Gilbert, may have been a settler who elected to hold his lands from the Bruce lords of Annandale, and possibly came with that family from Yorkshire. Gilbert was succeeded by another Gilbert, witness to a transaction of 1249. Sir John of Johnstone appears in the homage roll of 1296. Gilbert of Johnstone also signed the *Ragman Roll*, and was probably a brother, as the two men are mentioned in a charter of the lands of Comlongan and Ruthwell, between 1315 and 1332. Gilbert was alive in 1347, and was the father or grandfather of Sir John Johnstone, on record between 1377 and 1398. Adam of Johnston, who succeeded, was styled 'of that Ilk', and was evidently the chief of the clan. A descendant, John, had a brother James, who had a charter of the lands of Drumhaston, Skeoch and others, in 1545, on payment of 1000 merks to John, Commendator of Saulsett, and the convent there. In the time of John Johnstone of that Ilk, a bitter feud with the Maxwells began, and it lasted nearly a century. He was twice married, first to Elizabeth Jardine, and next to Nicola Douglas, and had a large family, including James, his heir; Robert, of Raecleuch; and Capt. James of Loch-house. John, son of James, must have come of age ca. 1570, and was held responsible by the government for the behaviour of his clan. His son James, however, continued the feud with the Maxwells and, on a day fixed for reconciliation, was shot and mortally wounded.

James, son of James, was a minor when his father was killed, and in his time peace with the Maxwells was established. He was created a peer, as Lord Johnstone of Lochwood in 1633. In 1643 he was created Earl of Hartfell, Lord Johnstone of Lochwood. His son James, 2nd Earl, resigned his titles in 1657 for a re-grant, becoming Earl of Annandale and Hartfell. He married Henrietta Douglas, and their eldest surviving son, William, succeeded, and in 1701 was created Marquess of Annandale and Earl of Hartfell. Henrietta, the eldest daughter, married in 1669, Charles Hope, created Earl of Hopetoun in 1703. When George, 3rd Marquess, died in 1792, he was succeeded by his grand-nephew, James, 3rd Earl of Hopetoun. A long contest for the titles ensued, in which a contender was John James Hope Johnstone, 1796–1876, son of Admiral Sir William Hope and Anne, daughter of James, 3rd Earl of Hopetoun. The claim was renewed by his grandson, John James Hope Johnstone, 1842–1912, but no decision was reached and the titles became dormant. The Hope Johnstones continued at Raehills and, in 1986, Patrick Andrew Wentworth Hope Johnstone, son of Major Percy Wentworth Hope Johnstone of Annandale and Raehills, *de jure* 10th Earl of Annandale, who died in 1983, was recognised by the House of Lords Committee of Privileges as 11th Earl of Annandale (Hartfell included), and was summoned to the Upper House. He is chief of Clan Johnstone.

JOHNSTON(E)S – VARIOUS The Johnstones of Galabank

once entertained a claim to the Annandale peerage, and proved their descent from the barons of Newby and Graitney, who branched off from the Lockwood cadets of Annandale. Lt. Col. James Johnstone, of Fulford Hall, Warwickshire, who represented this family, served with the Durham Light Infantry during World War II.

A Johnston family of Beirholm, Annandale, descended from Gavin Johnston, who received a charter of the lands of Clerk Orchard, Thornick and others, in 1555. He was ancestor of Archibald Johnston, 1611–63, of Warriston, Edinburgh, a distinguished lawyer, who became Lord Advocate in 1646. He was unfortunately induced to take office under Cromwell, who made him Lord Clerk Register and advanced him to the peerage as Lord Warriston. At the Restoration, having supported Cromwell and also the Covenanters, he fled to France. An act of forfeiture being passed against him, he was condemned to death, discovered at Rouen, and brought back to Edinburgh where he was hanged without trial. A descendant, Sir Patrick Johnston, was three times Lord Provost of Edinburgh, but was mobbed by the citizens for supporting the Union of 1707. However, he became a member of the first parliament of Great Britain. Lt. Col. George Richard Johnston, who represented this family, served in World War I with the Royal Horse Artillery. He became a qualified interpreter in six languages, and was granted arms by the Lord Lyon in 1950.

The Johnstones of Westerhall are an important branch of the Johnstones of Annandale, and descend from Matthew, second son of Sir Adam Johnstone of that ilk. Matthew had a charter of lands in Westeraw, Lanarkshire in 1455. The family had a long history as MPs for Dumfries and other seats. Sir James Johnstone of Westerhall, MP, was knighted by Charles II, and his son Sir John, was created a Baronet of NS in 1700. He married Rachel Johnstone, co-heiress of Sheens but, dying without issue, the title devolved on his brother, Sir William, who married Harriet, the other co-heiress. His son, Sir James, was a claimant for the Annandale title in 1792. His brother, Col. John, was ancestor of the Barons Derwent. Sir William, 5th Baronet, was a member of seven successive parliaments, and acquired the great Pulteney property through his first wife, Frances, whom he married in 1760, heiress of Daniel Pulteney. Their daughter Henrietta became Countess of Bath. The 10th Baronet is George Richard Douglas Johnston, who succeeded his father, Sir Frederick, in 1994.

The Johnstons of Caskieben possess a baronetcy of NS, conferred in 1626 on George Johnston, Sheriff of Aberdeen. This family appears to be a collateral line of the Annandale Johnstones, and erroneously use the style 'of that Ilk'. The 11th Baronet emigrated to Alabama, USA, where his descendant, Sir Thomas Johnston, 13th Baronet, became partner in the legal firm. He died in 1984, and the present and 14th Baronet is his son Thomas Alexander Johnston.

It is difficult to pinpoint Johnstons or Johnstones descended from those who took their name from Jonyston, East Lothian, or from St John's-toun (Perth). Gilbert, son of Thomas Johnstone, who received the forfeited lands of Whiteriggs and Redmyre, in Kincardineshire, was probably of a family which derived the name from St John's-toun. The Rt Hon. Thomas Johnston, 1881–1965, Secretary of State for Scotland (1941–45), founded in the latter year, the Scots Ancestry Research Society. Lyndon Baines Johnson, 1908–73, who acceded to the presidency of the USA in 1963, when President John F. Kennedy was assassinated, is said to have been descended from Johnstones of Dumfriesshire.

KEITH It has been said that 'there is hardly a Scotch noble family who have not the blood of the Keiths in their veins'. Certainly, with such an illustrious old family, there were many alliances with other families. The surname derives from the lands of Keith, in Humbie parish, East Lothian. Hervey Keith, who possessed part of the lands, held the office of Marischal (Keeper of the Royal Mares) under Malcolm IV (1124–53). His son Malcolm, a witness to Eschina's gift of the church of Molle to the Abbey of Kelso in 1185, appears a witness to other deeds up to 1203. His brother David held the office of Marischal, conjunctly with his brother Philip and nephew Hervey. Hervey had a son, Sir John, who inherited all of Humbie. Around 1250 he witnessed a gift to the Hospital of Soltre (Soutra). His grandson, Sir Robert, was a supporter of Robert the Bruce, who granted him lands in the Forest of Kintore, in the Garioch, and lands in Buchan, in 1309. Later, he bestowed upon him lands forfeited by the Comyns, Earls of Buchan.

Sir Robert Keith was elevated to the peerage as Lord Keith, and his son, Sir William, 2nd Lord Keith, was created Earl Marischal in 1458. The 3rd Earl, William 'of the Tower', lived at Dunnottar, where he entertained King James IV in 1504. His grandson, George, 4th Earl, founded Marischal College, Aberdeen, in 1593. The 5th Earl, William, was educated in Europe, and was interested in the colonisation of Nova Scotia. He had a grant of lands there, to be called the barony of Keith-Marischal (in New Brunswick), in

1625. According to the *Scots Peerage* (vi, 54), there was no grant of the title of Baronet, but he is listed as Baronet of NS by Sir E. MacKenzie and other writers on the subject. Incidentally, the numbering of the earls in the *Scots Peerage*, will be found to differ from this work. Sir William, 6th Earl, sympathised with the Covenanters, and led them into Aberdeen, where he proclaimed himself governor. It was this earl who saved the Scottish Regalia from Cromwell by hiding the items at Dunnottar. His brother George, 7th Earl, was a Royalist, as was his son William, 8th Earl. The 9th and last Earl Marischal, George, was a Jacobite, attainted for treason in 1715, along with his brother, Maj. Gen. James Keith, who went into Russian then Prussian service, and was killed at Hochkirchen in 1758. Since the Earl's death in 1778, the Earls of Kintore (see FALCONER article), have been held to represent the House of Keith Marischal, through descent from Sir John Keith, third son of the 5th Earl.

A Keith who went to Sweden, rose through merit to great honour. He was Sir Andrew Keith of Forsa, a natural son of Sir Robert Keith, a younger brother of the 4th Earl Marischal, and was in Swedish service from ca. 1567 to 1583, when he came home. King James VI created him a peer with the title of Lord Dingwall, ratified in 1584. George Keith, ca. 1650–ca. 1715, the Quaker controversialist, a native of Aberdeen, founded a new body of his own in Pennsylvania, but on returning to Britain took orders in the Church of England and became rector of Edburton, in Essex. James Keith, 1663–1719, educated at Edinburgh and Leyden, lectured on anatomy at Oxford and Cambridge, and his younger brother, John, 1671–1721, was an astronomer and mathematician, who became a Professor at Oxford. Bishop Robert Keith, 1681–1757, descended from the Keith Marischals through the Pittendrum branch, was the author of *Catalogue of Scottish Bishops*, and other historical works. Thomas Keith, 1827–95, a physician, studied under Sir James Y. Simpson at Edinburgh, and became a house surgeon at the Royal Infirmary there. Later, he worked in Sardinia, but returned to Edinburgh where, apart from working in the Infirmary, he became a notable photographer.

KENNEDY Probably descended from the indigenous race who inhabited Galloway, Kennedys appear on record as early as the reign of William the Lion (1165–1214). Some authorities give the meaning of the name as the Gaelic *ceann eitigh*, meaning 'stern-headed', while others, less convincingly, say the name means 'son of

Kenneth'. Gilbert mac Kenidi witnessed a charter of lands in Galloway to the Abbey of Melrose ca. 1185. It was about this time that Henry Makenede led a rebellion in Galloway. In 1266, Fergus Makenedy rendered accounts to the sheriff of Ayr, for expenditure on the king's ships. Alexander Kenedy, clerico, witnessed John Baliol's renunciation of a treaty with France in 1296, and the same year swore fealty to Edward I of England.

In the time of Robert II (1371–90), the Kennedys of Dunure emerged as the principal family of the name, and obtained the lands of Cassillis, possibly through marriage. An advantageous union was made by James Kennedy of Dunure, ca. 1409, when he married Princess Mary, daughter of Robert II, and widow of George Douglas, Earl of Angus. Possibly because of this event, several lines of the family came to assume the double treasure on their seals. The celebrated James Kennedy, Bishop of St Andrews, third son of James and the princess, did so, and the *Lindsay Armorial* of 1542 shows the arms of Kennedy of Girvanmains with the tressure. The eldest surviving son, Gilbert of Dunure, succeeded and was created Lord Kennedy, 1457/58. David, the 3rd Lord, was created Earl of Cassillis in 1509, but perished at Flodden in 1513. When his son, Gilbert, was assassinated by Sir Hugh Campbell of Loudon in 1527, his brother William, Abbot of Crossraguel, became tutor to his nephew, Gilbert, 3rd Earl, whose son, also Gilbert, was a supporter of Mary, Queen of Scots. Tradition says that the wife of John, 6th Earl, the Countess Jean (Hamilton), was the lover of John Faa, a Gypsy captain, ca. 1622, but here chronology is the weak point, as she was then aged 15 and, although contracted, was not yet married. Archibald, the 9th Earl, erected the village of Straiton, in Ayrshire. The 12th Earl was created Marquess of Ailsa in 1831. His descendant, Archibald Angus Charles Kennedy, is 8th Marquess of Ailsa, Lord Kennedy and Earl of Cassillis. He is chief of the clan and resides at Cassillis House, Maybole.

An interesting group of Kennedys, said to be from Lochaber, settled around Dull, in Perthshire, ca. 1550, and it seems likely they were of Celtic ancestry. The Kennedys of Lochaber are known in Gaelic as *Mac Ualraig* (McWalrick). In Moray the Kennedys are said to be an offshoot of the Dunure family, and became known as *Ceannaideach*. Those of Arran came to be called *McCnusachainn* or possibly *McRusachainn*. Kennedys in Ireland because Baronets of Johnstown-Kennedy. The most famous Kennedy of Irish extraction was John F. Kennedy, 1917–63, the assassinated USA President. The Kennedys of Underwood, Symington, descend from

Robert Kennedy, of Liverpool, who purchased the lands ca. 1785. Of this family Neil James, 1866–1958, assumed the additional names of Cochran and Patrick when he married Eleanora, the heiress of Dr Roger Cochran-Patrick of Woodside. From them came the Kennedy-Cochrane-Patrick family of Ladyland, Beith, Ayrshire. The Kennedys of Knockgray descend from John Kennedy of Dalmorton, whose son Rev. Alexander Kennedy, minister of Straiton, 1691–1738, bought the estate. The Kennedys of Doonholm descend from Robert Kennedy of Tilliepowrie, in Angus. Peter Norman, of this family, is a company director. Sir Ludovick Kennedy, writer and broadcaster, who married Moira Shearer (King), star of the film *The Red Shoes*, is descended from Robert, brother of the 1st Marquess of Ailsa.

KERR ORIGINS It is often stated that the surname of Ker, Kerr or Carr, is derived from a Lanarkshire place-name, meaning a wood or copse, and that the earliest in Scotland so named were of Anglo-Norman extraction. The surname does appear in England before 1200, and came from Normandy or Brittany, but was probably brought there by Norsemen. The name 'Kari' is found in a saga of the 10th century.

While the two great families of Cessford and Ferniehurst, in Roxburghshire, are the best known, there must be many Kerr families in Scotland who are not descended from those houses, but may have similar origins. They appear in a number of Lowland shires. The earliest on record is Johannes Ker, venator (i.e. hunter), styled 'of Swynhope', in Peebleshire, who witnessed the perambulation of the bounds of Stobo manor ca. 1190. William Ker was witness to an agreement between the burgh of Irvine, Ayrshire, and Brice of Eglunstone (Eglinton), during the reign of William the Lion, who reigned 1165–1214. Thomas Kaurr was Sheriff of Roxburghshire in 1264. The ship of Thomas Ker, merchant-burgess of Aberdeen, was plundered by the English in 1273. Thomas Kayr swore fealty to Edward I at Kinghorn in 1291, and was a juror at Dysart in 1296. William Kerre of Ayrshire, Henry Ker of Edinburghshire, and Nicol Kerre of Peeblesshire, also signed the *Ragman Roll*. Wylliam Kerr appears on an inquest of the lands of Lady Elena la Zuche, in Conynham, Ayrshire, in 1296.

The Kers of Cessford and Ferniehurst descended from a family long in possession of Auldtounburn, Roxburghshire. John Ker obtained a charter of all the lands and tenements of Molle and Auldtounburn, in the barony of Sprouston, resigned by John de

Copeland in 1357. He was possibly the father of Henry Ker, who was Sheriff of Roxburghshire in 1369. Robert of Auldtounburn, the next on record, received a charter of the lands of Smailholm in 1404. He had sons Richard and Andrew, successively of Auldtounburn. Andrew's son, Sir Andrew of Auldtounburn, had two sons: Sir Walter of Cessford and Thomas of Ferniehurst. From them descended the earls and marquesses of Lothian, the lords Jedburgh, earls of Ancrum and the earls and dukes of Roxburghe.

Kers and Kerrs are widespread. In 1358, Richard Kerr had a charter by William, Earl of Douglas, of the lands of Samuelston, now in East Lothian. George of Samuelston and Elizabeth Carmichael, his spouse, witnessed a deed by George, Earl of Douglas, in 1450. By the reign of James IV (1488–1513), many are recorded in the *Register of the Great Seal*. Some of those in the west country may have been vassals of the Douglases. Henry Ker of Dundaff Hill, in Stirlingshire, was escheat for a period, and James Douglas obtained a charter of the property in 1364. Many farmed in Lanarkshire, Renfrewshire and Ayrshire, and on the island of Arran. The Kers of Kersland, seem to stem from Robert Ker, who embraced the Reformation in 1560. He left three daughters, the eldest of whom, Janet, married (as his second wife) Capt. Thomas Crawford of Jordanhill, descended from the Crawfords of Kilbirnie. Their son, Daniel, assumed the name and arms of Kersland. John Ker of Kersland became bankrupt in 1726, and the estate was sold by the creditors to William Scott of Bavelaw. Much research on those western families was done by Dr William Hogarth Kerr, who became a physician at Swansea, Wales, in 1919. He was the eldest son of Rev. Robert Kerr, 1857–1939, UF Church minister at Kirkmuirhill, Lanarkshire. Many Kerrs from Arran emigrated to New Brunswick, Canada between 1829 and 1842.

KER, DUKES OF ROXBURGH
Sir Robert Ker, created 1st Earl of Roxburghe in 1600, was son of William Ker of Cessford and Caverton, Warden of the Middle March, by his wife, Janet, daughter of Sir James Douglas of Drumlanrig. His sister Elizabeth married in 1601, Sir James Bellenden, knight, of Broughton, and had a son, William, created 1st Lord Bellenden in 1661, with destination to the heirs male of his body; but he resigned his peerage and obtained a re-grant, confirmed in 1673, in favour of his cousin, John Ker, second son of the 2nd Earl of Roxburghe, who succeeded as 2nd Lord Bellenden. Jean Ker, sister of William, Master of Roxburghe who died in his father's lifetime, married

John Drummond, Earl of Perth. Their eldest son, James, continued the Perth (and Melford) line, and their fourth son William succeeded as 2nd Earl of Roxburghe, assuming the name and arms of Ker. He fulfilled the stipulation of a deed of nomination, drawn up in 1648, and married ca. 1655 (delayed because of her tender years), his cousin Jean, eldest daughter of Harry, Lord Ker, youngest son of the 1st Earl by a second wife.

The 2nd Earl had two sons: Robert, 3rd Earl; and John, who succeeded to the Lordship of Bellenden in 1671, and continued that family. The 3rd Earl was drowned in 1682, when the ship *Gloucester*, carrying the Duke of York and some other noblemen, was wrecked off Yarmouth. By his Countess, Margaret Hay, daughter of the 1st Marquess of Tweeddale, he had three sons: Robert, 4th Earl; John, 1st Duke; and Lt. Gen. William, soldier and politician. The 4th Earl died unmarried and the honours devolved on his brother John, created 1st Duke of Roxburghe in 1707. His only son, Robert, 2nd Duke, in the lifetime of his father was created a peer of Great Britain by the title of Baron Ker of Wakefield. His elder son, John, 3rd Duke, was a celebrated book collector, and died unmarried in 1804, when the honours devolved on his kinsman, John, 7th Earl of Bellenden, 1728–1805. When he died there was a long contest for the succession between: Maj. Gen. Walter Ker, heir male of the 1st Earl; William Drummond, descended from Sir John Drummond of Logiealmond, as heir male of the 2nd Earl; and Sir James Innes, 3rd Baronet of Innes, who married Margaret, daughter of Harry, Lord Ker, only son of the 1st Earl by his second marriage with Jean, daughter of Patrick, Lord Drummond. The House of Lords Committee of Privileges decided in favour of the latter in 1812.

Sir James Innes, 1736–1823, the 25th feudal baron of Innes, sold his ancestral estates in 1767, and served in the 88th and 58th Regiments. He married first, in 1769, Mary, daughter of Sir John Wray of Glentworth, Baronet, and Frances, heiress of Fairfax Norcliffe of Langton, Yorkshire, and assumed the surname of Norcliffe. She died without issue, and he married in 1807, Harriet, daughter of Benjamin Charlewood of Windlesham, Surrey. They had an only son, James Henry Robert, who succeeded as 6th Duke of Roxburghe, and assumed the surname of Innes-Ker. (See also the article INNES.) The 7th Duke, named after his father, married in 1847, Lady Anne Emily Spencer-Churchill, daughter of John Winston, 7th Duke of Marlborough. She was Lady of the Bedchamber and Mistress of the Robes to Queen Victoria. The present and 10th Duke is Guy David Innes-Ker, also 11th Baronet of Innes. His son and heir is Lord George Alastair, Marquess of Bowmont and Cessford.

KERR, MARQUESS OF LOTHIAN Mark Ker or
Kerr, created 1st Earl of Roxburghe in 1600, was descended from Andrew Ker of Auldtounburn and Cessford, who died in 1444. Andrew's eldest son, Walter, was the father of Sir Robert of Cessford, who died in his father's lifetime, ca. 1500, leaving two sons: Andrew of Cessford, and George, from whom descended Sir Walter Ker of Fawdonside, who became heir male of Cessford, but resigned his rights in 1664. His line is extinct. Andrew of Cessford survived the Battle of Flodden, 1513, and was knighted. He married Margaret Crichton and had three sons: Sir Walter of Cessford; Mark, Commendator of Newbattle, father of the 1st Earl; and Andrew.

Mark, created 1st Earl of Lothian in 1606, was an Extraordinary Lord of Session, 1589, and had charters of the lands of Newbattle and Prestongrange, erected into the Barony of Newbattle in 1591. He married Margaret Maxwell, daughter of Lord Herries, and Scotstarvet alleges she caused her husband's death by witchcraft in 1609. Witch or not, she bore him three sons and five daughters. Robert, the eldest son, succeeded as 2nd Earl, and married in 1611, Annabella, daughter of Archibald, Earl of Argyll. They had a daughter Anne, who married in 1630, her kinsman, Sir William Kerr of Ancrum. Her father took his own life in 1624, and she was not allowed the earldom, but her husband, having redeemed Newbattle and other lands, was created Earl of Lothian and Lord Ker of Newbattle (of the second creation), in 1631. He was descended from Robert Kerr of Ancrum and Woodhead, third son of Sir Andrew Kerr of Ferniehurst. Sir Andrew was grandfather of Sir Thomas of Ferniehurst, father of Andrew, created 1st Lord Jedburgh, 1621/22, and Robert (Carr), created Earl of Somerset in 1613. William Kerr, son of Robert of Ancrum and Woodhead, had by his wife, Margaret Dundas, a son Sir Robert, created Earl of Ancrum in 1701, and he had two sons, William, created Earl of Lothian, as above; and Charles, 2nd Earl of Ancrum, who died without issue, when his title devolved on his nephew of the half blood, Robert Kerr, created Marquess of Lothian, with subsidiary titles, in 1701. William Henry, his grandson, 4th Marquess, fought at Fontenoy and in 1745 commanded the cavalry on the left wing of the Royal army at Culloden.

Schomberg Henry, 9th Marquess, and Keeper of the Privy Seal, married in 1865, Lady Victoria, eldest daughter of the 5th Duke of Buccleuch, and died in 1900. He was a director of the Lothian Coal Company, which had several pits around Newtongrange and Roslin. His general manager was James A. Hood, 1859–1941, but it was Mungo Mackay, the engineer and agent at Newtongrange who sunk the Lady Victoria Pit at Newtongrange, 1890–94, named after the wife and one of the daughters of the 9th Marquess. Mungo ruled the mining communities with a rod of iron, and his story has been told in Ian MacDougall's book, *Mungo Mackay and the Green Table* (Tuckwell Press, 1995). The Lady Victoria Pit was the jewel of the Scottish Coalfield, but it closed in 1981, and is now a fascinating mining museum.

Robert, 10th Marquess, died unmarried in 1930, and was succeeded by his kinsman, Peter Francis Walter Kerr, born 1922. His heir is the Rt. Hon. Michael Andrew Foster Jude Kerr, PC, MP. He represented Berwickshire and East Lothian as Michael Ancrum in 1974, and Edinburgh South, 1979–87, and since 1992 has sat in the House of Commons for Devizes, Wiltshire.

KIRKPATRICK Everyone conversant with Scottish History will be familiar with the stabbing at the altar of the Greyfriars Church of Dumfries, of Red John Comyn by Robert the Bruce, in 1306. This incident, mentioned in Barbour's *Bruce*, brought swift excommunication. An old tradition says that when he left the chapel, Bruce exclaimed, 'I doubt I have slain the Comyn', and a loyal supporter replied: 'You doubt? Then I'll mak siccar', and rushed into the building and stabbed the unconscious Comyn to death. Someone did 'mak siccar', and the story goes that it was Sir Roger Kirkpatrick of Closeburn. The crest of the family shows a bloody dagger, and the motto: *I MAKE SURE*. It is worth noting, however, that the seal of a later Sir Roger Kirkpatrick in 1498, is like the shield of today, but the crest was then a swan neck and head.

Ivo or Ivone, the earliest certain ancestor of the Kirkpatricks, witnessed a charter before 1141. The family settled at Closeburn, Dumfries, on lands adjoining a chapel dedicated to St Patrick: *Cell Patricii*, hence the surname Kirkpatrick. Stephen, grandson of Ivone, is styled in a deed of 1278, 'Stephanus Dominus Village de Closeburne, filius et heres Domini Ade de Kirkpatrick'. Sir Thomas, his son, died without male issue, and was succeeded by his nephew, Winfred, whose elder son, Sir Thomas, had a new charter of the lands of Bridburgh and Closeburn in 1409. Roger, his brother, succeeded, and was the father of Thomas, his heir, and Alexander of Carmichael, ancestor of the Kirkpatricks of Conheath, and of branches of the family in Kildare and Antrim, Ulster. Thomas was knighted, and he married Maria, daughter of the 1st Lord Maxwell. His grandson, Thomas, died soon after the Battle of Solway Moss, 1542, and was succeeded by his cousin Roger, whose great-grandson, Robert Kilpatrick of Closeburn, by his wife Grizel Baillie, was the father of Thomas, created a Baronet of NS in 1685. The 10th Baronet, Sir James Alexander Kirkpatrick served in the RAF in World War II, and was mentioned in despatches. His son, Sir Ivone, 11th and present Baronet, lives in Adelaide, South Australia.

That grand lady, the Empress Eugenia, 1826–1920, was of Scottish extraction. Her grandfather, William, second surviving son of William Kirkpatrick of Conheath and Mary Wilson, became American Consul at Malaga, in Spain. He married Dona Francisca Marie, daughter of Baron de Grevignees, with issue, Maria Manuella, Carlota Catalina, and Henriquita. The eldest married Don Cipriano Palofoj, Count of Teba, later Montigo, and had two daughters, Maria Francisca and Eugenie Maria de Guzman. Maria Francisca married James Francis Raphael Stuart Fitz James, Duke of Alba and Xerica; and Eugenie married at Notre Dame in 1853, the French Emperor, Charles Louis Bonaparte, King of Holland. She was a great beauty, with auburn hair, fair complexion and blue eyes. Her upbringing was cosmopolitan. The Empress visited Scotland in 1860, calling upon the Duchess of Hamilton and the Duke of Atholl. At Edinburgh and Glasgow she was welcomed enthusiastically, and when at Dumfries was presented with a genealogical chart of the Kirkpatricks. Her only son, Napolean, 1856–79, Prince Imperial, was killed in Zululand.

Herbert James Kirkpatrick, 1910–77, son of Maj. Gen. Charles Kirkpatrick of Larchwood, Pitlochry and Elsie Isobel Fasson, had a conspicuous career in the RAF, rising to the rank of Air Vice-Marshall. In World War II he was twice mentioned in despatches and awarded the DFC. He was made CBE in 1945 and CB in 1957.

KNOX　John Knox, 1505–07, the priest who brought about the Reformation in Scotland, has stamped his name indelibly on the Scottish nation. The story is forcibly told in his *History of the Reformation in Scotland*, first published in 1573. He was born near Haddington, probably son of William Knox, a small farmer, and

Marion Sinclair. William may have been descended from the old family of Knox of Ranfurly, in Renfrewshire.

The surname is mentioned in the reign (1214–49) of Alexander II, when Adam, son of Uchtred, had a grant of the lands of Knock, named after a hillock of that name (Gaelic *Cnoc*), in the Barony of Renfrew. John de Cnoc witnessed a document relating to the lands of Ingliston, in Renfrewshire, ca. 1260. In 1328, Alan de Cnoc received payment from the royal exchequer of 44s. 10d. for conveying the royal stud to the Forest of Ettrick. A family named Knox appear in the north-east in the 15th century, and have no known connection with the Renfrewshire group. They derived their name from the Aberdeenshire place-name of Knock, and must have considered themselves chiefs of the surname as John Knox of that Ilk is mentioned in 1538. Another John Knox, 'grassman' of Knock is recorded in the *Poll Tax Record* of 1696. The Renfrewshire family must also have thought of themselves as chiefs, since Johne Knox of that Ilk is mentioned as an arbiter in a dispute between the town of Renfrew and the Abbey of Paisley in 1408. Knollis seems to be a variant surname. Sir William Knollis was Preceptor of Torphichen and Lord St John of the Knights Hospitallers before 1500.

The Earls of Ranfurly descend from Marcus Knox, merchant-burgess of Glasgow (1585), through his son Thomas, who married Elizabeth Spang. Their son Thomas, a merchant in Belfast, matriculated arms at the Lyon Office in 1693, as the male representative of the Ranfurly family. He died in 1728, leaving only two daughters, and was succeeded in his lands of Dungannon, Co. Tyrone, by his nephew Thomas, son of his brother John. Thomas married Hester Echlin, and they were the parents of Thomas Knox, who was created Baron Wells of Dungannon in 1791. His son, another Thomas, was made Baron Ranfurly in 1826, and created Earl of Ranfurly in 1831. The 7th Earl is Gerald F.N. Knox, in Nayland, Colchester, Essex. An Irish family, Knox of Palmerston, Killala, Co. Mayo, appear by their arms to be related to the Earls, but it is uncertain where they branched from the Knox family of Renfrewshire.

Jack Knox, RSA, RSW, son of Alexander Knox in Kirkintilloch (d. 1986), is a well-known artist, and has exhibited in Glasgow, Edinburgh and Aberdeen. He lectured at the Glasgow School of Art, 1981–92. Some of his work is in permanent collections. David Laidlaw Knox, a Lockerbie man, was Conservative MP for Leek, 1970–83, and has represented Staffordshire Moorlands since 1983. He was knighted in 1993. Ian Campbell Knox, a freelance writer and director, who resides in London, was educated at Anstruther and Edinburgh. He has a number of BBC credits, including *Sweet Nothings*, 1983 and *Spender*, 1991. He gained a BAFTA award for the best play, *The Privilege*, in 1983; this work also won an award at the Bilbao Festival.

LAIDLAW The name Laidlaw, or some variant of it, is thought by some to derive from an unknown place-name in southern England, but the scarcity of it there in early times makes this doubtful. Names like Laidlaw, Laidly Ludlow and Lodelaw, have appeared consistently in the eastern border counties of Scotland. An Ettrick laird, William of Lodelaw, was charged with concealing a horse from the English in 1296, and it is worth noting there is a farm called Laidlawstiel near Clovenfords. The maternal ancestors of James Hogg, 1770–1835, 'The Ettrick Shepherd', were Laidlaws. His mother, Margaret Laidlaw, was of assistance to Sir Walter Scott when he was collecting material for his *Minstrelsy of the Scottish Borders*. Her father was the far-famed sheep farmer, Will o' Phaup, who 'for feats of frolic, agility and strength, had no equal in his day'. Hogg had a relative named William Laidlaw, who is mentioned in his sketch entitled 'The Shepherd's Dog'. Robert Laidlaw, 1710–1800, tenant of Hopehouse, was probably of the same stock. Probably Walter Laidlaw in Chapelhope, with his wife Marion Linton and children John, William and Catherine, who are mentioned in 'the Brownie of Bodsbeck', were also relatives. William Laidlaw, who was the son of the farmer at Blackhouse who employed James Hogg as a shepherd for ten years, became a friend, brother poet and amanuensis of Sir Walter Scott. James Cameron Laidlaw, born at Ecclefechan in 1937, is Emeritus Professor of French, University of Aberdeen, and has lectured in England, Ireland and New Zealand. Irving Laidlaw, a Monaco based multi-millionaire, was born at Keith, Banffshire, in 1943, and has been a benefactor of the Conservative Party of Great Britain.

LAMONT The Lamonts or Lamonds derive their name from Laumon or Ladman, a chief who was living in the Cowal district of Argyll in the second half of the 13th century. He was a grandson of Ferchar (from whom the Macerchars were named), who descended from Anrothan, son of Aodh O'Neill, King of Northern Ireland, 1030–33. Between 1230 and 1246, Duncan, son of Ferchar, and his nephew, Laumon, son of Malcolm, gave the monks of Paisley lands at Kilmun, and the patronage of the church of St Finan (Kilfinan).

The grants were confirmed by Engus, son of Duncan, and Malcolm (died before 1295), son and heir of Lauman. The name Lauman is probably derived from the Norse *Logamor*, 'lawman', and may indicate his maternal descent.

The Lamonts became powerful, and their chiefs were called 'the great Mac Lamonts of Cowal'. Their territory stretched from the Dunbartonshire border to Loch Fyne, and probably included some islands. Malcolm, son of Lauman, married Christian, daughter of Alexander of Ergadia, only to learn she was within the fourth degree of consanguinity and, in 1290, they obtained a dispensation. From the 13th to the 17th century, the chiefs lived at Toward Castle. In 1446, the Campbells ravaged the district, causing much loss of life, and the chiefs moved to Ardlamont. Around 1463 the lands of the chief fell to the Crown by non-entry, and the Lamonts of Inveryne held sway. John Lamond, Sheriff-Depute of Argyll, had a dispute with the monks of Paisley in 1466, over the patronage of the kirk of St Finan, and it was resolved on production of the old charters. He had confirmation of Ardlamont in 1472, when his wife was 'Donaldis doc(h)ter'.

Sir John Lamont of that ilk married Jean, daughter of Archibald, Earl of Argyll. In the 1587 'Roll of Landlords and Bailies' where broken men dwelt, appears James Lamont of Inveryne. Sir James Lamont sat in Parliament, 1639–40, as one of the Commissioners for Argyll. He established a parochial school at Toward in 1646. Not long after this, Campbell cadets in Cowal ravaged his lands, and 'most barbarously, cruelly and inhumanly murdered several young and old, yea, and suckling children, some of them not one month old'. Furthermore, they carried people from Toward and Escog to Dunoon and hung 'near the number of thirty'. The atrocities formed one of the charges against the 9th Earl of Argyll, as chief, although he was not personally involved.

From 1685 to 1686, Archibald Lamont of Invernye was MP for Argyll. He married Margaret Henry, but left no issue, and when he died in 1697 was succeeded by Dugal Lamont of Stilaig, the heir male. His daughter Margaret married another cadet, John Lamont of Kilfinan, and their son Archibald succeeded to the estates, now smaller because of depredations by the Campbells. His descendant, Archibald James Lamont, 1818–62, married Adelaide Dawson, with issue, a daughter Adelaide. He married next, Harriet, daughter of Col. Alexander Campbell of Possil. Their elder son, John Henry Lamont, sold Ardlamont in 1894. He was awarded the chiefly arms as heir of line, and was allowed supporters in 1909. On his death the chiefship passed to the Monnydrain branch of the family, of whom Ronald Coll Lamont, 24th chief, died in Australia. Following resignations by his daughter Marian and her cousin, Keith John Lamont, the chiefship was awarded in 1953 to their cousin, Alfred Grenville Lamont, residing in Australia. The present chief is Peter, son of the late Noel Brian Lamont, residing in New South Wales.

LANDSBOROUGH The surname Landsborough or

Landsburgh is not ancient, but several bearers of it have distinguished themselves. The nearest reference to the name occurs in 1703, when Samuel McClamroh was at the University of Glasgow, appearing as McLanburgh, and this may be a transitional stage. The original name was in fact McClamroch, and was prevalent in the south-west, especially in the Glenkens district of Kirkcudbrightshire. Variants are MacClameroch (1455), McClanrouth (1500), McClameract (1530), McGlainroch (1637), McKlamroch and even Mackclamyaugh (1684), McClamro (1703), and Maclamrock (1747). The correct rendering is MacLamroch, 'son of the ruddy (or bloody) handed'. As so often happened in Galloway, the 'c' in Mac was capitalised and attached to the suffix, while Mac was shortened to Mc. In a marriage contract of 1750, the laird of Stranfasket signed himself as 'John McClambroch', and his son signed as 'Alexr. McClamroch'. The meaning of the name is supported by the fact that the family crest was a hand couped, holding a bloody dagger. The MacClamrochs of Stranfasket and the collateral line of Craigenbay were vassals of the Viscounts Kenmure.

It has been stated that the reason for the change to Landsburgh by the brothers and kin of Alexander MacClamroch was because he contracted debts through horseracing and other habits, and lost Stransfasket to John Newall younger of Barskeoch, about 1759. Alexander borrowed heavily, and even owed the Kirk-Session of Kells money. Moreover, he married in 1750, Margaret, daughter of Robert McMillan of Nether Holm, and uplifted her dowry of £100 Sterling in 1753, although she died in December, 1751, probably in childbirth. It would seem as if his brothers and sisters were attempting to distance themselves from him, but it was probably their father's bond in their favour of 6th August, 1751, which finally ruined him.

Descendants of Alexander's brothers, Andrew and John, are of interest. Andrew's sons moved to Otley, Yorkshire, and founded families there. One member, Andrew, born in 1822, emigrated to Ohio, later to Iowa, USA. John, a weaver, had a son, David Landsborough, 1775–1854, who became minister of Stevenson parish, Ayrshire and, after 1843, pastor of a Free Kirk congregation at Saltcoats. He was an accomplished naturalist: author of *Natural History of Arran*, and other works. Three of his sons emigrated to Australia and one of them, William, 1825–86, explored in Queensland. He also crossed Australia from the Gulf of Carpentaria to Melbourne in 1862. William became a member of the Upper House of Legislature in Queensland in 1864, and was Government resident in Burke District, 1865–69. He received a gold watch from the Royal Geographical Society, a service of plate from inhabitants of NSW and £2000 from the Legislature of Queensland. Many places in Australia have been named after William: as 'Landsborough Town', Victoria; 'Landsborough County', NSW; and 'Landsborough River', Westland, South Island, NZ. He died on his estate, 'Lochlamborough', near Brisbane. William's youngest brother, Rev. David Landsborough, 1826–1912, was minister of Henderson Free Church, Kilmarnock, and also a fine naturalist. His son, another David, was a medical missionary in Formosa.

Robert McClamroch, who emigrated to Virginia ca. 1755, may have belonged to the Craigenbay line of the family. He was the ancestor of James G.W. MacLamroc, of Greensboro, NC, an eminent lawyer and family historian.

LAW The meaning is usually 'hill' or 'summit', but in some cases the surname is a diminutive of Lawrence, and in others may be a variant of Low, on record in 1331. Those considerations account for the fact that the surname is of comparatively late origin. It was quite common in Glasgow in the 16th century. In 1428 Robert de Law had a safe conduct through England on his return from Spain, and James of Law was an accuser at a court in Prestwick in 1488. Rev. James Law, minister at Kirkliston, 1585–1610, was rebuked by the Synod for playing football on the Lord's Day, but became Bishop of Orkney in 1605 and Archbishop of Glasgow in 1615. William Law of Waterfitt was admitted burgess of Glasgow, *gratis*, in 1632. John Law, 1671–1729, of Lauriston, Cramond, a financier and speculator, became Comptroller-General for France. A grandnephew, Gen. James A.B. Law, 1768–1828, was a favourite aide-de-camp of Napoleon I, and was created Compte de Lauriston. The British Prime minister (1922–23), Andrew Bonar Law, 1858–1923, was born in New Brunswick, Canada, but brought up by his mother's relations in Glasgow, where he attended the High School. He was elected Conservative MP for Blackfriars, Glasgow, and was Opposition leader in 1911. He partnered Lloyd George in conducting the war in Europe, and in 1922 he gained the highest office. The strain of the war years probably contributed to his died in office.

LEARMONTH An old surname in the Merse, deriving the name from lands so-called in Berwickshire. Variants include Learmont, Learmond and Leirmonth. William de Learmonth was a juror in an inquest held at Swinton in 1408. Andrea de Lermwth appears in Edinburgh, 1413. Alexander Leremonthe was clerk of works of the town and castle of Berwick in 1434. George Learmonth in Edinburgh was admitted guildbrother there in 1538 in right of his wife Jonet, daughter of the deceased Robert Henrisone. The master of the household to King James V, was Sir James Learmonth of Dairsie Castle, who was provost of St Andrews in 1546. A number of Lermonts are listed as tenants of the Abbey of Kelso in 1567. The Russian poet, Michael Lermontoff, was descended from a Scot who was a mercenary in the Polish army. Other Lermontoffs in Russia are probably of Scottish extraction. Learmonth Gardens, Grove, Terrace and Place, Edinburgh, are named after John Learmonth of Dean, died 1856, who was Lord Provost (1831–33), and a partner of the firm of John Learmonth, Junr. & Co., coachbuilders. Sir James Learmonth, 1895–1967, born at Girthon, Kirkcudbrightshire, graduated as a physician at Glasgow, and became a Fellow of the Royal College of Surgeons of Edinburgh in 1928. He was awarded various other distinctions, including being made a Chevalier of the Legion of Honour, in France. Dr Learmonth attended King George V during his last illness, and was appointed surgeon to Queen Elizabeth.

LEITH Those who first bore the surname of Leith were of Flemish extraction, probably from Boulogne, and were possibly of the same ancestry as the Setons and Bethunes. The surname comes from the port of Leith, so closely connected with Boulogne as to share the arms of the cathedral there. They may have landed in Leith, but soon moved to Aberdeenshire, near the Leslies, who also came from Flanders.

The first Leith of note was William of Barns, Provost of Aberdeen, 1351–53 and 1373–74, who held the lands of

Caprinton. He represented the town in Parliament, 1357 and 1367, and was sometime Collector of Customs. To achieve such positions his family must have been well established in the burgh. William Leith is said to have married Christian, (?natural) daughter of Donald, Earl of Mar, but, although just possible, it seems unlikely as Donald died in 1332. However, the cross-crosslet in the Leith arms does lend support to a marriage with the Mar family and, in 1359, William Leith received a charter of Rothens, Harebogge and Blackboggis, from Thomas, Earl of Mar.

Laurence of Barns, son of William, had a charter of the lands of Caprinton in 1388, and was an alderman of Aberdeen in 1401. His brother John, armiger, was an ambassador to England, 1412–16, and had a charter of Ruthrieston. The descendants of a later William Leith, who died in 1480, are usually styled 'of Barns'. Laurence Leith of Barns, son of William, had sons: Norman of Barns; Gilbert, alive in 1505; and John, ancestor of the Leiths of Overbarns of Overhall. Henry Leith, VIth of Barns, who died before 1499, had by his wife Eliza Gordon, George of Barns; William of Edingariok, who succeeded his nephew John of Barns; and Patrick of Harthill, whose son Patrick sold Edingariock. His brother Laurence held Kirkton of Raine, sold by his son, John, who purchased New Leslie and Peill, where a new house was built by his son James, called Leith Hall, and this became the chief seat of the family. From him descended the later Leiths of Leith Hall, and the Leiths of Freeland. John, XXIInd representative of the family, was succeeded by his brother, Gen. Alexander Leith, who married in 1784, Mary, eldest daughter of Charles Forbes of Ballogie. He was succeeded by his son Andrew, who assumed the name of Leith-Hay, borne by later lairds. General Alexander's second son, John James, was the father of Alexander, created Baron Fyvie in 1905. His grandson, Sir Andrew George Forbes-Leith, 3rd Baronet lives at Dunachton, Kingussie.

From the Leith family of Harthill descended Alexander Leith of Freefield, who married Martha, daughter of John Ross of Arnage. Their son John Ross, 1777–1839, WS, was heir to his aunt, Christian Ross of Arnage, and assumed the surname of Leith-Ross. He married Elizabeth, daughter of William Young of Sheddocksley, Provost of Aberdeen. From Alexander Leith of Freefield, his half-brother, descended the later Lords Burgh, in the peerage of England, whose arms are quartered with those of Leith.

Ronald Leith, the talented organist and campanologist of St Nicholas Church, Aberdeen, is a pillar of the Aberdeen & North-

East Scotland Family History Society. As manager of their Family History Centre at 164 King Street, Aberdeen, he has done much to encourage the publication of genealogical material by the Society, and to enlarge their library.

LESLIE It was appropriate that in 1993, the anniversary of the death of the saintly Queen Margaret of Scotland, a useful history of the Leslies, by Alexander Leslie Klieforth, should appear. Titled *Gripfast: The Leslies in History* (Phillimore: Chichester), it is the best account of the family since 1869. Their ancestor, Bartolf the Fleming, came to England in the retinue of Edward the Exile, who died soon after his return in 1057, and then to Scotland with Edward's daughter, Princess Margaret, and her brother Edgar. She married Malcolm *Canmore*, King of Scots. Bartolph witnessed charters concerning the lands of Voormezele, in Flanders. His son Malcolm was Constable at Inverurie, and his grandson Norman assumed the surname of Leslie, from Lesslyn, in the Garioch, where the family raised a motte. The ruined castle and title of baron was purchased in 1979 by David C. Leslie, an architect and burgess of Aberdeen, who has tastefully restored the building. Until recently, when the castle was advertised for sale, he and his wife Lesley Margaret (Stuart), utilised it as a private hotel.

About 1458 George Leslie was elevated to the dignity of Earl of Rothes. His grandson, George, 2nd Earl, succeeded, and in 1490 was infeft in the barony of Ballenbriech and other lands. The Leslies obtained the lands of Balmuto, and gave their name to a Fife town and parish. William, 3rd Earl, perished at Flodden in 1513. The 6th Earl, John, signed the National Covenant in 1638. His son, John, 7th Earl, was imprisoned as a Royalist during the Commonwealth period, but obtained a new charter of his honours in 1663. In 1680 he became a duke. As he died without male issue, only the earldom passed to his daughter Margaret, who married Thomas, Earl of Haddington. Their eldest son became Earl of Rothes, and their second son Earl of Haddington. John, 10th Earl of Rothes, died without issue, and the title passed to his sister Jane, 1750–1810, who married George Raymond Evelyn Glanville. Their son George succeeded as 11th Earl. The 21st Earl is Ian Lionel Malcolm Leslie, who is chief of the clan and resides at West Tytherley, in Wiltshire.

Sir Alexander Leslie, a famous general during the Civil War, was created Earl of Leven in 1641. His title is now united with that of Melville, and the family muniments are in the National Archives. Ronald, 11th Earl of Leven and 10th of Melville, succeeded his half-brother Alexander in 1889. Alexander Robert Leslie Melville, 14th Earl of Leven and 13th of Melville, is chairman of the board of governors of Gordonstoun School, and resides at Glenferness House, Nairn. Two sons of Patrick Leslie of Pitcarlie and Lady Jean Stewart were raised to the peerage in the 17th century. The elder, Patrick, was created Baron Lindores, but this title has been dormant since 1775. His brother, General David Leslie, served in the German Wars under King Gustav Adolph of Sweden, and returned to Scotland when the Civil War broke out. He commanded the Scots cavalry at Marston Moor in 1644, when the Royalists were defeated. In 1661 he was created Lord Newark. This title has been extinct since 1694. Another notable branch of the family are the Leslies of Balquhain, Aberdeenshire, with their important offshoot, the Leslies of Wardis, whose baronetcy (NS, 1625), is dormant. The heir presumptive is Percy Theodore Leslie, residing at Kingston Hill, in Surrey. The Leslie Baronets of Glaslough, Ireland, descend from the Wardis family.

LINDSAY The Scottish House of Lindsay, of which the Earl of Crawford and Lindsay is chief, was founded early in the 12th century by Sir Walter de Lindsay, who accompanied Prince David (later King David I) when he took possession of the Principality of Cumbria. He was one of the advisers at an inquisition of the See of Glasgow, ca. 1120. This knight was of Flemish extraction: a descendant of the Count of Alost. Some believe the surname to have come from De Limesay, Pays de Caus, near Pavilly, which would indicate a Norman connection. Others say the name comes from Lindsey, in Lincolnshire.

Sir David Lindsay of Glenesk, born 1359, succeeded to the Lordship of Lindsay and Barony of Crawford on the death of his cousin James, and in 1398 was created Earl of Crawford. David Lindsay of Edzell succeeded as 9th Earl on the death of his namesake, the 8th Earl, through the exclusion of his son Alexander, the 'Wicked Master', in 1542, but re-conveyed the earldom to the son of the latter, David, 10th Earl. David of Edzell's second son by Catherine Campbell was John, founder of the Balcarres line of the family. He was a statesman during the reign of King James VI, and on his appointment to the Court of Session took the judicial title of Lord Menmuir. David, second son of Lord Menmuir, who had bought the lands of Balcarres and Pitcarthy, in Fife, was created Lord Lindsay of Balcarres in 1633. His son Alexander was created Lord Lindsay of Balneil and Earl of Balcarres in 1651. Alexander, his great-grandson, became the 6th Earl of Balcarres, and was always known by that dignity, but became *de jure* Earl of Crawford in 1808. Succeeding Earls of Crawford and Balcarres have played important roles in national history. The 28th Earl of Crawford and 11th of Balcarres, David Alexander Robert Lindsay, was a trustee of the Tate Gallery, 1932–37, and of the National Gallery for several terms. He became a trustee of the British Museum in 1940 and of the National Library of Scotland in 1944. He was senior Vice-President of the Scottish Genealogy Society from 1953 until his death in 1975. Many honours were bestowed upon him. The present holder of the titles is Robert Alexander Lindsay, who was chairman of the Board of the National Library, 1990–99.

One of the most famous names in Scottish History is that of Sir David Lyndsay, ca. 1485–1555, of the Mount, Lord Lyon King of Arms from 1542 to 1555, and previously Lyon Depute. His *Satyre of the Thrie Estaitis* is still performed on stage. His nephew, Sir David Lyndsay of the Mount, also held the office of Lord Lyon, as did this man's son-in-law, Sir Jerome Lindsay of Annatland. Sir Jerome had a daughter Rachel, who married in 1640, Capt. Bernard Lindsay, of Leith. Their eldest son Robert was progenitor of Lindsays in Virginia and North Carolina.

There are many branches of the family and some two hundred spellings of the name, eighty-four of which are given in Lord Lindsay's admirable *Family of Lindsay* (1840). The Lindsays of Dowhill, Kinross, descend from Sir William Lindsay of Rossie, half-brother of the 1st Earl of Crawford. Sir Martin Alexander Lindsay, 1905–81, 22nd of Dowhill, was created a Baronet in 1962. His son, Sir Ronald Alexander Lindsay, 2nd Baronet, lives at Reigate, Surrey. Dr John Maurice Lindsay, born 1918, and residing at Milton, Dumbarton, is a prolific journalist, author and poet. Some McLintocks ('sons of Findan's gillie'), from around Lorne and Luss, are said to have Englished their name to Lindsay.

LIVINGSTON Leving or Leuing, ancestor of the Lowland Livingstons, came to Scotland from Hungary in the retinue of the Saxon Princess Margaret, in 1057. Like others who came to Scotland at that time, they seem to have been briefly in Flanders awaiting a ship. Leving appears to have some relationship with the East Flanders family of Gavere, closely allied to Count Lambert of Lens. The arms borne by Leving's descendants are blazoned: Argent, three gillyflowers (carnations) Gules, within a double treasure flory-counter-flory, Vert, the very device in that unusual green tincture of the family of Gavere.

The descent from Leving to Sir Andrew Livingston, Sheriff of Lanark, and ancestor of the Earls of Linlithgow, is nebulous. Levin's son, Thurston, had sons Alexander and William. About 1200, one William de Levystone witnessed a charter by Malcolm, Earl of Lennox, and in the *Ragman Roll*, 1296, appear Andrew de Levingston, Lanarkshire; Sir Archibald de Levingston, Edinburghshire, and Master Archibald de Levingston, chevalier. Their designations imply relationships, and there can be no doubt the place-name Levingestun (Livingston in West Lothian), derives from Leving. William of Gorgyn (Gorgie), a descendant, held the lands of Levingestun before 1328. His son William married Christian, heiress of Patrick de Callander, on whose forfeiture he had a charter of the barony of Callander, in Stirlingshire. William was one of the commissioners appointed to treat with the English for the release of David II in 1357, and his son Patrick was one of the hostages for the ransom.

Sir John Livingston, IIIrd of Callander, who was killed at Homildon Hill in 1402, left a son and heir, Alexander, and was also ancestor of the Livingstons of Kinnaird, Westquarter and Barnton. Alexander's grandson, James of Callander, was created Lord Livingston of Callander in 1455. Alexander, 5th Lord Livingston, accompanied Queen Mary to France in 1548, and his daughter Mary became one of the Queen's 'Four Maries'. His son, William, 6th Lord, entertained the Queen at Callander House in 1565 and again in 1567. The 7th Lord, Alexander, was high in favour and was created Earl of Linlithgow in 1601. His second son, Alexander, succeeded, and James, the third son, a distinguished soldier, was created Earl of Callander in 1641. The 4th Earl of Callander, James, succeeded as 4th Earl of Linlithgow in 1695, but becoming involved in the Jacobite rising of 1715, had his estates and honours forfeited. The Kilsyth branch, created Viscounts, 1661, suffered the same fate. The Kinnaird line, created Viscounts Newburgh in 1647, ended in an heiress. The Livingstons of Dunipace and of Teviot are presumed extinct.

The people who have been termed the 'Highland Livingstones' have a very different origin. A member of this group is called in Gaelic, Mac-an-Leigh ('son of the physician'). From this we have the surname Macleay. The Macleays of the north-west are thought to be descended from *Ferchar Leighiche*, who held land in Appin in 1386. He was of the famous MacBeths, physicians to the Lords of the Isles. The Mac-an-Leighs of Appin, followers of the Stewarts of that place, Anglicised their names as Livingstone: the most famous of them was

Blantyre born David Livingstone, 1813–73, the missionary and African traveller. This family received in early times a grant of lands in Lismore, which they held as keepers of the bishop's crozier.

LOCKHART Many Lockharts have been conspicuous in Scottish affairs. Forenames and surnames of Lockharts survive in the place-names Stevenson, Simonston (Symington) and Craiglockhart. Originally *Locard* or *Lockard*, the name is of Teutonic origin and appeared in Scotland about the middle of the 12th century. Eventually they owned several estates. Sir Simon Lockhard of Lee accompanied Sir James Douglas on his expedition with the heart of Robert the Bruce to the Holy Land. Sir James was killed in a conflict with the Moors in Spain, in 1333. Ever since the Lockharts have borne on their arms a heart and a padlock, and for a time they spelled the name Lockheart. Sir Simon went to the Holy Land as a soldier of the cross, and brought back the celebrated 'Lee Penny', upon which Sir Walter Scott founded his novel, *The Talisman*. Sir William Lockhart of Lee, 1621–175, a notable military man, held a commission in the Royalist Army, and fought bravely at Worcester in 1651. Sir George Lockhart of Carnwath, 1673–1732, a well-known lawyer and author of *Memoirs of Scotland*, was killed in a duel. John Gibson Lockhart, 1793–1854, an eminent critic and novelist, married Sophia, elder daughter of Sir Walter Scott, whose biography he wrote. In 1957 the Lord Lyon recognised Angus Hew Lockhart 'of the Lee' as chief of the surname.

LOGAN There are several places named Logan in Scotland, but Dr George F. Black, in his *Surnames of Scotland*, was of the opinion that the surname came from Logan, in Ayrshire. The derivation is probably from the Gaelic *lagan*, meaning 'little hollow'. The Logan Water in Ayrshire prompted the poet Burns to write *Logan Braes* in 1793. Robert Logan appears as a witness in Roxburghshire in 1204, and in 1226 Adam de Logan witnessed a charter of land in Gowrie. Wautier Logan in Lanarkshire swore fealty to Edward I of England in 1296. John de Logan held the lands of Grugar, in Ayrshire, in 1304. A charter of John Logan to William Douglas of Kingscavil, of lands at West Linton, was inspected in 1340. Logans held lands in Angus for generations. The bones of Robert Logan of Restalrig, Edinburgh, who died in 1606, were exhumed in 1609 and exhibited in court, when sentence of forfeiture was pronounced against him, thus depriving his family of Fast Castle and other lands. Logie and Loggie are probably variant surnames.

LUMSDEN The surname Lumsden or Lumsdaine derives from a place-name in Coldingham parish, Berwickshire. The earliest reference to the name is ca. 1170, when Gillem and Cren de Lumisden witnessed a charter by Waldeve of Dunbar. Adam and Roger Lummesdene rendered homage to Edward I in 1296. A branch of the family settled in Fife before 1350, and obtained lands in Aberdeenshire. John Lumsden of Ardhuncar owned the lands of Towie-Clatt, and died before 1740. A son of the same name was killed at Culloden in 1746. The Clova line ended with an heiress, Catherine, who married in 1754, John Leith. From them descended the Leith-Lumsdens. John Lumisden, eldest son of Rev. Andrew Lumisden or Lumsden, minister of Duddingston, Edinburgh, 1681–91, consecrated a bishop of the non-jurors in 1727, married Catherine Craig, and their eldest son, John, featured in the Jacobite honours in 1740, when King James III and VIII, created him a knight and baronet. He married Mary, Dowager-Viscountess of Kenmure (having been tutor to her son), widow of William Gordon, 6th Viscount Kenmure, who was executed on Tower Hill in 1716. John Lumsden died in France, without issue, in 1716. His cousin Andrew Lumsden was also a Jacobite, attainted in 1746. He became assistant secretary to James III and VIII in 1751, and was sole secretary, 1751–63. He was, moreover, secretary to Charles III (Charles Edward Stuart), 1766–68, and died at Edinburgh. In 1985, Patrick Gillem Sandys Lumsden, then of Innergellie, Kilrenny parish, Fife, was recognised by the Lord Lyon as chief of the name and arms.

MACALISTER/ALEXANDER Under their own patronymic, Clan Alister of Kintyre are the senior cadet branch of Clan Donald. They descend from Alasdair (or Alexander) *Mor*, younger son of Donald of Islay, and grandson of Somerled. They were given lands in Kintyre, and after Alasdair was killed by his cousin, Alasdair MacDougal, in 1299, they cultivated the friendship of their kinsmen, the MacDonalds, and the Campbells. This allowed them to survive in Kintyre. Alasdair's descendant, Charles, son of Ean-Dubh, was appointed Steward of Kintyre in 1481. Angus Vic Ean-Dhu McAlister of the Loup, Loch Tarbert is on record as chief in 1515. His son, Alasdair was forfeited for abiding from 'the raid of Solway', but had a remission in 1550. The MacAlisters supported Clan Donald in their feud with the MacLeans, and in 1591 Gorrie

MacEachinne Vic Alester Vic ean-Dubh, received a charter of the lands of Loup and others from the Earl of Argyll. His son Alasdair was a Jacobite and fought at Killiecrankie under Viscount Dundee. He afterwards served with the Royal army in Ireland against William of Orange. He married Jane, daughter of Sir James Campbell of Auchinbreck, Baronet. Among their family were Hector and Charles, successively lairds of Loup, and Duncan, whose son, Gen. Robert MacAlister commanded the Scots Brigade in Holland. In 1792, Charles MacAlister of Loup married Janet, heiress of Somerville of Kennox, and moved to Ayrshire. Their grandson, Charles Somerville McAlester, was awarded arms in 1846 as chief of the clan. His son, Charles Godfrey Somerville MacAlester of Loup and Kennox, barrister-at-law (Inner Temple, 1892), died without issue in 1931, and his nephew of the same name, son of William, succeeded.

The MacAlisters of Glenbarr, Argyll, an old cadet branch, descend from John MacAlister of Ardnakill, who married Flora, daughter of Lachlan MacNeill of Tearfergus. Their son Ranald married in 1742, Anne, daughter of Alexander MacDonald of Kingsburgh, and had seven sons. The youngest, Col. Matthew MacAlister, 1758–1824, fought against Hyder Ali and was imprisoned at Seringapatam for nearly four years. He was the first MacAlister of Glenbarr. By his second wife, Charlotte Brodie, he had a son Keith, father of Matthew, IIIrd of Glenbarr. By his second wife, Edith Dudgeon, Matthew had a son Ranald MacDonald Brodie MacAlister of Glenbarr and Clachaig. The MacAlister-Hall family of Torrisdale, Carradale, Argyll, descend from William Hall, 1785–1865, of Dalintober, Campbeltown, who married Grace, daughter of Peter MacAlister. Their grandson, Major William Hall of Torrisdale, served with distinction in the South African War, 1900–01, and in World War I. He matriculated arms in 1895, and assumed the additional surname of MacAlister. His son, Donald Stuart MacAlister-Hall of Torrisdale, married in 1939, Caroline Mary Begg, and their eldest son, Donald, was born in 1940.

The Alexanders who settled in Clackmannanshire in the 16th century, claimed descent from Clan Alister. The Alexanders of Menstrie became Viscounts in 1630, and Earls of Stirling from 1633 to 1739; also Viscounts Canada. Sir William Alexander, the 1st Earl, a poet and courtier, was granted lands comprising modern Nova Scotia and New Brunswick. This historic deed is in the Sigmund Samuel Canadiana building of the Royal Ontario Museum, in Toronto. He was instrumental in founding the Order of Baronets of NS. At Menstrie Castle there is a commemoration room, one wall of which is adorned with the arms of 107 Baronets of NS, grouped round a portrait of Charles I.

MACALPINE The MacAlpins are said to descend from Alpin, King of Dalriada, whose son Kenneth united the Scots and Picts in 1843. Alpin's Queen may have been a Pictish princess. Along with several other families termed the *Siol Ailpin*, there is scant evidence of an autonomous clan. John MacAlpyne witnessed a charter by Malise, Earl of Strathearn, ca. 1260, and in 1271 Monach filius Alpine witnessed a charter by Bricius de Ardrossane to Insula Missarum (Inchaffrey). He also witnessed a charter by Thomas of Munimuske, ca. 1285, and several Atholl charters between 1284 and 1290. He is probably Monaghe fiz Alpyn of Perthshire, who appended his seal to the *Ragman Roll* in 1296. Duncan Alpynsone of Augh(in)tulos, of Dunbrettan, also attached his seal. Sir John Macalpyn was escheat for his part in the rebellion of the deceased James Stewart, youngest son of the Regent Albany. Down through the years MacAlpins/MacAlpines have played significant parts in the affairs of the kingdom, none more so than the family of Robert MacAlpine of Newarthill, Lanarkshire, in the latter part of the 19th century, and in the present century. His son Robert, 1847–1934, founded the large civil engineering firm of Sir Robert MacAlpine & Sons. He was created a Baronet in 1918, and left a large family. Sir Robert, the 2nd Baronet, did not long survive his father, and was succeeded as 3rd Baronet by his son, Alfred Robert, who died unmarried His title then passed to his cousin, Sir Thomas McAlpine, 1901–83, 4th Baronet, who was succeeded by his brother, Robert Edwin McAlpine, created Baron Moffat of Medmenham, Buckinghamshire, in 1980. His son, Hon. William Hepburn McAlpine, 6th Baronet, lives in London. Baron Moffat's second son, Robert Alister McAlpine, was created a Life Peer in 1984.

MACARTHUR For long it was argued that the MacArthur Campbells of Strachur were not only of the same stock as the House of Argyll, but represented the senior line of the family. A number of early Campbells certainly bore the forename of Arthur, and there can be no doubt they were of the same stock. Their claim to chiefship, however, has long been abandoned. They migrated from the district of Lennox, part of the old kingdom of Strathclyde, into Argyll. The late Sir Iain Moncreiffe suggested they came of mixed British-Dalrriadic dynastic stock, but their close relationship to the Campbells points to descent from the Baldwins, Counts of Flanders. The House of Argyll descended from Gilleasbuig (Archibald), who held the lands of Menstrie and Sauchie, in Stirlingshire, in 1263, whose offspring obtained the lands of Loch Awe, in Argyll. Duncan Dhu, probably his brother, was the father of Arthur, from whom the MacArthurs of Innestrynich, on the horses of Loch Awe, took their name. The Campbells of Strachur were known as MacArthur Campbells to distinguish them from the descendants of Gilleasbuig and from their kinsmen at Innestrynich, but are usually named as Campbells in historical documents. There seems originally to have also been some link with the MacAulays of Ardincaple, in Dunbartonshire.

Arthur Campbell, progenitor of the Strachur line, swore fealty to Edward I of England in 1296 but, like other Scottish lairds, afterwards espoused the cause of Robert the Bruce. He probably fought at Bannockburn in 1314 along with the followers of his kinsman, Sir Neil Campbell of Lochawe. Arthur was made constable of Dunstaffnage Castle, with Mains thereof, and Bruce also granted him the lands of Torinturke and others in Lorne, also Kinlochlyon and Auchingewall, for the service of a galley of twenty oars. The MacArthur Campbells had a long association with Strachur and came to be represented by Ian Niall MacArthur Campbell, XXIVth of Strachur, residing at Newtonlees, Kelso.

John MacArthur of Innestrynich, contempory with Arthur MacArthur Campbell of Stracchur, fell victim to a campaign by King James I to rid the Highlands of chiefs considered too powerful. The historian Tytler calls him 'a potent chief', and he is said to have been the leader of 1000 men. In 1427 his lands were forfeited and he was beheaded. Duncan Makarthure de Turrywadiche, witness to a charter in 1529, received a charter to him, his spouse Janet Campbell and son John of the two-merk land of Auchencrywe, in the barony of Phantilands, from Malcolm, son of Eugene Makcorquidill, in 1542. Nigel MacArthur, notary public, witnessed a charter of lands in Roseneath, in 1558, and a few clergymen were probably of *Clann-Artair-na-tir-a-cladich ile* – 'of the shoreland' – but when their chief lost his lands most clansmen became rentallers. It has been suggested that the chiefship passed to MacArthurs of Proag, Islay, some of whose ancestors were armourers to the MacDonalds of Islay. One family of MacArthurs were hereditary pipers to the MacDonalds of Sleat. Charles MacArthur, piper to Sir Alexander MacDonald, perfected his piping under Patrick Og MacCrimmon. His brother Neil was the father of John MacArthur, grocer-burgess of Edinburgh who became piper to the Highland Society of Scotland, founded in 1784, and he died in 1792. There was another MacArthur family at Kilmuir, Skye, one of whom was an excellent piper.

Arthur MacArthur, who emigrated from Glasgow to Massachusetts in 1825, was the father of Arthur MacArthur, 1845–1912, a soldier who attained the rank of Lt. General. His son, Gen. Douglas MacArthur, 1880–1964, commanded the US forces in the Far East in World War II, and occupied Japan.

MACAULAY Curiously, there were two MacAulay clans: one at Ardencaple, in Dunbartonshire, and the other in Lewis and Harris. The Ardencaple family may have derived their name from *Amhalgadh*, meaning in Irish Gaelic 'Aulay'. Sir Aulay MacAulay of Ardencaple, a vassal of the Earl of Lennox, appears in a roll of landlords and bailies in 1587. The MacAualy lands passed to the Duke of Argyll in 1767. The MacAulays of the Western Isles derived the name from *MacAmhlaidh*, a Gaelic form of the Norse *Olafr*, and may have been related to a group at Lochbroom. The Hebridean MacAulays may all have come from a common ancestor, Donald *Cam*, grandfather of Rev. Aulay MacAulay of Harris, from whom sprang a talented family, many of whom were clergymen. His son Rev. John, 1720–89, minister successively at South Uist, Lismore and Appin, Glenaray, and Cardross, had by his second wife, Isobel MacNeill, a large family, of whom Lt. Gen. Colin, 1760–1836, fought at Seringapatam. Another son, Zachary, was the father of Thomas Babington MacAulay, 1800–59, the eminent Anglo-Scottish historian, created Baron MacAulay of Rothley, Leicester. An ex-RAF Squadron Leader, Iain MacAulay, has been recognised as commander of the clan, and hopes to be elected chief.

MACBAIN/MACBEAN Those were probably separate surnames at an early period – MacBain (McBane etc.) being *Mac a' Ghilliebhain*, 'son of the fair servant', and MacBean being *Macbheathan*, 'son of Beathan' (see also the article BEATON/BETHUNE) – but have become so confused as to be treated alike, including variants such as MacBane. Ferquhard McBane took part in the second depredation of Petty in 1513. According to tradition, a father and four sons came from Lochaber, and settled in the Inverness-shire parish of Petty, placing themselves under the protection of Mackintosh. They became loyal supporters of the Clan Chattan federation. A number of them were killed at the Battle of Harlaw in 1411, when Mackintosh attempted to gain his rights to the Earldom of Ross. Duncan mc behan in Dunmaglass was bailie to James Stewart, Earl of Moray, in 1539. Alexander McBen in Balquhidder was accused of theft in 1621. In a sasine of 1650, John McBean, alias McAngus vic Phaill vic William appeared, and from this patronymic we can identify William McGillies McFaill of the Clan Chattan bond of union, 1543. The MacBeans of Kinchyle took prominent parts in the history of Clan Chattan, although at one period they acknowledged Cameron of Lochiel as their chief. The MacBeans of Tomatin were successful East India merchants. The first of Faillie was Donald mac Gilliphadrick, who held his lands from the Earl of Moray in 1632. The lands were sold to MacGillivray of Dunmaglass in 1771. Farquhar McBean alias McCoilbea, leased the 'half-auchten' part of Leald in 1725. The MacBeans in Alvie parish may have been distantly related to the MacBeths. Most MacBeans were Jacobites, and because Gillies MacBean of Kinchyle was a major in the Mackintosh batallion, he could raise one hundred followers. At Culloden in 1746, this gigantic Highlander was beset by a party of government troops, and with his back to a wall defended himself with his targe and claymore cutting down thirteen of them, although severely wounded. An officer, observing his heroism, ordered his men to spare the brave man, but he was too late. The following are lines from Logan's work, *The Gael*:

> With thy back to the wall, and thy breast to the targe,
> Full flashed thy claymore in the face of their charge;
> The blood of the boldest that barren turf stain,
> But alas! thine is reddest there, Gillies MacBane!

The Gaelic scholar, Dr Alexander MacBain, 1855–1907, of Inverness, compiled *An Etymological Gaelic Dictionary* (1895), and among other literary work is his revised edition of William Forbes Skene's *Highlanders of Scotland* (1902), originally published in two volumes in 1836.

MacCALLUM It is generally agreed that the original homeland of the MacCallums was the district of Lorn, in Argyll. Their early history is not well documented, but the main line of the family came to be represented by Donald McGillespie vich O'Challum, who had a charter of Poltalloch, in Kilmartin parish, from Duncan Campbell of Duntrune in 1562. Archibald MacCallum, VIIIth laird, died without issue in 1758, and was succeeded by his brother, Alexander of Glennan, who, apparently for aesthetic reasons, preferred Malcolm as a surname. It is usually thought of as an Englishing of Calum or Callum, but in fact derives from the Gaelic *Maolcolum*, or 'devotee of St. Columba'. John Wingfield Malcolm, XVth of Poltalloch, was created Baron of that place in 1896. Lt. Col. George Ian Malcolm, XIIIth of Poltalloch, was a man of wide interests, including farming and breeding of pure bred Arabs. He died in 1976, and was succeeded by his heir, Robin Neill Lochnell Malcolm, residing at Duntrune Castle, Lochgilphead.

MaCCRIMMON There is scarcely a family of the Western Isles that has aroused so much controversy as the MacCrimmons. They may have been in Harris and Skye from the early years of the MacLeods, and were one of the lesser families on their lands. Dr George F. Black derives their name from Old Norse: *Hromund (Hro(p)mundr)*, 'famed protector'. The eponymous ancestor is given as Finlay *a breachan*, 'Finlay of the plaid'. It cannot be said that the next few generations are well documented, but it seems likely they were pipers to the MacLeod chiefs.

Donald Mor MacCrimmon, ca. 1570–1640, was piper to Sir Roderick MacLeod of Dunvegan, famed as Rory *Mor*. He is said to have gone on a course to Ireland and listened in secret to all the students, so that when he returned to Skye he was highly skilled, and is credited with having developed the advanced piping called *piobareachd*. Donald went again to Ireland to join Hugh O'Donell in the uprising, and composed a lament for the death of the Earl of Antrim. His son Patrick *Mor*, and his grandson, Patrick *Og*, composed many pipe tunes, and improved others. The sons of Patrick *Og* – Malcolm, ca. 1690–1769, and Donald Ban, ca. 1710–46 – were both pipers, sometime in Harris, and the latter was sometime piper to a MacLeod Independent Company, raised to keep the peace in the Highlands. Malcolm's sons, Iain *Dubh*, 1731–1832, and Donald *Ruadh*, 1742–1845, were also fine pipers. Iain *Dubh* MacCrimmon witnessed the decline of piping caused by the Jacobite Rising of 1745, and perhaps annoyed with a chief in need of cash, he decided to emigrate, but could not leave his native land. Donald *Ruadh*, his young brother, went to America, and had a colourful military career for which there is ample evidence.

The MacLeods of Harris and Dunvegan fostered piping, and there are many proofs in their accounts. In 1706 it is on record that Patrick *Og* MacCrimmon was paid 228 merks, and in 1711 there is an entry for 'two pypes brought to MacCrimmon, MacLeod's principal pyper'. Patrick Morrison, merchant, was paid for 'livery cloths to MacCrimmon' in 1714. According to tradition, a MacCrimmon college of piping was established as far back as the time of Alastair *Crotach* MacLeod, who died ca. 1547. The whole concept of a MacCrimmon college was censured in 1980 by Alastair K. Campsie in his book, *The MacCrimmon Legend*, but it certainly existed: perhaps not always at Boreraig. While Campsie has credited Dr Samuel Johnson, who visited Dunvegan in 1773, with 'acuity', he skips smartly over the great man's words: 'There has been in Skye beyond all time of memory a college of pipers, under the direction of MacCrimmon, which is not quite extinct'. His comments on what he calls the 'alleged' indenture by which Simon, Lord Lovat, sent a piper, David Fraser, to be 'perfected' under Malcolm MacGrimon in 1743, shows his ignorance of documents of this kind. He stated that the authenticity of it was 'conjectural', but the manuscript was unearthed at the Scottish Record Office in 1981, and certified as genuine by archivists. Despite Campsie's nit-picking, it does prove the existence of a college.

Lt., later Capt. Donald *Ruadh* MacCrimmon and his sons Patrick and Donald, are well documented. Donald emigrated to Ontario, Canada, ca. 1820, and his descendant, Malcolm Roderick MacCrimmon, an expert piper in Alberta was in 1941 made hereditary piper by Dame Flora MacLeod, 1878–1976. He has passed on the tradition to his son, Iain Norman, born 1952, who lives at Monifeith, in Angus. Initially taught at Edmonton by Harry Lunan, he now plays for the City of Dundee Pipe Band, and also composes. Who said *MacCrimmon no More*? A genealogical account of the family appears in *Notes & Queries* of the Society of West Highland and Islands Historical Research, 1995.

MacDONALD OF MacDONALD

MacDONALD OF MacDONALD Clan Donald is the largest of Highland clans and has played a conspicuous part in Scottish history. The old seanachies proclaimed descent from Conn of the Hundred Battles, who flourished in Ireland ca. AD 125, and from *Colla Uais*, a Celtic prince with influence in the Western Isles before the establishment of the Scots kingdom of Dalriada, ca. 503, by Fergus mac Erc. There is more support for descent from Angus, a brother of Fergus, who founded a dynasty in Argyll called the *Cinel Aonghais*, credited with intermarriage with the Pictish royal house.

The clan of Angus were driven out of Islay (to which island they later returned) by the Vikings ca. 850, and settled beside kinfolk in Argyll. By the 1100s the Scots were resisting the Norseman, and eventually the mighty Somerled drove them from the mainland. A son of Gillebride, who may have had some Norse blood, he also – perhaps to end feuds with the Norse kings of Man and the Isles – married Ragnhild, a natural daughter of Olaf of Man. At times, Somerled, aided by his brother-in-law, Malcolm McHeth, came into conflict with the Scottish monarchs. In 1164 he invaded Renfrew, and was killed there: some say assassinated by a page. His mainland possessions were divided among his sons: Reginald of Islay and Kintyre; Dougal of Mull and Lorn, progenitor of Clan MacDougal; and Angus of Arran and Bute. There were some natural sons. Reginald's son Donald was the name father of *Clann Domhnuill*, and was 'Regulus' of Argyll and the Isles. Donald in the Gaelic tongue is a combination of two words: *Domh*, 'house', and *Nuall*, 'noble', signifying 'Noble House', an apt description for the clan which ruled in Islay and the Isles for nearly 500 years. Reginald's great-grandson, 'Good' John of Islay, ruled as Lord of the Isles for half a century, and was confirmed in his mainland possessions. He married first Amie MacRuaridh, from whom descended the MacDonalds of Clanranald and Glengarry; and secondly, Lady Margaret, daughter of Robert the Steward, who, after becoming King Robert II in 1380, induced him to settle the Lordship on a son of this union, Donald *Og*, who also laid claim to the Earldom of Ross.

Under the Lords of the Isles evolved a remarkable culture. They had a 'parliament' or council, which met at Finlaggan, in Islay. Alexander, Lord of the Isles, was made Earl of Ross, but the inbuilt power of the Lords was seen as a threat to the monarchy, and his son John was forfeited in 1493. After the fall of the Lordship, the representation passed to the Glengarry line of the family, who favoured the spelling MacDonell: more in line with Gaelic phonetics. Some writers maintain that the Dunyveg line should have succeeded; others that the Clanranald lairds were heirs of line. Aneas, IXth of Glengarry, a Royalist, became Lord MacDonell and Aros at the Restoration in 1660. At his death in 1680, Glengarry passed to his cousin, Reginald of Scotus, and the high chiefship to the Sleat line, descended from Hugh, son of Alexander, Lord of the Isles, probably by a daughter of Patrick O' Beolan. The Sleat chieftains were Baronets of NS (1625), and in 1776 the 9th Baronet was created Baron MacDonald in the peerage of Ireland. Ronald

Archibald, 1853–1947, 6th Baron, succeeded as chief of the name of MacDonald and (until 1910) chief of Sleat. His grandson, Alexander Godfrey, 7th Baron, was recognised as chief of the clan in 1947 and officially restored to the ancient arms. His son, Lord Godrey, 8th and present Baron, resides at Kinloch Lodge, Isle of Skye, and much of the old family territory is owned by the Clan Donald Lands Trust. The old MacDonald home at Armadale, designed by James Gillespie Graham, 1777–1855, was badly damaged by fire, but part of it was restored as an excellent Clan Centre.

MacDONALD OF THE ISLES

The MacDonalds of Sleat, who style themselves 'of the Isles', descend from the same ancestor as the clan chief, Lord MacDonald. Their history requires explanation. The lairds of Sleat, in Skye, were held to have been chiefs from the latter part of the 17th century, and premier Baronets of NS from 1625. The story of the division into two families begins with Sir Alexander MacDonald, 9th Baronet, who was elevated to the peerage of Ireland as Baron MacDonald of Slate, in Antrim. He married in 1768, Elizabeth, eldest daughter, and in her issue co-heir of Godfrey Boswell of Gunthwaite, Yorkshire, by his wife Diana, daughter of Sir William Wentworth, Baronet. They had, with other issue, Alexander Wentworth, 10th Baronet and 2nd Lord MacDonald, who died unmarried, and his brother, Godfrey, 11th Baronet and 3rd Lord MacDonald of Slate, who succeeded his brother in 1824.

Sir Godfrey, on the death of his maternal uncle, William Bosville of Thorpe and Gunthwaite, succeeded to these estates for life, and assumed the name Bosville. On the death of his brother he assumed the name MacDonald after that of Bosville, and succeeded as 11th Baronet and as the Irish Baron. He married apparently by declaration in Scotland, Louisa Marie la Coast, natural daughter of the Duke of Gloucester and Lady Almerie Carpenter, daughter of the Earl of Tyrconnel. They had three children – Alexander, William and Louisa – before their marriage at Norwich in 1803, and had ten other children, including Godfrey William Wentworth. Under Scottish law the first three children were legitimised in view of the subsequent marriage of their parents. Alexander (William Robert), *de jure* 12th Baronet, entered into possession of the Yorkshire lands, but did not assume any title. The father sought to separate the Skye and Yorkshire inheritances. This would make Alexander owner of the Yorkshire estates, with the arms of Bosville, and

Godfrey William Wentworth proprietor of the Skye lands, with the territorial barony, the Irish peerage and chiefship of the clan. A special act of Parliament was passed in 1847 to regulate the position.

Although the squires of Thorpe, father and son Godfrey, did not assume any title, when the grandson, Alexander Wentworth Bosville MacDonald, petitioned the Scottish Court of Session in 1910, they were found to be *de jure* 12th and 13th Baronets. Alexander thus became the 14th Baronet, and 22nd chief of Sleat. He and his children all assumed the designation of 'MacDonald of the Isles'. This has been criticised, since younger children do not normally use the chief designation. The present Sleat chief is Sir Iain Godfrey Bosville MacDonald, 17th Baronet, who lives at Rudston, in Yorkshire.

MacDONALD OF CLANRANALD

The Clanranald line of the MacDonalds looms large in the history of the West Highlands and Islands. Like the MacDonells of Glengarry, they descend from John, Lord of the Isles, and his first wife, Amie MacRuaridh. Ronald, the eldest surviving son, from whom the generic appellation arose, was the father of Allan of Garmoran, who left at least three sons. Roderick, the eldest by his first wife, Margaret, daughter or grandaughter of Donald *Balloch*, progenitor of the MacDonalds of Dunyveg, died in 1481, and was succeeded by Allan (numbered 8th of Clanranald by the clan genealogists). Allan married Florence, daughter of Alexander MacDonald of Ardnamurchan, and had two sons. Ronald Bane and Alexander. Ronald had charters of lands in Uist, Eigg and Arisaig. His son Dugal was murdered and left issue but was succeeded by his uncle, Alexander, styled 'Captain of Clanranald' in 1498. His son, John or Ian of Moidart, legitimated in 1530, became 8th chief. He was imprisoned in Edinburgh Castle in 1540, and at that time Hugh Fraser, 3rd Lord Lovat, invaded Moidart and installed his uncle (of the half-blood), Donald *Gallda* MacDonald, in Castle Tirim, situated on a prominence in Loch Moidart. John escaped, and aided by the Camerons, defeated and killed Donald *Gallda* at Loch Lochy in 1544.

By his first marriage to Margaret, daughter of MacDonald of Ardnamurchan, John left a son, Allan, 9th of Clanranald. He married secondly a daughter of Angus MacDonald of Knoydart, and had with other issue a son John, from whom descended John MacDonald of Glenaladale, who led colonists to Prince Edward

Island, Canada, in 1771. Allan married (?Flora) daughter of Alastair MacLeod of MacLeod, and had five sons. From Ranald, fifth son, came the MacDonalds of Belfinlay, Balivanich and Boisdale. Flora MacDonald, 1722–90, the heroine of the '45 Jacobite Rising, was a daughter of Ranald of Balivanich and his second wife, Marion MacDonald, of the Griminish family. Allan was succeeded by his third son, Angus, whose issue failed, and his brother Donald became 11th of Clanranald and Moidart. He was knighted in 1617, and succeeded by his son John, a Royalist, who married Sarah, daughter of Sir Rory *Mor* MacLeod of Dunvegan. Her dowry was a fully equipped galley of twenty-four oars and one hundred and eighty head of cattle.

The Clanranald family were involved in the '15 and '45 Jacobite Risings, and Allan, 14th chief, was killed at Sheriffmuir in 1715. His cousin Donald, 16th laird, had fought under Dundee at Killiecrankie in 1689. Donald, his son, took no active part in the '45, but it was in Clanranald country that the Young Pretender landed in 1745. Ranald, 18th chief, gave a bond which enabled Prince Charles to leave Edinburgh, although it seriously impaired the family fortunes. He fought in the '45 and later in the American Revolutionary War. Under his son John, over three hundred people emigrated from the impoverished Clanranald estates to Prince Edward Island in 1790. Ranald, 20th of Clanranald, was forced to sell his estates between 1813 and 1830. Although the family believed they were heirs of line of the Lords of the Isles, he matriculated arms in 1810 as chief of Clanranald. The 23rd chief, Angus MacDonald, died in 1944, as was succeeded by his kinsman, Ranald Alexander, who also matriculated arms in 1956. He is a company director and a former chairman of the Clan Donald Lands Trust. Ranald married in 1961, Jane Campbell-Davys, and has issue. The old home of the Clanranalds was Arisaig House, in Lochaber. Ranald resides in Selkirk.

MacDONELL OF GLENGARRY

MacDONELL OF GLENGARRY The MacDonells of Glengarry and the MacDonalds of Clanranald descend from John, Lord of the Isles (d. ca. 1387), and his first wife and cousin, Amie MacRuaridh. Ranald, their second son, from whom Clanranald is named, had several sons, including Allan of Garmoran, from whom descended the chiefs of Clanranald; and Donald, Steward of Lochaber, progenitor of the MacDonnells of Glengarry. A dispute over precedency long agitated the two houses. Donald died in 1420, having had at least three sons; John, who left no issue or was passed over in the succession; Alexander, who held lands in Morar and Glengarry, and died in 1460; and Angus. John, son of Alexander, held Glengarry, and was succeeded by his son Alexander, styled in 1501 Alastyr MacEean vic Allyster. He married Margaret, daughter to Sir Alexander MacDonald of Lochalsh, included with him in a charter of Glengarry and Morar, with parts of Lochalsh, Lochcarron and Lochbroom (including Strome Castle), in 1538/39. They had five sons and were succeeded by Angus, laird of Glengarry, numbered 7th in the clan genealogies.

Donald, 8th of Glengarry, obtained a charter of Glengarry in 1627, incorporating the lands into a free barony. Relations with the collateral line improved after his marriage to a MacDonald of Clanranald. Their son, Aneas or Angus, a Royalist, who adhered to Montrose throughout his campaign, was created a peer at the Restoration in 1660, by the title of Lord MacDonnell and Aros. He married Margaret, daughter of Sir Donald MacDonald of Sleat, 1st Baronet. In 1672, the Privy Council charged him to find caution according to the laws, for 'the whole name and clan'. When he died in 1680, Glengarry passed to his cousin Reginald or Ranald McDonell of Scotus, and the representation became vested in the Sleat line. The peerage became extinct.

Ranald, 10th of Glengarry, was succeeded by his son Alastair, a Jacobite who carried the Royal Stuart standard at Killiecrankie, and was attainted by the government in 1690, but managed to retain his estates. He fought again at Sheriffmuir in 1715, and was again attainted in 1716; in recognition of his great services, the exiled King James VIII and III, created him a peer in 1716, as Lord MacDonell. His son John, and grandson Alastair, were confined in the Tower of London. The latter died unmarried in 1761, and was succeeded by his nephew, Duncan, 4th baron, and 14th of Glengarry. His son Alastair raised a regiment in 1794, by which time he was chief. He treated the men shabbily when they were discharged in 1802, and many of them emigrated to Glengarry County, Ontario. A Glengarry Regiment, founded there, distinguished themselves in the War of 1812. Alastair attempted to live in the grand style of his ancestors, and his character is drawn as 'Fergus McIvor' in Scott's *Waverley*. He matriculated arms in 1777, and the following year killed Lt. MacLeod, of the Black Watch, in a duel. However, he was pardoned and in 1802 married Rebecca, daughter of Sir William Forbes of Pitsligo. His son Aneas succeeded him in 1828, and in 1840 was forced to sell and ancestral lands and emigrate to Australia. Only Knoydart remained, and after his death in 1852 his widow, Josephine Bennett, and the other trustees evicted the tenants. Knoydart was later sold to a family of Bairds. The 22nd chief (and 12th titular Lord MacDonell) was A/Cdre Donald MacDonell, 1913–99, who served in the RAF and Fleet Air Arm, and became an industrialist. He retired to Fortrose. His eldest son, Aneas Ranald Euan MacDonell, who lives in London, is the present chief.

MacDONELL OF KEPPOCH Another branch of the MacDonalds which favoured the spelling MacDonell, descended from Alastair, third son of John, Lord of the Isles (d. ca. 1837), by his second wife, Lady Margaret, daughter of Robert the Bruce, and held the lands of Keppoch, in Kintail. He fought at Harlaw in 1411 and at Inverlochy in 1431. From him descended Alastair MacDonell, 10th of Keppoch, who assisted Sir James MacDonald in escaping from Edinburgh Castle in 1615. The family were devoted to the Stuarts, and the 16th chief, Alastair, was created a knight and Baronet by James VIII and III in 1743. He was killed at Culloden in 1746. Angus MacDonell, 20th chief, resided at Keppoch, which had been sold to the Mackintoshes, and d. in 1838. Donald Nicholas, 21st chief (and titular 6th Bt.), spent several years in Ceylon and Australia. On his death in 1889 the baronetcy became dormant. His youngest sister, Claire, the clan bardess, came to represent the family.

MacDOUGALL The MacDougalls of MacDougall and Dunollie descend from Somerled, 'regulus' of the Isles: progenitor also of the MacDonalds. His son Dugall (or Dougall) was ruler of the south isles, having been given Argyll and Lorn, with some of the adjacent islands. His chief fortresses were Dunstaffnage and Dunollie, still the family residence. Parts of their territory were held under the kings of Norway. Dugall, name-father of the clan, had three sons – Duncan, Gillespic and Dugall – who, along with King Haakon, attacked Bute, which had fallen into Scottish hands. At this time the Norwegian king was still prepared to intervene in the islands. Around 1249, Dugall's son Duncan had a temporary commission from Haakon to govern all the islands from Man to Lewis. All the Western Isles were ceded to Scotland in 1266. Duncan was the first to assume the surname of MacDugall (MacDougall). Alastair, his son, attended a council at Perth in 1284 as a baron of the realm. When Argyll was made a sheriffdom in 1292, he was appointed sheriff.

In favourable circumstances, Robert the Bruce, crowned king in 1306, could expect support from Gaeldom, but his slaying of John Comyn altered matters. Comyn's kinsman, Alastair MacDugall, defeated him at *Dal-Righ* the same year. It was on this occasion that John of Lorn, son of Alastair, in attempting to seize the king, grasped and held the celebrated reliquary brooch, still in existence. Bruce confronted the clan again in 1308, and obtained the submission of Alastair. It was untrustworthy, as his son John adhered to Edward of England. Bruce, better organised, broke the power of the MacDugalls at Brander Pass in 1309. The Campbells, not then a power in Argyll, received part of their estates, and Sir Neil Campbell was permitted to marry the king's sister, Mary. However, the MacDugalls made a pact with their kinsmen, the MacDonalds, in 1354, and re-entered Gaelic society. Their position was strengthened by Robert the Steward, before becoming king, and some of their lands were restored. Ewen, 6th chief, married Joanna, daughter of Sir Thomas Isane by the Princess Mathilda, daughter of Robert the Bruce, but died without issue.

John, son of Allan, succeeded his cousin, and in 1451 the Stewart Lord of Lorn granted him lands near Oban, down the coast to Loch Melfort. By the 16th century the chiefs were acknowledging Campbell of Argyll as their superior. After the execution of Archibald Campbell in 1685, it seemed as if the MacDugalls would recover their old territory, but the Campbells rose to power again. James VII, however, gave the chief a charter of part of Lorn. John MacDugall of that Ilk fought at Sheriffmuir in 1715, and was forfeited. As a prisoner, he just escaped transportation, and the estates were restored to his son Alexander who, wisely heeding the advice of John, Duke of Argyll, kept out of the Jacobite Rising of 1745.

MacDougall became the favoured spelling, and the chiefs came to serve in the British armed forces. Sir John MacDougall, 1789–1865, served in the Royal Navy and rose to the rank of Vice-Admiral. His heir, Capt. Alexander, served in the Royal Artillery, and another son, Charles, was in the Navy. Captain Alexander's heir, Lt. Col. Charles MacDougall, served in the Bengal Staff Corps. Alexander James, 29th chief, served in the Royal Army Medical Corps in World War I. He was succeeded by his daughter, Madam Coline, 1904–84, who married in 1949, Leslie Graham Thomson, RSA, 1896–1974. The present chief is her niece Morag, who married in 1966, Richard Morley, MICE.

MACDUFF　The early members of Clan MacDuff are literally seen through the mists of time. Although indistinct, the vital thread links us with Aedh or Ethelred, a son of Malcolm III and Queen Margaret. He was born ca. 1170 and debarred from the throne either through infirmity or as an abbot. Clergymen could marry in those days and his wife was a granddaughter of Queen Gruoch (the Lady MacBeth of Shakespeare), herself the heiress of line of King Dubh or Duff, killed in 967. Aedh was Earl of Fife, and among his children was probably a son Dubh or Duff, who died in his father's lifetime, leaving two sons: Constantine, 2nd Earl, who died ca. 1129, and Gillemichael MacDuff, 3rd Earl, who did not long survive him. Gillemichael had two sons: Duncan, 4th Earl, and Hugh, whose son Michael was ancestor of the Wemyss family (still representers). Hugh may also have been ancestor of the Duffs of Banffshire.

Duncan, who died in 1154, was made hereditary Earl by David I, in return for military service. The position of the earls as magnates of the important province of Fife, and their privileges later enshrined in the 'Law of Clan MacDuff', all reflected compensation for exclusion from kingship. The 'Law' gave them the honour of enthroning kings at their coronations; leading the vanguard in battle, and remission for homicide, with sanctuary at 'MacDuff's Cross', Duncan was succeeded by his son Duncan, father of Malcolm, 6th Earl, who was succeeded by his nephew Malcolm, 7th Earl, who married Helen, daughter of Llewwllyn, Prince of Wales, with issue two sons, Colban, 8th Earl, and MacDuff of Reres. Colban had a son Duncan and also a daughter Isabella, who, extending the 'Law of Clan MacDuff', crowned Robert the Bruce in 1306. Duncan, son of Colban, had a son Duncan, 1285–1353, who was followed by his daughter Isabella, Countess of Fife. When she died childless ca. 1398, the earldom passed by an entail made by her father, to Robert Stewart, Earl of Menteith. His third son, Robert, succeeded, but as he was forfeited, the earldom was annexed to the Crown.

The genealogy of the Duffs becomes reliable after a grant to David Duff of the lands of Muldavit and Baldavy, in Banffshire, in the reign of Robert III (1390–1406). After the direct line of Craighead-Muldavit expired, Alexander Duff of Keithmore's son Alexander assumed the chiefship. He had three sons: Alexander of Braco, who died in 1718 without male issue; William of Dipple; and Patrick, from whom descended the Duffs of Hatton and Fetteresso. William of Dipple, a wealthy landowner, was succeeded by his son William, who was created Baron Braco of Kilbryde in 1735, also Viscount MacDuff and Earl of Fife, both in the peerage of Ireland. He erected Duff House, 1740–45. During the '45 he was on the government side. His son James, 2nd Earl Fife, was created a peer of Great Britain in 1790, as Baron Fife. He enlarged his estate and changed the town of Doune to MacDuff: procuring for it a burgh charter. He died in 1809, when the title Baron of Fife expired, and the other honours devolved on his brother. Alexander, 6th Earl, was created Duke of Fife in 1889, on his marriage to the Princess Louise, daughter of King Edward VII. All the peerages save the dukedom and the representation of Duff of Braco, became dormant in 1912. The present and 3rd Duke, James G.A.B. Carnegie, was already 11th Earl of Southesk, and has other honours. His son and heir, David Charles Carnegie, was styled Earl of MacDuff, 1961–92, but is now known as Earl of Southesk.

Other surnames associated with Clan MacDuff are Abernethy, Spens or Spence, Fife, and of course Wemyss.

MacDUFFIE/MacFIE

The ancestors of the MacDuffies probably came to Scotland as early as the 12th century. Some historians give them Norse origin, but it is almost certain they were Celts from Ireland, where variants such as MacAfee, MacHaffie and Duffy are common. They probably derived their name from *Duibhside*, who appears in the *Annals of Ulster* in 1164, as lector of Iona. Another possibility is that they descend from Murdoch, son of Ferchar, son of Cormac, Bishop of Dunkeld, ca. 1130. The clan may descend from Duffy (*Dubhsithe*, 'son of the dark spirit'), third in descent from Murdoch. At any rate the principal family settled in the Hebridean islands of Colonsay and Oransay, where a member of the family was a clergyman. Traditionally, the Augustinian priory of Oransay was founded by John, Lord of the Isles, before 1353.

No certain genealogy can be drawn before Christinus, who flourished towards the middle of the 15th century. He appears to have had three sons: Donald, Niall and Malcolm. 'Donaldi Mcduffee' appears as a charter witness in 1463, and again as 'Donaldo Christini Makduff' in 1472. His youngest brother, Malcolm, 'Lord of Dunevin', succeeded as chief, and he is named on a graveslab at Iona to his wife's brother, Ian MacIan of Ardnamurchan. Malcolm also appears as 'son of Christinus MacDuffee' on a cross at Oransay. It was possibly the MacDuffie/MacIan (MacDonald) marriage which resulted in some clansmen settling in Lochaber. The MacPhees (sometimes MacFie or MacFee), formerly MacDuffies, of Glendessary, held their lands prior to the forfeiture of the Lords of the Isles. The chiefly family of Colonsay were hereditary keepers of the records of the Lords of the Isles, but unfortunately these registers are not extant.

Murroch was the name of the McDuffie chief in 1531, and he was probably grandson of Malcolm. In 1609, Malcolm MacFie of Colonsay was one of twelve chiefs and gentlemen who met at Iona with Andrew, Bishop of the Isles, and formulated the *Statutes of Iona*. Malcolm joined Sir James MacDonald of Islay, who had escaped from prison at Edinburgh, and was one of the leaders in his rebellion. He and eighteen others were delivered by Coll Kitto MacDonald (*Colla Coitach*) to the Earl of Argyll for trial by the Privy Council. Coll, however, was charged in 1623 for the murder of Malcolm MacFie, Donald *Oig* MacFie (brother of Murdoch in Islay), Dougald McFie and others. Malcolm left a widow, Marie MacDonald, and children Donald *Oig*, Katherine and Finvola. MacFies at this time scattered to Mull, Jura, Gigha and other islands.

Subsequent chiefs were obliged to place themselves under the protection of the MacDonalds of Islay. Their ancestral lands passed to the Duke of Argyll, who exchanged Colonsay and Oransay for Crerar, in South Knapdale, with Donald MacNeill, some of whose descendants shed lustre on the islands. The names of the MacFie chiefs since 1623 appear to be Donald *Oig*, Dougald, Donald, Angus and Malcolm, 1786–1854, whose son John emigrated to Mariposa Township, Victoria County, Ontario, Canada. Many clansmen remained in Scotland, and among these were the MacFies of Dreghorn and those of Langhouse. The latter family were prominent landowners, and their cadets included the MacFies of Gogarburn and Borthwick Hall, Mid Lothian, and of Airds, Argyll.

MACEWEN The MacEwans (MacEwans, MacEuens, MacEwings, etc.) have a long history, and were associated with the district of Cowal, in Argyll. They were recognised in Gaelic as *Clann Eoghain na h-Oitrich*: the MacEwens of Otter. MacEwens appear in different parts of the country from about 1219, and the earliest chief flourished in the latter part of that century. He was succeeded by Severn of Otter, and the chief, ca. 1315, was Gillespie, ancestor of Sweine, last of the Otter family, who had a re-grant of the lands in 1432, with remainder to Archibald Campbell, Earl of Argyll. When the lands passed out of MacEwen hands, the clan scattered. Some took new names, such as MacLaren and Mac-Dougal. There was a family of MacDougalls alias MacEwens, who were seannachies to the Campbells of Argyll, but it is thought they were originally MacDougalls. John Helias Finnie MacEwen, MP for Berwick and Haddington, 1931–45, and a Parliamentary Under-Secretary of State for Scotland, 1939–40, was created Baronet of Marchmont, Berwickshire and of Bardrochat, Ayrshire, in 1933, and died in 1962. The present and 5th Baronet is Sir John Roderick Hugh MacEwen.

MACFARLANE The MacFarlanes of Arrochar, or of that Ilk, were proud of their descent from Gilchrist, a younger brother of Maldouin, Earl of Lennox, who flourished in the reign of Alexander II (1224–49), and were granted by his brother a charter of the lands of Upper Arrochar and Luss, with some islands in Loch Lomond. For centuries the lands were known as Arrochar McGilchrist. Later lairds appear to have been the male representatives of the Celtic earls of Lennox, but the title of earl was assumed by Sir John Stewart of Darnley ca. 1473, and recognised by 1488.

A fighting race, and fine archers, they fought in the War of Independence and were involved in the conflict at *Dal Righ*, near Tyndrom, in 1306, when MacDugall, Lord of Lorn, gained the celebrated brooch worn by Robert the Bruce. From Parlane, the fourth chief, the surname arose, but some members of the clan kept the surname MacGilchrist. This patronymic is now, but not always corrrectly, believed to be associated with the MacLachlans and Ogilvys.

Under Duncan MacFarlane of that Ilk, the clan suffered losses when they fought along with the MacDugalls against the Stewarts and MacLarens at Stalc, in Appin, in 1468. The clan lost its chief, Sir John, at Flodden in 1513. His son Andrew, earned the soubriquet of 'The Wizard'. He had learned many sleight of hand tricks when he visited the Continent, and these 'astonished and frightened the country people who ascribed these things to witchcraft'. Andrew is regarded as the composer of the famous clan pibroch,' Thogail nam bo theid sinn', to which words were later added to note the clan's reputation as cattle rustlers. These include the words: 'Wasps o' the west, be sparin' o' rest, when to the west fare we; That ye shall be shorn o' fleece and o' horn; 'tween this and the morn, swear we.' Those raiding exploits led to the moon being called 'MacFarlane's lantern'.

The clan fought at Glasgow Muir when their superior, the Earl of Lennox, took up arms in 1544 to oppose the Regent Arran. Hollinshed described them as 'well armed in shirts of mail, with bows and two-handed swords'. Many clansmen fought at Pinkie in 1547, where their chief, Duncan, was slain. They distinguished themselves at Langside in 1568 when they supported the Regent Moray against the Queen's party. It is said that the Regent gave them their crest, a crown, with a warrior armed with arrows, and the motto: THIS I'LL DEFEND. The armorial bearings remained unchanged until the famous clan chief and antiquary, Walter MacFarlane, re-matriculated in 1750. The war cry of the clan was 'Loch Sloy', from their rallying place, the loch of that name, opened as a reservoir by Queen Elizabeth (now the Queen Mother) in 1952.

Walter MacFarlane, 1698–1767, was an unusual chief, with antiquarian leanings. He became a competent Latinist and palaeographer, and a zealous collector of historical material, most of which is preserved in the National Library. He married in 1760, Lady Betty Erskine, some thirty-five years his junior. Walter was succeeded by his brother, Dr William, who sold the estate of Arrochar in 1784. His eldest son, John, is supposed to have been the last chief, and to have emigrated to America, but this is an error caused by a misreading of a document of that time. John seems to have died in his father's lifetime, and his son William was 22nd chief. He was succeeded by his son Walter, 1792–1830, whose son William, 24th of that Ilk, who died in 1886, without issue, was the last landless chief of the MacFarlanes. His sister, Jane Watt MacFarlane, married James Scott, an architect and builder, and the heir to the chiefship may be among their descendants.

MacGILCHRIST The surname comes from the Gaelic *MacIlleChrioste*, 'son of the servant of Christ'. Maldouen, 3rd of the Celtic earls of Lennox, gave the land of Arrochar, in Dunbartonshire, to his brother Gilchrist in the first half of the 13th century. His son Duncan MacGilchrist was ancestor of the MacFarlanes, but some descendants retained the patronymic MacGilchrist. One of the oldest charters (1243) relating to Argyll, grants to Gillascop MacGilcrist the five pennylands of Fyncharne and others. Donald MacGilchrist, *dominus de Tarbard*, granted the monks of Paisley the right to cut timber in his territory for the building and repair of their monastery. He was progenitor of the MacGilchrists of North Barr and others in the west of Scotland.

Some MacGilchrists probably settled in MacLachlan territory, and others in Perthshire and Angus. Some books on clans and tartans say they are associated with the MacLachlans and Ogilvys. Gilechreist McGilechreist and Donald McGilchreiste in Glenlyon, Perthshire, were fined in 1613 for sheltering MacGregors. Some other MacGilchrists were tenants of Campbell of Glenorchy in 1638. John MacGilchrist was clerk-depute to the Justices of the Peace for Glasgow, in 1709. In many cases the name has been shortened to Gilchrist, and that name is thought to have often been rendered into English as Christie and Christison.

MacGILLIVRAY When King Alexander II (1214–49) subdued Argyll in 1222, the forebears of the MacGillivrays were one of the principal tribes he dispersed. Some settled in Mull, and others probably in Lochaber and Morvern. By some accounts their chief, ca. 1263, was Gabra or Gillebride, who migrated into Strathnairn 'from the west', and placed himself and his followers under the protection of Farquhar, the Mackintosh chief who was killed in 1265. Thus, by Celtic law, they were indigenated into Clan Mackintosh, and subsequently, by Mackintosh inheritance, into Clan Chattan.

Duncan MacGillivray, who flourished around 1500, is considered to be the first of the family styled 'of Dunmaglass'. He appears to have been a tenant, but his followers were known as *Clann Mhic Gillebhrath*. In 1609, Farquhar of Dunmaglass was a minor, and his uncle, Duncan, along with two others, took burden 'for the haill kin and race of MacGillievray', and signed the famous Clan Chattan Bond. In 1626 Farquhar was granted a feu charter of Dunmaglass by John Campbell of Calder.

The MacGillivrays took on active part in the Jacobite Rising of 1715. The chief, Capt. Farquhar of Dunmaglass and his brother, Lt., later Capt. William, served in the Clan Chattan Regiment. The Clan Chattan and Mackintosh chief remained loyal to his Hanovarian commisson in 1745, but his wife Ann Farquharson, raised the clansmen for Prince Charles. They fought at Falkirk and at Culloden, in 1746. Alexander, the MacGillivray chief, led a fierce charge which almost overwhelmed the left wing of the Hanovarian Army. He fell near the well which still bears his name. After the '45, two important members of the chiefly line emigrated to Georgia. Lachlan MacGillivray became an Indian trader and married Sehoy, mixed race daughter of Capt. Marchand and a Creek princess. Their son Alexander, 1758–93, was educated by his kinsman, Rev.

Farquhar MacGillivray, in Charleston, and became a member of the Council of the Creek Nation at the age of twenty-two. He kept the Creeks out of the War of Independence, and enabled them to survive better than any other tribe against the ruthless white man. Another clansman, William MacGillivray, 1764–1825, emigrated to Canada and engaged in the fur trade. His story as chief superintendent of the North-West Company is told by Marjorie Campbell in her biography, *MacGillivray: Lord of the Northwest* (Toronto, 1962).

Dunmaglass was in a precarious financial state when William MacGillivray succeeded his brother who was killed at Culloden, and he obtained a captaincy in the Gordon Regiment. His son, John Lachlan, served in the 16th Light Dragoons, and died without issue in 1852. The estates then passed to his fourth cousin, John MacGillivray, 1777–1855, also a Nor' Wester in Canada. He did not actually come into possession of the estates because of prolonged litigation. It was a kinsman in Canada, Lt. Col. George B. MacGillivray, a newspaper proprietor, who matriculated posthumously in 1967, arms for Farquhar, chief in 1672 when the official *Lyon Register* commenced. Captain Neil John Mac-Gillivray, who succeeded his father in 1855, was also involved in litigation and had to sell Easter Gask and Wester Lairgs, leaving only Dunmaglass. His son, John William MacGillivray, was obliged to dispose of the remaining parts of his inheritance. He went to India, where he lived comfortably, but died without issue. There is now a Clan MacGillivray Association, engaged through the internet in a search for a chief. A cadet branch in the Invergordon district has kept the name to the fore in the north by building up a famous herd of cattle.

MacGOWAN/SMITH
From early times there have been workers in metal, and in the Scottish burghs they formed Incorporations of Hammermen, which included those working in gold, silver, iron and copper. In their ranks were blacksmiths, whitesmiths, coppersmiths, swordsmiths, bucklemakers, and even (sometimes with reluctance) clock and watchmakers. Little wonder then that Smith is the most prolific surname in the country.

The Gaelic form is *gobha* or *gobhainn*, and usually relates to blacksmiths. MacGown or McGowan is simply *mac a ghobhainn* or *MacGhobhainn*, 'son of the smith'. Some clan books say that Macgowans are septs of MacDonald or Macpherson, but there must have been a smith in every large clan. An exception is found in

Dumfriesshire in the reign of David II (1329–32), and it appears there was a small Clan Macgowan in Nithsdale. The clan was represented by Donald Edzear, a descendant of Dunegal of Strathnith whose home was at Morton. It has been suggested that they descended from Owen the Bald, King of the Strathclyde Britons. Many people surnamed Macgowan appear in the records of the south-west, and unless other evidence is forthcoming, we must treat them as descended from smiths. Gilbert Makgowin, a follower of the Earl of Cassillis, was respited for murder in 1526. In 1626, the Earl of Cassillis gave a precept for infefting John McGowne as heir to his father in the five-merkland of Skeoch, at Whithorn. John McGowan, son of William McGowan, town clerk of Whithorn, was admitted WS in 1713. The surname appears elsewhere. In 1503, Gilcallum McGoun had a remission for rapine and other crimes on the lands of the Abbot of Cupar. William McGown, a follower of Ross of Pitcalny, is recorded in 1592, and Murchiey McGowne in Fanmore, Mull, appears in 1629. In modern times, Iain Crichton Smith, 1928–98, reared in Lewis, but residing at Taynuilt, was a distinguished writer in prose and verse. Ian Duncan McGowan has been Librarian of the National Library of Scotland since 1990.

Smith or Smyth is rendered in old Latin writs as *Faber* and *Ferro*. Adam Faber held a croft on the lands of Swaynstoun ca. 1225, and William faber de Karel was a witness ca. 1250. Thomas Smyth, Scotsman, had a safe conduct in England in 1398, and in 1401, another Scot, Patrick, was imprisoned in the Tower of London. Elizabeth and Margaret Smythe were heirs portioners of Alexander Smythe in Greinholme in 1621. The surname increased around Glengarry in the first half of the 18th century, when the woods there were used in the smelting of iron ore from Lancashire. It is said that in the 1841 census, enumerators in Lewis who could not understand Gaelic names, entered them as Smiths. There were Smiths there before 1841, and a number had emigrated to Canada. Others who were smiths kept *Gobha* in their names. John *Gobha* Murray, of Tolsta, Lewis, emigrated to Compton County, Quebec in 1855.

Adam Smith, 1723–90, the eminent political economist and moral philosopher, whose book *The Wealth of Nations* is still hailed as a landmark in the study of economics was a native of Kirkcaldy. Donald Alexander Smith, 1820–1914, from Archieston, in Moray, had a remarkable career in the fur trade in Canada, commencing as a junior clerk with the Hudson's Bay Co., and rising to high office. He was Deputy Governor, 1888–89, and was created Baron Strathcona and Mount Royal in 1897. He was Governor, 1889–1914. John Smith, 1938–94, QC, from Dalmally, Argyll, qualified as an advocate, but turned to politics. He was an MP from 1970–94, latterly for Monklands East, and Leader of the (Labour) Opposition in Parliament from 1992. But for his sad death, he would almost certainly have become Prime Minister when Labour was returned to power in 1997. He was buried at Iona.

MacGREGOR The crest of the MacGregors bears the proud motto: *S'rioghail Mo'Dhrem*, 'My Race is Royal', and for centuries the ancestor was believed to be Alpin, the king of Dalriada slain in battle in 832, and whose son Kenneth united the Scots and the Picts ca. 843. However, the old genealogies of the clan cannot now be accepted. It is possible their name comes from the shadowy figure of Gregor of the Golden Bridles, who lived in the 14th century. Clan leaders often took their name from an ancestor noted for some outstanding trait or exploit, and Gregor was quite possibly of royal descent. Gregor's son Iain *Cam*, who died in 1390, held the glens of Orchy, Strae and Lochy, on the opposite watershed of Strathfillan and Glendochart. He had three sons: Patrick, who held the ancient homeland of Glenorchy and lands of Strathfillan; Ian *Dhu*, ancestor of the Macgregors of Glenstrae; and Patrick, progenitor of the MacGregors of Brackley, Roro and Glengyle. Patrick's son Malcolm lost the Strathfillan lands to the Campbells of Breadalbane, and the Glenstrae line came to be recognised as chiefs, but not universally. Some writers, such as Sheriff John MacGregor, 1877–1967, maintained that in olden times they never had a chief, but he also claimed there were no clansmen called Magruder outside America! Evidently he had never seen the *Old Parochial Registers* of Comrie.

The MacGregors lost possession of all their lands except Glenstrae. The land-hungry Campbells of Argyll annoyed and oppressed them; reducing them virtually landless and to a state of lawlessness. Naturally they retaliated, but were represented in Edinburgh as having an untameable ferocity which nothing could remedy save 'cutting off the tribe of MacGregor, root and branch'. An act of 1488 injured the clan, but they were still numerous over a wide area, and it seems their fighting spirit and pride of race sustained them.

By the slaughter of Drummond of Drummondernoch in 1589, and their part in the conflict at Glenfruin in 1603, the former leading to an incident related in Scott's *Legend of Montrose*, the very name of MacGregor was proscribed by the Privy Council. They were forced to adopt other names such as Drummond, Murray, Graham, Grier, Stewart, Grant, and even Campbell. A later act pronounced death on any who had borne the name if they assembled in groups of more than four. Remarkably, they fought under Montrose, and this led to a relaxation in 1661, but the surname was not fully restored until 1774.

In 1714 the Balhaldie line – cadets of Roro – claimed chiefship, but were frustrated. This family were staunch Jacobites, and in 1740 Alexander MacGregor alias Drummond of Balhaldie was created a Knight and Baronet by James III and VIII. His successors held the estate for several generations. At length, the Brackley line, with others, entered into a deed recognising John Murray (later MacGregor) of Lanrick as chief. He was created a Baronet, 1795. The position of chief was not conceded by the MacGregors of Glengyle, from whom descended the famous Rob Roy MacGregor alias Campbell, but the chiefship being *de jure* and *de facto* vacant, John was recognised by the Lord Lyon as chief, and matriculated arms in 1775. Several books have been written about Rob Roy MacGregor, a mediocre one by Sir Walter Scott. The best is *Rob Roy MacGregor: His Life and Times*, by W.H. Murray (1982). The present chief is Brigadier Sir Gregor MacGregor, 6th Baronet of Lanrick and Balquhidder, whose heir is Maj. Malcolm Gregor Charles MacGregor. There is a flourishing Clan Society, and the informative magazine, *The Quaich*, is published at Edinburgh.

MACINNES The MacInnes's – *Clann Aonghais* – are of Celtic origin, and were among the earliest inhabitants of Ardnamurchan and Morvern. They suffered when Alexander II (1214–49) conquered Argyll. They became highly favoured by the Lords of the Isles. Their last chief is said to have been murdered at Ardtornish in 1390. Part of the clan became attached to the Campbells of Craignish. Some others went to Skye and became hereditary bowmen to the Mackinnon chiefs. Descendants of the murdered chief seem to have recovered his castle of Lochaline: at least as constables. It is one of the most picturesque ruins on the west coast, overlooking the rocky estuary of the Gearabháinn. Possibly a MacInnes governed it for the tutor of Kintail, during the siege by Young Colkitto in 1645. In the 17th and 18th centuries, the Kinlochine branch came under the patronage of the Campbells of Argyll, and supported Covenanting and Hanovarian interests. A few followed Stewart of Ardshiel in 1745. The MacInnes's of Rickersby descended from *Neil an Bogha*. Many clansmen emigrated to the USA and Canada. David M. Mackinnes, married at Edinburgh in 1780, Rachel Rebecca Mathieson, and emigrated to Virginia in 1814, later moving to North Carolina. Angus MacInnes, from Inverlussa, Jura, Argyll, emigrated to Cumberland County, North Carolina, ca. 1820, with his wife, Mary Shaw, and several children. Scores of clansmen emigrated to Canada, some with the name rendered MacInnis. Alexander MacInnes emigrated from Glendale, Duirinish, Skye, to Southeast Mabou, Inverness County, Cape Breton, ca. 1822, and became a builder, including the construction of bridges. Another who went, ca. 1822, was Angus MacInnis, from Glenfinnan, Inverness-shire. He settled in Inverness County, Cape Breton, and became a farmer and magistrate. Donald MacInnes, a native of Oban, became a merchant in Dundas, Ontario, in 1840; later a senator at Hamilton.

MACINTOSH In Gaelic, the surname MacIntosh is *Mac-an-Toisich*, meaning 'Son of the Chief (or Thane)', and the principal family, who favour the name with the intrusive 'k', thus Mackintosh, is believed to be descended from Shaw, a younger son of Constantine, 3rd Earl of Fife (MacDuff), who died before 1130. Writers on titles are silent about Shaw, but heraldic evidence gives some credence to the story. Different chiefs gave their style to other MacIntosh families. Those of Tininnie, in Atholl, descended from the thanes of Glentilt, and the Toshes of Monzievard came from the thanes of Strowan.

In 1234, Ferquhard, son of Shaw, witnessed a charter of the Bishop of Moray, and held the office of seneschal. His extensive lands comprised Petty and Breachley, with the forest of Strathdearn. After the marriage of the 6th Mackintosh chief to Eva, heirtrix of Clan Chattan, in 1291, he and his successors represented the old Clan Chattan. Ferquhard, 9th chief of Mackintosh, abdicated in 1409, giving up all claims of his issue to Malcolm Beg, a strong chief whose leadership inspired confidence. As 10th chief, he had a dispute with the Cummins about the lands of Meikle Geddes and Castle Rait, but obtained a charter of those subjects. The rival claims may have brought about the famous conflict at Perth in 1396, but no historian has conclusively proved who the combatants were.

William, 1521–1550, the 16th chief, styled 'of Dunachtonmore', had the misfortune to quarrel with his superior, the Earl of Huntly, and was tried at Aberdeen for conspiring against him. A packed jury found him guilty, and he was put to death. For the next two centuries the Mackintoshes had feuds with the Gordons, the Camerons and the MacDonnells of Keppoch. In 1688, Lachlan, 19th chief, took part in the last clan battle against the MacDonnells at Mulroy. His son Lachlan was created Lord Mackintosh in the Jacobite peerage in 1717, but died childless in 1731. His cousin and successor, William of Daviot, supported King George during the '45, while his wife and followers took the field for Prince Charles. His successor, Aneas, created a Baronet, died in 1812, without issue. By an entail the estate went to Alfred Donald Mackintosh, 1851–1938, who, by tanistry, settled the *duthus* of Moy and the chiefship on his cousin, Vice-Admiral Lachlan Mackintosh, the 29th chief. The representation of Clan Chattan passed to his granddaughter, Arabella, but as she did not bear the ancient name the honour passed to Duncan Alexander Mackintosh of Torcastle, descended from Angus, 29th chief, and he thus became the 31st Captain of Clan Chattan. Lachlan Donald Mackintosh, 30th Mackintosh chief, had a distinguished naval career, and sold a large part of the estates. He retained the family home of Moy Hall, and died in 1995. The present chief is his son John.

A branch of the Mackintoshes, sometime at Spittal, Old Aberdeen, went to England, and a descendant, Harold Vincent Mackintosh, 1891–1964, was knighted in 1922, became a Baronet in 1935, and was created Viscount Halifax in 1957. His son, Sir John, was head of the well-known confectionary firm of Mackintosh. The 3rd Viscount is Sir John Clive Mackintosh. One of the most colourful clansmen was Waldo E. Mackintosh, chief of the Creek Indians, who visited Moy in 1964. He was descended from John Mackintosh of the Borlum line of the family, who emigrated to Georgia, USA, before 1775. His grandson William became a Creek chief, and ancestor of Waldo, known to his tribe as *Tustanuggee Mico*. A new edition of *The Clan Mackintosh and The Clan Chattan* (Edinburgh, 1948), by the wife of the 30th chief, was published in 1997.

MacINTYRE This name derives from the Gaelic *Mac an-t-Saoir*, 'son of the carpenter', and this accounts for its appearance in many parts of the Highlands. It is associated particularly with Glen Noe, near Bonawe, Argyll, but tradition brings them from the Hebrides in a galley with a white cow in the latter part of the 15th century. Curiously, the reddendo they were due annually to the

Campbells of Argyll for Glen Noe, was a snowball and a white calf. This arrangement continued until early in the 18th century, when the MacIntyre of Glen Noe was a tenant and paid rent in money. When they could no longer pay rent increases the clansmen lost the glen. James MacIntyre of Glen Noe in 1783 had three sons, the eldest of whom emigrated to Canada, having passed the lands to his youngest brother, Capt. Donald MacIntyre, who lost Glen Noe in 1808. The emigrant chief and his sisters Ann and Catherine, settled in Fulton County, New York State, and he left descendants. Some MacIntyres in Badenoch became attached to Clan Chattan in 1496, in the time of William MacIntosh, 13th chief. A family of MacIntyres were hereditary pipers to Menzies of Menzies, and another family piped for Clanranald. MacIntyres fought under Stewart of Appin in 1745. The MacIntyres of Sorn Castle, Ayrshire, produced a High Court judge. He was James Gordon McIntyre, 1896–1983, who was educated at Winchester, Oxford (Baliol College), and Glasgow. After serving in the Ayrshire Yoemanry in World War I (1914–18), with the rank of captain from 1917, he passed as an advocate. He was Dean of the Faculty of Advocates, 1939–44, and a Senator of the College of Justice, 1944–63. Donald MacIntyre, 1891–1954, was a distinguished obstetrician. The son of Donald MacIntyre, in Greenock, he served in World War I, then studied to become an obstetrician and gynaecologist. He worked in a number of hospitals and was the author of several textbooks.

MacKAY The surname Mackay is derived from the Gaelic *MacAoidh*, 'son of Aodh'. Aoidh was a popular Celtic name, meaning 'fire'. Early chroniclers wrote the name Ed, Eth or Heth. it was often spelt Y or Iye, hence MacIye, which owing to the intrusion of 'k' became Mackay. There is some confusion about the clan origins, but a distinct trace of some ancient link with the Kings of the Scots. Aethelred, son of Malcolm III and Queen Margaret, was known as Aedh, Abbot of Dunkeld and 1st Earl of Fife (see the article MACDUFF). Malcolm McHeth, Earl of Ross, was possibly a son, but a competent historian has suggested that Malcolm was a natural son of Alexander I (1107–24), son of Malcolm III. Some idea of his status may be gained from the fact that he married a daughter of Somerled of the Isles.

When the MacWilliams attempted to gain the throne, Malcolm MacHeth was associated with them. He was captured in 1134 and imprisoned at Roxburgh. His eldest son, Donald, was also kept there after 1156, and the fact they were not executed tends to support the impression they stemmed from the royal family. They were released in 1157, and Malcolm was restored to his earldom. It does not appear that his offspring succeeded him, and there were further uprisings along with the MacWilliams. As they sought the crown, it seems probable the MacHeths were attempting to regain the earldom. Kenneth MacAht, grandson of Donald, rebelled in 1215, and was slain at Cupar. It seems likely the family held Strathnaver at that time.

Iye MacEth in Strathnaver may be considered the first chief of Mackay. In 1263 he was chamberlain to the Bishop of Caithness, and married his daughter. Their son Iye *Mor*, obtained land at Durness from the Bishop. His son Donald married a daughter of Iye MacNeill of Gigha, and had a son Iye, who was murdered along with his own son Donald at Dingwall in 1370. He was succeeded by his grandson, Angus, who had grants of lands in Sutherland and Caithness. Strathnaver itself was known as *Duthuc Mhic Aoidh*, of 'The Mackay Country'. About 1415, Angus *Dubh* Mackay or Strathnaver married Elizabeth, sister of Donald, Lord of the Isles, and granddaughter of King Robert II. Subsequent chiefs strove hard to keep their estates from being absorbed by the Earls of Sutherland. Eventually, the power of gold prevailed.

In 1627, Sir Donald Mackay, a fine soldier, was created Baronet of NS, and about two years later made Baron Reay. He raised 'MacKay's Regiment', for Danish and Swedish service, and consequently did much to advance the Protestant cause in Germany. A younger son of the 2nd Lord Reay, being maternally a nephew of Gen. Hugh Mackay of Scourie – who commanded the army of William of Orange at Killiecrankie in 1689 – entered the Danish service himself and became a Brigadier General. His grandson, Col. Angus Mackay, married the eventual heiress of the Barons van Haeften of Ophemert, whose castle was inherited by the Mackays. In 1875, Baron Mackay van Ophemert succeeded his distant cousin, Eric, 9th Baron Reay, as 10th Lord Reay. The present and 14th Baron Reay and chief of the clan is Sir Hugh William Mackay, who is also Baron Ophemert. He was a Member of the European Parliament, 1973–79, and sits as a Conservative in the House of Lords. The Master of Reay is his son and heir, The Hon. Aneas Simon Mackay.

To Mackays in the south belonged Brian Vicar Mackay, to whom the Lord of the Isles granted a Gaelic charter in 1408. The Mackays of the Rhinns, in Islay, were lieutenants to the Lords of the Isles, and were sometime at Ugadale, in Kintyre.

MacKENZIE Unlike clans such as Chisholm, Fraser and Gordon, the MacKenzies are of Gaelic origin, and probably descended from Gilleoin of Aird. Indeed, a genealogy of 1450 gives the descent as follows: 'Murdoch, son of Kenneth, son of John, son of Kenneth, son of Christian, son of Adam, son of Gilleoin-Oig of the Aird'. The surname in Gaelic means 'son of Coinnach', or of Kenneth, and means fair or bright. The earliest known Kenneth was closely related to the Earls of Ross, and in 1267 resided at Eilean Donan, Loch Duich, one of Scotland's most photographed castles. Succeeding generations were vassals of the Earls, but by an advantageous marriage the Lords of the Isles became superiors.

About 1463, Alexander MacKenzie had grants from John, Lord of the Isles, of lands including Garve and Kinlochluichart, and the family came to be styled 'of Kintail'. He was succeeded by his son Kenneth, who had a charter under the Great Seal of Scatwell and other lands, 1508/9. After the forfeiture of the Lordship of the Isles in 1493 the MacKenzies rose to prominence in the north and north-west.

In 1508, Kintail was erected into a barony, and this gave the chief jurisdiction over his clan. Additional lands were obtained between 1528 and 1542, and more land and influence through good marriages later in the 16th century. Further tracts of land were acquired through less honourable means. A feud with the MacDonnells of Glengarry led to the acquisition of lands at Lochalsh and Loch Carron, and eventually they came to hold lands on the east coast. King James VI, ostensibly to civilise the island of Lewis, gave rights to some Lowlanders called the Fife Adventurers, in 1599, who soon found themselves in trouble with the MacLeods of Lewis. The king prevailed upon Kenneth MacKenzie of Kintail, newly raised to the peerage, to intervene, and by some duplicity he received a grant of Lewis. About this time he had a dispute with MacLeod of Raasay over Gairloch.

Descendants of Lord Kintail obtained two earldoms: Seaforth and Cromartie, and numerous cadets founded landed families and left thousands of people who can claim to be of the Clan MacKenzie. The Earls of Seaforth were Royalists and suffered losses in the Jacobite Rising of 1715. The title and estates were forfeited. In the '45, the Earl of Cromartie was involved, and his title and estates were forfeited. The lands were restored to his son, Lord MacLeod, whose daughter Isabella inherited his estates in 1796. Her husband, Edward Hay, assumed the surname and arms. They left an heiress, Anne, created Countess of Cromartie in 1861, who married Lord Elibank. Their daughter Sybil became countess, and married Lt. Col. Blunt-MacKenzie. The male line of the Seaforth family having failed in 1818, their son, Roderick, 4th Earl of Cromartie, was recognised as chief of Clan MacKenzie by the Lord Lyon in 1979. His son John Ruaridh Grant MacKenzie is 5th Earl and clan chief. John Hugh Munro MacKenzie of Mornish, born 1925, descends from the old chiefs through the Gairloch and Letterewe Cadets.

Among MacKenzies who achieved lasting fame may be counted Coinneach, the Brahan Seer, who lived in the 17th century. Many of his prophecies came true. Sir George MacKenzie, 1636–91, of Rosehaugh, was a distinguished lawyer, and founded the Advocates' Library in Edinburgh, since 1925 the National Library of Scotland. The famous explorer of the Canadian north-west, Sir Alexander MacKenzie, 1764–1820, emigrated from Stornoway with his father Kenneth to New York, ca. 1772. He made historic journeys to the Arctic Sea and the Pacific coast, and wrote an account of his epic travels. Sir Alexander retired to Scotland in 1808 and obtained the estate of Avoch, in Ross-shire.

MACKINLEY The name is synonymous with Finlayson, 'son of Finlay', and the first of the name is believed to have been a son of a Buchanan of Drumakil. There can be no doubt they originated in the district of Lennox, and in Gaelic orthography the name is *MacFionnlaigh*. Although distinctly Scottish it was taken to Ulster by Presbyterian settlers. A variant is McGinley. William McKinley, 1843–1901, 25th President of the USA, was descended from Stephen McKinley, 1730–1819, an Ulster-Scot. Some MacKinlay families migrated into Glenorchy and Glen Lyon. Sir John Finlosoun alias McAlan McKewella (the attempt by a non-Gaelic scribe to write *MacFionnlaigh*), was vicar of Kilmorich in 1511. In 1574, Sir Andrew Finlayson was chaplain of an altar in St Machar's Cathedral, Old Aberdeen. Donald McKindlay appears at Innerchocheill, Perthshire, in 1696. Peter McKinlay was a clock and watchmaker in Edinburgh, around 1840. Col. Hamish Grant McKinlay, from Tillicoultry, is Deputy-Governor (Security) of the Tower of London.

MACKINNON Many of the genealogies in the Gaelic Manuscript of 1467 are suspect, but the Mackinnon descent given there, from Cormac, son of Airbertach, cannot easily be dismissed as it is supported by Highland monuments. Finguaine, son of

Cormac, may be accepted as the name-father of the clan, and ancestor of Nial, down to whom the manuscript brings the line. Nial was probably related to Lachlan Mackinnon, who in 1409 witnessed a charter by his superior, the Lord of the Isles, to Hector MacLean of Duart. Either he or a later Lachlan was the father of John MacKinnon, last Abbot of Iona, who died in 1500, and whose tomb effigy survives, as well as a sculptured cross erected by Lachlan at Iona in 1489.

The Mackinnons held important posts under the Lords of the Isles. They were sometime Masters of the Household, and entrusted with the the supervision of weights and measures. Possibly it was their skill in measuring liquids that led to Prince Charles Edward Stuart passing on to the chiefly line the recipe for Drambuie (Yellow Drink). The Mackinnon chiefs received a charter in the 16th century of the twenty-merkland of Mishnish, in Mull, and the twenty-merkland of Strathardal, in Skye. They were loyal to their superiors and took part in attempts to restore the Lordship of the Isles. Ewen, the chief in 1513, was a member of the Council of Donald *Dubh*, the claimant. The Mackinnons became a clan in their own right, and although noted as troublesome in 1587, the chief accepted the *Statutes of Iona*, and bound himself to keep his people in good order. There were some unrest in 1696, when the Royalist chief, Sir Lachlan, created knight-banneret by Charles II at Worcester, died leaving a son who was a minor. His kinsman, Mackinnon of Corriechatachan, helped to stifle the disturbance.

John *Dhu* Mackinnon was 'out' with his clansmen in the '15, and joined Prince Charles in 1745 with 120 followers. He served throughout the campaign, but was not at Culloden, being elsewhere engaged; but he was arrested at Morar. After a long spell in prison he died in 1757. A nephew, John of Elgol, was also a prisoner, and died in 1762. The chief's estate was impoverished and sold by his son in 1756. He held Strathaird until 1791, and left a son John, the last of the direct line, who died in 1808. William A. Mackinnon, MP for Dunwich, descended from a cadet in Antigua, obtained a decree in Lyon Court in 1811 recognising him as chief. Mackinnon of Corry asserted a claim, but the matriculation was not reduced. William was succeeded by his son, Francis Alexander Mackinnon, 1848–1947. His son Cmdr. Arthur Avalon Mackinnon was 36th chief, and died in 1964. The next chief was Alastair Neil, 1926–83, who had no issue. There is a younger brother, Lt. Col. Ian K. Mackinnon, but the present chief is Alastair Neil's only surviving child, Ann Gunhild Mackinnon (Mrs Alan Jeffrey), an occupational therapist, who resides in Bridgewater, Somerset.

Colonel Daniel Mackinnon, 1791–1836, of the chiefly line, wrote a history of the Coldstream Guards (1832). William A. Mackinnon, 1830–97, son of a Skye minister, became a Surgeon-General in the army and founded the Mackinnon Scholarship at the University of Glasgow. Another William Mackinnon 1823–93, a Glasgow merchant, founded the British East Africa Co., and was created a Baronet in 1889. Professor Donald Mackinnon, who died in 1914, held the chair of Celtic Languages at Edinburgh University from 1882. Lachlan Mackinnon, author of *Recollections of an Old Lawyer* (1935), represented an old legal family in Aberdeen. Rev. Donald Mackinnon, 1890–1966, Free Church minister at Portree, later at Kennoway, Fife, was a noted genealogist. Numerous Mackinnons from Skye, Mull, Rum (clearance, 1828), Arran and other islands emigrated to Canada.

MacLACHLAN The MacLachlans are one of the oldest recognisable clans in Scotland. Ancient genealogies bring them from the O'Neill kings in Ireland, through Niall of the Nine Hostages, who flourished around AD 400. Their descendant, Anrothan, is said to have married into one of the old dynastic families of Dalriada, and obtained lands in Cowal. The evidence for this is weak, but Gilpatrick, possibly his grandson, witnessed a charter whereby his cousin, Lauman, progenitor of Clan Lamont, gave church livings to the Abbey of Paisley about 1238. Gilpatrick had a son Lachlan, from whom not only the clan is named, but Lachlan Water and Lachlan Bay, the village of Strathlachlan, and the barony thereof, with Castle Lachlan.

Richard, son of Lachlan, is mentioned in 1327 as custumer of Stirling, and the following year he appears as 'Ricardus filius Lochlane', Sheriff of Stirling. He appears to have had a son Gillescop; possibly also Ewen, who rendered homage to Edward I in 1296. A younger Gillescop requested lands from that king, but later adhered to Robert the Bruce, and was present at his first parliament in 1308. In 1314 he granted to the preaching friars of Glasgow, 40 s. sterling annually from his Pennylands of Kilbride, in Strathlachlan. Later MacLachlan cadets held local benefices. In 1410, Iain MacLachlan, the chief, witnessed a charter, from which it appears that his cousin, Allan, crowner of Glassary, was ancestor of the MacLachlans of Dunadd. A 'nobleman', Donald MacLachlan, seemingly of the chiefly line, had a dispensation in 1411, to marry Affrica Nigelli, related to him in the fourth degree of affinity. Ferquhard, natural son of another Ferquhard MacLachlan, was Bishop of the Isles, 1530–44. The MacLachlans of Coire-uanan held the position of standard-bearers to the Camerons of Lochiel. Of this family came the MacLachlans of Drumblane, in Mentieth. Another important cadet was MacLachlan of Kilchoan.

The MacLachlans prospered through their attachment to Bruce, and through intermarriage with the Campbells. In 1536, Lachlan MacLachlan of that Ilk had a safe conduct to France, along with the Earl of Argyll, in connection with the marriage of the Scottish king and Madeleine de Valois, daughter of King Francis I. By the time the chief's lands were enumerated in 1633, these contained thirty farms, with the patronage of the church of Kilmory. The lands were erected into a free barony in 1680. In 1666 Archibald MacLachlan of that Ilk signed a bond by which 10 s. was to be paid out of every merkland in Argyll, for maintaining an armed watch. In 1679, Capt. MacLachlan, as laird, raised fifty men for his company in the Ardkinlas Regiment. He died in 1687. The MacLachlans were Jacobites, and involved in the Risings of 1715 and 1745. The chief, Lachlan, was fatally wounded at Culloden, and because of this his lands were not forfeited. In 1747, his son Robert, aided by the Argyll family, was able to take possession of the estates.

Major John MacLachlan, 1859–1942, XXIIIrd laird, married Marjorie, daughter of the deceased Albert C. Macpherson of Cluny, and widow of Donald Nicol of Ardmore. Their eldest daughter, Marjorie (called Marnie), 1920–96, was next chief, but had to sell a large part of the estate of Strathlachlan. She married in 1948, George S. Rome, who assumed the surname of MacLachlan, and died in 1994. Their eldest son Euan is 25th chief of the clan.

MacLAREN

The MacLarens formed a small clan in West Perthshire, mainly in the parish of Balquhidder and in parts of Comrie and Callander. Loch Voil and Loch Earn were parts of their territory. The surname derived from Lawrence or Lachrain, Abbot of Achtow in the 13th century. In those times the Celtic church permitted the marriages of the clergy. At an early period MacLarens were allodial holders of land under the Celtic earls of Strathearn, and they were probably of the same stock. Indeed the arms of the earls from the middle of the 12th century, with the two chevronels, are similar to those borne by the MacLachlan chiefs. It it is possible they were all descended from the ancient dynastic rulers of Fortrenn

(Strathearn and Menteith), one of the seven old provinces of Alba.

The *Ragman Roll* was signed in 1296 by Conan de Bethweder (Eoan of Balquhidder), and his cousin, Lorin de Ardbethey (Ardveach). A third name, Morice de Tyry, has been confused with MacLarens in Tyree, but he belonged to the Perthshire family of Tyrie. The eminent mathematician, Colin MacLaurin, 1698–1746, son of the Rev. John MacLaurin of Kilmodan, claimed descent from the Tyree family, and his son John of Dreghorn, Ayrshire, a Lord of Session, matriculated arms in 1781, blazoned: Argent, a shepherd's crook, Sable.

Clan Labhran was never strong after the fall of the earls of Strathearn and, when their jurisdiction became vested in the Crown, the chiefs never obtained charters of the lands they held. Eventually the superiority was held by the Murrays of Tullibardine, Lord Drummond and Campbell of Glenorchy. Reduced to rentallers, with no ancestral castle and no tenant cadets of their own, they had little use for a charter chest, and it is not surprising that so little is known about them. Although 'Clanlawren' is credited with having a captain or chief in 1587, his jurisdiction must have been limited. Local feuds with the MacGregors and Campbells did nothing to strengthen the clan, and they were forced to seek the protection of the Campbells of Glenorchy, later of Breadalbane. Some even settled in Breadalbane. In 1769 there were fourteen MacLaren tenants on the south side of the Loch Tay, and three on the other side.

The MacLarens supported Montrose and Dundee in their campaigns, and along with their Jacobite friends, the Stewarts of Appin, were 'out' in the '15 and '45 Risings. At Culloden in 1745, thirteen were killed, fourteen wounded, and a number taken prisoner. Their leader, Donald of Invernenty, escaped when being taken to Carlisle for trial. At one period they were accused of resetting MacGregors, but in 1736 bad feelings were aroused. Robin *Oig*, a son of Rob Roy MacGregor, fatally wounded John MacLaren of Wester Invernenty while he was ploughing. He became a fugitive, but was executed in 1754 for the abduction and forcible marriage of Jean Key, heiress of Edinbellie. In spite of all their troubles the chiefly line of Achleskyne held on to their farm until 1892, and in 1957, the recognised chief, Donald, 1910–66, son the Rev. Duncan MacLaren, of Turriff, purchased Craeag an Tuirc, and matriculated arms. His Lady, Margaret (Miller) wrote a readable clan history, published in 1960. The senior branch of Ardveach tenanted their farm until 1888. Invernenty was next in importance. The Barons Aberconway descend from John MacLaren, who farmed on the island of Lismore, in Loch Linnhe, Archibald MacLaren, 1755–1826, a prolific dramatic writer, who fought in the American Revolutionary War, died in London, leaving a wife and family in poor circumstances. Ian F. MacLaren, born 1927, soldier and surgeon, and a chieftain of the clan, resides in Edinburgh, and was chairman of the Clan MacLaren Society, 1968–91.

MacLEAN/MacLAINE

In old writs the MacLeans appear as MacGilleain, 'son of Gilleain', and derived their name from Gilleain-na-Tuaighe, 'Gilleain of the Battle-Axe', a renowned Celtic warrior of the 13th century, probably descended through an abbot of Lismore, from the old royal house of Dalriada. They may have been followers of the Lord of Lorn, and settled early in Morvern, but they became vassals of the Lords of the Isles. There must have been some blood relationship before 1367, when consanguinity caused Lachlan *Lubanach* MacLaren of Duart or Dowart, to petition the Pope for a dispensation to marry Mary, daughter of MacDonald, Lord of the Isles. It is possible an earlier link was through the MacRuaries, since the MacLeans have always shown a sable galley in their armorial bearings.

The Lochbuie family favour the spelling MacLaine, and descend from Hector *Reaganach*, a brother of Lachlan *Lubanach*, of the Duart family. Hector had a son Charles, progenitor of the MacLeans of Dochgarroch and Glen Urquhart. Fearcher, son of Charles, also had a son Charles, who was a close friend of his kinsman, Lachlan *Bronnach*, the grandson and successor of Lachlan *Lubanach*. Lachlan's son, Donald, obtained Ardgower from Alexander, Lord of the Isles, thus founding that important branch of the family, represented until 1996 by the veteran soldier, diplomat and author, Sir Fitzroy Hew MacLean, created a Baronet in 1967. He had an adventurous life and some people erroneously think he was the prototype of Ian Fleming's James Bond, played so well in several films by Sean Connery. His son, Sir Charles, the 2nd Baronet, resides at Dunconnel, Strachur.

Twice married Hector *Og* MacLean of Duart had four sons: Hector of Duart; Lachlan, created a Baronet of NS in 1631; Donald of Brolas; and John, ancestor of the Counts MacLean of Sweden. The MacLeans of Duart and the MacLaines of Lochbuie were ardent Jacobites. Sir John of Duart, 4th Baronet, led the clan at Killiecrankie and Sheriffmuir and died in 1716. His castle and lands were seized by the Campbells. His son, Sir Hector, 5th Baronet, was created Lord Maclean by James III and VIII, in 1716. The clan was led in the '45 by Charles MacLean of Drimnen, and Lord MacLean was arrested and sent to the Tower of London. He was released in 1747, and died unmarried in 1751. His titles devolved on his cousin, Sir Allan MacLean of Brolas. Sir Fitzroy Donald MacLean, 1835–1936, during his long life, succeeded in re-purchasing the castle of Duart and restoring it. He was succeeded by his grandson, Sir Charles, 1916–90, Baron MacLean, whose son, Sir Lachlan, is the 12th Baronet and 28th chief of the clan.

Donald MacLaine of Lochbuie, born 1816, a rich merchant in Batavia, Java, bought back the estate of Lochbuie, and it remained with his descendants until the 1920s, when his grandson, Kenneth, lost it to an English bondholder. The MacLeans of Dochgarroch have been influential in the north since the middle of the 16th century. Until recently they were represented by the Rev. Donald A. MacLean, an Episcopalian, residing at Hazelbrae House, Glen Urquhart, whose widow Loraine is a keen historian. Lieutenant Col. Alexander MacLean, 1880–1930, representative of the Ardgour family, served in the Argyll & Sutherland Highlanders. Alistair MacLean, 1922–87, was a leading Scottish novelist, some of whose books have been the basis of films. Present day MacLeans who have achieved eminence or fame include: Ranald Norman Munro MacLean, who has been a High Court judge since 1990; John Ruairi McLean, an expert typographer, who advises HM Stationery Office and is a trustee of the National Library; Jack McLean, journalist and broadcaster; and the actress, Una McLean.

MACLEOD The MacLeods can claim Norse ancestry. Olaf the Black, 1177–1237, eldest son of Godfrey, King of Man and the Isles, by his third wife Christina, daughter of Farquhar, Earl of Ross, had a son Leod, fostered by Paul Balkeson, Sheriff of Skye, who bequeathed to him his lands of Harris and North Uist. From his maternal grandfather, he received part of the barony of Glenelg, and by his marriage to the heiress of MacRiald Armuin, he obtained Dunvegan, Bracadale, Duirinish, Trotternish and other lands in Skye. His sons Tormod (Norman) and Torcul (Harold), were the progenitors of the MacLeods of Harris and Dunvegan, and those of Lewis. It is not certain which of them was the elder, but in time the MacLeods of Dunvegan became recognised as chiefs of the clan. Leod died ca. 1280.

In 1343 Torquil MacLeod, the Lewis chief, had a grant of four davachs of land in Assynt, 'together with the fortress on the island', of Loch Assynt. His descendants were loyal to the MacDonald Lords of the Isles, and although the chief made his submission to the King of Scots after the forfeiture of the Lordship in 1493, the family joined in attempts to restore the principality. Towards the end of the 16th century the MacLeods of Lewis were weakened by a curious fratricidal conflict, and this may have been a factor in the decision of King James to colonise the island with Lowlanders. In 1597 the chiefs, having failed to produce their charters (which they had), the king granted Lewis for a substantial rent to a company called the Fife Adventurers. The scheme failed, but MacKenzie of Kintail bought them out and obtained possession. The chiefly line became extinct, but came to be represented by the MacLeods of Raasay.

The MacLeods of Dunvegan rose to strength. Malcolm, son of Norman, had a grant of parts of Glenelg in 1343. He was the progenitor of the old MacLeods of Berneray, and those of Gesto. Alastair *Crotach* MacLeod, the chief who died in 1547, is credited with having established a college for his MacCrimmon pipers, and he built for himself a sculptured tomb at Rodil, in Harris. One of the greatest MacLeod chiefs was Roderick, called Rory *Mor*, who was knighted ca. 1613. He was patron of the arts, and lived at Dunvegan, where he supported his pipers, bards and harpers. The clan took no part in Montrose's campaign, but supported the Royalists at Worcester. The chief in 1715 was Norman MacLeod, a child of nine years of age, but the exiled Stewarts evidently expected much support from the tutor, as James III and VIII created him Baron MacLeod in 1716. Their faith was shattered in 1745 when the chief refused to join Prince Charles, and in fact raised his clan for the government, only to be defeated by Lord Lewis Gordon at Inverurie in December, 1745. Other MacLeod chieftains, notably those of Raasay, Galtrigal and Glendale, supported the Prince. On the death of Sir Reginald MacLeod of MacLeod, 27th chief, in 1935, the representation passed to his elder daughter, Flora, in terms of an entail. This remarkable woman was the last person to be born at 10 Downing Street, London. Her father had been Registrar-General for England and Wales, 1900–02, and her maternal grandfather, Stafford Henry Northcote, was Chancellor of the Exchequer, 1874–80. She married Hubert Walter, who died in 1933, and on becoming chief resumed her maiden name. Her second daughter, Mrs Joan Wolridge Gordon, had twin sons: John, the present clan chief, and Patrick, of Hallhead and Esselmont.

Flora (DBE, 1953), instituted 'MacLeod Days' at Dunvegan during 'Skye Week' in 1950, and a clan 'parliament' at Dunvegan in 1956. As a result, the old castle has become a world centre for the clan. It houses precious relics such as the Fairy Flag, the medieval Dunvegan Cup, and the famous Drinking Horn used when chiefs are inaugurated.

MacMILLAN The MacMillans descend from Gilchrist, one of the six sons of Cormac, Bishop of Dunkeld, ca. 1107, son of Airbertach, who belonged to one of the dynastic families of Dalriada. Gilchrist, called *Gillie-Maolin*, 'the little tonsured one', was a monk of the Celtic church of Kintrae, Old Spynier, in Moray, and he may have built a Culdee shrine at Kilmallie (*Cill-Maolin*), where he left descendants. Malcolm IV, King of Scots, ca. 1160, removed MacMillans from Lochaber to Lawers, in Perthshire, to make room for the Gilliechattan family. Some also migrated to Knapdale, Argyll. A return to Lochaber is said to have been made ca. 1300, when a MacMillan in Breadalbane fled there after killing his father-in-law. This might be a distorted story as, ca. 1335, John, son of Malcolm *Mor* MacMillan, 1st of Knap, and six of his followers sought refuge in Lochaber after the killing of Marallach *Mor* at Kilchamaig, Loch Tarbert. According to the late Rev. Somerled MacMillan of Paisley, they and their families were none other than the Clan Qwhevil, outlawed in 1392, who proved victors over the Clan Ha (*Clann Sheadhgh*, 'offspring of Shaw', i.e. the people who adopted the surname of Mackintosh), at the clan battle at Perth in 1396.

The headship of the MacMillans was vested in the descendants of the above Malcolm *Mor* MacMillan. Gilchrist, grandson of his son John, was the father of Ewen, on whom Cameron of Lochiel bestowed Murlaggan. The family became attached to Clan Chattan, although at times they seemed more comfortable with the Camerons, whose tenants they were for centuries. Iain MacMillan, IXth of Murlaggan, however, refused to follow the 'Gentle' Lochiel on the side of Prince Charles in 1745. Curiously, tradition says it was two sons of Iain who carried the wounded Lochiel off Culloden Moor. The attitude of Iain of Murlaggan may have influenced Lochiel's son, who evicted many MacMillans from their ancestral homes. John in Murlaggan gave up his farm ca. 1760, and it was taken by Alexander MacMillan of the Glenpean family. Archibald, eldest son of John, along with his cousin, Allan of Glenpean, emigrated to Canada in 1802 with over four hundred other tenants.

In Lochaber there were numerous cadets: Glendessary, Kenmore and Sallachan, Lagganfern and others.

The direct line of the Knap family failed, and Duncam MacMillan of Dunmore, Loch Tarbert, came to represent the family. He matriculated arms in 1742. His son, Alexander of Dunmore, settled his estates on his cousin, Duncan, of the Laggalgarve family, by whom these were lost. In 1951, the recognised chief of the line was Gen. Sir George MacMillan, 1897–1986, of Finlaystone, Renfrewshire. His son, George MacMillan of MacMillan and Knap, is the present chief.

The MacMillans of the south-west are well known. Those of Holm and Dalquhairn, and of Glencrosh, descended from John MacMillan of Brockloch and Holm of Dalquhairn, who died in 1830. His son Robert was the father of John Holm of Glenquhairn and Glencrosh, who died in 1895. He was succeeded in Holm by his eldest son, Robert, and the younger sons, Thomas and John, were joint proprietors of Glencrosh.

Hugh Pattison MacMillan, 1873–1952, son of a Greenock minister, was a brilliant student of law, and became Lord Advocate of Scotland in 1924. In 1930 he was created a Life Peer. Malcolm Macmillan, a tacksman on the island of Arran, was father of Duncan, whose son Alexander, 1817–96, along with his brother Daniel, founded the publishing house of Macmillan. Of this family came Harold Macmillan, PM of Great Britain, 1957–63, created Earl of Stockton. The 2nd Earl is his grandson, Alexander Daniel Macmillan chairman of Macmillan Publishers, 1980–90, and president of Macmillan Ltd since 1990. His son and heir is Daniel Maurice Macmillan, Viscount Ovenden.

MacNAB

MacNAB The name, in Gaelic, means 'son of the abbot', and Sir Iain Moncreiffe of that Ilk, 1919–85, Baronet, describes the chiefs as 'the descendants and heirs of the Celtic hereditary Abbots of Glendochart, themselves the *coarbs* or heirs of St. Fillan mac Geradach, who was a prince of the Dalriadic royal house of Lorn,' and died in 703. His principal abbey was in Glendochart, the upper part of which became known as Strathfillan. If they were the heirs, one might think they would be custodians of the seven relics of the saint, but these were placed in the care of others. The *coigerach* or quigrich, for example, was found at an inquest in 1428 to be in the keeping of Finlia Jore (Finlay Dewar), *coarb* of St Fillan, and it passed with some vicissitudes, down through that family (see DEWAR). John, son of Alexander MacNab, the chief who died before 1407, attended the inquest. It seems probable that the MacNabs and Dewars were of the same stock. When the Celtic church was dismantled, the MacNabs continued to hold their lands as the barony of Glendochart. In 1365 their chief, Gilbert, had received a charter of the lands of Bovain, and others in Glendochart.

The MacNabs chose the wrong side in the War of Independence, but their chief, Alexander, who died before 1407, received a charter of the lands of Bovain, Invermonichele, Ardchyle and Downich, in Glendochart. Patrick Macnab, his grandson, disponed the above lands to his son, Finlay, in 1487. Finlay's grandson, another Finlay, is styled 'of Bovain' in 1503. He married Mariota Campbell, to whom he granted a liferent charter of the lands of Ewer and Leiragan, ca. 1522. The IXth laird, John MacNab, married Eleyn Stewart, and died before 1558. Finlay, Xth chief resigned his lands in favour of Colin Campbell of Glenorchy in 1553. His son Finlay married Katherine, a natural daughter of Colin, who conveyed the lands to him ca. 1548. Their son Alexander succeeded to the lands, and his son, Finlay, was the last of the family to bear that forename. He became involved in the Civil War and deserted the Campbells to join Montrose. His son Ian *min Macanaba*, 'smooth John' led the clan, and was killed in Breadalbane in 1653.

Major John MacNab, XVth laird, served in the Hanovarian Army in 1745, and was taken prisoner at Prestonpans. He was released after the Jacobite defeat at Culloden. His eldest son, Francis, 1734–1816, XVIth of Bovain, is well-known from his full length portrait by Sir Henry Raeburn. He was never married, but had a number of natural children. He inherited an encumbered estate, but continued to live the life of a feudal lord. When he died the chiefship devolved on Archibald, 1777–1860, son of Dr Robert MacNab of Bovain. He married Margaret Robertson, and had six children who all predeceased him, except Sarah Anne who died unmarried in 1894. Archibald, to avoid a writ of caption, emigrated in 1823 to Renfrew County, Ontario, Canada, where he attempted to establish a feudal lordship. This involved him in various problems, and he fled to the Orkneys, later to France, where he died in 1894. His cousin, Allan Napier MacNab, became Premier of Upper Canada.

James William MacNab, 1831–1915, of Arthurstone became *de jure* 19th chief, and in time his grandson, Lt. Col. James Alexander MacNabb, was 20th *de jure* chief. He transferred his right to James William MacNab's fourth son, Archibald Corrie MacNab,

1886–1970, who had prospered as a civil servant in India, and bought back 7000 acres of the old clan territory. He married Alice MacLeod (Dunvegan) and was recognised as *de facto* 21st chief of the clan in 1954. Having no children, he was succeeded as 22nd chief by the above Lt. Col. James Alexander MacNab, whose son James Charles MacNab, born 1926, is 23rd chief. His heir is James William Archibald MacNab.

MacNACHTAN The MacNachtan or MacNaughton clan is of undoubted antiquity, but its history has been much neglected. The name means 'son of Nechtan', an ancient Pictish name which also appears in the *Cinel Loarn*, a branch of the Scottish royal house of Dalriada. A similar name, *Naiton*, was known among the Britons of Strathclyde. The resemblance to MacNaught, MacNitt and MacNaught, prolific names in the south-west, is noteworthy. Families such as McNaught of Kilquahnity and McNeight of barns, may have no connection with the MacNachtons found in Argyll, Perthshire and Fife, and probably earlier around the Moray Firth and on the island of Lewis, where a castle was named Macnauchtane. There is also a place called Macnaughton, near Irongray, Dumfriesshire. The Macnachtans were thanes of Loch Tay, possessing land between there and Lochawe. The earliest reference to them makes their eponymous ancestor *Neachtain Mor*, of the *Cinel Loarn*, who lived about the beginning of the 9th century. The earliest printed source says they descend from Nauchtan, an eminent man in Argyll in the time of Malcolm IV (1153–65), who received lands at Lochawe.

Malcolm, the 1st chief, was father of Gillechrist, Aith, and Sir Gilbert. Gilliechrist was of baronial rank, and gave a church at the head of Loch Fyne to Inchaffray Abbey, in Perthshire, ca. 1246. His brother gave a church on an island in Loch Awe to the same Abbey. Gillechrist, who held the lands at Lochawe, had a charter ca. 1267 appointing him hereditary keeper of the royal castle of Fraoch Eilean. The family lands made up of twelve baronies which were formed in 1292 into the new sheriffdom of Argyll. They came to hold land in Glenshira and Glenlyon, from whence they spread to Kenmore and Fortingal. On Lochtayside as late as 1769, there were thirteen MacNaughton crofters, including John of Portban, whose descendants lived at Remony, Pitlochry and Aberfeldy. Numerous MacNaughtons went to the USA in the 18th century and to Canada in the 19th century.

Donald MacNachtan of Dunderave, Loch Fyne, opposed Robert

the Bruce, who deprived him of some land when he became king in 1306. However, his son Alexander received a charter of entail in 1343 of lands which had belonged to the deceased John, son of Duncan, son of Alexander of Islay, and some which had belonged to John, son of the parson. These were presumably kinsmen, and the lands helped to restore the family fortunes. Alexander, 6th chief, was the father of Duncan, the next chief, and by Mariota de Cardney, mistress of King Robert II, he had a natural son, Donald MacNachtane (?1385–1440), Dean of Dunkeld, who was elected Bishop in 1437, but died while on a journey to Rome for confirmation. A MacNachtan chief is said to have died at Flodden, 1513, but this has not been proved. Gilbert MacNachtan of Dunderave appears in the *Treasurer's Accounts* during that year. In 1617, Alexander MacNachtan had a commission to raise 200 bowmen to serve in the war against France. The last MacNachtan of Dunderave lost his lands and died at Edinburgh in 1773, without issue. A scion of the family, Shane *Dhu*, went to Ireland ca. 1580 and the name came to be spelled MacNaghten. In 1818, Edmund Alexander MacNaghten (1762–1832), of Dunderave, in County Antrim, a barrister, at the desire of 400 clansmen, was recognised as chief by Lyon Court. He died unmarried, and his brother, Francis, assumed the additional surname of Workman and was knighted in 1809. He was created a Baronet in 1836. The 4th Baronet, Sir Edward, a distinguished lawyer, was created a Lord of Appeal and a Life Peer in 1887. The 11th and present Baronet and clan chief is Sir Patrick Alexander MacNaghten, born 1927, who resides at Dunderave, Bushmills, C. Antrim. His son and heir is Malcolm Francis MacNaghten.

MacNEIL   There are reasonable grounds for accepting that the MacNeils or MacNeills descend from Aeod Athaeuch, who ruled in Aileach before 1033, and whose ancestor was Niall of the Nine Hostages, who ruled Tara, in Ireland, ca. AD 400. They may have arrived in the Western Isles as early as the 11th century, and married into the old royal house of Dalriada. The genealogies of the MacNeils of Barra may, however, be viewed with reservations; so also their claim to cheifship of the clan from an early date. Possibly their residence in Barra resulted from marriage to a MacRuari heiress of the old Norse Celtic sea kings before 1427, when Gilleonan, son of Ruari, son of Murchard MacNeill, obtained a charter of the island, and of Boisdale, in Uist, from Alexander, Lord of the Isles. The sable galley of the MacNeil arms certainly suggests some link with the MacRuaries.

The genealogy is fairly accurate from the time of Marchard and his son Ruari, said to have been chief of the *Clann Niall*. As late as 1530, Torquil MacNeil, of the collateral line of Gigha, was referred to by the Privy Council as 'chief and principal of the clan and surname of Macnelis'. The power of the Gigha line waned in the days of Campbell expansion into the Inner Hebrides, and evidently that of the MacNeils of far off Barra, in the Outer Isles, increased. That line has long been recognised as the chiefs. The MacNeils of Colonsay are a branch of the MacNeils of Gigha and Taynish, whose pedigree has been proved back to Torquil MacNeil, who had a grant of Gigha and Danna in 1440 by Alexander, Lord of the Isles, and at the same time certain lands in Knapdale, with the constabulary of Castle Sween. Recent research suggests there was some relationship with the MacLeans of Duart and Lochbuie. Another branch of the MacNeils of Taynish are those of Kippilaw, later of Nonsuch. An early member was Lachlan of Tearfargus and Losset, in Kintyre, who was the first chieftain of the clan to record his arms in *Lyon Register*.

Roderick *Dhu* MacNeil was a Jacobite, known in song and story. He supported Dundee in 1689, and James III in the '15. His son Roderick also fought in the '15, and in the '45 was captured and taken to London, but was released in 1747. The MacNeil ownership of Barra continued until 1838, when the island and castle were sold by Gen. Roderick MacNeil. He died without issue and the chiefship passed to his kinsman, Hector Edward, son of his third cousin, Hector MacNeil of Ersary. In 1937, Robert Lister MacNeil, 1889–1970, upon whom the chiefship had devolved by tanistry (established in Lyon Court, 1915), with the help of his second wife, Marie Stevens, recovered and restored the old stronghold on Barra, and also recovered some of the lands. His son, the present chief, who had a distinguished legal career in the USA, is Prof. Ian Roderick MacNeil of Barra, born 1929, who now lives in Scotland. The heir is his son Roderick.

Several members of the Colonsay family were also eminent in the legal profession. Duncan MacNeill, 1793–1867, became Lord Justice General as Lord Colonsay. A younger brother, Archibald, 1803–70, WS, was one of the Clerks of Session, and for a time Keeper of the Registers of Scotland. Wallace MacNeil, of Brevaig, PEI, Canada, entered a caveat in connection with the undifferenced arms granted to Robert Lister MacNeil, but has not prosecuted his claim to the chiefship.

MACPHERSON Macpherson means 'son of the parson'. Clerical celibacy was late in being enforced in the Highlands, and in any case was often ignored by old families who traditionally filled sacred offices in their own territory. Many people called *Mac a phearson* descended from different parsons: thus Macphersons appear in many parts of Scotland.

The principal kindred of the name are the famous *Clan Mhuirich*, who were of Celtic origin and migrated from Lochaber into Badenoch, and gradually settled mainly in Strathnairn and Strathdearn. Their eponymous ancestor was Muriach, chief of the old Clan Chattan, whose younger son, Ewen *Ban*, was prior of Kingussie ca. 1173. The descendants of three brothers – Kenneth, Ian (or John), and Gillies – traditionally offspring of the parson, formed the three great divisions of the clan: the *Sliochd Choinnich*, the *Sliochd Iain*, and the *Sliochd Ghilliosa*, from all three of which sprang numerous cadets. Kenneth's descendants included families in Cluny, Nuide, Blairgowrie, Dalraddie and Brin. The Cluny line came to be recognised as chiefs, although their position was later challenged. Duncan, parson of Laggan ca. 1438, was the father of Donald *Mor*, who seems to have been the first to adopt the name Macpherson. He was succeeded by his son Donald *Dall*, reckoned 5th chief, and his second son was ancestor of the Macphersons of Breakachy. Andrew, 8th chief, who defended Ruthven Castle against the Earl of Argyll in 1594, had a son, Lt. Col. Ewan, who died before him, leaving two sons, Andrew, 9th chief, and Duncan, 10th chief, who recorded arms in 1672. He left an heiress, Anna, who married Archibald, son of Sir Hugh Campbell of Calder. When it appeared by the marriage settlement that Duncan intended his son-in-law to succeed him, the clansmen, fearing that the estate would be tailzied away to a stranger, signed a protest in 1689, in favour of William Macpherson of Nuide, the heir male, whose son Lachlan became 11th chief. His natural brother was Andrew, father of James 'Ossian' Macpherson. Ewen, the 12th chief, was involved in the '45 Jacobite Rising, and was some time in hiding, with a price on his head. His lands were forfeited, but restored to his son Duncan. Three sons of Ewen, 14th chief, succeeded in turn, and their nephew, Ewen George, became 18th chief. Cluny was the home of the chiefs until 1932, and passed from the clan some ten years later. Ewen George emigrate to Adelaide, Australia, where he died without issue, and the chiefship became vested in William Alan MacPherson, styled 'of Cluny and Blairgowrie', 27th representative, an eminent jurist and soldier, knighted in 1983. The heir is his son Alan Macpherson.

Of several branches flourishing today may be mentioned that of Michael Alastair Fox Macpherson, a director of several companies, who has a home at Duror of Appin. He is the son of Stephen M. Fox and Margaret Gertrude Macpherson of Pitmain. Thomas Macpherson, 1888–1965, of Warley, Essex, son of James Macpherson, Muirhead, Chryston, Lanarkshire, was MP for Romford Borough, 1945–50, and in 1951 was created Baron of Drumochter. His son, James Gordon Macpherson, the 2nd Baron, resides at Kyllachy, Tomatin, Inverness-shire. A Clan Macpherson Association was formed in 1947, and in 1952 the first ever clan museum was opened at Newtonmore.

MacQUARRIE

Although a small clan, the MacQuarries or MacQuarrys have made their mark in places far from their homeland: the isle of Ulva and adjacent part of Mull, in the Western Isles. The surname is derived from the Gaelic 'son of Guaire', itself an old personal name meaning proud or noble. According to the old genealogies, Guaire was a brother of Fingon, name-father of the Mackinnon chiefs, and descended from Cormac, son of Airbertach, descended from one the dynastic families of Dalriada. The MacQuarries, like larger clans, married into neighbouring families and founded cadet houses.

Two charters by John, Lord of the Isles and Earl of Ross, were witnessed by John McGeir of Wlua, in 1463. This is probably Jon Makquhory of Wlway, who died ca. 1473. When rebellion broke out under Donald *Dubh* of the Isles in 1503, Makcorry of Wllowa (Dunslaf, son of John), and others, were several times summoned before parliament to answer for treasonable acts, but did not compear. In 1509, along with several others, he was ordered to pay Duncan Stewart of Appin and his tenants for goods and cattle they had taken. Dunslaf or *Donn-sleibe*, 'Lord of the Hill', had a natural son, John, legitimated before 1540. He had a remission in 1546, for assisting the English in burning the islands of Bute and Arran.

In 1630, Donald Makquoyrie in Ulway was served heir to his grandfather, Hector, in the lands of Ulva, the Isle of Staffa (famous for its coastal caves), and some lands in Mull. He married Christian, daughter of Lachlan *Oig* MacLean of Torloisk, and was succeeded by his eldest son Alan, who was involved in the Civil War, and lost his life at Inverkeithing in 1651. In 1689, when his son Alan was chief, the family writs were burned, and this suggests he was probably involved in the Revolution. John, the next laird, seems to have lived quietly at Ulva, where his son, Lachlan, entertained Johnson and Boswell on the night of 16/17 October, 1773. The English moralist found the chief 'intelligent, polite and much a man of the world'. However, Lachlan was forced to sell his encumbered estate in 1777, retaining only Little Colonsay, which was sold later. He became an officer in the 75th Regiment, and died at Pennygown, Mull, in 1818, reputedly a centenarian. His eldest daughter, Marie, married Gilleon MacLaine of Scallastle, a cadet of Lochbuie, and became known as the 'Mother of Heroes', four of her seven sons having fought in the Napoleanic Wars. The main cadets of the clan were the MacQuarries of Ormaig, Laggan and Bellighartan. Some MacQuires descend from MacQuarries.

The most famous clansman was Maj. Gen. Lachlan Macquarrie who, after a relatively obscure army career, was Governor-General of New South Wales, Australia, where he made many changes, including reducing the number of licensed premises in Sydney from seventy-five to twenty! His popularity is reflected in the naming of Macquarrie River, and other places in Australia. His brother Charles, also a soldier, was for several years laird of Ulva, but not clan chief. The population was reduced and the clan became scattered. Sir Albert MacQuarrie, son of Algernon Stewart MacQuarrie, served in the army during World War II, and became MP for Aberdeenshire East, 1979–83, and for Banff and Buchan, 1983–87. He was knighted in 1987, and resides at Troon. Robert William Munro, the Edinburgh octogenarian journalist and author, has done much research on the MacQuarries.

MacQUEEN The surname comes from *MacSuibne*, 'son of Siubne', a personal name meaning 'good going', and is of Celtic origin. Hector MacSouthyn attended an inquest at Dunbarton in 1271, and Duncan McQuene was a burgess of Perth in 1613. The 'hanging judge', Robert MacQueen, 1722–99, of Braxfield, was born in Larark, and died in Edinburgh. It is generally agreed that the Skye MacQueens are of Norse/Celtic stock, probably from the personal name *Sveinn*. They produced numerous clergymen, who ministered at Durinish, Uig, Snizort, Kilmuir-in-Trotternish, and other Hebridean parishes. Reverend Adam MacQueen, son of Murdo in Uig, emigrated to Ontario, Canada in 1849. It was probably a branch of the Skye MacQueens who migrated to Moidart and early in the 15th century rose to the status of a minor clan, and attached themselves to Clan Chattan. The name appears frequently in the Hebrides as MacSween. Professor John

MacQueen, born 1929, served in the RAF, 1954–56, and was director of the School of Scottish Studies (University of Edinburgh), 1969–88. He is author or editor of a number of historical works. Hector MacQueen, born 1956, is Professor of Private Law in the University of Edinburgh, and has also written several books.

MacRAE The surname MacRae, with variants such as MacRae, McRae, and Mackrae, is not a patronymic like MacDonald and other Highland names. It is probably of ecclesiastical origin, and in Gaelic is rendered *MacRath*, 'son of grace'. It appears in Scotland and Ireland from the 5th century to the 13th as such, and originated independently in more than one place and time, with people in no way related to each other.

Macraith de Ospitali witnessed a gift of the church of Dunrod by Fergus, Lord of Galloway, to the canons of Holyrood, confirmed before 1165. Macracht, deacon of Carrick, ca. 1202, was possibly the same person. Alexander Macrad witnessed a charter of lands in Luss to Maldoon, son of Gillemore, by Maldouen, 3rd Earl of Lennox, ca. 1225. Macrath ap Molegan of Dumfriesshire rendered homage to Edward I in 1296, and had his lands restored. In 1376, Patrick McRey was a tenant in Tibbers Penpont. Christinus McRath, the first on record at Inverness in 1386, was probably ancestor of the tribe which moved from Clunes, in the lordship of Lovat, to Wester Ross when there was pressure on land. After this time MacRaes appear also in Perthshire and in the south-west.

In Kintail, the Macraes were at first vassals of the Earls of Ross, then became loyal to the MacKenzies. They formed a bodyguard for the chief, and were known as his 'shirt of mail'. In the 15th century the MacKenzie chiefs moved to Kinellan, in Strathpeffer, leaving the MacRaes as constables of the picturesque Eilean Donan Castle, in Loch Duich, and as chamberlains of Kintail. Some were clergymen in the district. The Rev. Farquhar MacRae, 1580–1662, son of Christopher MacRae, constable of Eilean Donan, was parson of Kintail, 1618–62, and sometime constable of Eilean Donan. His son Donald was his assistant and successor, and died ca. 1681. Another son, Rev. John, became minister at Dingwall. Reverend Farquhar was the progenitor of the MacRaes of Conchra and Inverinate.

At the Battle of Auldearn in 1645, the MacRaes fought under the MacKenzie chiefs in the army of Montrose, and it is recorded that more of them fell than the Maclennans, who were the standard bearers. At the commencement of the 18th century, Duncan

MacRae, a clansmen of immense strength and a poet, gained local fame when he recovered stolen cattle from reivers in Lochaber. He was killed with many other MacRaes at Sheriffmuir in 1715. Except for a few individuals, they took no part in the '45, perhaps because they lacked a chief. A large number enlisted in the Seaforth Highlanders when that regiment was formed in 1778. They took part in a mutiny at Leith, claiming they had only joined for a limited period and not for overseas service. However, in 1781, they agreed to embark for the West Indies. Writing in the *Old Statistical Account*, in 1793, the minister of Kintail recorded that the natives of the parish 'are all MacRaes, except two or three families'. Emigration considerably thinned their numbers in Kintail, but they are found all over Scotland, and in the USA, Canada, Australia and New Zealand.

MacRae of Inverinate, in Kintail, claimed chiefship and Sir Colin MacRae, 1844–1925, WS, of this line of the family, petitioned Lyon Court in 1909 for recognition. The claim was opposed by MacRae of Conchra, who alleged there was no chief, and no decision was made. Sir Thomas Innes of Learney, Lord Lyon, 1945–69, considered the idea of 'no representer' to be untenable. The Inverinate and Conchra families are both armigerous. Lieutenant Col. John MacRae of the Conchra line purchased the ruined castle of Eilean Donan, and did restoration work.

MacTAVISH The surname derives from the Gaelic MacTomais, 'son of Thomas'. Variants are MacThomas, MacComb, MacCombich and MacCombie. A distinct group lived around Kilmartin and Glassary, in Argyll. In 1533, John, son of Ewen MacTavish, and his son, Dugal, had a feu charter of lands at Tonardare, Dunnavis, Barddarroch, Barinloskin and Barindaif, from The Earl of Argyll. It is reckoned that ten generations of the family held Dunardry for over 200 years, and members of that family spread all over Knapdale. Duncan McThomais is recorded at Glassary in 1355, when he served on an inquest regarding the lands of that parish. The MacTavishes were suspected of Jacobite sympathies. Dugal, son of Archibald, the chief of the family, was arrested in 1745, but released under the amnesty of 1747. The Duke of Argyll made him one of his factors and chamberlains, with the office of Baron Baillie. Dugal purchased the estate of Inverluss in 1757, but his successor Lachlan failed and Dunardry was sold in 1785.

Another group of McTavishes settled in Stratherrick, and became a sept of the Frasers. A number of them became fur traders in the USA and Canada. Simon MacTavish, 1750–1804, from Garthbeg, son of John MacTavish, of the 78th Regiment, emigrated to New York, and settled in Albany County. Later, he went to Montreal and became a clerk with the North-West Co. He became wealthy and in 1800 purchased the old MacTavish estate of Dunardry. Among others in the Canadian fur trade was Donald McTavish, from Stratherrick, a cousin of the above Simon, who became a partner of the North-West Co. by 1799. He commanded an expedition to Fort Astoria in 1813, and brought the post under the care of the North-West Co. He was drowned near the mouth of the Columbia River in 1814.

MacWILLIAM/WILLIAMSON The earliest MacWilliams
of note were of the blood royal. Malcolm Canmore, King of Scots (1057–93), had a son Duncan, probably by Ingebiorge, widow of the northern jarl, Thorfin. Some historians state that she was his first wife, while others, including Lord Hailes, considered Duncan to be illegitimate. He was probably a hostage in England from 1072–87, and knighted by King William Rufus on his release. Duncan expelled his uncle Donald *Bane*, who had asserted his claim to the throne after the death of King Malcolm and Queen Margaret, in 1093; their children being all under age. In 1094 Duncan reigned, but was assassinated and Donald *Bane* again occupied the throne until ousted in 1097 to allow Edgar, son of Malcolm and Margaret, to be King of Scots.

The descendants of Duncan II, in more than one generation, put forward claims to the Scottish crown. Duncan's son William Fitz Duncan, claimed, and he had two sons, William and Donald, surnamed MacWilliam. Donald invaded Ross and Moray, but was defeated and killed in 1187 at Mangarve, Inverness, by forces led by Roland of Galloway. Donald MacWilliam left at least two sons: Donald *Ban*, slain in an insurrection in Moray in 1215, and Guthred. The latter led a revolt in the north in 1211, and was captured by an army commanded by an English nobleman: probably Saier de Quincy, Earl of Winchester. Guthred was executed at Kincardine and hung up by the feet. It seems there was a government attempt to exterminate the MacWilliams, and there is a confused account of a rising in 1230, and of an infant of the race having its brains dashed out against the market cross at Forfar.

The name William became prolific in England after the Norman Conquest and, in spite of the fate of the above MacWilliams, was also popular in Scotland, resulting in various families of MacWilliams, Williamsons and Wilsons, not of common ancestry. Many MacWilliams and Williamsons lived in Glenlivet, and are found there in old records as MacWillie, MacWullie, MacKullie and MacVillie. The Glenlivet tribe became attached to Clan Macpherson, and others are supposed to be of MacFarlane ancestry, but this is disputed. It is also said that a branch of the MacLeods of Dunvegan, descended from William, 5th chief, who died ca. 1402, took the name MacWilliam, and were known as *Clann Mhic Uilleim*. The Robertsons of Pittagowan, early in the 16th century, were known as MacWilliams. In the south-west the name often took the form of Macuilam and MacQuilliam.

In 1317, John Williamson held land in Peebles, and Adam, son of William, rendered the accounts there in 1343. Between 1620 and 1680, the burgh was frequently represented by Williamsons. James Williamson, Provost of Peebles in 1638, signed the *National Covenant*, and James of Hutcheonfield recorded arms, 1672–78. He purchased the estate of Cardrona, on which many members of the family resided. Major Gen. William Williamson, who died in 1815, served with the HEIC.

Thomas Williamson, an archer in the Scots Guard in France in 1495, obtained property there, and ca. 1506 married Marguerite, heiress of Guillaume Raolt, seigneur of Mesil Hermey, and his descendants flourished. The pedigree of the family traces Thomas from Duncan Williamson who, in 1381, married Alice MacKenzie of the Kintail family.

John David McWilliam, educated at Leith Academy and Napier University, is Labour MP for Blaydon.

MATHESON The Mathesons claim descent from Gilleon of the Aird, who lived in the first half of the 12th century, and is also said to be ancestor of the MacKenzies. Gilleon is believed to have belonged to a branch of the old royal house of Lorn. Those Mathesons of the north-west, who point to Lochalsh as their homeland, were known in Gaelic as *MacWhathain*, collectively as *Mathanach*. Old genealogies give the meaning as 'son of the bear'. The clan should not be confused with Lowland Matthewsons, 'sons of Matthew', who appear in Galloway, Ayrshire, Kintyre and Fife, where, around Kilconquhar, there was a notable family of Matthewson clockmakers in the late 18th and early 19th century.

The earliest reference to a Matheson is in 1264, when Kermac MacMaghan in Inverness received twenty cows of the fine of the

Earl of Ross, for services rendered. In the Norse sagas he is called Kjarmak, son of Makamel (Cormac Manmathan). Matheson and sometimes Mathieson have been adopted as English forms of the name. The old pedigrees give the descent of the chiefs as Christin, father of Kenneth, father of Mahan, father of Kenneth, father of Murdoch, father of Murdoch of Bower, chief in 1427. John, a succeeding chief, was appointed Constable of Eilean Donan Castle, and sustained attacks by Donald *Gorm* MacDonald of Sleat, in one of which he was killed. The Matheson possessions were greatly reduced, and his son Dugal had no more than a third of Lochalsh. He engaged in squabbles with his turbulent neighbour, MacDonell of Glengarry, in whose dungeon he perished. His son, Murdoch *Buidh*, in an effort to avenge the death of his father, gave up all his farms except Balamcara and Fearnaig to MacKenzie of Kintail, for a body of men to attack Glengarry, but met with little success.

Murdoch had two sons, Roderick of Fearnaig, and Dugal of Balmacara, who was chamberlain of Lochalsh in 1631. The former had only one son, John, father of John *Mor* of Fernaig, who made money in cattle droving and bought Bennetsfield in the Black Isle in 1688. His grandson, John fought at Culloden in 1746, and his grandson died in 1843, leaving encumbered estates. His successors were his nephew and his nephew's son.

John Matheson of Attadale, descended from Dugal of Balmacara, was succeeded by his son Donald, who was in turn succeeded by his brother Alexander of Attadale, who died in 1804. His son John married Margaret, daughter of Capt. Donald Matheson, and sister of Sir James Matheson, 1796–1887, who purchased the island of Lewis, and whose property passed to his nephew, Donald Matheson. Alexander of Attadale's grandson, Alexander, bought in 1839 and 1844, the lands of Ardintoul and Inverinate, and in 1851, the barony of Lochalsh. He was created a Baronet in 1882. The 5th Baronet, Gen. Sir Torquil George Matheson, 1871–1963, was nominated as *Tanastair*, and the chiefly arms tailzied accordingly. The 7th and present Baronet, Major Sir Fergus Matheson, born 1927, served in the Coldstream Guards, and his son, Lt. Col. Alexander Fergus Matheson, serves in the same regiment.

MAXWELL
The surname is of territorial origin, derived from lands on the Tweed, near Kelso Bridge. The lands (now Springwood), were granted to Maccus, son of Undewyn, a Saxon lord, and from whom an attached fishery (OE, *wael*, a pool or

whirlpool) became known as Maccusweil. Maccus witnessed a charter of David I ca. 1149, and in 1159 it is recorded that Herberti Macchuswel donated the church of Macchuswel to the Abbey of Kelso. Sir John de Maccuswel was Sheriff of Roxburgh and Teviotdale early in the 12th century, and became Chamberlain of Scotland. His son Aymer obtained through marriage lands in Renfrewshire and Lanarkshire, and from him descended cadets in the west and south-west. His eldest son, Herbert, rendered homage to Edward I in 1296. His splendid baronial castle of Caerlaverock was captured by the English, but restored to his son Sir John. A descendant, Herbert, was created Lord Maxwell before 1445. Robert, 10th Lord, was created Earl of Nithsdale before 1581. The 5th Earl was forfeited for his part in the Jacobite Rising of 1715. Families possessed of baronetcies are the Stirling-Maxwells of Pollock (dormant), the Heron-Maxwells of Sprinkell, represented by Sir Nigel Mellor Heron-Maxwell, 10th Baronet, residing at Old Harlow, Essex, and the Maxwells of Monreith, represented by Sir Michael Eustace George, Maxwell (*de jure* 9th Baronet), residing at Monreith House, Port William, Newton Stewart. He is a nephew of the novelist, Gavin Maxwell, 1914–69.

MELVILLE The name Maleuile appears on the *Roll of Battle Abbey*, 1066, and derived from Malleville in the Pays de Caux, Normandy. It came early to Scotland. Geoffrey de Melville (variants include Meleuile, Meleville, Maleville and Maleuile), appears to have been a justice under Malcolm IV (1153–65), and with others perambulated various lands, including his own lordship of Liberton. His son Gregory had a grant of lands at Ednam, near Kelso, for the service of a mounted archer. The Melvilles came to be styled 'of Raith'. John of Raith had a charter of the lands of Pitscottie, in Fife, from William Scott of Balweary, in the reign of Robert III (1390–1406). A descendant, Sir John and his wife, Helen Napier, had charters of the lands of Murdocarney in 1536 and 1542. Sir Robert Melville of Murdocarny, 1531–1621, was an extraordinary Lord of Session, by the title of Lord Murdocarny, 1594. He was created Lord Melville of Monymaill. He was succeeded by his only son, Sir Robert. George, 1636–1707, 4th Lord Melville, was created 1st Earl of Melville in 1690. He married in 1655, Catherine Leslie, daughter of Lord Balgonie, and granddaughter of the 1st Earl of Levin, Sir Alexander Leslie, 1590–1661, one of the most noted soldiers of his time. Their second son, David, became 2nd Earl of Melville and eventually inherited as 3rd Earl of Leven. Succeeding earls have served in the House of Lords and in the army. Alexander Robert Leslie Melville, born 1924, 14th Earl of Leven and 13th of Melville, served in the Coldstream Guards during World War II, and was ADC to the Governor-General of New Zealand, 1951–52. He married in 1953, Susan, elder daughter of Lt. Col. Ronald Steuart-Menzies of Culdares, and has issue. The heir to the earldoms is their elder son, David Alexander Leslie Melville, Lord Balgonie.

A number of Melvilles have left their mark on history. Andrew Melville, 1545–1622, was among the courageous band of reformers mentioned in McCrie's *Life of John Knox* (1824). His nephew, James Melville, worked with him in resisting episcopacy. Robert Melville, 1723–1809, was a military officer and antiquarian. The Viscounts Melville belong to the Dundas family.

MENZIES The surname Menzies is of Norman origin, being originally de Meyners, and probably derived from Mesniers, north of Rouen. In England it assumed the form of Manners, and is found there ca. 1180. Robert de Meyners witnessed charters between 1217 and 1249, when he was appointed Great Chamberlain of Scotland. He granted the lands of Culdares, in Glenlyon, to Sir Matthew Moncreiffe, ancestor of the late Sir Iain Moncreiffe of that Ilk, who possessed the deed. Robert also held lands in Rannoch. Members of his family may have married into the blood royal, and the names David and Alexander favoured by them, crop up in the Menzies pedigree. Sir David Menzies was one of the retinue of the Scottish Queen in 1248.

Letters patent were granted to Alexander de Meygneys by Edward I in 1297, and he is probably the man who witnessed the grant of the office of High Constable of Scotland to Sir Gilbert Hay in 1314. Alexander de Meyneris held the lands of Durisdeer, in Nithsdale, but resigned these in the hands of Robert the Bruce, who granted them to James, brother of Walter the Steward. Thomas de Meineris was one of those who signed the Declaration of Independence in 1320, and he was probably the knight to whom Bruce granted the lands of Unwyn (?Oyne) in the Garioch, and other lands in Atholl. Bruce also granted to Alexander Menzies the barony of Glendochart and some land at Finlarig. Robert Maynhers had a charter of half of the barony of Culter from Robert II in 1385. David de Meygnes was one of the hostages for James I in 1425.

John de Mengues who died in 1487, was succeeded by his son Sir

Robert, who obtained a new grant of the family estates, erecting these into the barony of Menzies. In 1665, Sir Alexander Menzies of that Ilk was created a Baronet of NS. The dignity became extinct in 1910, on the death of the 8th Baronet, Sir Neil James Menzies. The Steuart-Menzies family of Culdares descended from Patrick Steuart of Cardney, who married Agnes, daughter of Col. James Menzies, brother of the 1st Baronet. The lineal heir of the Menzies chiefs, Lt. Col. Ronald Steuart Menzies, 1884–1961, petitioned Lyon Court in 1957, and obtained the name and arms of Menzies of Menzies. He had a son David. The clan has links with Australia. Sir Robert Menzies, 1894–1978, born in Victoria, was PM of Australia, 1939–41. Moreover, Sir Douglas Ian Menzies, 1907–74, was Justice of the High Court of Australia.

Two brothers, Gilbert and William, possibly sons of Sir Robert Menzies of Weem, migrated to Aberdeen early in the 15th century. Gilbert became Provost of Aberdeen in 1423 and again in 1439, and obtained the estate of Pitfoddels in 1457. From him descended a long line of lairds who wore the provost's robes over the next 200 years. John Menzies of Pitfodddels gave his estate of Blairs to the RC Church in 1810, and the mansion became Blairs College.

Castle Menzies, the old home of the chiefs near Aberfeldy, became ruinous, but between 1972 and 1977 essential restoration work was done by the Clan Menzies Society. Prince Charles Edward Stuart slept in the Menzies home in 1746, and interesting relics of yesteryear survive. A death-mask of the prince made by the modeller Berdardine Lucheese, was at one time in the castle and came into the possession of a descendant of the antiquarian, Sir David Menzies. It was sold at auction in Glasgow in 1996 for £8000 to Ms Gemma Howard of Wormiston House, Crail. A member of the Menzies family of Culdares introduced the larch tree to Scotland.

MERCER This is an occupational surname, deriving from a draper or dealer in fine cloths (French *Mercier*), and is probably of Norman origin. The name appears in Scotland ca. 1200, when William le Mercer witnessed charters in favour of the Abbey of Kelso. Aleumnus Mercer was party to a bond given by Alexander II to Henry III in 1214 to keep the peace. He had a grant of Tillicoultry from Walter, son of Allan. Duncan Mersar appears in Aberdeen, 1272–81. Two old families, the Mercers of Aldie, near Fossoway, and those of Innerpeffray, near Crieff, made their marks locally. An old rhyme runs:

Sae sycker 'tis as onie thing on earth
The Mercers aye are aulder than auld Perth.

Thomas Mercer held property from the Abbey of Scone, and his son John was Provost of Perth, and sat in the General Council of Scotland, 1364–67. He had charters of Aldie and Meikleour in 1362 and 1364, which descended in the female line to the Landsdowne family. Several Mercers were clergymen. Reverend Laurence Mercer became parson of Fossoway in 1607, and his son, also Rev. Laurence, was minister there, 1647–58. His son, another Rev. Laurence, was minister at Findogask. He was a non-juror and became factor of Aldie. The Rev. William Mercer, 1696–1767, brother of Rev. John Mercer of Tyrie, was minister at Pitsligo, and father of Hugh Mercer, 1725–77, who became a Brig. Gen. in the American Revolutionary War, and died of wounds at Princeton. John Francis Mercer, 1759–1821, descended from the Mercers of Aldie, was eleventh governor of Maryland. The principal family were long styled 'of Gorthie', sold in 1913, but came to be styled 'of Huntingtower', near Perth (now a hotel). Major Laurence Walter Mercer, 1900–51, CIE, had two sons by his first wife, Irene Hind: John Laurence, born 1932, who married Ann Katherine Parker, and has issue; and Andrew Philip, born 1938, a chartered architect and town planner. Sir Walter Mercer, 1890–1971, was a distinguished orthopaedic surgeon, whose home was in Edinburgh. He was the recipient of many honours, including a knighthood in 1956.

MILLAR/MILLER
An occupational name, Millar or Miller, derives from the Latin word *molendino*, and appears all over the country. At one time on large estates, tenants were bound to grind their grain at a particular mill, and to uphold the mill, repair dam dykes, lades or aqueducts, and even to supply the millstones. This was termed thirlage, and the system ensured that the miller would continue in business to the benefit of the community. At some sites generations of millers are found. Surnames such as Milne usually refer to people who lived near a mill.

The earliest references are found in Latin documents, hence an inquest at Dumfries Castle in the reign of Alexander III (1249–93) records the death of Adam Molendinarius. Probably Millar or Miller did not become a hereditary surname until much later. John and Harry Millare were jurors at an inquest regarding fishing in the Tweed, 1467. Margaret Myllar was a tenant of the Bishop of Glasgow in 1509, and Robert Millare held lands at Irvine in 1540. John, 1735–1801, son of the Rev. James Millar, minister of Shotts, was admitted advocate in 1760, and became an eminent lecturer on law at the University of Glasgow. He wrote several legal works, important in his time, including the *Distinction of Ranks in Society*, which was translated into French. Hugh Miller, 1802–56, born at Cromarty, began life as a stonemason and devoted his winter nights to writing, reading and natural history. He became Scotland's first geologist, and his works include *The Testimony of the Rocks* (1857).

Several Miller families became landowners. Among these may be mentioned the Millers of Glenlee, in Galloway, descended from Matthew Miller, who married Agnes, daughter of Rev. William Guthrie, of Fenwick. William, his second son, WS (1719), had three sons: John, Professor of Law at Glasgow, who died unmarried, in 1780; Thomas, admitted advocate, 1742, who rose to be Lord President of the Session; and Patrick, 1731–1815, of Dalswinton, a pioneer of steam navigation, and owner of Ellisland Farm, tenanted by the poet Burns from 1788 to 1791. Thomas became a Baronet in 1789. He was succeeded by his son Sir William, 2nd Baronet, a Lord of Session with the title of Lord Glenlee. The 5th Baronet, Sir William Frederick Miller, served in the South African War and as a staff captain in World War I. Sir Frederick, the 7th Baronet, served in World War II, and his son, the 8th Baronet of Glenlee, is Stephen William MacDonald Miller, a physician, of Shebbear, Beaworthy, in Devon.

A Miller family, styled 'of Monk Castle', Ayrshire, stemmed from William Miller, a Glasgow merchant, whose brother Alexander, also a merchant, purchased the lands of Monk Castle and Craigmill, but these subjects passed to William, served heir in 1725. William Miller, Vth of Monk Castle, married Anna Maria, daughter of Admiral Campbell, of the Portuguese Navy, and had a son, William Augustus Cunningham Miller. Another interesting family, of whom came George Miller, CE, bought the estate of Leithenhope, in Peebleshire, in 1852. Sir William Miller, MP for Berwickshire, 1873–74, was created a Baronet in 1874. He purchased the estate of Manderson, near Duns, and his son, Sir James, 2nd Baronet, built the magnificent mansion there, now owned by Sir Adrian Bailie Nottage Palmer, 4th Baronet of Reading (created 1916), and 4th Baronet (created 1933). His heir is his son, the Hon. Hugo Bailie Rohan Palmer.

MITCHELL The surname Mitchell comes from the Hebrew Michael, through the French form *Michel*. It was a common baptismal name in several countries, and its introduction to Scotland was probably due to French influence. Malcolm IV confirmed to the hospital of St Andrews, one carucate in Kedlock, Fife, granted by Simon, son of Michael. Micheal *Flandrensis*, was clerk to King William, and Sheriff of Edinburgh between 1198 and 1214. An early appearance as a surname occurs in the indenture of the treaty drawn up at Berwick in 1357, for the release of David II, where Thomam Mitchell is mentioned. Robert Michael de Hyrmanston was a charter witness in 1438, and Richard Michel was admitted burgess of Aberdeen in 1475. In 1489, John Michell had a remission for his part in holding Dunbarton Castle against the king.

Mitchells appear as landowners in Ayrshire, where the surname is still prolific, and in various locations all the way to the Shetland Isles. The Mitchells of Bandeth, Stirlingshire, traced their ancestry to James Mitchell, who had the lands confirmed to him in 1578. John Mitchell, Vth of Bandeath, became archdean of Tingwall, Shetland in 1629, and his descendant, John Mitchell, was created a Baronet in 1724. The title became extinct ca. 1783. Thomas Mitchell, Lord Provost of Aberdeen, 1668–1700 and 1702–04, who purchased Thainston, Kintore in 1717, was second son of Thomas Mitchell of Tilliegreig. His descendant, John Forbes-Mitchell, 1843–1882, left a widow, Jane M. Rawson, who was in possession of the estate in 1925. The Mitchells of Carwood, Biggar, produced James D. Mitchell, 1853–1910, one of Lanarkshire's foremost educationalists. Probably the wealthiest landed family became Mitchell-Innes of Stow. William Mitchell, younger son of Alexander Mitchell of Darrahill, Aberdeenshire, inherited in 1839 (following litigation) the estate of his cousin, Jane Innes of Stow. He assumed the surname of Mitchell-Innes. William held the lands of Aytoun and Whitehall, Berwickshire, and inherited Parson's Green. He also owned Bangour and Ingliston, and in 1846 he built the mansion there, since 1958, the mansion of the Royal Highland & Agricultural Society of Scotland. William Mitchell-Innes of Whitehill, married in 1933, Mary Gibson, daughter of George Robert Fortune of Rosebank, Colinsburgh, and had a daughter, Janet Julia, who married in 1955, Matthew W.B. White.

Scots emigrants surnamed Mitchell, who settled in Norway, adopted the form Mitzel. Andrew Mitchell, a Scot, introduced the steam engine to Denmark in 1790. Sir Thomas Livingston Mitchell, 1792–1855, who had a distinguished military career, emigrated to Australia in 1827, where he became an explorer and Surveyor-

General in NSW. Stephen Mitchell, of the famous tobacco firm of Stephen Mitchell & Son, and originally from Linlithgow, bequeathed £66,998 10s. 6d. to the Town Council of Glasgow to create a library bearing his name. By the time they obtained premises at East Ingram Street, interest had enlarged the sum to £70,000. In 1891 the library moved to Miller Street, and in 1911 to its present location at North Street. Next to the National Library of Scotland, it is the most important repository in Scotland. In recent years it has been enlarged and now has conference facilities.

MOLLISON The surname Mollison is associated mainly with north-east Scotland, and especially with Aberdeen from the 15th century. It is derived from the personal name Malise, recorded in Scotland as early as the reign of David I (1124–53). Malise was a marischal under that monarch, and is stated by the eminent medievalist, Geoffrey W.S. Barrow, to have been of Celtic origin. Probably the meaning of the name in Gaelic was *Mael Iosa*, 'shaveling' or 'tonsored servant of Christ'. Malisio or Malisius, son of Leod, appears as a witness to a charter of Lundin, in Fife, by Malcolm IV in 1164, to Philip the Chamberlain and his heirs. Malise, son of Ferteth, Earl of Strathearn, gave to the Abbey of Arbroath, half a merk annually from the fishery at Meiklour, in Perthshire, confirmed by William the Lion in 1199. The name Malise was much favoured by the old earls of Strathearn and by the Stewarts who succeeded them. It passed also to the Grahams of Menteith through Euphemia, Countess Palatine of Strathearn.

Malison or Malyceson appears as a surname in 1391, when Malcolm, so named, witnessed an agreement between the bishop of Aberdeen and the laird of Forbes, regarding the land of Lurgyndespok. Robert Malisei was a juror in an inquest over a third part of Ledyntushe and Rothmais in 1413. In 1445, Thomas Malison was admitted a burgess of Aberdeen, and Willim Malitesone appears as a witness in 1469. John Malison witnessed a charter by William Futhus to the chaplains of the choir, of two annualrents, in 1500. In the early part of the 16th century, John Malison, a priest, appears as master of a music school at Cantore (Kintore). Patrick Malyson was admitted burgess of Aberdeen, 1551/52. He was a goldsmith, and died ca. 1590, leaving a son Thomas. Alexander Malison, related to Provost Alexander Reid, had a son Gilbert, who became an influential burgess of Aberdeen, and was the ancestor of numerous Mollisons who were involved in municipal affairs. His eldest son, John, was killed at the Battle of

Pinkie in 1547, and a younger son, Thomas, became clerk to the Town Council. He was chosen in 1602 to represent the burgh in purchasing a discharge from the king, of their taking part in his prosposed colonisatian of Lewis by Lowlanders. The douce folk of the Granite City wanted no part in such a hazardous enterprise. Gilbert, 1613–89, son of Thomas, became an officer of militia and was a commissioner to the Convention of Royal Burghs in 1673 and 1676. His daughter Christian married the Quaker apologist, Robert Barclay, 1648–90, of Urie. Gilbert's son Gilbert, 1659–1730, went to London, where he became a draper-freeman and Quaker correspondent. Another son, John, emigrated to Piscataway, New Jersey, USA. Other members of the family remained at home.

Patrick Molleson was teacher of a Grammar School at Campbeltown, Argyll, ca. 1775, and had issue by his wife Jean Doig. In the present century, Glasgow born Jim Mollison, 1905–59, distinguished himself as an aviator, breaking many records, including Australia–England, 1931; first solo westward flight, South Atlantic, 1933. With his wife, the famous aviator, Amy Johnson, who died in 1941, he undertook the first UK–USA flight in 1933, and again with her made a record-breaking flight (22 hours), England–India. A film, based on some of their flights, called *They Flew Alone*, was made starring Anna Neagle and Robert Newton. Mollison published *Death Cometh Soon or Late* (1932), in which his portrait appears, and *Playboy of the Air* (1937). He received many awards overseas, and in 1946 was made MBE. Dr Denis Mollison has been Professor of Applied Probability at Heriot Watt University since 1986.

MONCREIFFE

The centre of the old Pictish kingdom was around Perth, the crowning place being Scone and a royal residence at Forteviot. This is the home of the Moncreiffes, and the name is derived from *Monadh Craoibhe*, ' the hill of the sacred bough'. The Moncreiffes, have always borne the royal red lion in their armorial bearings, as did Roger Moubray, who gave a charter to Matthew Moncreiff of the lands of Moncreiff and Balconachin, which were erected into a free barony by a subsequent charter from Alexander II in 1248. Matthew was knighted and held the lands of Culdares and Duneaves, incorporated under a descendant with the barony of Moncreiffe in 1455. In 1296, William de Monncrefe of Angus and John de Moncref of Perthshire appear on the *Ragman Roll*. During the same year, Thomas de Mouncref was a prisoner of war taken at

Dunbar Castle. The Moncreiffes of that Ilk and the barons of Tulliebole, Kinross, descend from the above Sir Matthew Moncreiff. Sir John Moncreiff, who was MP for Perthshire' 1639–41, was created a Baronet of NS in 1626. Sir Hugh Moncreiff, the 6th Baronet, died unmarried in 1744, and the baronetcy devolved upon his kinsman, the Rev. Archibald Moncreiff, minister of Blackford, who married Catherine, daughter of Robert Wellwood of Garvock. Their son, the Rev. Sir Henry Wellwood Moncreiff, the 8th Baronet inherited from his maternal great-uncle, the estate of Tulliebole and assumed the additional surname of Wellwood. He was Moderator of the General Assembly of the Church of Scotland in 1785. The 10th Baronet, the Rev. Henry Wellwood Moncreiff, 1809–83, was succeeded by his brother, James, created Baron Moncreiff of Tulliebole, Kinross-shire, in 1874. He was a distinguished lawyer, and held successively the posts of Solicitor-General, Lord Advocate and Lord Justice Clerk. He died in 1895. The 15th Baronet and 5th Baron Moncreiff is Col. Sir Harry Robert Wellwood Moncreiff, born 1915, residing at Tulliebole Castle. His heir is his son the Hon. Rhoderick Harry Wellwood Moncreiff, born 1954.

The Moncreifff(e)s of that Ilk descend also from Sir Matthew Moncreiff, whose son, Sir John, resigned Easter Moncreiffe in 1312 to a younger son, Mathew, progenitor of the Moncreiffes of Easter Moncreiffe. John Moncreiffe, VIIth of Moncreiffe, was squire to the young King James III, in 1464, and married Beatrix, daughter of James Dundas of that Ilk. Sir John, the IXth laird, was killed at Flodden in 1513, and his son, William, Xth of Moncreiffe, supported the the Earl of Angus at the Battle of Linlithgow Bridge in 1526. He was fined for refusing to sit on the assize that condemned Lady Glamis to be burnt as a witch in 1532. The XIIIth laird, Sir John, sold Moncreiffe to his kinsman, Thomas Moncreiffe, who was created a Baronet of NS in 1685 as Moncreiffe of that Ilk. Under Sir Thomas, who was XIVth laird, the baronies of Moncreiffe and Easter Moncreiffe were united. Sir Thomas Moncreiffe, 3rd Baronet and XVIth laird, eloped in 1730 with Katherine, daughter of the Jacobite Sir William Murray of Ochtertyre, 3rd Baronet, and descended through her grandmother, Margaret Haldane of Gleneagles, from several Highland chiefs. Another Sir Thomas, 7th Baronet and XXth laird, was captain of the Royal & Ancient Golf Club, St Andrews, and a gold medalist. He married in 1843, Lady Louisa Hay, daughter of Lord Lyon, the 11th Earl of Kinnoull. His fourth son was the late Sir Rupert Iain

Kay Moncreiffe, who succeeded as 11th Baronet. He was a brilliant historian, herald, genealogist and author. By his first wife, Diana (Hay), Countess of Erroll, 27th Hereditary Lord High Constable of Scotland, he had two sons and a daughter. The eldest son, Sir Merlin Serald Victor Gilbert Hay, succeeded his mother, and the second son, the Hon. Peregrine David Euan Malcolm Moncreiffe is fiar of the Barony of Moncreiffe and Baron of Easter Moncreiffe.

Moncreiffs (and variant surnames) have left their marks abroad. One of them was involved and died in the plot of 1574 to restore the deposed King Eric of Sweden. Three branches of the family were ennobled in France. One was an eminent scholar and another died in battle. The Marquis de Moncrif was executed during the French Revolution. Thomas Moncreiffe, 1861–87, a grand-uncle of Sir Iain, mentioned above, was a planter in India, and his immediate younger brother, William Moncreiff, 1863–1944, was a rancher in Wyoming, USA. He knew 'Buffalo' Bill Cody and and President 'Teddy' Roosevelt.

MONTGOMERY EARLS According to Dr G.F. Black, the surname Montgomery or Montgomerie is derived from the old castle of Saint Foy de Montgomery, in the diocese of Lisieux, in Normandy. Roger de Montegomerie, ca. 1025–94, described himself as a Norman, but he was probably of mixed blood, as he commanded the powerful Flemish wing of William the Conqueror's invading army. He is probably the 'Mountgomerie' who appears on the *Roll of Battle Abbey*, 1066. His heir was Robert, Earl of Shrewsbury, who married Agnes, heiress of Guy, Count of Ponthieu, and their son William inherited the Countship. Robert Mundegumrie, who was in Scotland with Walter Fitz Alan, was probably a younger son of the Earl, and may have come north in the retinue of his sister's kinswoman, Ada de Warenne, when she married Prince Henry in 1139. His arms were blazoned Azure, a fleur-de-lis Or, denoting his Ponthieu connection. He had a grant of the manor of Eaglesham, in Renfrewshire.

Sir John Montgomerie, who signed the *Ragman Roll* in 1296, was probably VIth of Eaglesham. John Montgomery, the next on record, had sons Alexander and Alan. Marjorie his daughter, appears with another Marjorie (? Yr.), in 1363, conveying the lands of Cassillis to John Kennedy. Alexander's son, John, VIIth of Eaglesham, fought hand to hand with Sir Henry Percy, called 'Hotspur', heir to the Earl of Northumberland, at Otterburn in 1388, and made him captive. He profited from an enormous ransome. John married Elizabeth, heiress of Sir Hugh Eglinton of that Ilk, and it was probably through this union he obtained the lands of Eglinton and Ardrossan. He then quartered the arms of Eglinton with his own.

Alexander, grandson of John, was created a Lord of Parliament in 1445, and was frequently an envoy to England. Hugh, son of his eldest son Alexander was the 2nd Lord, and in 1506/07 was created Earl of Eglinton. From him came the later earls and the Montgomeries of Lainshaw. Hugh's brother George was ancestor of the now extinct line of Skelmorlie. Hugh, the 3rd Earl, was one of those who escorted Queen Mary from France to Scotland in 1561, and he remained loyal to her throughout her troubled reign. His elder son Hugh succeeded as 4th Earl, and his elder daughter Margaret (with a dowry of 10,000 merks) married in 1582, George, 6th Lord Seton, afterwards Earl of Winton. Their third son, Alexander, succeeded his cousin Hugh as 6th Earl of Eglinton. After some problems about recognition he became a favourite of King James, whom he entertained at his house in Glasgow in 1617. Yet another link with the Setons took place in 1662, when Mary, daughter of the 7th Earl of Eglinton, married George, 4th Earl of Winton.

Hugh, 12th Earl of Winton,was created a peer of the UK in 1806, as Baron Ardrossan. He had previously rebuilt Eglinton Castle. His grandson, Archibald William, is remembered as the promoter of the Eglinton Tournament in 1839, intended to honour the ancient code of chivalry. It was attended by Lady Seymour, appearing as the 'Queen of Beauty', but heavy rain marred the event. The 5th Earl of Winton, an attainted Jacobite, died unmarried in 1749, and in 1840 Archibald William Montgomerie had himself served heir male general and heir male of provision to him, but did not establish his right to the peerage dignities. However, in 1859, he was created Earl of Winton. Archibald George Montgomerie, the 18th Earl of Eglinton, is also Lord Montgomerie, Lord Seton and Tranent, Earl of Winton, Baron Ardrossan and Hereditary High Sheriff of Renfrewshire.

MONTGOMERIE OFFSHOOTS Branches of the Eglinton family are found spelling the name Montgomerie and Montgomery. The Montgomerys of Stanhope, Peeblesshire, descend from Robert, younger brother of the 1st Lord Eglinton. He had a grant by his father, Sir John Montgomerie, of Ardrossan, Giffen and other lands in Ayrshire, confirmed by charter, 1413/14. Robert was ancestor of a line of Montgomerys of Giffen, from whom the Montgomerys of Stanhope, in Peeblesshire descended through a cadet branch who purchased Coldcoat, which was renamed Magbiehill. William Montgomery of Magbiehill, passed advocate in 1707, and married Barbara Rutherford. They were the parents of Sir James Montgomery, 1721–1803, also an advocate, who was Solicitor General, 1764–74, and Chief Baron of Exchequer, 1775–81. He promoted a scheme for colonising Lot 34 in Prince Edward Island, Canada, in 1770. His second son, Sir James, was an eminent lawyer, and the family has given the country local and national politicians, soldiers and clergymen. The 8th Baronet, Sir Basil, died without issue and was succeeded by his nephew, Sir Basil Henry David Montgomery, in 1964. He was a Tayside Regional Councillor, 1974–79, and Vice-President of COSLA, 1978–79. George, second son of the 1st Lord Montgomerie, was progenitor of the family of Skelmorlie. Sir Robert, VIIth of Skelmorlie, was created a Baronet of NS in 1628. The male line ended in 1735, and Lilias, daughter of the 5th Baronet, was heiress and carried the estates to her husband, Alexander Montgomerie of Coilsfield, descended from Col. James, fourth son of the 6th Earl of Eglinton. It was their eldest son. Hugh, who inherited the earldom of Eglinton in 1796, and was created Baron Ardrossan. His brother Alexander was ancestor of the Montgomeries of Annick Lodge, Ayrshire.

The Montgomeries of Lainshaw descended from Sir Neil, third son of the 1st Earl of Eglinton. He married Margaret Mure, and their elder son John died without male issue. The younger son, Neil, married Jean, heiress of Lord Lyle, and their son Neil assumed the title of Lord Lyle, but was refused the vote in the election of representative peers in 1721 and 1722. By his wife, Barbara Kennedy, he had a daughter Jean, who married David Laing, who assumed the surname of Montgomery. Their daughter and ultimate heiress Elizabeth, married Capt. Alexander Montgomerie Cunningham, Corsehill. He also assumed the title of Lord Lyle, and was refused the vote in the election of peers in 1784. Lainshaw was sold to the Cunninghams of Bridgehouse.

Branches settled in Ireland. The family Montgomery of Grey Abbey, Co. Down, descended from Sir Hugh Montgomery of Braidstane, descended from Robert, second son of Alexander, Master of Montgomerie, and grandson of the 1st Lord Montgomerie. Hugh, elder son of Adam, Vth of Braidstane, was raised to the peerage of Ireland in 1622 as Viscount Montgomery of Ardes, but the dignity expired with the death of Thomas, 7th Earl, in 1758. Robert Montgomery, cousin of Hugh, went to Ireland early in the 17th century, and continued the Braidstane line, now represented by William Howard Clive Montgomery of Grey Abbey, Newtownards, Co. Down. Another Montgomery family settled near Dunkineely, Co. Donegal, in 1628, and prospered. From them descended the famous Field-Marshall of World War II, Sir Bernard Law Montgomery, 1887–1976 created Viscount Montgomery of Alamein in 1946.

Glasgow-born Colin Montgomerie is currently Scotland's top golfer. For the past six seasons, 1993–98, he has led the European Order of Merit.

MORRISON
Morrisons in various parts of the country do not descend from a common ancestor. The usual interpretation of the name is 'son of Maurice', a common name in medieval times. The Maurice or Mourice, the eponymous ancestor of the Morrisons of Lewis – the *Clann MhicGillemhoire* – is thought to have been a natural son of Olaf the Black, King of Man and the Isles from about 1226. His mother appears to have been Lauon, daughter of a Kinttyre chief, and his wife was a daughter of the chief of the Gows. Mourice was a natural brother of Leod, progenitor of the MacLeods of Lewis and Harris.

The heirs of Mourice became hereditary brieves or justices of Lewis. Hutcheon (Gaelic *Uisdean*), brieve of Lewis, was summoned to Inverness with Rory MacLeod in 1551 for harbouring rebels. The brieves were well versed in Gaelic law, and prior to the fall of the Lordship of the Isles in 1493, there was probably a right of appeal to the Council of the Isles. John Morrison, brieve of Lewis, was a supporter of Torquil Cononach during the troubles caused by the Fife Adventurers in the time of King James VI. Another Hutcheon appears as brieve in 1616. Those later brieves were MacDonalds by blood, as the Morrison heiress married ca. 1346, Cain MacDonald of Ardnamurchan. The only Hebridean Morrisons who recorded arms were those of Ruchdi, North Uist, who traced their descent from the Morrisons of Dun of Pabbay, descended from the brieves. William Shepherd Morrison, 1893–1961, was a younger son of John, son of John Morrison of Ruchil and Ann Ross. He served in World War I in the RFA, and was wounded and mentioned in despatches three times. He afterwards studied law, and became MP for Cirencester and Tewkesbury, 1929–59. He rose to become Speaker of the House of Commons, 1951–59, the only Gaelic speaker ever to hold that post.

In 1959 he became Viscount Dunrossil of Valaquie, North Uist. His widow, Catherine Alison, daughter of the Rev. Dr William Swan, of South Leith, born in 1893 was survived by four sons. John Morrison, eldest brother of the Viscount, married her sister, Dorothy Mary Swan. He was granted arms in 1959 as chief of the Morrisons. A Lewis man, Alexander, son of Alexander Morrison in Habost, Ness, graduated at Aberdeen in 1908 and had a distinguished teaching career in South Africa.

In Aberdeenshire, a notable family descended from Alexander Morison, who obtained the lands of Bognie in 1635. His son George married Christian, Viscountess Frendraught, and he redeemed the wadset of the estate. In 1673 he had a grant of arms: Azure, three saracen's heads conjoined on one neck Argent. The arms are similar to those recorded, 1672–78, for Alexander Morrison of Prestongrange, a Lord of Session, whose kinsman, Henry Morrison, WS, also registered arms. Theodore Morison of Bognie, son of George, attended Aberdeen Grammar School, and excelled at archery, for which he provided a medal bearing his father's arms. From his second son, James, of Strewberry Vale, Finchley, Middlesex, descended the later lairds of Bognie and Frendraught.

The Hon. Lord Morison (Alastair Malcolm Morison), a Senator of the College of Justice since 1985, comes from a family who have been prominent in legal circles. His father, Sir Ronald Peter Morison, 1900–76, QC, was admitted advocate in 1923 and to the English Bar in 1940. He was a son of the Rt Hon. Thomas B. Morison, 1868–1945, PC, who was admitted advocate in 1891 and to the English Bar in 1899. He became a KC in 1906, and was Solicitor-General for Scotland, 1913–20, and Lord Advocate, 1920–22. In 1922 he became a Senator of the College of Justice, and retired in 1937. He was a son of Peter Morison, SSC.

Morrison is a prolific surname around Durness, in Sutherland, and according to tradition the ancestors came from Lewis. Their tartan is that of their Mackay neighbours, with a red line added.

MOWAT Of Norman-French origin, the earliest Mowats took their name from *Mont Hault*, Latinised *Monte Alto*. They settled in North Wales, where Monteralt, reduced to Mold, is a form of the name, which first appears in Scotland in the reign of David I (1124–53). The family rose to power in their new home. In the reign of William the Lion (1165–1214) they obtained lands in Angus, and spread out from there all the way to the Orkneys and south as far as the Lothians. William de Montealto witnessed an inspection of the marches of Arbroath Abbey in 1219. Sir Bernard de Monte Alto and other knights accompanied Princess Margaret to Norway, and on the return journey was drowned. In 1296, Willielmus de Monte Alto signed the *Ragman Roll*. Axel Mowat, 1593–1661, a scion of the Mowats of Balquholly, Aberdeenshire, became an admiral of the Norwegian-Danish Fleet. Another branch of the family, through the Dumbreck line, obtained Ingliston, in Mid Lothian (site of the Royal Highland & Agricultural Show since 1959), in 1664, when George Mowat, Knight, was created a Baronet of NS. A daughter of Sir George married William, son and heir of William Mure of Glanderston, in Renfrewshire. The baronetcy descended to George Mowat's grandson, Sir Alexander, but became extinct. Several Orkney Mowats, variously spelled Moat and Mouat, served in the Canadian fur trade.

MUNRO Modern historians, while agreeing that the early Munros were of Celtic origin, are sceptical of the idea they were descended from one of the indigenous tribes of Moray, such as the *Vacomagi*, and scorn the old story that the name signifies 'Man from Roe', meaning a man from the foot of the River Roe, Derry, Ireland. Old genealogies bring them from Ewen, son of Donald *Dhu*, and traces them up to Milan, the son of Neil. Moreover, the tradition that Donald, from whom their territory of Ferindonald (roughly equivalent to the Ross parishes of Alness and Kiltearn), is supposed to have been named, came to Scotland with some forces to assist Malcolm II (1004–34) against the Danes, and was rewarded with some lands to the east of Dingwall, no longer has credibility. In Gaelic the Munros form *Clann Rothaich*, and their origin has been described as one of the great problems of clan history. The title of the chiefs has always been Munro of Foulis.

At first the Munros were vassals of the Lords of the Isles and Earls of Ross, and were becoming established as a clan in the reign of Alexander III (1249–86). Robert de Monro had a charter from Robert the Bruce of Counetis, in Strathspey, and the lands of Cupermakcultis, and in 1338, George Munro witnessed a charter of lands in Badenoch. In 1364, Robert Munro was given a charter by William, Earl of Ross, 'of the haill clavoch of land of Easter Foules and the fortar of Strathskea, with the milne, fishings and other pertinents'. He married Jane Ross, a niece of Queen Euphame, consort of Robert II. Robert Munro was killed in 1369 in a scuffle in defence of his superior. After this time the Munros are well documented. Hugh Munro had grants of land from his cousin, Euphame, Countess of Ross, in 1394, and these were confirmed to his son, George, in 1426. In 1453, John Munro had sasine of Easter and Wester Foulis, as heir to George, his father. Hugh, a younger son of George, was ancestor of the Munros of Coul. A relative, Fr Thomas Munro, sub-dean of Ross, acted at times as secretary to the Lord of the Isles.

In the time of Queen Mary, Robert *Mor* Munro of Foulis was firmly attached to her cause, and as a reward had a tack of the Crown customs of the town and shire of Inverness. His grandson, Robert, was in favour with James VI. A later laird, Robert, greatly encumbered the estate, but his brother Hector did much to restore prosperity. He fought in the German Wars, and on his return was in 1634 created a Baronet, of NS. His son, Sir Hector, died at the age of sixteen and the honour passed to his kinsman, Sir Robert, grandson of Robert Munro of Obsdale. This family came to be styled 'of Foulis-Obsdale'. Sir Harry, 7th Baronet, was MP for Ross-shire, 1746–47, and for Wick Burghs, 1747–61. By the will of her father, Sir Hector, 11th Baronet, his daughter Eva, having survived her two brothers, and married Lt. Col. Cecil Orby Gasgoigne, assumed the surname Munro of Foulis in 1935, and relinquished it in 1938. The baronetcy passed to Sir George Hamilton Munro, 12th Baronet, and his grandson, Sir Arthur Herman Munro, 1893–1972, of Foulis-Obsdale, 14th Baronet, was succeeded by his cousin, Ian Talbot Munro. Eva Marion Munro's son Patrick, 1912–95, became chief of the clan, and was succeeded by his eldest son, Hector W. Munro of Foulis. The Munros of Lindertis, in Angus, descend from Hugh Munro, the clan chief who fought at Harlaw in 1411.

Brothers of the 1st Baronet of Foulis fought against Cromwell, and one of them, William, with some clansmen, was captured at Worcester in 1651 and transported to New England. A descendant, Ebenezer Munro, 1752–1825, claimed to have fired the first shot in the American Revolutionary War. From another prisoner, Andrew Munroe, taken at Preston in 1648, descended James Munroe, 1758–1831, 5th President of the USA. There was a branch of the clan in France, and another at Lower Iveagh, in Ireland.

MURE/MOOR Since Mure, and variants such as Mure, More, Moore and Muir, usually stem from people who lived on or beside a moor, it is not surprising that the surnames are prolific in the Scottish Lowlands. In Gaelic, however, *Mor* means big, and possibly some surnames derived from that descriptive name. The earliest reference to the surname appears during the reign of Alexander II (1214–49), when David de Mure, of the house of Polkelly, Ayrshire, witnessed a charter. He may have been the father of Reginald of Craig (of Rowallan), and others who swore fealty to Edward I in 1296. Gilchrist More, another who signed the *Ragman Roll*, was ejected from Rowallan, in Ayrshire, by Sir Walter Cumyn, and ordered to keep to his castle of Polkelly. Eventually he retrieved Rowallan and other lands by his marriage to Isobel, daughter of Sir Walter Cumyn! The remote ancestry of those landed men is obscure, but they may have come from Kent, the original home of the Irish peers of Drogheda, surnamed Moore.

Archibald Mure of Rowallan, who was slain at Berwick in 1297, left a son William, his heir, and possibly another, Reginald, progenitor of the Mures of Caldwell. An important member of the family was Sir Adam of Rowallan, who married his distant cousin, Janet, heiress of Polkelly, and had two sons, Sir Adam and Andrew, and a daughter Elizabeth, who married in 1348, Robert, Steward of Scotland, afterwards King Robert II. The parties were within the fourth degree of consanguinity, and although a dispensation was obtained, arguments regarding the legitimacy of their son Robert III, were once commonplace. Sir William Mure of Rowallan, 1594–1657, was a notable poet, and he translated Boyd of Trochrig's Latin poem, 'Hecatombe Christiana'. His main work was his *True Crucifix for Catholics* (1629). Sir William became a Covenanter. He was twice married and had seven sons and eight daughters. His heir, William, was also a Covenanter, and the youngest son, Sir Patrick, was created a Baronet of NS in 1662. The title ended with Sir William Mure, who died in 1700.

Sir Reginald Mure of Caldwell, by his marriage to Sybilla, daughter of Sir John Graham of Dalkeith, obtained extensive lands. Sir Adam, a later laird, who died ca. 1513, was the father of John, who married Lady Margaret Stewart, grand-aunt of Lord Darnley, who married Mary, Queen of Scots. They had two sons, John of Caldwell and William of Glanderston. In 1666, Sir Robert Mure of Caldwell raised a troop of horse for the Covenanters, and was forfeited. His estates were restored to his daughter Barbara, who married John Fairlie, without issue. Caldwell was inherited by William Mure, IVth of Glanderston, who in turn was succeeded by a nephew of the same name, eldest son of James Mure of Rhoddens, in Ireland. The Mures of Caldwell have distinguished themselves in many fields, including the army, literature, the law and politics.

Sir John Moore, 1761–1809, son of Dr John Moore, a Glasgow physician and miscellaneous writer, was a celebrated military commander, and fell at Corunna. Thomas Muir, 1765–98, of Hunterston, a 'political martyr' of 1793, was transported to Australia, but escaped and died in France. The surname was spelled Moar in Orkney and Shetland, and several men of this name served in the Canadian fur trade with the Hudson's Bay Co. Lesmahagow born Alexander Muir, 1830–1906, went to Ontario, Canada, in 1833, and wrote the words and music of 'The Maple Leaf Forever'. John Muir, 1838–1914, a native of Dunbar, emigrated to the USA in 1849, settling in California. He was an explorer, naturalist and pioneer coservationist, largely responsible for the creation of Yosemite National Park.

MURRAY OR MORAY, ANCIENT The great families of Moray of Bothwell, whose castle is an impressive ruin, and Murray of Tullibardine, from whom came the Earls and Dukes of Atholl, descended from William of Petty, son of William of Moravia, son of Freskin the Fleming. He died before 1226, when his second son, Sir Walter, made an agreement with Andrew, Bishop of Moray, his cousin, regarding lands and tiends granted to the abbey by his father. Sir Walter's grandson, also Sir Walter, inherited estates in Moray, and probably through his wife, a daughter of David Olifard (Oliphant), obtained Bothwell, in Lanarkshire, and lands in Berwickshire. His sons, William and Andrew, who were supporters of Sir William Wallace and Robert the Bruce, succeeded in turn to the estates. Andrew's son, Sir John, Lord of Bothwell, was a hostage for King David II, and died in an English prison before 1351. Leaving no issue, he was succeeded by his brother, Sir Thomas, who was the last of the Bothwell line of whom anything is known. His widow, Joanna, heiress of Sir Maurice Moray of Drumsargard, Strathearn, married ca. 1362, Sir Archibald Douglas, 'The Grim', afterwards Lord of Galloway.

The Perthshire line of Tullibardine favoured the spelling Murray. They descended from Sir Malcolm Murray, grandson of William of Petty, and held the lands of Llanbryde and others in Moray: probably also farms in Roxburghshire. His son, Sir William, obtained the lands of Tullibardine, east and west, half through his marriage with Ada, daughter of Sir Malise, Steward of Strathearn, ca. 1284. For Sir David Murray, VIIth of Tullibardine, the lands were erected into a feudal barony in 1443. His son William was scutifier or esquire to King James III, and sat frequently in

Parliament. In the time of his son William there was a bitter feud with the Drummonds, who set fire to the church of Monzievaird. They made peace before 1500. Sir William, XIth of Tullibardine, was Comptroller of Scotland, and had a hand in the escape of Queen Mary from Lochleven Castle in 1568. Sir John, his son, was created Earl of Tullibardine in 1606. By his wife, Catherine Drummond, he had five sons: William, 2nd Earl; Capt. John, who died before 1607; Sir Patrick of Redcastle, who became 3rd Earl; Sir Mungo of Drumcairn, who became 2nd Viscount Stormount; and Robert, who was alive in 1618. The 2nd Earl resigned Tullibardine in the hands of his brother Patrick, seemingly on the promise of the king to make his issue by Lady Dorothy Stewart, Earls of Atholl. The Tullibardine line was continued by Sir Patrick, who had a charter of the earldom in 1628. James, his son, Earl of Tullibardine, died in 1670, without issue, and his titles and estates passed to his kinsman, John Murray, 2nd Earl of Atholl.

The Earls of Dunmore descend from John, 1st Marquess of Atholl. Cadets of the Tullibardine line include the Earls of Dysart (1643), and those of Mansfield (1776), also the baronets of Ochtertyre (NS, 1673). Other associated families include the Murrays of Glendoick, Ayton, Pitcaithly, Dorrary, Lintrose, Arbenie, Pitcullen and Woodend, Strowan and Tippermore. Important families in the south include the Murrays of Cockpool, who came to be Earls of Annandale (1642), and their cadets, Touchadam and Polmaise, in Stirlingshire, and Falahill, Mid Lothian, from whom came the baronets (NS, 1628) of Blackbarony, in Peeblesshire, and their cadets, not least Dunerne, also baronets (NS, 1630), The Morays of Abercairny, who kept the old spelling, claimed descent from the Drumsargart line of the Morays of Bothwell.

MURRAY OF ATHOLL John, son and heir of William, 2nd Earl of Tullibardine, was created Earl of Atholl in 1629. His sons John and Mungo were Royalists. John succeeded to the titles and estates of Tullibardine on the death of his kinsman, James Murray, in 1760. In 1676 he was created Marquess of Atholl and Earl of Tullibardine. His son John was created Duke of Atholl and Marquess of Tullibardine in 1703. John, his eldest son, was killed at Malplaquet in 1709, and William, the second son, along with his younger brothers, Charles and George, played significant roles in the Jacobite Risings. William, styled Marquess of Tullibardine, fought at Sheriffmuir in 1715, and was attainted for high treason.

His brother Charles commanded a regiment of the Atholl Brigade, and was taken prisoner. He was sentenced to death, but reprieved and died in 1720. William and George escaped to the Continent. The latter was pardoned in 1724, but his Jacobite sympathies were as strong as ever in 1745, and he joined the army of Prince Charles. William returned from France with the Prince, and raised the standard at Glenfinnan. He and the *de jure* Charles III, took up quarters at Blair Castle. William took possession of the family estates and assumed the title of Duke of Atholl. His brother, Lord George, commanded the left wing of the army at Prestonpans, and the right wing at Culloden in 1746. It has been remarked that if the Prince had slept during the campaign and left full command to Lord George Murray, he would have found the crown of Great Britain on his head when he awoke. William sought refuge in Dunbartonshire, but was betrayed by a Buchanan of Drumakil, and died in an English prison. Lord George escaped to Holland, and died in 1760, leaving issue. His eldest son, John of Strowan, succeeded as 3rd Duke of Atholl on the death of his uncle, James, 2nd Duke.

John, 3rd Duke, 1729–74, regained the honours by petition, and became a representative peer. In 1767 he was created a Knight of the Thistle. He married in 1753, his cousin, Charlotte, daughter of the 2nd Duke, on whose death she inherited the barony of Strange and the sovereignty of the Isle of Man. The latter was sold to the crown, reserving patronages, and with a reddendo of two falcons to the kings and queens of England on the days of their respective coronations. Their eldest son, John, raised the regiment in 1777, called the 77th or Atholl Highlanders, which saw service in Ireland, and was disbanded in 1783. When Queen Victoria visited Blair Castle in 1845, and a guard was turned out in her honour, she granted permission for the Duke and his descendants to muster their own private army, known as the Atholl Highlanders. It is still in existence: the only private army in Europe. The 4th Duke, John, was created Baron Murray of Stanley and Earl of Strange in 1786.

The 7th Duke, John James, served in the Scots Guards before 1865. He succeeded to the barony of Percy in right of his grandmother, Lady Glenlyon, on the death of his uncle, Algernon, Duke of Northumberland, in 1865, becoming senior co-heir of John, 14th Earl of Oxford. He was already co-heir of Henry, 18th Earl, and as such claimed unsuccessfully to entitlement to execute the office of Great Chamberlain at the King's coronation. His son, John George, 8th Duke, 1871-1942, was chairman of the committee that planned the Scottish National War Memorial.

James Thomas, 9th Duke, died unmarried, in 1957, when the honours and estate passed to his third cousin, George Iain Murray, 1931–96. He was 6'5" tall, and affectionately called 'Wee Iain'. The dukedom passed to his third cousin, John Murray, a land surveyor, living in South Africa, and the estates were inherited through a trust, by his twelve-year-old half-nephew, Robert Troughton.

NAPIER The old surname of Napier is occupational: coming from 'naperer', a person in a great household charged with keeping and handling table linen; perhaps also with making it. The first recorded in Scotland was John Naper, who obtained some land in the Lennox ca. 1290. He appears on the *Ragman Roll* in 1296. One Alexander Naper was a peace commissioner in 1451, and his son, Sir Alexander of Merchiston, was several times Provost of Edinburgh between 1453 and 1472. His descendant, the celebrated John Napier, 1550–1617, of Merchiston, was the inventor of logarithms. Archibald, his eldest son by his first wife Elizabeth Stirling, was a Lord of Session and created a Baronet of NS, 1627, and the same year, Baron Napier of Merchiston. The 3rd Lord, also Archibald, obtained a new patent, extending the honour to heirs female. He died unmarried in 1683, and was succeeded by his nephew, Sir Thomas Nicolson, 1669–86, of Carnock, whose aunt Margaret succeeded him as Baroness Napier. She married in 1676, John Brisbane, and their daughter Elizabeth married Sir William Scott of Thirlestane, Baronet, with issue an only son, Francis, who succeeded his grandmother as 6th Baron Napier, in 1706. He also succeeded his grandfather as 3rd Baronet of Thirlestane, and assumed the surname of Napier. The 14th Baron Napier of Merchiston, Sir Frances Nigel Napier, born 1930, is also 5th Baron Ettrick and 11th Baronet of Thirlestane. His son and heir, the Master of Napier, is the Hon. Francis David Charles Napier, who lives in London.

By his second wife, Agnes Chisholm, the inventor of logarithms was the ancestor of the Napiers of Culcreoch, Craigend and Blackstoun. The Culcreoch Napiers inherited the baronetcy of Merchiston, and the 14th Baronet is Capt. Sir John Archibald Lennox Napier, who resides in Marlborough, Wiltshire. The Napiers, Barons Magdala, in Abbysinnia, descend from Field Marshall Sir Robert Cornelius Napier, 1810–90, Constable of the Tower of London, and Commander-in-Chief of the Army in India, who was born in Ceylon.

NICOLSON/MacNICOL There are Nicolsons (with variant spellings) scattered all over Britain, and the only certainty about their origins is that they did not all descend from a common ancestor. In Scotland, Highland and Lowland Nicolsons carry the heads of hawks on their armorial bearings, but it is highly improbable that even those families had a common origin. The baronets of Kensington, Luddenham and Winterbourne, in England, do not have those charges on their arms, and it seems possible their surname mean 'son of Nicholas'.

It is reasonably certain that the Nicolsons of Wester Ross and the Hebrides came originally from Norway. Some authorities think those who bore the name Nicolson came first, and the name is really 'nic' Olsen, derived from a female ancestor. Later a wave of MacNicols arrived. Their chief is said to have died ca. 1340, leaving no sons, and both groups merged. There is ample evidence to show that the surnames became interchangeable, but probably the Nicolsons of Scorrybreac, vassals of the MacDonalds, were originally MacNicols. The Nicolsons obtained lands in Lewis, and may have been dispossessed by the MacLeods. Previously they may have been in Assynt and Coigach. Angus Nicolson, tacksman of Kirivig, in Lewis, was the ancestor of Alexander Morison Nicolson, a shipbuilder in Shanghai, who founded the Nicolson Institute in Stornoway. When the Nicolsons settled in Skye is uncertain, but one 'McNicail of Portree' is said to have been one of the sixteen men who formed the Council of the Lord of the Isles. In 1507, one Mulconil MacNicol appears in Trotternish. The eponymous ancestor was Greagall, whose descendants are given as Nicail, Neailbh, Aigi (Hugh), Nicail, John and Ewan. The list is possibly mythical before John, who seems to have been the ancestor of the *Clann Mhic Neacail Scorrabreac*, now Clan MacNicol. Malcolm Nicolson, 1727–1813, of Scorrybreac, was buried at Snizort, 'who, with his predecessors, had held that farm for many centuries back'. Norman Nicolson of Scorrybreac, a bard and head of the family, emigrated to New Zealand, and came to own an estate called Scorrybreac, in Tasmania. The line continues in the person of Iain MacNeacail, residing in NSW. There are other branches in the USA. Hammond Burke Nicholson, Junior, of Atlanta, Georgia, obtained in 1988 a grant of arms for his ancestor, Duncan Nicholson, who emigrated to North Carolina before 1809. Several members of the Nicholson family have since matriculated arms as descendants, and Hammond is now Baron of Balvenie, Banffshire, having bought the ruined castle there.

Nicolsons who were under the impression that Nicolson of Scorrybreac was chief of all the Nicolsons in Scotland, and not simply those of *Clann Mhic Neacail Scorrabreac*, were troubled in 1983 when Sir David Nicolson of Carnock petitioned Lyon Court for recognition as chief of the surname, or 'Nicolson of that Ilk'. The petition was granted, and rightly so, as he could prove his connection with the Nicolsons of Lasswade, who were styled 'of that Ilk'. These Lowland Nicolsons formed a prominent legal family. James Nicolson, a writer (solicitor) in Edinburgh, who died in 1580, was progenitor of the Nicolsons of Lasswade, Carnock and Cockburnspath. His son John was admitted advocate in 1586, and John, his eldest son, was created a Baronet of NS in 1629. The collateral line of Carnock were raised to the same status in 1636. Arthur Nicolson, 11th Baronet of Carnock, an eminent diplomat, had been created Baron Carnock in 1916, and it was his grandson, the 3rd Baron, who was recognised as 'Nicolson of that Ilk'. However, there is now a recognised Highland Clan MacNeacail Federation, with Iain MacNeacail of MacNeacail and Scorrybreac, armiger, as chief.

The Rev. Donald MacNicol, minister of Lismore, in Argyll, a fine Gaelic scholar, published in 1779 *Remarks on Dr Samuel Johnson's Journey to the Hebrides*, at which the great moralist 'growled hideously'.

NIMMO This name, the origin of which is obscure, was thought to be Huguenot, but occurs in Scotland long before the Massacre of St Bartholomew in 1572. The earliest notice found is that of Johannes Newmoch, juror on an assize at Liston (now Kirkliston), near Edinburgh, in 1459. Other forms of the name are Nemo, Nemmo, Nemmock, Nimoke and Nymmo. Alexander Nemok was a witness at Glasgow in 1587. Reverend John Nimmill, son of William in Dalkeith, was minister at Corstorphine, 1589–90. Alexander Nemo was retoured as heir to John Nemo de Myddilmount, in Kylestewart, in 1616. James Nimmo, the Covenanter from Bridgehouse, Torphichen, fought at Bothwell Brig in 1679. The name was prolific in West Lothian, with farming families at Philpstoun, Craigton and Duntarvie spanning a period of three centuries. James Nimmo, Receiver-General of Excise in Scotland, died ca. 1759. Kirkcaldy-born Alexander Nimmo, 1783–1832, was involved in building harbours, bridges and railways in many parts of Great Britain.

NISBET

Scottish Nisbets, the most common variants of which are Nesbit, Nisbett and Nesbitt, derive the name from the lands of Nisbet, in the Berwickshire parish of Edrom. William de Nesebite witnessed a charter of the town lands of Nesbitt, to the Priory of Coldingham, confirmed by David I in 1139. On a dower charter of Alexander II to his queen in 1221, occurs the entry: *Thomas de Nisbet et heredes sui pro villa de Nesbyt*. In 1480, Adam Nisbet held the lands of East and West Nisbet. The family were associated with those for centuries, but Sir Alexander Nisbet was in financial difficulties towards the middle of the 17th century. He was grandfather of the learned heraldic writer, Alexander Nisbet, 1657–1725, who published several works before his *System of Heraldry* appeared in one folio volume in 1722. A second volume, edited by R. Fleming in 1742, was marred by his interpolations and forgeries which remained undetected for 150 years. Several Nisbet families held estates in various parts of the country; some of them no doubt descended from the original Edrom stock. Henry Nisbet of the Dean family was Lord Provost of Edinburgh, 1597–98, and his son Sir William was Lord Provost, 1616–19. John Nisbet, 1627–85, was a Covenanter who fought bravely at Rullion Green in 1666. The More-Nisbitts of the Drum, Mid Lothian, and Cairnhill, Lanarkshire, descend from George Nisbitt, deacon of the Wrights of Glasgow in 1753, in which year he married Margaret More of Cairnhill. The representative of the family, George Alan More Nisbett, married in 1968, Patricia Evelyn Agar, a writer and broadcaster.

OCHTERLONY

The surname is derived from the lands of that name, in Angus, and is of considerable antiquity. According to tradition the origins are Pictish. The name is variously rendered Auchterlonie, Ochterlonie, Ochterlownie, Auchtirlownie and Ouchtirlony. The name survives as Lownie village in Dunnichen parish. It is said that about the middle of the 13th century, Walter, son of Turpin, exchanged his lands of Kelly for those of Auchterlowny, held by John de Ouchtirlowny. However, while many Ochterlony lairds are styled 'of Kelly', those lands became part of the barony of Ochterlony, and the Ocherlonys frequently appear as 'of that Ilk and Kelly', clearly establishing them as the principal family of the name. Wauter de Oghterloveny rendered homage to Edward I in 1296, but he may have been Walter, son of Turpin. The lands of Kelly came into the possession of Walter the Steward of Scotland, son-in-law of Robert the Bruce, and heir to the throne, and may have passed eventually to an armigerous Stewart heiress, 'Lady' Margaret, who married Sir William Ochterlony of that Ilk, towards the close of the 14th century. The arms were later quartered: 1st and 4th, Azure, a lion rampant Argent; 2nd, Or, a fess chequy Argent and Azure, within a bordure of the first, charged with eight buckles of the second; 3rd, Or a fess chequy Argent and Azure, within a bordure of the first, charged with six buckles of the second, as in the *Lindsay Armorial*.

In 1410, Alexander de Ucterlowny witnessed a charter by Robert, Duke of Albany. He had been served heir to his father, William, the previous year. He married Janet, daughter of William Maule of Panmure, and she had a grant from her family of the lands of Greinford, in 1434. The Ochterlonys had further alliances with the Maules, and with the Stewarts, Lyons, Scrimgeours, Arbuthnotts and other Angus families. In 1514, William Auchterlonye of Kelly was Sheriff of Forfar. Alexander Ouchterlowny of that Ilk and his spouse Elizabeth Leirmont had a charter of the lands of Balcathy, adjacent to Kelly, in 1530. The Ochterlonys acquired the lands of Guynd, near Arbroath, early in the 17th century, apparently having given up Kelly. John Ochterlony of Guynd wrote *An Account of the Shire of Forfar*, 1684–85, from which we learn that the family also held Muirhouse. John and two of his kinfolk registered arms, 1672–78, dropping the old quarters.

The Ochterlonys of Kintrokat and those of Pitforthy, in Angus, descended from the stem family. Alexander of Pitforthy, born 1695, married in 1721, Elizabeth, daughter of David Tyrie of Dunnydeer, and had issue. Two sons went to the USA: David, to Boston, Massachusetts, and James to Pennsylvania. David's eldest son, also David, 1758–1825, commanded the British Army in India, and was created a Baronet in 1816. The patent was recreated in 1823, extending the limitations to heirs female. Sir David Ochterlony, 3rd Baronet, was an accountant with the Scottish Education Department, and died in 1831. The honour became extinct on the death of Sir Charles Ochterlony, in 1946.

Captain John Ochterlony, a mariner, emigrated to Karlshamn, Sweden, in 1755, and married Margareta Maria Hulst. Their eldest son, Isaac, bore the quartered Ochterlony/Stewart arms. A later member of the family, Hannah, founded the Swedish Salvation Army in 1888. General Octherlony, of the Russian Army, fought at Inkerman in 1854, and claimed to be of the Angus stock. Willie Ochterlony, a 'displaced Briton', was a prominent figure in the early days of championship golf in the USA.

OGILVY/OGILVIE The Ogilvys or Ogilvies descend from Gillebride (Normanised Gilbert), Earl of Angus, who witnessed charters between 1150 and 1187. He was probably a descendant of the ancient mormaers of Angus, and from his third son, Gilbert, who received lands in Angus, descended the Ogilvys of that Ilk, Airlie and cadets, and Inverquharity. In the branches of Findlater, Boyne, Banff and Inchmartine, they spread themselves over large areas of Aberdeenshire and Banffshire. Among the lands granted to Gilbert were those of Ogilvy, deriving from *Ocel Fa*, meaning 'high plain'.

Patrick de Ogilvy rendered homage to Edward I in 1296, and from him descended a line of Ogilvys of that Ilk, which expired when the branch of Auchterhouse became the stem family. Their founder was Sir Partrick Ogilvy of Wester Powrie, ancestor of Sir Walter Ogilvy of Auchterhouse, who had two sons: Alexander, his heir, and Sir Walter of Lintrathen, from whom came the House of Airlie. Sir John, IInd of Lintrathen, received a charter of Airlie in 1491, and his son Sir James was created Lord Ogilvy of Airlie in 1639. Although not the heir male, he was recognised as chief of the surname and arms.

The Ogilvys had a deadly feud with the Lindsays, ostensibly because Sir Alexander Ogilvy of Inverquaharity displaced the Master of Crawford as justiciar of the regality of Montrose. The quarrel resulted in a battle at Montrose in 1646, in which the Ogilvys suffered heavy losses. They also had a feud with the Campbells of Argyll, who razed 'The Bonny Hoose o' Airlie'. During the troubles of the Stewart monarchs, the Ogilvys remained loyal. A French descendant of the Boyne family, Alexander, son of Patrick Ogilvy, living in Burgundy, was given a *Declaration of Noblesse* in 1737 by the exiled Stuarts. Several Scottish Ogilvys were Jacobites and took part in the Risings of 1715 and 1745, for which they were attainted. In 1778, a pardon was granted to Lord Ogilvy because of his youth at the time of the '45, and in 1826 the earldom of Airlie was restored to David Ogilvy, as 4th Earl. His son David married Henrietta, daughter of Edward, 2nd Lord Stanley, and had a son David, 6th Earl of Airlie, and several daughters, the third of whom, Henrietta Blanche, married in 1878, Sir Henry Montague Hozier of Stonehouse. They were the parents of Clementine Ogilvy Hozier, who married in 1928, Sir William S. Churchill, Great Britain's PM during World War II. Another notable marriage took place in 1963, when Angus, second son of David, 12th Earl of Airlie, married HRH Princess Alexandra of Kent. His brother, David George, is the 13th Earl.

The Ogilvys of Deskford and Findlater descend from Sir Walter Ogilvy of Deskford, younger son of Sir Walter of Lintrathen. James, 2nd Lord Ogilvy of Deskford, was created Earl of Findlater in 1638. In 1701, James, 4th Earl, was created Earl of Seafield. He supported the Union of 1707, but repented it by 1713. James, 7th Earl of Findlater, died without issue in 1811, and the title expired. The other dignities devolved on his cousin, Lady Margaret, daughter of the 5th Earl of Findlater and 2nd of Seafield, who married (as his second wife) Sir Ludovick Grant, Baronet. Their grandson, Sir James Grant, became 5th Earl of Seafield. The Earls of Findlater were acknowledged as chiefs in the north-east, but in 1641, the then Earl arranged that the succession should pass through his daughter to Ogilvy of Inchmartine. This was an older line, and the Earl of Airlie, fearing this family would claim precedence, obtained a royal mandate confirming him as chief.

The Inverquharity branch of the family possess a baronetcy (NS, 1626), and the 14th and present holder of the title is Francis Gilbert Ogilvie, surveyor and farmer.

OLIPHANT The first Oliphant to come to Scotland belonged to a family seated in Northamptonshire, and deriving their name from Killeford, a crossing on the River Nene, often given as Holyford, because the Abbot of Peterborough had a manor on one side. David Olifard, godson and namesake of David I, King of Scots (1124–53), was serving in King Stephen's army at the Rout of Winchester in 1141, and saved the monarch from being captured. Soon afterwards he appears in Scotland, and was rewarded with lands as well as being made a justiciar (probably of Lothian). David Olifard was probably second son of William, son of Roger Olifard, who witnessed a charter of Simon de Senlis ca. 1107. The landowner was the wealthy Countess Judith, widow of Waltheof of Northumbria, and the daughter of Adele, sister of William the Conqueror, by her second husband, Lambert, Count of Lens, in Flanders. Maud or Matilda, daughter of Waltheof and Judith, married David I, King of Scots. The armorial device of David Olifard – Argent, three crescents Gules – suggests some close link with the family of Lens, and probably also with the Setons.

Some Olifard lines remained in England, although for a time the manor of Lilleford was possessed by the Scottish family. David

Olifard had several sons, and the heir, Walter, justiciar of Lothian, held lands in East Lothian and Berwickshire. By his marriage to Christian, daughter of Ferteth, Earl of Strathearn, he obtained lands at Dupplin, in Strathearn. There appear to be two lines stemming from David Olifard: one from Walter, Yr., who died in 1242, and another coming from the son David, whose son William was progenitor of the Lords Oliphant. During the War of Independence there were two Sir William Oliphants, cousins, who fought bravely. From one of these came Walter Oliphant of Aberdalgie who married before 1365, Elizabeth, daughter of Robert the Bruce. From them descended Laurence Oliphant, created Lord Oliphant in 1463. His grandson Colin was killed at Flodden, 1513, and his great-grandson, Laurence, 3rd Lord, was captured at Solway Moss in 1542, and ransomed. The 4th Lord, also Laurence, was present at Bothwell's marriage to Mary, Queen of Scots. Another Laurence, 5th Lord, encumbered all his estates except Gask, which had passed to a cadet, descended from the 2nd Lord. He attempted to transmit his title to his only daughter, Anna, but failed, and the king bestowed it on his cousin Patrick, the nearest heir male. The 9th Lord, William, was a Jacobite, involved in the campaigns of 1688 and 1715. He died without surviving issue, and the title passed to Francis, younger son of the 6th Lord. He died without issue in 1748, and the title became dormant.

The Oliphants of Gask, Perthshire were also Jacobites. James of Gask married Janet Murray, and prevailed on his son Laurence, 1692–1767, to join Lord Mar, and he fought at Sheriffmuir in 1715. He joined Prince Charles at Atholl in 1745, but his tenants did not take part. At Falkirk and Culloden he fought alongside his son, and Gask was seized by the government. He escaped to Sweden, then to France. In 1760 he was created Baron Gask in the Jacobite peerage. He married in 1719, Lady Amelia, daughter of William Murray, Lord Nairne. Their son Laurence was ADC to Prince Charles and fought throughout the campaign: going afterwards into exile with his father, and later returned to Gask, having married in France, Lady Margaret, daughter of Sir Duncan Robertson of Struan, by Lady Nairne. It was their daughter, Carolina, 1766–1845, who became famous as a song writer. Among her lasting songs is 'The Auld Hoose', and 'Will ye no' come back again', which reminds us of the family's Jacobite sympathies. The honours became extinct in 1847, with the death of James Blair Oliphant, 5th Baron. Another interesting branch of the

Oliphants is that of Condie, descended from the 3rd Lord Oliphant through the Newton line. This family came to be represented by Lt. Cdr. Ralph Henry Hood Laurence Oliphant, who served with distinction in World War II.

PATERSON A prolific surname in Scotland, Paterson (sometimes spelt with a double 'tt') simply means 'Patrick's son'. As Patrick is often synonymous with Peter, the name is occasionally rendered Peterson. Patison and Paton are variants. At one time there was a group of Patersons on the north side of Loch Fyne, known as *Clann Pheadrean*. Patrick, being a popular name in the Middle Ages, appears all over Ireland and Scotland (Gaelic *Padruig*), and there is no question of a common ancestor. Nor – despite some similarities – can any credence be given to a tradition of Scandinavian origin. Among early references to the name are William Patrickson and John Patonson, 'gentillmen' witnesses at Aberdeen in 1446. In 1494, Donald Patryson was admitted burgess there. Robert Patryson was captain of a Dundee ship in 1544. In 1557, Fyndlay Patersoun had a lease of the lands of Ower Elrick from the Abbey of Cupar. George Peterson was a monk at Culross in 1569.

Castle Huntly, in Longforgan parish, Perthshire, belonged to a Paterson family from 1777 to 1948. It was probably built in the latter part of the 15th century by Andrew, 2nd Lord Gray, and it passed in 1615 to the Lyons, Earls of Kinghorn. George Paterson, who purchased the castle, married Ann, daughter of the 11th Lord Gray, and he made additions to the building, as well as renovating the interior. A later George Paterson married Jane, daughter of James Paterson of Longbedholm, Dumfriesshire, and left two sons, George Frederick and Charles James, successively owners of Castle Huntly. A kinsman, Col. Adrian G. Paterson, purchased the property from the executors of James Paterson, and it was sold by his widow in 1948.

A Jacobite Paterson family once owned the estate of Bannockburn. Hugh, son of John, was admitted WS in 1661 and created a Baronet of NS in 1686. He was succeeded by his son, Sir Hugh, whose younger daughter Katherine married John Walkinshaw, IIIrd of Barrowfield, and had ten daughters, the youngest of whom, Clementine, 1720–82, met Prince Charles Edward Stuart in 1746, probably at Bannockburn House. She later joined him in France and became his mistress. Clementine bore him a daughter, Charlotte, 1753–89, legitimated by him in 1784, and who was known as Duchess of Albany. Sir Hugh Paterson, 3rd Baronet of Bannockburn, was involved in the '15 Rising, and forfeited. He died in 1777, when the title became extinct.

In 1688, the estate of Granton, near Edinburgh, came into the possession of Sir William Paterson, Baronet (NS, 1687), son of John, Bishop of Ross, and brother of John Paterson, Archbishop of Glasgow. For a time he was Regent of Philosophy in the University of Edinburgh. His son, Sir John, sold the estate in 1708, and purchased that of Eccles, in Berwickshire. Among Paterson property owners in the south-west was the family in Balgray, Dumfriesshire. Robert Jardine Paterson, 1878–1942, of Balgray, served in the Coldstream Guards in World War I. His son, Capt. David Paterson, served with the Gurkha Rifles in World War II. A Dumfriesshire man who achieved lasting fame was William Paterson, 1658–1719, a farmer's son who became a financier. In 1691, he submitted to the London merchants a scheme for forming the Bank of England. Dissatisfied with lack of encouragement for other projects, he devised a grand scheme for colonisation of the Isthmus of Panama. It ended in disaster through poor supplies, the unhealthy climate, internal dissension and English subterfuge. David Paterson, a schoolmaster at Dolphinton, Lanarkshire, residing at Logiebank in that parish, was charged at the High Court in Edinburgh, in 1838, of culpable homicide. He was found guilty by the jury who, in respect of his previous good character, recommended leniency, and he was sentenced to eighteen months imprisonment.

PITCAIRN There are places called Pitcairn in the counties of Fife and Perth, but most Pitcairns took their names from the Fife estate, near Lochgelly. William de Petkaran was one of an assize at Dunfermline before 1149, and may have been the father of John de Petcarn, who had a charter of the lands of Innernethie in 1250. Pitcairns held the Fife estate for generations, but by 1846, John Pitcairn, a magistrate, was living at Pitcairns House, Perthshire. David Pitcairn was archdeacon of Brechin between 1524 and 1541. Edinburgh-born Archibald Pitcairn, 1652–1713, was son of Alexander Pitcairn, merchant-burgess of Edinburgh, and Janet Sydserf. He became an eminent physician and poet, and claimed descent from the Fife Pitcairns. He was Professor of Physics at Leyden, 1692–93. In the van of British troops converging on Lexington, Kentucky, in April, 1775, was Major John Pitcairn, who fired the first shot of the Revolutionary War. A volley killed a group of minute-men. This act was claimed by Ebenezer Munro (see MUNRO article), but Bancroft's detailed *History* clearly gives this dubious honour to Pitcairn, who was himself killed at Bunker Hill. His son, Dr David Pitcairn, 1749–1809, was sometime physician at St Bartholomews Hospital, London. Archibald Pitcairn, 1802–61, a native of Ceres, Fife, whose father owned an estate in that parish, was a well-known barrister in Hobart Town, Tasmania. Robert Pitcairn, who died in 1855, was the compiler of *Ancient Criminal Trials in Scotland*, 1488–1624, printed in three volumes in 1833: a work much admired by Sir Walter Scott. Pitcairn Island, in the Pacific Ocean, forever associated with the mutiny on the ship *Bounty*, was discovered by Robert Pitcairn, RN, in 1767.

PRIMROSE The place-name Primrose appears in 1150 in a charter relating to the Abbey of Dunfermline, and the meaning may have been 'tree on the moor', derived from the British *prenn*, 'tree', and *Rhos*, 'moor'. It is highly probable that the surname comes from the Fife place-name. John Prymros, mason in Edinburgh, was one of those who contracted in 1387 for building chapels at St Giles' parish church. Archibald Prymrose was a friar at Culross in 1569, and from him descended Sir Archibald Primrose of Carrington, clerk to the Privy Council in 1641, created a Baronet of NS in 1651. In 1662 he purchased the lands of Barnbougle and Dalmeny from the Earl of Haddington. He died in 1679 and was interred in a leaden coffin at Dalmeny Church. From him descended the Earls of Rosebery. His son, Archibald, by a second marriage, was created Viscount of Rosebery in 1700, and Earl of Rosebery, Viscount Inverkeithing, Lord Dalmeny and Primrose in 1703. The 5th Earl, Archibald Philip, was PM of Great Britain and First Lord of the Treasury, 1894–95, and created Earl of Mid Lothian in the UK peerage. Sir Albert Edward Primrose, 1882–1974, 6th Earl of Rosebery, was a celebrated sportsman and racehorse owner. His son, by a second wife, Sir Neil Archibald Primrose, is the 7th Earl. Hans Primrose appears in Sweden in 1644, and his son, Major Henry Primrose, was enobled in 1653. He became governor of Johannsborg, near Norkoping, and died in 1668. His line is now extinct.

PRINGLE The old form of this name was Hoppringle, from the lands of that name on the Gala Water, near Stow. The earliest notice found of the name is in a Soutra charter in which Robert Hoppryngil is a witness to a gift to the Hospital there, confirmed by

Alexander III (1249–93). Thomas de Oppringill or Hopyringhil occurs in 1368, and Johyn Pryngel appears in Fife in 1406. Robert of Hoppringill witnessed a charter ca. 1413. The leading family were the Hoppringles of that Ilk, afterwards of Torsonce. Other families of note were at Burnhouse, Hawtree, Glengelt, Rowchester, Lees, Stichell, and at Whitsome in Berwickshire. From the Pringles of Whitsome descended those of Whytebank. The male line of the Torsonce family failed in 1737, but a daughter of John Pringle had married Gilbert Pringle of Stitchell, near Kelso and carried the estates to that family. Robert Pringle of Stitchell was created a Baronet of NS in 1683. John, youngest son of Sir John, 2nd Baronet, was a distinguished physician. The 10th Baronet is Lt. Gen. Sir Steuart R. Pringle, who had a notable career in the Royal Marine Commandos, 1946–90. Thomas Pringle, 1789–1831, from Teviotdale, was a pioneer settler in South Africa, but returned to become secretary of the Anti-Slavery Society.

RAMSAY The first of this surname recorded in Scotland was Simon de Ramsay, who took his name from Ramsey, in Huntingdonshire, where he had an estate which was ravaged in 1140 by Geoffrey de Mandeville. He was probably of Flemish extraction, and related (possibly a son) to Walter de Lindsay, by his Seton wife. Simon was given an estate in East Lothian, under the protection of the Setons. He appears as a witness to charters between 1153 and 1140, and was ancestor of the Ramsays of Dalhousie and of Inverleith. Sir Alexander of Dalhousie was Warden of the Middle Marches, ca. 1342, and was succeeded by his brother, Sir William, ca. 1345.

The Ramsays established themselves firmly at Dalhousie, and in 1617 Sir George Ramsay was created a Lord of Parliament by the title of Ramsay of Melrose, but had the title changed to Dalhousie. His eldest son, William, was created Earl of Dalhousie and Lord Ramsay of Kerington in 1633. He led a regiment of the Covenanting Army at Marston Moor and at Philiphaugh. William, 8th Earl, succeeded to the estates of his maternal uncle, William Maule, Earl of Panmure, for life, with remainder to his second son by his first wife, Elizabeth, daughter of Andrew Glen, Linlithgow. He was William, who became Lord Panmure in 1831, assuming the name and arms of Maule. Elizabeth Glen was niece of Gov. James Glen of South Carolina, and she inherited his wealth. The Earl was succeeded by his eldest son, George, who was Lt. Gov. of NS, 1816, and Gov. of Canada, 1819–28. He was created Baron Dalhousie in

1815. His third son, James, 10th Earl, was Gov. Gen. of India, 1847–56, and was created Marquess of Dalhousie in 1849. He died in 1860, when the marquessate and barony (UK) became extinct. The Scottish honours devolved on Fox Maule, a noted politician, on whose death in 1874 the Maule honours became extinct, but the Dalhousie title devolved on his cousin, George. Simon Ramsay, 1914–99, KT, his brother, succeeded in 1950, and the 17th Earl is his eldest son, James.

By the middle of the 13th century, Ramsays appear in Perthshire and Angus. The lands of Bamff, Perthshire, were granted to Neis de Ramsay in 1232, by Alexander II, whose physician he was. From the Ramsays of Carnock, in Fife, descended Sir John Ramsay, Lord of Bothwell, who died in 1513, From him descended David Ramsay of Balmain, whose son Gilbert was created a Baronet of NS in 1625. The title became extinct in 1806, and the estates devolved on Sir Alexander Burnett Ramsay, created a Baronet (UK) during that year. The present Baronet is Sir Alexander William Ramsay, who resides in NSW, Australia.

Allan Ramsay, 1684–1758, a native of Leadhills and a wigmaker in Edinburgh, became a successful poet, best remembered for 'The Gentle Shepherd', but also produced a volume of songs: *Tea Table Miscellany*. His son, Allan, 1713–84, studied art at London and Rome, and on his return commenced a series of paintings, including John, 2nd Duke of Argyll. In 1761 he was appointed portrait painter to King George III. Alexander 'Dean' Ramsay, 1793–1876, an Episcopal clergyman descended from the Balmain family, was the author of *Reminiscences of Scottish Life and Character*. Sir Andrew Crombie Ramsay, 1814–68, became Director-General of the geological survey of Britain. A classical scholar, William Ramsay, 1806–65, became Professor of Mathematics at Glasgow in 1833, and Sir William Ramsay, an organic chemist who discovered new gases, was a Nobel prizeman in 1904. Major Gen. Charles Alexander Ramsay, of the Balmain line, a chief executive of Caledonian Eagle, had a distinguished post-war army career.

REID Reid, Read or Reed, is a prolific surname, originally indicating red hair or ruddy complexion. In Latin charters it is often rendered *Rufus*, in Gaelic, *Ruadh*. Writers on books about tartans tell us that Reids were a sept of *Clann Donnachaidh*, and this is sometimes correct. The name is borne by many families who do not have a common ancestor. Ade Rufus witnessed a resignation of the lands Ingilbriston in 1204, and William Rufus was a juror on an inquest on the lands of Padevinan (Houston) in 1259. Gilbert 'le Rede' of Coul died in prison in 1296. 'Red' is found as a surname at Kildrummy, Aberdeenshire, in 1317. John Reed was collector of the tithes in the deaneries of Stormonth and Atholl in 1362. Another John Reid had a charter of lands in the Park of Cardross in 1362, and in 1367 Simon Reed, Constable of Edinburgh Castle, had a charter of the lands of Lochendorbe, Inverness-shire. William, son of John Rede, had confirmation of the lands of Kyle in 1375. The lands of Wester Foddels, Aberdeenshire, were held in wadset in 1389 by William Rede from his cousin, Alexander de Moravia. In 1494, when Archbishop Blackadder summoned thirty members of 'genteel' Ayrshire families to be interrogated for heretical opinions, including the denial of papal indulgencies and adoration of images, Adam Reid of Barskimming, bold spokesman for the Lollards of Kyle, showed 'little respect for proud prelates'.

Down through the centuries Reids have distinguished themselves in many walks of life. John, 1656–1723, son of John Reid, gardener at Niddry Castle, Winchburgh, published his celebrated book, *The Scots Gard'ner*, in 1683, when he emigrated to East New Jersey with his Quaker wife, Margaret Miller. He became surveyor-general and owner of a large estate called Hortensia. Peter Reid, 1777–1838, physician, born near Leven, in Fife, was editor of Dr Cullen's *First Lines of the Practice of Physics*. A successful teacher of chemistry, Dr David Boswell Reid, 1805–63, was son of Dr Peter Reid, Edinburgh, and Christian, daughter of the historian, Hugo Arnot. He devised a method of ventilating public buildings, and in 1863 went to the USA to employ his system in military hospitals. Unfortunately he died in Washington DC. Bathgate-born Dr John Reid, 1809–49, became Professor of Anatomy and Medicine at the University of St Andrews, and published a volume of essays.

General John Reid, 1721–1807, composer of the air, 'The Garb of Old Gaul', left money to establish a chair of music at the University of Edinburgh. He was in fact a Robertson, whose ancestors held an estate in Strathardle for eleven generations. The progenitor of this family was Patrick Robertson of Lude, who bore the cognomen of 'Red'; second son of Duncan de Atholia. Dr James Reid, 1849–1923, Physician in Ordinary to Queen Victoria, 1889; to Edward VII, 1899–1910, and to George V, was created 1st Baronet of Ellon in 1897. His grandson, Sir Alexander, is the 3rd Baronet James Scott Cumberland Reid, 1890–1975, had a notable legal career, and served with the Royal Scots and the Machine Gun Corps during World War I. He was an MP, 1931–48, and appointed a Lord of Appeal in Ordinary in 1948, in which year he was created a Life Peer as Baron Reid of Drem, East Lothian. Hugh Reid, 1860–1935, Lord Dean of Guild of Glasgow, was created 1st Baronet of Springburn in 1922. The 3rd Baronet is Sir Hugh Reid, a travel consultant, who served in the RAF, 1952–56, in Egypt and Cyprus, and in the RAF (VRT), 1963–75.

ROBERTSON The Robertsons form one of the oldest documented clans. They descend from the Celtic earls of Atholl, who were of the royal line of the kings of Dalriada, themselves probably descended from Niall of the Nine Hostages, who ruled Ireland about the time the Romans left Britain. Conan, second son of Henry, 3rd Earl of Atholl, inherited extensive lands in Atholl, including Glenorchy. His descendant, Duncan de Atholia, 1275–1355, was the first chief of *Clann Donnachaidh*. At first the chiefs were called Atholl or Duncanson, but when surnames began to emerge, adopted Robertson from Robert *Riabhach*, 4th chief. Some kept the name Duncanson, and others became MacConochie, Macinroy or MacLagan, Stark or Collier, and Reid.

Robert received a charter in 1451, erecting his lands into the barony of Struan. His brother, Patrick *Ruadh*, obtained Lude, and his descendants formed the senior cadet branch of the clan. Patrick's youngest son married a kinswoman, Matilda Robertson, and was progenitor of the celebrated barons Reid of Straloch, from whom came the Durdin-Robertsons of Huntington Castle, in Co. Carlow, Ireland. Other cadets were Inches, Kindeace, Killichangy, Calvine, Auchleeks, Ladykirk, Faskally, Drumachuine, Woodsheal, Inverack and Trinafour. The Auchleeks line came to be represented by Robert Alexander Dundas, WS, who married in 1869, Emily Bridget, daughter of Robert Robertson, 10th laird. In olden times the Robertsons of Struan had castles in Rannoch and at Inverack.

The Robertsons chiefs were staunch supporters of the Stewart kings. Donald, Tutor of Struan, during the minority of the 12th chief, raised a regiment for Charles I in 1644. Alexander, 17th chief, and a noted poet, first joined Viscount Dundee in support of the Jacobites in 1688, for which he was attainted and had his estates confiscated. He was pardoned in 1703 by Queen Anne, but joined Lord Mar in 1715, and was taken prisoner at Sheriffmuir. He escaped to France, and James III and VIII made him a knight and baronet. His devotion to the Stuarts was such that he joined Prince Charles in 1745, but was too old to fight, although he watched the Battle of Prestonpans. The government, in respect of his age, took no action against him. When he died in 1749, his sister Margaret established Duncan Robertson of Drumachine in the estates, but his name was excluded from the Act of Indemnity, and he was dispossessed in 1752. His son Alexander obtained a restitution of Struan in 1784, as 15th chief. Captain Alastair Robertson, 20th chief, called 'Struan' Robertson, broke the entail of the barony, and sold the mansion of Rannoch Barracks to his sister Jean Rosine, who sold the remaining parts of the estate. On her death the representation passed to Robert Joseph Stewart Robertson, 21st chief, descended from Alexander, 16th chief. His brother, George Duncan Robertson, 22nd chief, was in the Colonial Civil Service at Kingston, Jamaica, and his son Langton George Duncan Haldane Robertson, matriculated arms in 1954. He was succeeded as 24th chief by his son, Alexander Gilbert Haldane Robertson of Struan. The Faskally line of the Robertsons were also involved in the Jacobite Risings. Alexander Robertson of Faskally, was created a knight and baronet by James III and VIII in 1725, and died in 1732. His son George succeeded to the estate. On the retreat of the army of Prince Charles from Stirling in 1746, he and his kinsman, James Robertson of Blairfetty, raised 140 men and, with 'seven pieces of cannon and four covered waggons', joined the Prince at Perth. He appears to have been the last of the direct line of Faskally.

A Clan Donnachaidh Society was formed in 1892, and in 1969 a Clan Museum was opened at Bruar Falls, between Blair Atholl and Struan. Biographical works show Robertsons as statesmen, soldiers, writers, actors, inventors, astronomers, lawyers, politicians and clergymen. The historian, Rev. William Robertson, 1721–93, was descended from the clan chiefs, through the Robertsons of Gladney. Lord Robertson (Ian Macdonald Robertson), was a Senator of the College of Justice, 1966–87. Dundee-born Sir Lewis Robertson is an eminent administrator and historian. Lord George Robertson, born in Islay, is Secretary General of NATO.

ROSE The Rose family has held the lands of Kilravock, near Nairn, for over seven centuries. They may have come to Scotland in the reign of William the Lion (1165–1214), with the Bissets, an Anglo-Norman family, who founded the Benedictine priory of Beauly in 1232. The name is obviously derived from *ros*, a promontory, but the headland must have been in their place of origin, possibly the Cotentin peninsula of Normandy. The bougets which appear on their arms may point to a more remote ancestor who fought in the crusades and carried water in leathern buckets or carriers.

Hugh Rose, who witnessed the charter of the priory of Beauly, held the lands of Geddes, and it was his son of the same name who obtained Kilravock through his marriage, ca. 1280, to Mary, daughter of Sir Andrew Bosco and his lady, Elizabeth, co-heiress of Sir John Bisset of Lovat. It was confirmed by King John Baliol ca. 1295. Hugh died ca. 1306. His son, William, IInd of Kilravock, fought at Bannockburn, and was knighted by Robert the Bruce. The next three lairds were all named Hugh, a favourite family name. The second of them married Janet Chisholm, and with her obtained some other lands in Strathnairn. In 1390, in the time of his son, the Vth laird, the family muniments kept at Elgin Cathedral were burned when Alexander Stewart, the 'Wolf of badenoch', made the building a ruin. John, VIth laird, resigned his lands (reserving the liferent) in the hands of his superior, John, Lord of the Isles and Earl of Ross, and his son Hugh received a new charter in 1440. He married Elizabeth Cheyne, and had four sons: Lachlan, a cleric; Hugh, the heir; Alexander of Dunearn, from whom descended several provosts of Nairn; and William, ancestor of some families in Mar.

The VIIth laird, Hugh, built Kilravock Castle ca. 1460, and additions were later made, particularly in 1553 by Hugh Rose, called 'The Black Baron'. He was the Xth laird, and was captured by the English at Pinkie in 1547, and ransomed. Hugh welcomed Mary, Queen of Scots, at Kilravock, on 15th September, 1562. William, his son, the XIth laird, was a peaceable man, but the clan, having many branches, were not always on good terms with their neighbours, and William and his son Hugh were imprisoned for a time in Edinburgh Castle. Hugh, XIIth laird, supported the Covenant, as did his son Hugh, who succeeded him in 1643. He led the fighting men of Auldearn in 1645, and died in 1649. His son Hugh was then a minor, and the Tutor was William Rose of Clava.

Hugh Rose, XVIth laird, was Sheriff of Ross, 1729–34, and one of his daughters was the mother of Henry Mackenzie, 1745–1831 author of *The Man of Feeling*. His eldest son was succeeded by his sister, Elizabeth, who married her kinsman, Hugh Rose of Brea. Their grandson Hugh, XXIst laird, died unmarried in 1847, and was succeeded by his brother, John. James, XXIIIrd of Kilravock, his half-brother, succeeded. His eldest son, Lt. Col. Hugh Rose, served in the Black Watch, and in 1922 entertained Queen Mary. He married Ruth Guillemard, a French lady, with issue two daughters. The elder, Anna Elizabeth, succeeded in 1946 at XXVth of Kilravock, and in 1967 opened the old castle as a Christian Centre. She wrote a useful pamphlet about the Rose family to commemorate a Rose Clan Gathering at Kilravock in 1970. Her sister Madeleine married in 1945, Hugh Heriot Baird, and in 1958 they and their four sons emigrated to NSW, Australia.

ROSS Hugh, a younger son of Hugh, 4th Earl of Ross, of the O'Beolin line, was the progenitor of the Rosses of Balnagowan, who were recognised as the chiefs of *Clann Rois*. From his father he received the lands of Rarichies, and his brother William, the 5th Earl, gave him Balnagowan, which became the designation of his heirs. The family probably came of the same stock as the O'Beolin abbots of Drumcliff, Ireland, whose ancestor was Cairbre, a son of Niall of the Nine Hostages.

The headland (*ros* in Gaelic) jutting into the north sea between the firths of Cromarty and Dornoch, gave its name to the clan, the county and the earldom. Under the Celtic mormaers, Ross formed part of the province of Moray, but the feudalising sons of David I (1124–53), separated Ross to form an earldom held in 1168 by Malcolm McHeth. Farquhar (*Fearchar Mac an t-Sagairt*, 'son of the priest') was the first of the O'Beolin line. He brought numerous warriors to the assistance of King Alexander II, against rival claimants to the throne, for which he was knighted in 1216. A decade later he was entrusted with the earldom of Ross.

When the 5th Earl died in 1372, Hugh Ross of Rariches continued the old line of the family. The honours passed to Euphemia, the earl's daughter, who married Sir Walter Leslie. Their line ended with an heiress, who resigned in 1415, and possibly entered a nunnery. From the late 15th century to the middle of the 16th century, there was a bitter warfare with the Mackays of Strathnaver. In a conflict at Alt a' Charrais, in Strathcarron, in 1486, Alexander Ross of Balnagowan was killed, and his followers defeated. During the time of a later Alexander Ross, the IXth laird, the clan embraced the Reformation. By 1587 the Rosses had become numerous.

The last laird, David, 1644–1711, was plagued with litigation about the succession and, ca. 1694, a new litigant appeared in the person of William, Lord Ross, of the Halkhead family, who claimed descent from the Balnagowan line, but who in fact belonged to a Lowland family which derived its name from the Norman *de Roos*. However, through various shady financial transactions, he obtained

Balnagowan Castle and extensive lands. The castle now belongs to business tycoon, Mohamed al-Fayed. The Pitcalnie line succeeded to the representation of the Ross family, and the present chief is David Campbell Ross, son of Sheriff Charles Campbell Ross of Shandwick, who succeeded his kinswoman, Miss Rosa Williamson Ross of that Ilk, in 1968. He is a grandson of Sir Ronald Ross, 1857–1931, a Nobel prizewinner in medicine.

The Rosses of Cromarty were descended from Hugh Rose of Glastullich, who married secondly, Catherine Ross, died 1852, heiress of her great-uncle, George Ross of Pitkerie and Cromarty, whereupon he assumed the name of Ross in terms of the entail of his wife's estate. Lieutenant Col. George Duncan Ross, of this family, joined the Seaforth Highlanders in 1923, and retired in 1926. He rejoined in 1939, and served in World War II.

William Ross, 1762–90, a schoolmaster at Gairloch, composed Gaelic songs which are still sung today. A contemporary, Col. George Ross, was a signatory of the American Declaration of Independence. In modern times, William Ross, 1911–88, Labour MP for Kilmarnock, Ayr and Bute, served as Secretary of State for Scotland, 1964–70 and 1974–76, and was created a life peer with the title of Baron Ross of Marnock. The Rt Hon. Lord Ross (Donald MacArthur Ross), son of a Dundee solicitor, is a distinguished Senator of the College of Justice (since 1977), and Lord Justice Clerk since 1985.

RUTHVEN The surname Ruthven is of great antiquity, and derives from the old barony of Ruthven, in Angus. Four generations of the family can be deduced from one document in the cartulary of the abbey of Scone. Sweyn, Thor's-son, feudal overlord of the district of Crawford, was at the court of Malcolm IV, ca. 1163, and settled in Perthshire before 1188, when he granted lands in Gowrie to the monks of Scone. The representatives of the family came to be styled 'of that Ilk'. Walter Ruthven of that Ilk was one of the Scots forced to capitulate with the 'Red Comyn' to King Edward I of England at Strathord, 1303/04, but he afterwards joined Robert the Bruce.

The Ruthvens have played important and sometimes stormy roles in Scottish history. Sir William Ruthven of that Ilk was, with Douglas, a leader of the moonlight victory over Harry 'Hotspur' and the other Percys at Otterburn in 1388. His son, also Sir William, was one of the Scots nobles sent to England as hostages for the payment of King James I's ransome, and was a prisoner there from 1424 to 1427. Sir William's great-grandson, William, fought with King James III against the rebel nobles at Sauchieburn in 1488, and around this time was created Lord Ruthven. His son William, Master of Ruthven, was killed at Flodden in 1513. Lord Ruthven was one of the four guardians of the boy king in 1515. Patrick, 3rd Lord Ruthuven, was implicated in the murder of David Rizzio, the Queen's secretary, in 1566. His son, William, 4th Lord, was created Earl of Gowrie in 1581, but kidnapped the king in 1582, leading to his arrest. However, he was pardoned after the monarch's release. Notwithstanding, the Lord Arran had him re-arrested and executed in 1584 for high treason. One of the curious episodes in the history of the family was 'The Gowrie Conspiracy' of 5th August, 1660, when James VI, enticed by Alexander, Master of Ruthven, into Gowrie House, was allegedly threatened with death. John, 3rd Earl, and his son William, were slain. The honours and estates were forefeited, and the very name of Ruthven abolished. The earl's cousin had the name restored in 1641, and ten years later was created 1st Lord Ruthven of Freeland. That title descended to Walter Patrick Ruthven, 10th Lord, 1870–1956, whose daughter, Bridget Helen, succeeded to the Scottish title as The Lady Ruthven of Freeland. Walter Patrick's brother, Alexander Gore Arkwright Ruthven, 1872–1955, a distinguished soldier, was created Baron Gowrie of Canberra in 1935, and in 1945 was created Earl of Gowrie in the UK peerage. His heir is Patrick, Viscount Canberra. Lady Ruthven of Freeland married first, 1918, George, 11th Earl of Carlisle (divorced 1947), and secondly, Viscount Monckton of Brenchley, who died in 1965. She died in 1982, when the heir presumptive to the Ruthven of Freeland title was her son, Charles James Ruthven, 12th Earl of Carlisle. He married Hon. Ela Aline, daughter of the 2nd Earl of Allendale, and has issue.

SCOTT   According to an old tradition, the first Scot(t)s on the borders of England and Scotland were of the race of the Scots of Galloway, who were of Celtic origin. Some authorities, however, with more justification, claim the family were of Northumbrian extraction, and point to the fact that the earliest known, Uchtred *filius* Scott, who witnessed the foundation charter of Selkirk ca. 1120, bore 'a good English name'. John *le* Scot, who was archdeacon of St Andrews and became bishop of Dunkeld late in the 12th century, is believed to have come from Podorth, in the earldom of Chester. His father was a Scot, and his mother was related to some other churchmen associated with Dunkeld and St

Andrews. In the same manner, John, Earl of Chester, who died in 1237, appears as *Johannes Scotus* in England, his father, Earl David of Huntingdon, grandson of David I, King of Scots, having married the heiress of the Earl of Chester.

Even in the 13th century, Scotts were widespread. Michael Scott, 'the wizard', who died ca. 1235, was probably born in the Tweed Valley. Ade *le* Scot was a burgess of Berwick (then in Scotland) in 1263. Among those who rendered homage to Edward I in 1296 were Alisaundre Scot of Perthayk, John *le* Scot, burgess of Haddington, Wautier *le* Scot of Peeblesshire, and Richard *le* Scot of Murthoxton (Murdostoun, Lanarkshire). The latter held also Rankilburn, in Selkirkshire, and may have acquired Murdostoun, in Lanarkshire, through marriage with the heiress of Murthoxton of that Ilk. He is said to have had a son Michael, father of Robert, who died ca. 1389, and was the ancestor of the Scotts of Buccleuch, whose cadets spread out between Ettrickdale and Liddesdale. Robert's son Walter had a charter from Robert II of the superiority of Kirkurd, in Peeblesshire. In the last quarter of the 13th century, Scotts appear in Fife. Michael *le* Scot or Lescot of Fife agreed to serve Edward I overseas in 1297. He may have been of the Scotts of Balweary, the first of whom married the heiress to that estate.

From the Scotts of Rankilburn and Murdostoun came Sir Walter Scott, who inherited half of Branxholm, near Hawick, and excambed Murdostoun in 1446 for the other half. From a cleuch at Rankilburn the family took the designation of Buccleuch. His descendant, Sir Walter of Buccleuch survived the Battle of Flodden in 1513, and was knighted. He also fought at Pinkie in 1547. His great-grandson, Walter, was appointed Warden of the West Marches in 1590, and was knighted by James VI. He rescued 'Kinmont Willie' Armstrong from the castle of Carlisle, and was delivered as a hostage upon an adjustment of the feuds with the English. In 1606 he was created Lord Scott of Buccleuch, and afterwards attained fame in the Netherlands as a military commander. His son Walter was created Earl of Buccleuch in 1619. The 2nd Earl, Francis, was succeeded in 1651 by his eldest daughter Mary, who married at the age of 11, Walter Scott of Highchester, and died without issue in 1661, when her sister succeeded. She married first, in 1663, the Duke of Monmouth, a natural son of Charles II, and secondly, in 1688, Baron Cornwallis. By her first husband she had three sons, the second of whom, James, Earl of Dalkeith, was father of Francis, 2nd Duke of Buccleuch. He also became Duke of Queensberry under the limitation to the heirs of

Lady Jane Douglas. The Scottish titles have descended to Walter Francis John Montague-Douglas Scott, 9th Duke of Buccleuch and 11th Duke of Queensberry, who lives with his Countess Jane at Drumlanrig.

The Polwarth line of the Scots has produced many eminent men, and the Harden branch of the family gave us Sir Walter Scott, 1771–1832, who became Scotland's greatest novelist. A definitive 'Edinburgh' edition of his novels is now being published.

SETON The surname of Seton appears in Scotland about 1146, when Alexander Seton witnessed a grant by David I of lands in Roxburghshire and Berwickshire to Walter Ryedale. The family originated in Flanders, and may have descended from the Counts of Boulogne. There were probably links with Normandy and, according to Dr George F. Black, the surname derives from Sai, near Exmes. Seytoune, Seyton and Seaton are variants, and Mrs Platts points out in *Scottish Hazard* that there are a number of places in England so called, notably Seaton Staithes (now simply Staithes), in the West Riding of Yorkshire, some nine miles from Whitby, which she favours as the place from which they took their surname.

Philip de Seton, probably son of Alexander, had a charter of the lands of Setune, Winton and Winchelburgh (Winchburgh), about 1282, confirming a grant to his father. These lands were again confirmed to his son Alexander ca. 1195, when the service was one knight. A valiant warrior, Sir Christopher Seton fought in the War of Independence, and was knighted by Robert the Bruce for rescuing him at the Rout of Methven in 1306. It seems that the reins of Bruce's horse were cut, and that Sir Philip de Moubray seized these and was making off with the king when Seton, 'to Philip sic rout he raucht, that thocht he wes of mekill maucht'. However, there is some doubt that he was in the direct line of the Seton family, but he was probably related as he was son of Sir John Seton, who held the manor of Seton, in Whitby Strand.

The succession to the Scottish estates of the Setons is nebulous in the latter part of the 13th century and early part of the 14th. Bertram de Seton, on record in 1201, and Serle, son of Dugal, are recorded ca. 1246. Alexander, son of Serle, is probably Alisandre de Seton, who signed the *Ragman Roll* in 1296. The family were prominent in the 14th and 15th centuries. The stem line ended with an heiress, Margaret, who married her kinsman, Andrew Wyntoun, ca. 1347. Their son William, styled 'Lord of that Ilk', was succeeded by his son Sir John, who had a charter of confirmation of the baronies of Seton and Tranent, and the lands of Winchburgh, 1410/11. His grandson, Sir George, was created a Lord of Parliament ca. 1445. The 2nd Lord built a castle at Niddry, near Winchburgh ca. 1500, doubtless to exercise his duties as hereditary bailie of the Regality of Kirkliston. Marie, a daughter of the 4th Lord, was the most devoted of the maids of honour of Mary, Queen of Scots, and the only one to go into captivity with her. George, 5th Lord, was involved in the escape of the Queen from Lochleven in 1568, and she rested at Niddry Castle before proceeding to Hamilton. The Setons paid dearly for their attachment to the House of Stewart, but Robert, 6th Lord Seton, was created Earl of Winton in 1600. The 4th Earl sold the Barony of Niddry and lands of Winchburgh in 1678 to John Hope of Hopetoun, progenitor of the Earls of Hopetoun, who built Hopetoun House, Abercorn.

The Gordon family of Huntly became merged with that of Seton through the marriage of Elizabeth Gordon and Alexander, son of William de Seton, in 1408. From them descended many titled and landed branches. Elizabeth succeeded her brother, John of Strathbogie, and their son, Sir Alexander, was created Earl of Huntly ca. 1454, and assumed the name of Gordon. The 6th Earl was created Marquess of Huntly in 1599. The Setons of Abercorn descend from a son of the 1st Marquess of Huntly, through the Setons of Touch, and gave rise to a baronetcy (NS) conferred on Sir William Seton in 1633. The 13th Baronet lives in Western Australia. Sir Alexander Seton of the Pitmeddan branch of the family was created a Baronet of NS in 1684. This family is now represented by Sir James C. Seton, Baronet.

SHAW There are two main groups of Shaws: one Lowland and the other Highland. The Lowland Shaws are of territorial origin, probably from a place in Lanarkshire. John de Schaw witnessed the resignation of the lands of Aldhus to the monks of Paisley in 1284. He reappears in 1294, again witnessing a Paisley document. Symon del Shawe, Fergus del Shaw and William de Shawe, all from Lanarkshire, signed the *Ragman Roll* in 1296. In 1331 John Shawe was a burgess of Dundee, and in 1409 there is a record of a payment by the monks of Melrose to James de la Schaw. James Schaw of Salquhi (Sauchie) witnessed a notarial attestation of the marriage settlement of James, son and heir of James, King of Scots, to the Lady Cecilia in 1474. The name became widespread in the west and south-west of Scotland. It is also on record in England, and was exported to Ireland. Of this family descended the eminent playwright, George Bernard Shaw, 1856–1950. Thomas, 1850–1937, son of Alexander Shaw, master baker in Dunfermline, was a distinguished lawyer. He was admitted advocate in 1875, and was Liberal MP for Hawick Burghs, 1892–1909; Solicitor-General, 1894–1905, and Lord Advocate, 1904–90. After a spell as a Lord of Appeal, he was created Baron Craigmyle in 1929.

The Highland Shaws are a branch of Clan Chattan, and the name derives from *Sithech* or *Sidheach*, meaning (son of the) wolf. Without Mac for 'son of', the name became Englished as Shaw. The first record of the name is on a margin of the 12th century *Book of Deer*, as 'Donnachac mac Sithig toesech clenni Morgainn' (Duncan mac Sithech toisech of Clan Morgan). A Culdee (*Celi De*) of Muthill, Perthshire, called Sitheach, witnessed a charter to the Bishop of Dunblane ca. 1178. The name was transformed into Shaw, but in Fife often appears as Seth or Seath, and as Shiach and Sheach in Strathbogie. Reverend Lachlan Shaw, 1686–1777, son of Donald Shaw, a farmer, was minister successively at Kingussie, Cawdor and Elgin, and a notable historian and genealogist. The Shaws are the second oldest sept of the Mackintoshes, being descended from John, second son of Angus Mackintosh, 6th of that Ilk, grandfather of Shaw McGilchrist Vic Iain, who obtained the lands of Rothiemurchus towards the close of the 14th century. Alan, 7th chief of Clan Shaw, sold Rothiemurchus to George Gordon of Ruthven, and married a daughter of Ferquhard, 12th Mackintosh chief. The chiefship then passed to Adam Shaw, progenitor of the Tordarroch line, who claim also to be chiefs of Clan Ay. Robert, 12th chief of the Shaws, signed the Clan Chattan bond with other chiefs in 1609. The 21st chief, the late Charles John Shaw of Tordarroch, published a *History of Clan Shaw* in 1983. The present chief is his son, John of Tordarroch, who is a Vice-President of the Clan Chattan Association and a member of the Royal Company of Archers.

SIBBALD The surname Sibbald comes from the Old English *Saebeald*, 'seabold', or from *Sigebeald*, 'victoriously bold'. Variants are Sibbet, Sebald, Sibald, Sybald, Sibbal and Sibbald. The form Sibbet is from the Norman-French pronunciation. Philip de Maleuille married ca. 1200, Eva, daughter of Walter, son of Sibald. Sir Duncan Sybald granted one stone of wax and four shillings for light to the monks of Cupar-Angus in 1286. The surname is found in various parts of Scotland, but mainly in Fife. Thomas Sebalde witnessed charters of the lands of Myrecairnie in Fife, 1386 and ca.

1390. A notable family was that of Balgony, who intermarried with the great House of Douglas. Sir Thomas Sibbald of Balgonie was treasurer to King James II (1437–60). The family failed in the direct male line during the reign of James IV (1488–1513), and the heiress, Helena, married Robert, son of Lundin of that Ilk. The Sibbalds of Rankeillor then became the principal family. Andrew Sibbald of Rankeillor married Margaret, daughter of George Lermouth of Balcomie and had three sons: Sir James, created a Baronet of NS in 1630; Dr George, of Giblistone, who married in 1648, Isobel Hunter; and David, 1589–1660, Keeper of the Great Seal, father of Sir Robert Sibbald, 1641–1722, of Kipps in West Lothian. Sir Robert was born in Edinburgh, and educated there and at Leyden for the medical profession. He afterwards studied botany at Paris, and gained his MD at Angers. In 1672, along with Sir Andrew Balfour, he established a botanical garden. He was also a founder member of the Royal College of Physicians, of which he was first president. He was also knighted, and became Professor of Medicine at the University of Edinburgh. Sir Robert was, moreover, an eminent historian and antiquarian writer, author of histories of Fife, Stirling and Linlithgowshire (West Lothian). He married first, in 1677, Anna Lowis, by whom he had a daughter Katherine, who married James Durham of Duntarvie. By his second wife, Anna Orrock, who died in 1722, he had six daughters, one of whom Elizabeth, born 1687, married (as his second wife), Alexander Falconer, advocate. The baronetcy of Rankeillor is extinct.

SINCLAIR LORDSHIP

The surname St Clair or Sinclair is derived from Saint-Clair-sur-Elle, in the Cotentin peninsula of Normandy. The progenitor appears to have been Walderne, Count de Sancto Claro, who came to England with the conqueror, and is named as Senclere in the *Roll of Battle Abbey*, 1066. His son by his wife Margaret, daughter of Richard, Duke of Normandy, was William de Sancto Claro, who came to Scotland. Sir Henry St Clair, a vassal of Richard de Morville in 1162, who obtained the lands of Herdmanstoun and Carfrae, must have been of the same stock, but the relationship is nebulous. Alan de St Clair, of this family, had a charter of lands in Lauderdale. William de Sancto Claro was knighted and had a grant of the barony of Rosslyn (Roslin). His son, Sir Henry, witnessed charters and died before 1270. He was probably the father of Sir William de St Clair, Sheriff of Edinburghshire in 1263. This man was high in favour with King Alexander III (1249–86), and was one of the magnates who, in

1285, negotiated the marriage of the king and Yolanda, daughter of the Count of Dreux. The king granted him the lands of Inverleith, Edinburgh. Sir William swore fealty to Edward I of England in 1296. He left three sons: Sir Henry, his heir; William, Bishop of Dunkeld, 1312–37; and Gregory, ancestor of the Sinclairs of Longformacus, Berwickshire.

Sir Henry Sinclair supported Robert the Bruce, who gave him lands at Pentland. He became butler to the royal family. His son, Sir William, died in Spain with Sir James Douglas in 1330. The young heir, Sir William, by his marriage to Isabel, co-heiress of Malise, Earl of Strathearn, much increased the family influence. Their son, Henry, obtained through his mother the earldom of Orkney. He was a noted seaman, and while conquering the Faroes in 1391, enlisted the aid of a shipwrecked Venetian mariner, Nicola Zewno. They crossed to Greenland, and are thought to have reached America. His grandson, William, 3rd Earl of Orkney, surrendered the earldom to the crown, and was created Earl of Caithness in 1445. He built the stately chapel of Rosslyn, famous in the world of freemasonry, and reputed to contain in its vaults holy relics, including even the holy grail. The family have always played a prominent part in freemasonry. The earl became a Lord of Parliament ca. 1449. By his first wife he had a son, William, 2nd Lord Sinclair, and, by his second, Sir Oliver of Rosslyn, ancestor of William, who sold his estate in 1736, and whose line failed during that year.

After the death of Henry, 10th Lord Sinclair, in 1723, a complicated situation arose. His son John, who died without issue in 1750, had been attainted for his part in the '15 Rising. He or his brother Gen. James Sinclair purchased Rosslyn in 1736. The latter died without issue in 1762, and his sister Grizel, and her issue by John Paterson of Prestonhall, became heirs of line. A younger sister, Catherine, married Sir John Erskine of Alva, Baronet, and their son, Col. James, succeeded his uncle, Alexander, as 2nd Earl of Rosslyn, and assumed the additional surname of St Clair. Charles St Clair of Herdmanston inherited a claim to the attainted Sinclair peerage by a patent of 1677, granted to the 10th Lord, and became *de jure* 12th Lord Sinclair, without descent from the original lords. His grandson, Charles, was recognised as 13th Lord in 1782. The 17th Lord Sinclair is Charles Murray Kennedy St Clair, born 1914, who served as a Major in the Coldstream Guards, 1937–45. He was Portcullis Pursuivant at the College of Arms, 1949–57, and York Herald, 1967–68. He was Hon. Genealogist to the Royal Victorian

Order, 1960–68. His heir is his son, Matthew, Master of Sinclair. The Rosslyn peerage has descended to Sir Peter St Clair-Erskine, Baron Loughborough (1780) and 10th Baronet (NS, 1666).

SINCLAIR EARLDOM William Sinclair, 1st Earl of Caithness, created 1455, was son of Henry, Earl of Orkney. He was Lord High Chancellor of Scotland, and by his second wife, Marjory, daughter of Alexander Sutherland of Dunbeath, had issue, including William, 2nd Earl, who received a new charter of the earldom in 1476. He was slain at Flodden in 1513, leaving by his wife, Mary Keith, two sons: John, 3rd Earl, and Alexander. George, 4th Earl, resigned the honour in favour of his son John. His second son was William of Mey, who left two natural sons: Patrick; and John, from whom descended the Sinclairs of Ulbster. The Master of Caithness died before his father, leaving by his wife, Jean Hepburn, three sons: George, 5th Earl; James of Murchil, ancestor of the 8th Earl; and Sir John, ancestor of the 10th Earl.

George, 6th Earl, son of John, succeeded his grandfather, and died in 1676, childless and bankrupt, with his estates mortgaged to John Campbell of Glenorchy, later Earl of Breadalbane. The heir was George, son of Francis Sinclair of Keiss, and he seized some of the lands. This led to John Campbell marching an armed force to Caithness, where he defeated George's small army at Old Marlack. The lands were purchased in 1719 by the Sinclairs of Ulbster and of Dunbeath. The 7th Earl died unmarried and the dignity devolved on John Sinclair, grandson of John of Murchil, an advocate who was raised to the bench in 1733 as Lord Murkle. His elder brother, Alexander, 1684–1765, died without issue and was succeeded by his cousin and heir male, William Sinclair of Ratter, recognised as 10th Earl of Caithness. He was descended from the Sinclairs of Greenland. His only surviving son, John, 11th Earl, soldiered in the American Revolutionary War and was wounded at Charlestown. When he died in 1789, the title went to a distant relative, Sir James Sinclair of Mey, who was the 8th Baronet of his line (created NS, 1631). His grandson James, was created Baron Barogill (UK) in 1866, but that title expired when his son George, 15th Earl, died without issue in 1889. The Scottish title then passed to his kinsman, James, descended from the Mey line. He was a CA in Aberdeen, and father of John, 17th Earl and of Norman, 18th Earl of Caithness. He was succeeded in 1965 by his son Malcolm Ian Sinclair, born 1948, 20th Earl of Caithness, Lord Berridale, 15th Baronet of NS, and clan chief.

Patrick, second son of William Sinclair of Mey, obtained the estate of Ulbster from his second cousin, the 5th Earl. He was twice married and had sons Patrick of Ulbster, and John of Brims. Patrick was succeeded by his son Patrick, whose son, John of Ulbster, married Janet, daughter of William Sinclair of Ratter. His cousin John of Brims succeeded as heir of entail. From him descended Sir John Sinclair, 1754–1835, voluminous writer and editor of the first *Statistical Account of Scotland*, who was created a Baronet in 1786. His family included George, 2nd Baronet; Alexandra, family historian; and Catherine, authoress to whom a memorial was erected in Edinburgh. The 4th Baronet, Archibald, was Leader of the Liberal party, 1935–45, and held government posts. He was created Viscount Thurso in 1952, and was succeeded in 1970 by his son, Robin, 2nd Viscount and 5th Baronet. His sister, Elizabeth, 1921–1994, who married Major Patrick Lyle, founded Butterstone House Preparatory School for girls in 1947.

Alexander Sinclair, OBE, is president of the Golf Foundation. A former Scottish gold internationalist, he was the recipient of the Frank Moran Award in 1979 for his services to sport.

SKENE Of territorial origin, this surname derives from the lands of that name in Aberdeenshire, erected into a barony in 1317. The meaning is not clear, but the family arms bear *sgians* or daggers, perhaps to mark some important event. Johan de Skene of Edneburk and Johan de Skene of Aberdeenshire, rendered homage to Edward I in 1296, and the seals prove they were of the same stock, if not one and the same person. The Skene family possessed the lands for over 500 years, but the direct line failed in 1827, and the estates devolved on a nephew, James, 4th Earl of Fife. The Skenes of Curriehill descended from James, second son of Alexander Skene of Skene. Sir John Skene of Curriehill, 1549–1611, was an eminent feudal lawyer, and William Forbes Skene, 1809–92, was Historiographer Royal for Scotland, and author of *Celtic Scotland*, the second edition of which was published at Edinburgh in three volumes, 1886–90.

STEVENSON This name means simply 'son of Steven', and should not be confused with Stevenston, which derives from the placename Stevens(t)on, in Newlands parish, Peeblesshire. The earliest known example of the name is that of Nichol fitz Steven, chaplain of Scotland, who had license to take shipping at London or Dovorre at pleasure, in 1372. Duncan Stewinson was a witness at Brechin in 1479, and Henry Stevinson there appears as Henry Steynson in 1505. Thomas Stevenson, last RC precentor of the metropolitan church of Glasgow in 1548, spelt his name as Steinstoune. Andro Steinunsone was treasurer of Edinburgh in 1580. The name appears in a number of forms, including Steinston, Stevinstine, Stevisone, Stevenstoune and Stivinsoun.

The best-known family of Stevensons descended from Robert Stevenson, admitted maltman-burgess of Glasgow in 1708. His son Robert, by his second wife, Elizabeth Cumming, was also a maltman. He married Margaret Fulton, and his testament was confirmed in 1765. They were the parents of Allan Stevenson, a Glasgow merchant who died in the West Indies when his son Robert, by Jane Little, was very young. Robert, 1772–1850, was (in conjunction with John Rennie) the architect of the Bell Rock Lighthouse. He was appointed sole engineer for the Board of Northern Lights. He married Jane Smith, and their son Thomas, also a CE, married Margaret Isabella, daughter of the Rev. Lewis Balfour, minister at Colinton, 1823–60. They were the parents of the much loved literary giant, Robert Louis Stevenson, 1850–94.

Sir Archibald Stevenson, 1640–1700, an Edinburgh physician, was associated with the founding of the Royal College of Surgeons. Reverend William Stevenson, 1805–73, born in Renfrewshire, became minister of Arbroath in 1833, and was translated to South Leith in 1844. In 1861 he became Professor of Divinity and Church History at the University of Edinburgh. William Graham Stevenson, 1849–1919, was a capable sculptor. Among his statues is one of Robert Burns at Kilmarnock, and that of Sir William Wallace at Aberdeen.

STEWART/STUART The Stewarts derive their name from the office of High Steward of Scotland, bestowed on their ancestor, Walter Fitz Alan by King David II (1124–53). Alan Fitz Flaald, the father, came from Brittany and was sheriff of Shropshire early in the 12th century. His father succeeded his brother Alan as Steward of Dol, in Brittany. Alan Fitz Flaald married Avelina, daughter of Arnulf de Hesdin, which was part of the county of Boulogne. The family had links with Flanders, and were related to William de Graham, who also came to Scotland. Walter was a younger son, and came to Scotland on the return of King David, from whom he received large grants of land in the west of Scotland, particularly in what became Renfrewshire. He founded the abbey of Paisley ca. 1136, and died in 1177, leaving by his wife Eschine de Molle, a son, Alan.

Alan Fitz Walter became hereditary High Steward of Scotland, and was the first to adopt the surname of Stewart. Besides being the ancestors of the Stewart kings, the family branched out and held at one time or another numerous estates and titles. The first four dukes and the first ever marquess to be created were all Stuarts. Others held the Earldoms of Angus, Atholl, Arran, Bothwell, Buchan, Bute, Caithness, Carrick, Fife, Galloway, Mar, March, Menteith, Moray, Orkney, Strathearn and Traquair. Walter, 6th High Steward, was the progenitor of the Stewart kings, having married as his first wife, Marjorie, ca. 1295–1315/16, daughter of Robert the Bruce by his first wife, Isabella, daughter of Donald, 10th Earl of Mar. Their only son became Robert II on the death of David II in 1371. On the death of King James V, the direct male line of the royal Stewarts was continued through Queen Mary's marriage in 1595 to her cousin, Henry Stewart, Lord Darnley, descended from a younger son of James, 5th High Steward. Their son, James VI, was heir male and heir of line to the House of Stewart, but it was as heir of line that he represented the Stewarts descending through Marjorie Bruce.

On the death of Prince Charles Edward Stuart (French spelling) and his brother Benedict, the male line of the royal Stewarts is believed to have ended. The chiefly line of the Stewarts is understood to be that of Randolph Keith Reginald Stewart, 13th Earl of Galloway, born 1928. A clever man, who has been addicted from an early age to the collection of empty titles, and who styles himself HRH Prince Michael of Albany, claims in his book, *The Forgotten Monarchy of Scotland* (Shaftesbury: Element, 1998), to be head of the House of Stewart, and seems to have a utopian desire to be King of Scots.

The present Earl of Moray, Douglas John Moray Stuart, descends from James Stuart, the Regent Moray, eldest surviving natural son of King James V. The Regent, by Agnes Keith, left a daughter Elizabeth, Countess of Moray in her own right, who married James Stuart, Master of Doune, who became Earl of Moray as well as Earl of Doune. He was slashed to death by the Gordons in 1592. This is the noble lamented in the old ballad, 'The Bonny Earl of Moray'. The present home of the family is Darnaway Castle, Forres. Another important branch of the family is represented by John Colum Crichton-Stuart, 7th Marquess of Bute ('Johnny Dumfries', the racing driver), who descends from Sir John Stewart, a natural son of King Robert II. The Stewarts of Appin spring from an allegedly natural son of John Stewart of Lorne, died

1463, descended from Sir John Stewart of Bonkyl. It is interesting to note that the Stewart heraldic *chequy*, which first appears on the seal of Alan, High Steward (1177–1204), is thought to represent the 'chessboards' used to calculate accounts: only one function of the ancient office.

STIRLING: ORIGINS AND HERALDRY The surname Stirling derives from the town of that name. It seems probable that those styled in early records, 'de Striueling', were important people in a key town, but not necessarily related. Petro clerico de Striueling, son of Walter, was a chamber official under Malcolm IV and William I, witnessing charters, 1153–77. Richard of Stirling was a chaplain of Malcolm IV, and held the benefice of Forteviot ca. 1175. When he died, this was to be attached to the abbey of Cambuskenneth. John of Stirling witnessed charters, 1204–10. Gilbert Stirling, whom Keith describes as a man well-born, was clerk to William I and Alexander II, and was bishop of Dunkeld, 1228–39. He may have been related to Thomas of Stirling, also a clerk and archdeacon of Glasgow. Robert of Stirling was a deacon of Dunkeld in 1263. Five men from Stirling swore fealty to Edward I of England in 1292–97, among them 'Mestre Henry de Striviling' of Stirlingshire. A family of Stirlings settled in the north at an early period, and one of those, 'Johannes de Striviling de Moravia', also signed the *Ragman Roll*. His seal displayed six stars.

The heraldry of the Stirlings has been subject to much confusion. Those – and this means most – whose arms show buckles, often on a bend, were of Flemish extraction, probably descended from the Malets, who ruled the lordship of Voormezele, near Ypres, and held estates adjoining Dixmude. Buckles go back to the time of Charlemagne and the dawn of heraldry. The seal of William of Stirling, 1296, shows, on a chief, three buckles. The shield, suspended from a tree, is flanked by two small lions rampant. Sir John of Stirling (of East Swinburne, Northumberland), sheriff of the Lothians and warden of Edinburgh Castle, ca. 1335, bore semee of crosses, three covered cups, and for crest on a helmet front face with coronet, a covered cup between two bull horns. The seal of William Stirling of Cadder, chief of the surname, ca. 1492, is couche, on a bend engrailed three buckles, and for crest on a helmet with mantling and coronet, a swan head, neck and wings. The legend is *S' villelmi striuelin de cadder*. When *Lyon Register* commenced in 1672, it seems there was some uncertainty, and the blazon for Cadder was entered as Argent, on a bend Azure (or rather Sable), three buckles Or. There is added a note to the effect that in old books the bend is found engrailed. In 1621, when John Stirling of Keir was knighted his arms were blazoned Argent, on a bend engrailed Sable, three buckles Or, as in the *Armorial of Sir David Lindsay*, 1542.

It seems clear that the progenitor of the Stirlings of Cadder, in Lanarkshire was Thoraldus, 'vicecomes [i.e. 'my minister'] de Strivelyn', on record in 1147. William his son was living 1165–1214, and his son Alexander died ca. 1244. All were sheriffs of Stirlingshire. John, IVth of Cadder, had three sons. The eldest was Sir Alexander of Cadder, and the youngest, Sir William was probably ancestor of the Stirlings of Keir. Sir Alexander's son, Sir John, was killed at Halidon Hill in 1333, and his son, Sir John, died ca. 1408. Sir William of Cadder, the next on record, also owned Redgorton. He died ca. 1434, having had issue, two sons: Sir William, IXth of Cadder, and Gilbert of Craigbernard, ancestor of the Stirlings of Glorat. Sir William, Xth of Cadder, held also Lettyr. He died ca. 1505. His grandson Andrew, 12th laird, left an heiress, Janet, who married (perhaps forcibly) Sir James Stirling of Keir. It was an unhappy marriage and she was divorced, having formed an attachment to Thomas Bishop, an adventurer. Cadder remained with her husband, but she retained Ochiltree, in Linlithgowshire.

STIRLING: THE LEADING FAMILIES
An influential family for over 500 years, the Stirlings of Keir have produced many fine soldiers. William Joseph Stirling, 17th of Keir, Perthshire, was Hon. Lt. Col. of the Scots Guards, and fought in World War II. His father Archibald was a much decorated soldier, having served in the Nile Expedition of 1899; the South African War as a Brig. Gen., and in Gallipoli and Egypt in World War I. The progenitor of this family was Lucas de Striveling, who died before 1462, and appears to have descended from the Stirlings of Cadder. William Stirling, IIIrd of Keir, espoused the cause of the nobles headed by Prince James, opposed to King James III, and was knighted by James IV. The VIth laird, Archibald, had, with other issue, James, his heir; Archibald, the progenitor of the Stirlings of Kippendavie; and John, from whom descended the Stirlings of Garden. George, son of James, followed his grandfather, but died without surviving issue, and was succeeded by his cousin, Sir Archibald Stirling of Garden, a Royalist who became a Lord of Session in 1661. His grandson James took part in the Jacobite Rising of 1715, and was

forfeited. Friends purchased the estates for his sons John, Archibald and William, who all followed one another as lairds. William, 1725–93, left a son and heir, Archibald, and another son, William, who married Jean Stewart, heiress of Castlemilk, in 1781. Their descendants are the Stirling-Stewarts. William Stirling, 1818–78, of Keir and Cadder, succeeded his maternal uncle, Sir John Maxwell of Pollock, as 9th Baronet in 1865, and assumed the surname Maxwell in addition to Stirling. Their second son succeeded to Keir and Cadder. He was the soldier associated with the Scots Guards and Lovat Scouts, and in fact married Margaret, daughter of the 10th Lord Lovat.

The Stirlings of Glorat, near Milton of Campsie, descended from Gilbert of Craigbernard, son of Sir William Stirling, XIth of Cadder. His grandson, Sir John, left two sons: George of Craigbernard, whose line expired in 1805, and William of Glorat. His descendant, George, was created; a Baronet of NS in 1666. The title came down to Sir George Murray Home Stirling, 1869–1949, but his sons died without issue and the title is extinct.

Another branch held the estate of Muiravonside, in Stirlingshire. This family descended from the Stirlings of Auld Keir and Lettyr. Of this family came Andrew Stirling of Drumpelier, recognised by Lyon Court in 1818, as heir male of the Cadder line, and allowed supporters to his arms. He married in 1778, Anne, daughter of Sir Walter Stirling of Faskine, RN. Their son John continued the line, and the second son, Charles, obtained Muiravonside, in Stirlingshire. He married in 1827, Charlotte, daughter of Vice-Adm. Charles Stirling. Their eldest son, Andrew sold the estate to his cousin, Thomas Mayne Stirling, who married his cousin, Anna, daughter of Charles of Muiravonside. Their eldest son, Thomas William Stirling, who sold the estate in 1927, was the father of Arthur C. Stirling. The family came to be represented by his cousin, Sir Charles Norman Strirling, 1901–86, a diplomat, who was knighted in 1957. Muiravonside house suffered a disastrous fire and was afterwards demolished. The grounds now form a country park. The old house was the first stop, on her way to St Kilda, of Lady Grange, kidnapped for political reasons. A prisoner for over 20 years, she died in Skye in 1745.

The Stirlings of Ardoch, Strathallan, baronets of NS (1666), and those of Garden, descend from the Keir line. The Stirlings of Gargunnock come from the Kippendavie family. The inventor of the Stirling Air Engine, patented in 1816, was the Rev. Robert Stirling, 1790–1878, minister at Galston, grandson of Michael

Stirling, inventor of the rotary thrashing machine. Many books, and a card index of Stirlings compiled by the late Matthew Stirling, an accountant in London, are preserved in the library of the Scottish Genealogy Society, 15 Victoria Terrace, Edinburgh.

STRACHAN A territorial surname, from the lands of Strachan, in Kincardineshire, it has numerous spellings. Sir James de Stratheyhan obtained the lands of Thorntoun, on his marriage to Agnes Quagie, an heiress. He had a charter of confirmation before 1153. Andrew Strachan, of this family, a favourite of Charles I, was created a Baronet of NS in 1625. The title has remained dormant since the death of Sir Richard John Strachan, 6th Baronet, in 1828. Waldeus de Stratheihan, with consent of his son Ranulf, gave the lands of Blarkeroch to the church of St Andrews ca. 1200. The son witnessed a charter by Thomas de Lundin before 1214. He is probably the man who, along with Michael de Strathkerkan, were appointed attorneys by Alexander, Earl of Buchan, in 1268. Ranulf's son, John, granted the lands of Beeth Waldef to the abbey and convent of Dunfermline in 1287. In 1424, Geffray Sterhaughan had a safe conduct to enter England. David Straughin was procurator of the 'Scottish Nation' at the University of Orleans in 1512. Landed Strachan families have owned the estates of Strachan itself, Carmyllie, Claypots, Glenkindie, Inchtuthil and Craigcrook. The latter place was purchased in 1698 by John Strachan, WS (d. 1719), who also held North Clermiston, and Boddoms, a house in Edinburgh, all of which he mortified for certain charitable purposes. John Strachan, 1778–1867 (pronounced Straun in Canada), was a schoolmaster at Kettle before emigrating to Canada, where he became an Episcopalian clergyman. He was consecrated Bishop of Toronto in 1839, and was a member of the powerful 'Family Compact'. Hew Francis Anthony Strachan, born in Edinburgh in 1949, is Professor of Modern History at the University of Glasgow, and a military historian.

SUTHERLAND Historians and genealogists are agreed that those who took the name of Sutherland – from *Sudrland* – the county south of the Northern Isles, were descended from Freskin the Fleming, whose family probably intermarried with the old dynastic House of Moray. He had several sons, the eldest of whom, Hugh, died before 1226, and was succeeded by his eldest son, William, created Earl of Sutherland ca. 1235. William, 2nd Earl, succeeded his father ca. 1248. In 1283/84 he attended the

Parliament at Scone which accepted the infant Margaret of Norway as Queen of Scots, failing direct issue of Alexander III. He signed the homage roll in 1296, and died in allegiance to Edward I of England ca. 1307.

Earl William was succeeded in turn by his sons William and Kenneth. The latter, who was killed at Halidon Hill in 1333, left two sons: William his heir, and Nicholas, who had a charter of Torboll in 1360, by his brother. He was ancestor of the Lords Duffus. William, 5th Earl, married ca. 1345, Margaret, daughter of King Robert I by his second wife, Elizabeth de Burgh. He had a charter of the earldom in free regality the same year, augmented by grants of land in Aberdeenshire and Kincardineshire. They had a son, John, party to a treaty made at Berwick in 1360. By a second wife, Joanna, three times widowed, he had two sons: Robert, who became 6th Earl, and Kenneth, ancestor of the Sutherlands of Forse or Forss.

Dunrobin, which simply means 'Robin's Castle', was named after Robert, 6th Earl, and it has since been the family home. Robert married, ca. 1398, Margaret, natural daughter of Alexander Stewart, Earl of Buchan, otherwise known as 'The Wolf of Badenoch'. King James IV gave the Gordons power to quell disorders in the north, and John, 8th Earl of Sutherland, was served with a brieve of idiotry in 1494. His son John, the 9th Earl, was also deemed incapable of managing his own affairs, which were placed in the care of his sister Elizabeth, who succeeded him, ca. 1514, as Countess of Sutherland. She married in 1550, Adam Gordon, second son of the 2nd Earl of Huntly. He assumed the courtesy title of Earl of Sutherland. Their eldest son, Alexander, was the father of John, 11th Earl, who was forfeited after the Battle of Corrichie in 1562, but rehabilitated in 1565.

In 1598, John, 13th Earl, caused the first pit to be sunk at Brora, where he also installed salt pans. Soon afterwards the earldom was erected into a regality. He had feuds with the Mackays and, in 1651, outfitted a contingent of his clan, who marched with Charles II to Worcester, where they were defeated by the forces of Oliver Cromwell. In the time of John, 16th Earl, 1661–1733, a wolf was killed within twelve miles of Dunrobin. It was he who resumed the surname of Sutherland, instead of Gordon. William, 18th Earl, was succeeded in 1766 by his surviving daughter, Elizabeth, who became Countess of Sutherland and Baroness Strathnaver in her own right. She married in 1765, George Leveson-Gower, Marquess of Stafford, who was created Duke of Sutherland in 1833. The

Duke and Duchess were responsible for improvements to their estates which, however well intentioned, led to notorious clearances and depopulation. After the succession of the countess, John Sutherland of Forse and Sir Robert Gordon of Gordonstoun contested a right to the honours other than those inherited by the Lady Elizabeth, but the House of Lords Committee of Privileges decided in her favour. On the death of the 5th Duke of Sutherland in 1963, the UK dignity passed to the Egerton Earls of Ellesmere, while the earldom and chiefship passed to his niece, Elizabeth Millicent, Countess of Sutherland, born 1921. Her son and heir is Alistair, Lord Strathnaver.

THOMSON 'We're all John Tamson's bairns', is a common saying when people are 'all in the same boat' or position, and points to the fact that Thomsons are numerous. Thomson simply means 'son of Thom'. As a forename Thomas goes back to biblical times. The usual abbreviations are Tom or Thom: hence the surnames Thomas, Thomson, Thompson and Tomlinson. The surname is not recorded in Britain until after the Norman Conquest, and there must be Thomsons of differing origins. *Mc k Chuin Tomson*, Baron of Pharnua, was associated with the Bisset family in Lovat, early in the 13th century. John Thomson, a man of humble birth but 'approved valour', led the men of Carrick in Edward Bruce's war in Ireland, in 1318. David Thomson was a student at St Andrews in 1408. Duncan Davidson, alias Thomson in Auchinlampers, married Bessie, daughter of William Leslie, IVth of Balquhan (d. 1476) and Euphame Lindsay. The Lord Lyon King of Arms, 1496–1512, was Henry Thomson, and Peter Thomson, who held various offices in Lyon Court between 1535 and 1571, was admitted burgess and guildbrother of Edinburgh, on 14th March, 1558/9, *gratis*, on condition that 'he sail in all tymes cuming be ready to serve in the townys effars'.

Thomsons of Argyll and Perthshire are really MacTavishes. The surname in those counties is an Anglicised form of the Gaelic *MacThomais*, 'son of Thomas', or *MacThomaidh*, 'son of Tommie'. The name was given as MacComie (and variants) in some areas, including Deeside. Alexander Thomeson in Strathdee is recorded in 1527. Thomsons in Banchory, Deeside, descended from Andrew in Cammachmore and Elizabeth Muir, married in 1736. Their descendant, Andrew Thomas, 1772–1806, was Professor of Mathematics in Marischal College, Aberdeen. Christie Thomson appears in Hoy, Orkney in 1502. The form Tomison is common in

South Ronaldsay. The Thomsons of Charleston held estates in Fife for several generations. Grizel, heiress of John Thomson of Charleston, married in 1774, Col. John Anstruther, of the Balcaskie family, and their descendants came to be known as Anstruther-Thomsons. An estate at Duddingston, Edinburgh was owned for six generations by a family of Thomsons. Thomas, son of Alexander Thomson of Duddingston, was created a Baronet of NS in 1636. His son Sir Patrick sold the estate in 1668 and died ca. 1674. The title is dormant.

James Thomson, 1700–48, the poet of 'The Seasons', was a native of Oxnam, in Roxburghshire. In association with David Mallet, he composed *The Mask of Alfred*, in which his song 'Rule Brittania' appeared. George Thomson, 1757–1851, editor of a five-volume collection of songs, was a friend of the poet Burns. Thomas Thomson, 1768–1852, was an eminent record scholar, and was Deputy Clark Register for Scotland, 1806–39. An annexe of the National Archives at Sighthill, Edinburgh, recently opened, has been named in his honour. Reverend John Thomson, 1778–1840, minister at Duddingston, Edinburgh, was a landscape painter. Thomas Thomson, 1773–1852, from Whittinghame, was a noted chemist. Many fine buildings in Glasgow were designed by Alexander 'Greek' Thomson, 1817–75. William Thomson, Baron Kelvin, 1824–1907, was an eminent scientist and inventor who was born in Belfast but educated in Glasgow. The 2nd Baron of Fleet, the newspaper magnate, descends from Archibald Thomson, a stonemason who emigrated from Bonese, Westerkirk, Dumfriesshire to Scarborough, Ontario, Canada ca. 1802. Dr George Morgan Thomson, a journalist and politician, was made a life peer in 1977 as Baron Thomson of Monifieth.

TURNBULL This surname may derive from Old English *Trumbald*, 'strongly bold', but an old tradition says that a man named Rule, in Roxburghshire, saved the life of Robert the Bruce at Stirling by twisting the head of a bull which attacked the monarch, and was rewarded with lands at Bedrule, in Roxburghshire, and a new name. Curiously, near the village of Bedrule, stood a castle of the Turnbulls where, ca. 1494, 200 members of that unruly clan were brought before James IV, with halters round their necks and naked swords in their hands. The Turnbulls of Bedrule were reckoned to be chiefs of the surname, and the Minto branch was powerful. In the *Register of the Great Seal* there is a charter of land to the west of Fulhophalche (Philiphaugh), in 1513, in favour of

William Turnbull. John Turnbull had a charter of the lands of Hundleshope ca. 1358. The name spread throughout the eastern border counties, and some moved to Angus. The earliest Turnbull arms, those of Agnes, spouse of William Merlzone, Junr., mason in Edinburgh, 1497, are blazoned: Ermine, three bars, the centre one charged with a star flanked by two ermine spots. In 1603, William Turnbull in Dalkeith bore arms, simply a bull's head erazed: possibly canting arms. The old tale about the bull is recalled in the arms of several branches, including one in France. William Paterson Turnbull, 1830–71, the American ornithologist and author, hailed from Gladsmuir, in East Lothian. Frederick Turnbull, 1847–1909, born in Glasgow, pioneered turkey-red dyeing in the USA.

TWEEDIE For well over 200 years the valleys of the Upper Tweed were inhabited by an unruly family named Tweedie. Tradition says that the first of the name was a water-sprite of the River Tweed, but in fact they derived their name from the lands of Tweedie, at Stonehouse, Lanarkshire. Finlay de Twydyn of Lanarkshire rendered homage to Edward I in 1296. Roger, son of Finlay, had a charter of the lands of Drumelzier, in Peeblesshire, ca. 1320, and the family held the lands until the reign of Charles I (1600–49). In 1948, John Tweedie and others were fined by the Privy Council for ejecting Oswald Porteous and his spouse from Upper Kingledores. They came into conflict with the powerful Flemings in 1524, and in 1582 the 'wild bunch' were again in trouble when James Tweedie murdered an old foe, James Geddes, in Edinburgh. After James Tweedie was killed in single combat with a Veitch in 1608, peace came, but the encumbered family estates had to be sold.

URQUHART This surname is usually stated to come from the lands of Urquhart, lying on the north side of the Great Glen (*Glenmore nan-Albin*), a magnificent Highland valley, chiefly in Inverness-shire, and a great castle there is thought to have been built by the Urquhart chiefs, one of whom is supposed to have married Castalda, daughter of Banco, Shakespeare's Thane of Lochaber. It seems more likely the surname derives from Urquhart in the Black Isle, Ross-shire, especially as the clan chiefs were the Urquharts of Cromarty, in the united county of Ross and Cromarty. The family came into prominence as sheriffs of Cromarty, and seem to have held the post before it became hereditary ca. 1357. In 1305 William de Monhaud was heritable sheriff, but in the reign of Robert the Bruce William Urchart was sheriff. His first wife is said to have been Lillias, daughter of Hugh, 4th Earl of Ross, and mother of Adam Urquhart of Cromarty, who had a charter of the lands of Inch Rory in 1338. Hugh Ross of Philorth, son of the deceased Hugh, Earl of Ross, granted Adam the land of Fishrie, in Buchan, together with Clochforbie, in fee and heredity, dated at Alness, in 1357. His son, John Urchard, was alive in 1368, and was the father of Sir William of Cromarty, knighted by Robert III. His elder son, William, died without issue and was succeeded by his brother Alexander. He had a son Thomas, his heir, and another, Col. John Urquhart, who fought in the Swedish wars. Thomas married Helen, daughter of Alexander, Lord Abernethy, and had a large family. Seven of his sons fell at Pinkie in 1547. The eldest son, Alexander, had by his wife Beatrix Innes, two sons: Walter of Cromarty, and John, 1577–1631, who became tutor to his grand-nephew, Thomas of Cromarty. From the tutor descended the later chiefs of the clan. Walter was succeeded by his son Henry, father of Thomas, noted in 1626 as soldiering under Gustav Adolph of Sweden. His son, Sir Thomas, 1605–61, was the eccentric translator of *Rabelais*, and in 1652 compiled a genealogy of the *Family of Urquhart since the Creation!* He was captured at Worcester and died apparently unmarried, when the chiefship passed to his third cousin, John of Craigston, descended from the Tutor of Cromarty. His line descended through Patrick of Lethnelie to James Urquhart, born 1759, last of his line.

The estate passed to a kinsman, Lt. Col. George Urquhart, who married in 1784 Bridget, daughter of Beauchamp Colclough of Bohermore, Co. Clare. Their son, Major Beauchamp Colclough Urquhart of Meldrum and Byth, died of wounds at Atbara in 1898, when the chiefship became dormant. George Urquhart, ca. 1733–99, descended from a collateral line coming from the Tutor of Cromarty, through his third wife, Elizabeth, daughter of Alexander Seton, heir apparent of Meldrum, emigrated to Florida, USA, ca. 1766, and their great-grandson, Charles Robert Urquhart, residing in New Orleans, became *de jure* representer of the Urquharts of Braelangwell. Their son, Wilkins Fisk Urquhart, was recognised as Urquhart of Braelangwell in 1957 and matriculated arms at the Lyon Office. In 1959 he was adjudgd chief of the name and arms of Urquhart. Wilkins was succeeded by his fourth son, Kenneth Trist Urquhart, born 1932, who lives in New Orleans, Louisiana.

WALLACE Despite the fact that a Shropshire knight, Sir Richard Walency, attested a charter by Walter Fitz Alan at Paisley ca. 1170, it is still generally believed that the Wallaces derive their name from the old British kingdom of Strathclyde, the inhabitants of which were called *Walensis*. Richard Wallensis, not certainly the same man, was a vassal of Walter Fitz Allan in 1174, and obtained the lands of Riccarton, in Ayrshire. His younger grandson, Malcolm, obtained the lands of Elderslie. He was the father of Sir William Wallace, ca. 1270–1305, the patriot. The lands of Craigie came to the elder branch of Riccarton, by marriage early in the 14th century. Sir William was the most famous bearer of the name, and he commenced the War of Independence in earnest by slaying the English governor of Lanark, who had caused the death of his wife. Wallace, after a gruelling campagin, came to a barbarous end at London after being betrayed, but his aims were later achieved by Robert the Bruce. Other early Wallaces include Adam Walleis, a charter witness between 1212 and 1249, in favour of the monks of Cupar, and John Walens, who attested gifts to the abbey of Paisley, before 1228. In the Elderslie line William Wallace had a charter from his namesake in Craigie in 1554. In 1669 Hugh Wallace of Craigie was created a Baronet of NS, but his title is now believed to be extinct. Hugh Wallace of Elderslie, sold his estates in 1678 to Sir Thomas Wallace of Craigie, who conveyed them to his own son, Sir Thomas, who in turn disponed the lands to John Wallace, son of William Wallace, of Glasgow, brother of John Wallace of Neilstonside. He died without issue. John Wallace of Ferguslie married his cousin, Margaret, daughter of John Hamilton of Ferguslie, and died in 1651. Their eldest son, William Wallace of Neilstonside and Drumgrain, Renfrewshire, married Elizabeth Stewart and had two sons: William, the heir; and William Wallace, merchant in Glasgow, father of Thomas Wallace of Cairnhill, whose eldest son was William, 1711–63, an advocate. The family produced a number of military men, including Capt. Henry Ritchie Wallace, of the Gordon Highlanders, who established in Lyon Court in 1888 his representation of the House of Wallace in Scotland. His son, Col. Hugh Robert Wallace of Busbie, had several children, the eldest of whom, Hugh, 1887–1938, died unmarried. His younger brothers, Archibald Malcolm and Charles John, along with their sister Matilda, became portioners of Busbie. When the son, Maj. Gen. Charles John, died in 1943, the chiefship passed to his cousin, Col. Robert Francis Hunter Wallace, 1880–1970, who matriculated appropriate arms in 1950. He was succeeded by his son, Lt. Col. Malcolm Robert Wallace of that Ilk, residing at Hilton of Gask, Auchterarder.

George Wallace, SSC, has been Hon. Sheriff of Hamilton since 1950. A director of the South of Scotland Electricity Board, 1966–69, he has been associated with a number of other organisations. In 1974 he was created a Life Peer as Baron Wallace of Campsie.

WEMYSS The sea coast at Wemyss, in Fife, has a group of caves, from which the surname is derived: *weem* in Scots, and *uaimh* in Gaelic meaning cave. Wemyss must be among the oldest place names in Fife, and gave its name to a family who owned lands. The earliest accredited ancestor was Michael of Wemyss and Methil, who died ca. 1202, but there is strong circumstantial evidence that the family descended from the ancient earls of Fife (see CLAN MACDUFF article), whose progenitor was Eathelred or Aedh, lay abbot of Dunkeld and 1st Earl, who was a son of Malcolm III and Queen Margaret. The succeeding earls were men of substance, with lands on both sides of the Firth of Forth, but their line ended with an heiress, Isabella, Countess in her own right. The above Michael was probably descended from Hugh, second son of Gillemichael, 3rd Earl.

Michael was succeeded by his son John, who flourished in the reign of Alexander II, and died ca. 1263. His descendants took the surname of Wemyss, from the caves containing Pictish drawings, below the ruins of MacDuff's Castle. A later Wemyss, Sir David, was one of the ambassadors sent to escort Margaret, 'The Maid of Norway' to Scotland in 1290. He was also a signatory of the *Declaration of Arbroath* in 1320. The family obtained further estates in Fife, and in the time of Sir David Wemyss, who perished at Flodden in 1513, these and other lands were erected into the barony of Wemyss. His grandson, Sir John, fought under Arran at Pinkie in 1547, and at Langside in 1568 for Mary, Queen of Scots.

Sir John Wemyss of Wemyss was in 1625 created a Baronet of NS, by which time Nova Scotia had been ceded to the French. He was elevated to the peerage as Lord Wemyss of Elcho in 1628, and in 1633 advanced to Earl of Wemyss. He was owner of a coal pit and salt works. His son David, 2nd Earl, entertained King Charles II to dinner at Wemyss Castle in 1650 and again in 1652. Having no surviving sons he resigned the earldom to the Crown in 1672, and obtained a new patent conferring the honours upon his only surviving daughter, Margaret. He died in 1679 when the baronetcy became dormant. Lady Margaret Wemyss married in 1672 her distant kinsman, Sir James Wemyss of Wemyss, created the same year Lord Burntisland for life. Their son David, who succeeded his father in 1682, and his son James, were leading officers in the Royal Company of Archers, the latter winning the silver bowl for shooting in 1720. David, 5th Earl, married in 1720, Janet, heiress of Col. Francis Charteris of Amisfield. His eldest son, David, was a Jacobite and was attainted in 1745. He fled to France and died in 1787. His brother Francis assumed the surname of Charteris on being adopted as heir to his maternal grandfather, and was *de jure* 7th Earl of Wemyss. His grandson, Francis, 8th Earl, inherited the earldom of March in 1810, on the death of the 4th Duke of Queensberry. He was created Baron Wemyss in the UK peerage in 1821, and restored to the earldom of Wemyss in 1826. Another descendant of the 5th Earl, Michael John Wemyss of Wemyss Castle, an inheritor of the ancestral estates, was recognised officially by Lyon Court as chief of the Clan Macduff (Wemyss of that ilk), in 1910. The present representative is his son, Capt. David Wemyss, residing at Invermay, Forteviot. He married in 1945, Lady Jean Bruce, a daughter of the 10th Earl of Elgin, and has issue.

Francis David Charteris, born 1912, 12th Earl of Wemyss and 8th Earl of March, served in the Lovat Scouts in World War II. He was chairman of the Royal Commission on Ancient Monuments and Constructions in Scotland, 1949–84, and has been Lord Clerk Register of Scotland and Keeper of the Signet since 1974. He lives at Gosford House, Longniddry. The heir is his son, James, Lord Neidpath.

WEST A prolific name in various parts of Scotland, and is also found in Eire, especially around Limerick. It is thought to have originally meant someone from the west of Scotland, but some may have come from Ireland. The name is found also around Turriff, Aberdeenshire, in parts of Fife and Perthshire, and notably in the West Lothian parishes of Linlithgow, Ecclesmachan and Kirkliston. Andrew West in Toddishaugh (Foxhall), Kirkliston, died ca. 1594, and his wife Margaret Forrester predeceased him ca. 1578. William West in Carlowrie, Kirkliston, was apprenticed to David Hog, baxter in Edinburgh, in 1597. James, son of James West in Toddishaugh, Kirkliston, was apprenticed to Patrick Douglas, baxter in Edinburgh, in 1619. James West in Nether Carlowrie, married Isobel Wilson, whose testament was confirmed in 1594. Several West families farmed in the Bathgate Hills. John West from Riccarton Farm emigrated to Quebec ca. 1850, and moved to Oregon, where he had a sawmill on the Columbia River, and also engaged in salmon-canning. He married Margaret, daughter of another John West, who emigrated to Quebec with his family ca. 1832. David West, 1868–1936, RSW, a native of Lossiemouth, worked there as a landscape and seascape painter, exhibiting frequently at principal exhibitions. He arranged a private exhibition of his paintings in the Argentine, travelled on the Continent and wintered in Alaska. Thomas Summers West, born at Peterhead, Aberdeenshire, in 1927, is a disinguished chemist, now emeritus Professor of Aberdeen University, and has been the recipient of many awards.

WHITE/WHYTE The surname White or Whyte is found all over Britain. It appears in Old English charters as a personal name in the form of *hwit*, 'white', and as a byname. As a surname it appears as early as the 10th century. Uuiatett Hwite witnessed King Eadgar's charter of Coldingham between 1097 and 1107. In Latin documents the name is rendered as *Albus*. Adam Albus appears as a charter witness between 1180 and 1214. John Albus was steward to Matilda, Countess of Angus, ca. 1242, and Adam Albus held lands in Kincardineshire during the reign of Robert II (1371–90). The surname White or Whyte was prolific in the north-east during the 15th century. Several Quhytes were admitted burgesses of Aberdeen in that age. Andrew Qwhit was a citizen of Brechin in 1472.

According to Sir Robert Douglas, the Whytts of Bennochy were of French extraction, descended from the *Les Blancs*, whose armorial bearings are similar. Matthew Whytte of Maw, in Fife, alive ca. 1490, was related to John Whytte, who held the lands of Maw and Lumbenny by charters dated in 1451. His son Robert, a merchant and first provost of Kirkcaldy, purchased Bennochy and part of Abbotshall. His son John married Jean, daughter of Thomas Melville of Murdocarney, and they were the parents of Robert, an advocate who died in 1714, leaving a son George, succeeded in 1728 by his brother Robert Whytte, 1715–66, who was a physician to George I and was knighted. He was Professor of Medicine in the University of Edinburgh. Sir Robert had a large family by his second wife, Louisa Balfour, of the Pilrig family, and was succeeded by his sons: Robert, who died in 1776, and John Whyte-Melville, who owned also the estate of Strathkinness. His second son, John, who served in the 9th Lancers, was the last Whyte of Bennochy, as his son, George John Whyte-Melville, the novelist, died in his lifetime without issue. Those later family members dropped the double 'tt' spelling.

The Whites who owned Kellerstain, in Mid Lothian, were supposed to be of the same stock. They descended from John White of Millthird, Clackmannan, whose grandson, John, married Elizabeth Logan. One of their daughters married Henry, son of the eminent painter, Sir Henry Raeburn, and their eldest son, William Logan Whyte, 1793–1877, an advocate, purchased Kellerstain in 1823. On the death of his son, James Maitland Whyte, in 1914, the property passed to two nephews.

Whytes were prolific around Rutherglen and Carmunnock. Walter Whyte, born ca. 1677, was a baillie of Rutherglen, and married late in life, Elizabeth, daughter of Provost John Spence. His eldest surviving son, George, became owner of Bankhead, and registered arms in 1786: Argent, a martlet between three quatrefoils Sable, on a chief as many quatrefoils Or. Motto: *Vincit qui curat*. Walter, 1780–1847, his son, matriculated at the University of Glasgow in 1794, and besides Bankhead, owned lands at Whitburn, Kenmure and Shettleston. His only son, Walter, was served heir to him and to his aunts, Jane Whyte or Reddoch and Elizabeth Whyte, in 1895. Jane Whyte, a member of the Faculty of Procurators of Glasgow in 1835, was probably of the same stock. He became a chemical manufacturer, and was the father of John Campbell Whyte, raised to the peerage in 1893 as Baron Overtoun. The title became extinct when he died in 1908.

Whytes were numerous in the Cowal district of Argyll, and two versions of their origin may be confusions of one. They appear in rent-rolls at Inveraray as MacIllebhains ('sons of the fair gillie') alias Whites, and were probably the people who often appear as Macilvans in parish registers; 'bh' in Gaelic being sounded as 'v'. They should not be confused with MacGilvanes. An old tradition fetches them from John McGillichallum, forester in Coire-an-T-Sith, Loch Eck, who died ca. 1646. He is sometimes confused with a later forester, Robert Campbell in *Tigh Chura*. The 'fair gillie' may have been John's son, Donald *Ban* (fair-haired), buried at Kilmun beside other Whites or Whytes.

WISHART The writer of the inscription on the tomb of Rev. George Wishartt, 1599–1671, Bishop of Edinburgh, believed the name meant 'wise-heart'. Although not strictly correct, the derivation was not far wrong. The name is recorded in England as Wischard (Latinised *Wiscardis*) in 1170, and appears in similar forms in Scotland in the 13th century: *Wiscard*, *Wischard* and *Wyschard*, and is from Old Norman French, *Guischard*, meaning 'prudent or sagacious'. The Wischards probably came from Normandy. William Wischard witnessed a grant of the mill tiend to the Abbey of Cambuskenneth ca. 1200. William Wischard, recorded in 1271 as bishop elect of Glasgow, was consecrated Bishop of St Andrews in 1273, and died in 1279. He was son of John Wischard, sheriff of the Mearns ca. 1230, ancestor of the Wisharts of Pitarrow. Another William Wischard was a canon of Dunkeld in 1280, and was probably brother of Mary, spouse of William Oliphant of Aberdalgie. Robert Wischard, a nephew of Bishop William Wischard, became Bishop of Glasgow in 1272. He was a cousin of William Wishcard, archdeacon of Lothian. John Wycard del Mierns, Gilbert Wichard, Forfarshire, John Wischard, Kincardineshire, and Master John Wischard, chevalier, all signed the homage roll in 1296.

The Wisharts came to own lands in Kincardineshire, and while some were later landowners elsewhere, they are best known for producing clergymen. Sir John Wishart of Pitarrow went on a mission to France in 1434. His second son, David, was vicar of Brechin, ca. 1453, and his grandson, Sir John of Pitarrow, was forfeited in 1499. Sir James Wishart of Pitarrow and Carnbeg was joint King's Advocate with James Henderson of Fordell, in 1513, and seems to have been Advocate and Justice-Clerk after Henderson was killed at Flodden. By his first wife, Janet Lindsay, he had sons John and James, successively lairds of Pitarrow and Carnbeg, and by his second wife, Elizabeth Learmont, he was the father of George Wishart, ca. 1500–46, the Protestant itinerant lecturer and preacher, burned at the stake in St Andrews as a heretic. Sir John Wishart, who succeeded to the estates in 1607, sold Pitarrow to his brother, Capt. Wishart, who disponed the lands to Lord Carnegie, and died in Ireland without issue. His brother, Rev. William Wishart, a graduate of Aberdeen, came to represent the family. He was minister at Fettercairn, and later at South Leith. His son John, a royalist soldier, was killed at Edgefield in 1642, when the representation passed to his cousin, Rev. William Wishart, 1621–92, minister at Kinneil, in West Lothian. He married Christian Burne, and from them descended many distinguished Wisharts.

Lieutenant Col. George Wishart of Cliftonhall, in Mid Lothian, eldest son of Rev. William Wishart, was created a Baronet of NS in 1706. The third son, Rev. William Wishart, 1660–1729, was Principal of the University of Edinburgh, and had two sons in the ministry, one of whom, Rev. William, also became Principal of the

University. From him descended the Wisharts of Foxhall, Kirkliston. Reverend George Wishart, brother of the second Principal Wishart, was minister of the West Kirk of Edinburgh (St Cuthbert's). He married Ann, daughter of John Campbell, 1682–1768, of Orchard, and had a son George, and five daughters, only two of whom were wed. Janet, the elder, married Maj. Gen. John Beckwith, and had issue. Jane, the younger sister, married in 1865, Baron Christian Heinrich von Westphalen. Their son Ludwig von Westphalen, married Carolina Heubal, with issue a daughter, Johanna Julia Jenny, who married in 1843, Dr Karl Marx, 1818–83, the political reformer, and left issue. The chaplain, Rev. George Wishart, 1609–71, was the historian of the wars of Montrose.

WYLIE The surname Wylie or Wyllie may derive from 'Willie', a diminutive of William, or from personal trait, 'Wiley' or shrewd. Donald Wyly, tenant in Thornhill, Dumfriesshire, is on record in 1431, and William Wyly was a witness at Prestwick in 1446. Thomas Wylie, merchant-burgess of Edingburgh, recorded arms in 1672. A number of Wylies achieved fame. Sir James Wylie, 1768–1854, educated at Aberdeen, entered Russian service as a regimental surgeon, and became physician-in-ordinary to the Grand Duke Alexander. He was the founder of the Medical Academy of St Petersburg, 1804, and its first president. General Sir William Wyllie, born 1802, son of John Wylie of Holmhead House, Kilmarnock and Amelia Hutt, had a brilliant military career in India, and retired in 1877. His son, Lt. Col. Sir William Hutt Curzon Wyllie, 1848–1909, also served in the Indian army, and was military secretary to the Rt Hon. W.P. Adam, Governor of Madras, in 1881.

Norman Russell Wylie, an advocate in 1952, was MP for Pentlands, 1964–74, and Solicitor-General in 1964. He was Lord Advocate, 1970–74, as Lord Whylie, and retired in 1990. Alexander Featherstonhaugh Wylie, a native of Perth, was admitted an advocate in 1978, and was Advocate-Depute, 1989–92. He was called to the English Bar in 1990, and became a QC for Scotland in 1991. He has been a member of the Scottish Legal Aid Board since 1994.

FURTHER READING

—◄○►—

I N HIS *MEMOIRS*, Sir Walter Scott wrote: 'Every Scottishman has a pedigree. It is a national prerogative, as unalienable as his pride and his poverty.' Robert L. Stevenson had much the same thoughts when he wrote in *Weir of Hermiston*, 'That is the mark of the Scot of all classes – that he stands in attitude to the past unthinkable to Englishmen, and remembers and cherishes the memory of his forbears, good and bad.' The learned authors of three of the four volumes of *The Edinburgh History of Scotland*, show with the use of drop-line charts how important to the understanding of national history is a clear view of family relationships.

While Scotland did not have a national body interested in such matters until the founding of the Scottish Genealogy Society in 1953, it must be remembered that numerous clan associations existed, the earliest dating from 1725. An age of more leisure, if not affluence, is reflected in the fact that Scotland now has more than twenty family history societies, all producing newsletters or magazines. It is therefore essential for those interested in family history to have a broad view of the past, much of which, preserved in those slim volumes, might otherwise have been lost. This book will also be of value, containing outline histories of some two hundred surnames, Highland and Lowland. Honours and titles – if we include chiefships – are more widely spread in Scotland than elsewhere, and some families will find links with landed families; others with the soil they owned. In the vast ocean of printed works it is therefore helpful to know what to read.

The first essential in any genealogical library, and a most important book to consult is Dr George Fraser Black's monumental work, *The Surnames of Scotland* (New York, 1946), reprinted several times and now available in paperback. While much new material has been uncovered since that book was written, notably the acts of our early kings in the 'Regesta Regum Scottorum' series, covering 1124 to 1424, and Mrs Platt's two-volume work, *Scottish Hazard* (London, 1985 and 1990), Black's book is still of immense value. Bibliographers have provided valuable finding aids. *Scottish Family History* (Edinburgh, 1930; reprinted at Baltimore, 1978), is still worth consulting. The main guide to printed family histories is now *Scottish Family Histories* (Edinburgh, 1986), edited by Miss Joan P.S. Ferguson, and published by the National Library of Scotland. A splendid guide to the numerous genealogical publications of John and Bernard Burke (Burke's Peerage, Ltd), is titled *Burke's Family Index* (London, 1976), compiled by Rosemary Pinches. The peerage articles often supplement the families treated in *The Scots Peerage*, in nine volumes (Edinburgh, 1904–14), and the landed gentry volumes are very useful: the families being less stable than the aristocracy.

Clanship and kinship being of paramount importance in Scotland, *Clans, Septs and Regiments of the Scottish Highlands* (8th edn, Edinburgh, 1984), revised by the late Sir Thomas Innes of Learney, is well worth consulting. So also *The Highland Clans* (London, 1967), by the late Sir Iain Moncreiffe of that Ilk. For the related subject of heraldry, Sir Iain's *Simple Heraldry* (Edinburgh, 1953, and reprints), illustrated by the late heraldic artist, Don Pottinger, is an excellent introduction. The standard work is *Scots Heraldry*, by the late Sir Thomas Innes, third edition by Malcolm R. Innes (Edinburgh, 1978), now Lord Lyon King of Arms.

People starting out on a search for their ancestors would do well to consult *In Search of Scottish Ancestry* (2nd edn, 1983), by the late Gerald Hamilton-Edwards. Also of assistance is Kathleen B. Cory's *Tracing Your Scottish Ancestry* (Edinburgh, 1990).

Serious students would find it worthwhile to join the Scottish Genealogy Society (Library and Research Centre at 15 Victoria Terrace, Edinburgh), and/or one of the local family history societies. These all publish magazines.

ANCESTRY RESEARCH

–‹o›–

GETTING STARTED Many people at home and overseas, seeking their roots, head for repositories such as New Register House, Edinburgh, without doing any homework. This is often a complete waste of time and money. The best place to begin is at home, and it is surprising how much information can be gleaned from family sources which, apart from old bibles, may include degrees, diplomas, references, testimonials, school reports, service discharge papers, medals, rings, seals, letters, journals, photograph and postcard albums (which can reveal changes of address), heirlooms, bank pass books, insurance papers, property deeds, stock transactions, silverware, proclamations of marriage, baptismal certificates, funeral intimations and obituary notices, telegrams, rent books or leases, newspaper cuttings and samplers.

In every family there is always one member – perhaps a maiden aunt – who is knowledgeable, and has preserved items such as those mentioned, and who may have kept in touch with relatives who have emigrated. A personal visit is best, and if there are initial difficulties the production of family photographs is fairly easy to encourage. You can then seek to identify people and gather details. It is worthwhile taping conversations, but it is also best to ask permission first. On the other hand, there might be less objection to taking notes. A good notebook is essential, one with opaque paper opening right to left, rather than the flip-over type; and write on the right hand page, leaving the left for future additions at the appropriate places. Write clearly and do not attempt to invent a new form of shorthand. Four 'keys' which unlock many doors are NAME, RELATIONSHIP, DATE and PLACE. Record the information systematically, and remember to add the name of the informant and the date.

When you have digested the information, it is worth attempting a 'drop-line' chart, or arranging the data on genealogy charts and family group sheets, such as those obtainable from the Scottish Genealogy Society Library at 15 Victoria Terrace, Edinburgh. If you are a 'computer-buff', it is worth investigating what software programmes are available for making family records. There are usually a number advertised in *Family Tree Magazine*. You may now be ready to visit record repositories. Scottish records are mainly centralised in Edinburgh. In New Register House, the Registar-General for Scotland has charge of the *Old Parochial Registers of Scotland*, pre-1855, available on microfilm; the decennial census records, 1841–91; and the statutory registers of births, marriages and deaths from 1855. The indices for the latter group are computerised and the record pages are on microfiche. Fees are charged for access to the records.

Practice will bring familiarity with old handwriting, but a useful aid is Grant G. Simpson's *Scottish Handwriting, 1150–1650* (Edinburgh, 1973, and reprinted). Having extracted all the information available at New Register House, you may visit the Historical Room of the National Archives in HM General Register Office. Here are preserved the public records of Scotland: a vast array of documents of various kinds. Those usually sought first are testaments. The earliest were recorded in commissariots and there are indices down to 1800 printed in volumes issued by the Scottish Record Society. In the Archives are typed indices which carry us forward to around 1823–30, when the jurisdiction was transferred to the sheriff courts. There is a register of confirmations from 1876, and for some areas there is a printed *Register of Defuncts*, mainly 1830–65. Before going on to consult other records in this repository, such as deeds and sasines, searchers should consult (better still purchase) a splendid guide compiled by Cecil Sinclair, *Tracing Your Scottish Ancestors in the Scottish Record Office*, published by HM Stationery Office in 1990. When some skills in palaeography have been achieved, the style of old documents can be followed by consulting *Formulary of Old Scots Legal Documents*, compiled by Peter Gouldsbrough, and printed by the Stair Society (Edinburgh, 1985).

SCOTTISH ASSOCIATION OF FAMILY HISTORY SOCIETIES

—◄o►—

WITH THE FORMATION OF family history societies it was deemed useful to have an 'umbrella' organisation, under which progress could be monitored and views exchanged: hence the founding of an Association of Scottish Family History Societies, which has an annual conference, and publishes the lectures delivered.

Full member societies are:

Aberdeen & North-East Scotland F.H.S.
Family History Centre, 164 King Street, Aberdeen AB2 3BD
Alloway & District F.H.S.
4 Broadwood Park, Alloway, Ayrshire KA7
Anglo-Scottish F.H.S. (an offshoot of Manchester & Lanarkshire F.H.S.)
Clayton House, 59 Picaddilly, Manchester M1 2AQ
Association of Scottish Genealogists & Record Agents
c/o James A. Thompson, 84 Gilmore Place, Edinburgh EH3 9PF
Borders F.H.S.
c/o Mrs Carol Trotter, 'Pentennen', 15 Edinburgh Road, Greenlaw, Berwickshire TD10 6XF
Central Scotland F.H.S.
c/o Mrs C. Sergeant, 4 Fir Lane, Larbert, Stirlingshire FK5 3LW
Dumfries & Galloway F.H.S.
Family History Research Centre, 9 Glasgow Street, Dumfries DG2 9AF
East Ayrshire F.H.S.
c/o Dick Library, Elmbank Street, Kilmarnock, Ayrshire KA1 3BU

Fife F.H.S.
c/o Mrs Janet Ross, 30 Duddingston Drive, Kirkcaldy, Fife KY1
Glasgow & West of Scotland F.H.S.
Unit 5, 22 Mansfield Street, Glasgow G11 5QP
Guild of One-Name Studies
Box G, 14 Charterhouse Buildings, Goswell Road, London EC1M 7BA
Highland F.H.S.
Hon. Secretary, C/o Reference Room, Public Library, Farraline Park, Inverness IV1 1NH
Lanarkshire F.H.S. (Formerly Hamilton & District F.H.S.)
Hon. Secretary, C/o Hamilton Central Library, 98 Cadzow Street, Hamilton, Lanarkshire ML3 6HQ
Largs & North Ayrshire F.H.S.
c/o Mrs C. Craig, 2 Raillies Road, Largs, Ayrshire KA30 8QZ
The Lothians F.H.S.
c/o Miss Anne Agnes, Lasswade High School, Eskdale Drive, Bonnyrigg, Mid Lothian EH19 2LA
Orkney F.H.S.
c/o Mrs M. Scott, Leckhelm, Annfield Crescent, Kirkwall, Orkney KW15 1NS
Scottish Genealogy Society
Library & Research Centre, 15 Victoria Terrace, Edinburgh EH1 2JL
Shetland F.H.S.
Family History Centre, 12 Lovers Loan, Lerwick, Shetland ZE1 OED
Tay Valley F.H.S.
Family History Centre, 179 Princes Street, Dundee, Angus DD4 6DQ
Troon & District F.H.S.
c/o MERC, Troon Public Library, South Beach, Troon, Ayrshire KA10 6EF

Associate members are:
British Columbia Genealogical Society
PO Box 88054, Lansdowne Mall, Richmond, BC, Canada V6X 3T6
British Isles Family History Society (Los Angeles)
2531 Sawtelle Blvd, #134, Los Angeles, CA 90064-3123, USA
British Isles Genealogical Research Association
5858 Blacksmith Road, Bonita, CA 91902-3003, USA

British Isles Family History Society of Greater Ottawa
PO Box 38026, Ottawa, Ontario, Canada 2KC 1N0
Catholic Family History Society
2 Winscombe Crescent, Ealing, London W5 1AZ
Genealogical Society of Queensland (Scottish Group)
PO Box 84233, Woolloongabba, Queensland, Australia, 4702
Genealogical Society of Victoria
252 Swanston Street, 5th Floor, Melbourne, Victoria, Australia, 3000
International Society for British Genealogy & Family History
PO Box 3115, Salt Lake City, UT 84110-3115, USA
New Zealand Society of Genealogists
PO Box 8795, Symonds Street, Auckland, New Zealand, 1035
Scottish Historical & Research Group of Ballarat
11b Elliott Street, Ballarat, Victoria, Australia, 3350
Shoalhaven Family History Society, NSW
PO Box 591, Nowra, NSW, Australia, 2521
Society of Genealogists
14 Charterhouse Bldgs, Goswell Road, London EC1M 7BA
Western Australia Genealogical Society (Scottish Group)
6/48 May Street, Bayswater, Western Australia, Australia, 6053

ASSOCIATION OF SCOTTISH GENEALOGISTS AND RECORD AGENTS

<o>

Founded in 1981, the Association is open to experienced and well-qualified professional genealogists and record agents working personally in Scotland. All members on joining accept the Association's strict CODE OF PRACTICE, and there is a complaints procedure. Members available for private commissions are as follows:

Bigwood, Mrs Rosemary, MA, MLitt
38 Primrose Bank Road, Edinburgh EH5 3JF
Brown, Mrs Doreen, FSAScot.
64 Orchard Road, Edinburgh EH4 2HD
Burns, David G.C.
17/7 Craigmount Hill, Edinburgh EH4 8HW
Dignall, Maggi
67 Comely Bank Ave, Edinburgh EH4 1ET
Fenwick, Robert, BA (Hons)
St Leonards Manse, 112 Dundee Road, Perth PH2 7BB
Garven, Anne
8 Lixmount Avenue, Edinburgh EH5 3EP
Iggo, Dr B.J.
5 Relugas Road, Edinburgh EH9 2NE
Lawson, William M., BL, FRICS, FSAScot
The Old Schoolhouse, Northton, Harris HS3 3JA
MacLeod, Allan J.L., FSAScot
51/3 Mortonhall Road, Edinburgh EH9 2HN
Miller, Mrs Susan, BSc
36 Branziert Road North, Killearn, Glasgow G63 9RF

Mortimer, Mrs Elizabeth, MA, FSAScot
Kilcomb, St Thomas's Well, Stirling FK7 9PR
Mowat, Mrs Alison, S.B., MA
14 Blacket Place, Edinburgh EH9 1RL
Poole, Mrs Julie, MA, Mem AGRA
Queens Gardens, St Andrews, Fife KY16 9TA
Shippey, Ms Daniella, MA (Oxon)
3 Warriston Crescent, Edinburgh EH3 5LA
Thompson, James A.
84 Gilmore Place, Edinburgh EH3 9PF
Weir, Mrs Hazel, MA
34 Swanston Terrace, Edinburgh EH10 7DN

INDEX OF SURNAMES

◄○►

T HE FOLLOWING NAMES (kings and queens – well documented – excepted), appear where indicated.